DIGITAL SYNERGY

In an era where technological progress redefines the boundaries of business and management, 'Digital Synergy - Innovative Management in the ICT Era' emerges as a guide for current and aspiring leaders. This book delves into the heart of modern management practices, illuminated by the transformative power of Information and Communication Technologies (ICT) and digital synergy. Facing the relentless pace of change, adaptation, innovation, and the utilization of digital synergy are no longer optional; they are the bedrock of sustainable success. Through a carefully selected collection of theories, case studies, expert insights, and examples of digital synergy, this book provides the foresight and tools necessary to navigate through the complexities of a globalized, digital marketplace.

The book is divided into four sections:

1. Financial and Strategic Management in Uncertain Times
2. Global Trends and Management Challenges
3. Corporate Social Responsibility and Effective CSR Managemen
4. The Future of Logistics, with a Special Focus on Military Logistics

Designed for business leaders, managers, students, and anyone keen on deepening their understanding of how ICT and digital synergy shape management strategies, this book is a call to action. It challenges to not just keep pace with technological progress but to lead the charge in leveraging it for strategic advantage.

PROCEEDINGS OF THE INTERNATIONAL RESEARCH CONGRESS - CANWEST 2023, 11–13 SEPTEMBER 2023, MADRID, SPAIN

Digital Synergy

Innovative Approaches of Management in ICT Era

Edited by

Ibrahiem M.M. El Emary

King Abdulaziz University, Jeddah, Saudi Arabia

Anna Brzozowska

Częstochowa University of Technology, Częstochowa

Piotr Maśloch

War Studies University, Warsaw

CRC Press
Taylor & Francis Group
Boca Raton London New York Leiden

CRC Press is an imprint of the
Taylor & Francis Group, an **informa** business
A BALKEMA BOOK

First published 2025
by CRC Press/Balkema
4 Park Square, Milton Park, Abingdon, Oxon, OX14 4RN

and by CRC Press/Balkema
2385 NW Executive Center Drive, Suite 320, Boca Raton FL 33431

CRC Press/Balkema is an imprint of the Taylor & Francis Group, an informa business

Typeset by Integra Software Services Pvt. Ltd., Pondicherry, India

British Library Cataloguing-in-Publication Data
A catalogue record for this book is available from the British Library

Library of Congress Cataloging-in-Publication Data
A catalog record has been requested for this book

ISBN: 978-1-032-57658-9 (hbk)
ISBN: 978-1-032-57660-2 (pbk)
ISBN: 978-1-003-44040-6 (ebk)
DOI: 10.1201/9781003440406

Digital Synergy – El Emary et al. (eds)
© 2025 The Editor(s), ISBN 978-1-032-57658-9
Open Access: www.taylorfrancis.com, CC BY-NC-ND 4.0 license

Contents

Digital Synergy – El Emary et al. (eds)
© 2025 The Editor(s), ISBN 978-1-032-57658-9
Open Access: www.taylorfrancis.com, CC BY-NC-ND 4.0 license

Preface

In the face of an ever-evolving world where information and communication technology (ICT) plays a pivotal role, management becomes a discipline that requires not just knowledge but continuous innovation. This book, "Innovative Management in the ICT Era," responds to these challenges by offering readers a compendium of knowledge on modern management practices essential for effective navigation in today's globalized world. In an era where change is the only constant, adaptation and innovation become the foundations of success. The book is designed for managers, business leaders, students, and anyone interested in a deeper understanding of how technology shapes modern management. Presenting both theoretical foundations and practical case studies, it aims to equip readers with the tools necessary to anticipate trends, leverage new opportunities, and overcome challenges. The goal of this publication is not only to convey current knowledge on management in the context of ICT technologies but also to inspire the search for innovative solutions in daily management challenges. We want our readers to not just keep up with changes but to be pioneers, setting new directions for development in their organizations and industries. The book covers a wide range of topics, from financial and strategic management to global trends, corporate social responsibility, and the future of logistics. Each chapter is prepared by scholars and experts in their field, ensuring the reliability and timeliness of the information provided. This gives readers a comprehensive picture of the challenges and opportunities presented by the ICT era.

Section 1: Financial and Strategic Management in Conditions of Uncertainty
The first section focuses on the fundamental aspects of financial and strategic management in the context of uncertain economic environments. Each chapter presents unique perspectives and analyses, emphasizing the importance of adaptive and predictive management strategies.

Section 2: Global Trends and Challenges in Management
The second section of the book discusses a broad spectrum of topics crucial for understanding current and future trends in global management. Each chapter focuses on a different aspect, offering readers a comprehensive overview of the challenges and opportunities facing contemporary organizations and leaders.

Section 3: Corporate Social Responsibility and CSR Management Systems
The third section concentrates on corporate social responsibility (CSR) and presents CSR management systems and management at the regional level, showcasing case studies and analyses of CSR practices in various geographic and sectoral contexts.

Section 4: The Future of Logistics (Military Logistics)
The fourth section focuses on the future of logistics, with special attention to military logistics. This part includes case studies and analyses regarding contemporary trends in military logistics, as well as challenges and opportunities for the future.

Each section of the book is closely linked to the theme of "Innovative Management in the ICT Era," highlighting how ICT technologies impact various aspects of management and business.

Scientific justification for linking each section to the book title "Innovative Management in the ICT Era":

Section 1: Financial and Strategic Management in Conditions of Uncertainty

In the era of rapidly changing ICT technologies, financial and strategic management faces new challenges. Market uncertainty, price volatility, dynamic changes in demand and supply require organizations to be flexible and quick in adapting strategies. ICT technologies enable the gathering and analysis of large amounts of data (big data), allowing for better prediction of trends and risk management. The introduction of tools such as Enterprise Resource Planning (ERP) systems or customer relationship management (CRM) tools enables more efficient strategic and financial planning.

Section 2: Global Trends and Challenges in Management

The ICT era is characterized by globalization and digitization, which are crucial for global-level management. ICT technologies facilitate international communication, supply chain management, or the implementation of global marketing strategies. Analyzing global trends and challenges, considering the role of information technologies, is essential for effective management of contemporary organizations. This section emphasizes how ICT innovations support companies in adapting to the global business environment.

Section 3: Corporate Social Responsibility and CSR Management Systems

In the context of corporate social responsibility (CSR), ICT technologies offer tools for better monitoring and reporting of CSR activities, as well as engaging stakeholders and customers through digital platforms. CSR management systems using ICT enable organizations to communicate their CSR actions more effectively and align these actions with social and environmental expectations. The ICT era increases transparency and information availability, which is significant for CSR practices.

Section 4: The Future of Logistics (Military Logistics)

ICT innovations play a key role in transforming logistics, including military logistics. Modern supply chain management systems, real-time monitoring, autonomous vehicles, and drones are just some examples of how technology affects the future of logistics. In the military context, where precision, speed, and security are crucial, ICT technologies allow for more efficient and effective planning and execution of logistical operations.

Each section of the book, precisely, each chapter belonging to a specific section, analyzes different aspects of management and business, highlighting the importance of innovations and ICT technologies in the digital era. Information and communication technologies not only change the way companies operate but also impact financial management strategies, global operations, corporate social responsibility, and logistics, including military logistics. Integrating ICT in each of these areas enables organizations to better adapt to the changing world, increasing their efficiency, competitiveness, and capacity for innovation.

The world of management in the ICT era is full of challenges, such as the rapid pace of change, increased competition, or rising customer expectations. However, each challenge also brings opportunities - for those who are ready to see and seize them. Our book aims not only to highlight these challenges but also to show how they can be turned into success.

We address this publication to a wide audience, from experienced managers immersed in daily professional practice, through students seeking solid theoretical foundations, to business theorists for whom innovative management is the subject of scientific research. "Innovative Management in the ICT Era" provides readers with key competencies and knowledge that will enable them to manage effectively in a dynamically changing world. We believe that the strategies presented here will make our book a valuable source of inspiration for leaders ready to face the challenges of the future.

We would like to express our sincere thanks to all those who contributed to the creation of this book. The input of scholars and experts, valuable comments from reviewers, and the support of the editorial team have allowed for the creation of a publication that, we hope, will become an important reference point in the field of management in the ICT era and innovative solutions.

Digital Synergy – El Emary et al. (eds)
© 2025 The Editor(s), ISBN 978-1-032-57658-9
Open Access: www.taylorfrancis.com, CC BY-NC-ND 4.0 license

Editor Biographies

Ibrahim M. M. El Emary received the Dr. Eng. Degree in 1998 from the Electronic and Communication Department, Faculty of Engineering, Ain shams University, Egypt. From 1998 to 2002, he was an Assistant Professor of Computer sciences in different faculties and institutes in Egypt. From 2002 to 2010, he worked as visiting professor of computer science and engineering in two universities in Jordan. Currently, he is a visiting Professor at King Abdulaziz University, Jeddah, Kingdom of Saudi Arabia. His research interests cover: various analytic and discrete event simulation techniques, performance evaluation of communication networks, application of intelligent techniques in managing computer communication network, and performing a comparative study between various policies and strategies of routing, congestion control, subnetting of computer communication networks. He published more than 200 articles in various refereed international journals and conferences. Also, in the current time, he is too interested in making a lot of scientific research in wireless sensor networks in view point of enhancing its algorithms of congestion control and routing protocols. He extends his research interest to cover Big Data, IoT and Edge Computing as well as Quantum & Fast Computing, BI and KM in decision making process.

Anna Brzozowska, Ph.D., associate professor in the field of economics, in the discipline of management science. Currently, he works at the Department of Logistics at the Faculty of Management of the Częstochowa University of Technology. Since 2000, the professor's research and teaching activity has been associated with the Częstochowa University of Technology, where I worked as an assistant, and since February 2005 as an assistant professor. From 2015 until now as an associate professor.She is the author or co-author of about 180 scientific publications. Its scientific and research activity focuses on organization management processes, primarily logistic, marketing, information and IT aspects as well as the institutional environment influencing management in the light of integration activities. The main directions of research and studies concern four key issues: the broadly understood concept of marketing and logistics management, IT in business, EU project management, management and marketing in agribusiness and the processes of integration with the European Union. He systematically develops these issues by conducting national and international research, participation in thematic groups and research and development teams, as well as through cooperation with business and local and regional authorities.

Piotr Maśloch is Professor at War Studies University in Warsaw, Management and Command Faculty. Prof. Piotr Maśloch is an officer of the Polish Army and Dean's Representative for EU projects. He is an author and manager of international projects (founded by UE) in the field of new technologies and modern education. He is an active teacher and researcher in management, sustainable energy, sustainability and environmental impact. He is a reviewer of scientific publications of the best Polish Universities and international publishing houses,he is an author and co-author about 100 publications as a paper contribution on international journals, book chapters and conference proceedings. His research interest includes management, global aspects of management, globalization and new trends in management (AI, VR, MR).

SECTION 1
Financial and Strategic Management in Uncertain Environments

Digital Synergy – El Emary et al. (eds)

Chapter 1
Municipal financial management in conditions of uncertainty – selected aspects

Wioletta Bień
Podhale State College of Applied Sciences, Nowy Targ, Poland

Marcin Surówka
Cracow University of Economics, Cracow, Poland

Contents

The possibilities of increasing local government revenues depend to a large extent on the efficient management of local government units, as well as on macroeconomic conditions and unpredictable events that may significantly disrupt the process of economic and social changes. The appearance of the Covid-19 pandemic in 2020, numerous restrictions related to combating it, and the observed inflationary processes intensified by the war in Ukraine had a negative impact on the activities of local governments in Poland, especially municipalities, which account for over 75% of local government finances.

The aim of the article is to assess the level and structure of municipalities' budget income and expenditure in the aspect of financial management in conditions of uncertainty and to attempt to determine the key elements of effective management of the municipality's financial resources. The study adopted research methods based on literature studies, analysis of financial indicators and inference. A comparative analysis of basic measures illustrating the state of local finances during the period of destabilization in 2020-2022 was carried out against the background of two previous years, characterized by good economic conditions. The results of research on the budgets of municipalities in Poland for the years 2018–2022 were used, prepared on the basis of numerical data from the Reports on the activities of the Regional Chambers of Audit and the implementation of the budget by local government units and information from the Ministry of Finance.

The analysis confirms the impact of events related to the COVID-19 pandemic and the war in Ukraine on the state of local finances and reduced financial stability of municipalities. This is evidenced, among other things, by the reduced importance of tax revenues in the structure of budget revenues and reduced investment activity.

1 INTRODUCTION

The manifestations of activities of local government units (LCU) to improve residents' quality of life are tightly related to their financial position, including the ability to systematically

DOI: 10.1201/9781003440406-1

increase budget revenues and the opportunity to perform new public tasks. Possibilities of increasing revenue are largely dependent not only on efficient management of local government units, but also the macroeconomic conditions that shape the economic situation of the country as well as unforeseeable events, which strongly interfere with the current process of economic and social developments. Such an occurrence was the emergence of Covid-19 in 2020, during which numerous restrictions related to combating the pandemic had serious economic and social repercussions. Additionally, the observed inflationary processes which grew more intense due to the war in Ukraine could have had an adverse impact on the activities of local governments in many instances. Over 75% of local government finances are at the municipal level, including cities at county rank, and most investments and public services are carried out at this level. In the case of municipalities, the changes observed since the beginning of 2020 are far less favorable.

Only municipalities have taxing powers, i.e., the right to impose local taxes and fees. The amount of these taxes and fees is set by the municipality itself, but it must comply with the framework and rates of taxation laid down by the legislation. Municipalities also have the highest share in the PIT income tax transfer.

The main aim of this article is to assess the level and structure of municipal budgetary revenues and expenses in the context of financial management in conditions of uncertainty and to attempt to determine the key elements of effective management of financial resources in municipalities. For the realization of the aim formulated in this way, a comparative analysis was made of basic measures illustrating the condition of local finances in the period of destabilization in 2020-2022 against the background of the two previous years, characterized by a robust economic situation. The article uses the results of research into municipal budgets in Poland for the years 2018-2022, based on numerical data from the activity reports of regional accounting chambers and budget implementation by local government units, as well as information from the Ministry of Finance.

The hypothesis formulated for the purposes of this article was that the uncertain economic environment determines the condition of local finances and, consequently, decisions taken in the process of managing the financial resources of the municipality.

2 THE NATURE AND SCOPE OF MUNICIPAL FINANCIAL MANAGEMENT

The problem of municipal finance management is currently one of the biggest concerns regarding the functioning of local authorities, especially in the context of increasing the utilization of modern management in administering local government units, including financial resources. Issues crucial for the sound management of local finances include: expenses and their structure, priorities of development projects, obtaining funds for the implementation of tasks and deciding on the sequence thereof in time. Local finance represents an area where the consequences of inefficient management are clearly revealed. The premise of ensuring self-governance is having a sufficiently high amount of financial resources to cover the costs of current operations and capital expenditure.

Municipal financial management can be defined as a complex process consisting in making numerous decisions by its legislative and executive bodies, under which the adopted financial policy tasks are implemented, monitored and coordinated, and the effects of the measures taken are assessed and, if necessary, corrected. Management covers regulating and directing the sources of funding and activities for their optimal use in accordance with the objectives set out in the local development strategy (Jastrzębska 1999: 15; Król 2016: 45; Wyrębek 2010: 143). This concept can also be understood as part of the general management of local government units, including financial planning, budget implementation, and financial audit (Zioło 2013: 45).

The decisions taken as part of managing local government finances concern, on the one hand, managing fund collection, and this is reflected in budget revenues; on the other hand, they concern managing the ways of using these funds, which is reflected in the structure and directions of budget expenditures (Kożuch 2008: 122-123; Gwoździcka-Piotrowska 2012: 102-103). The decision-making process is conditioned by economic and social factors determining local community needs and the resources available to the municipality, as well as the organizational structure of local authorities, which depends on central legal regulations.

The process of financial management allows for shaping the capital and property structure, ongoing day-to-day assessment of the financial and asset standing of the local government, enabling the assessment of compliance of current, investment and financial activities with the adopted assumptions and setting the financing strategy (Filipiak 2011: 25-33). This definition of financial management emphasizes the conduct of financial policy and budgetary management of the municipality – geared to manage, rather than merely to govern finances.

According to the literature on the subject, there are two models of financial management: traditional and active (Król 2016: 52; Wiatrak 2018: 56-57). The traditional (administrative) model of financial management focuses mainly on cash resources in a one-year cycle, as a result of which investment decisions are often made beyond financial capabilities. It covers financial resources, starting from the budget, through planning the implementation of budget revenues and expenditures, ending with the schedules for their implementation. It is based on providing local government units with rules, processes and information necessary to ensure effective and efficient use of resources.

The active financial management model is characterized by a holistic approach to financial management and covers all the processes of collecting and spending cash, as well as making decisions in this regard in an annual and multiannual cycle. Professional municipal management uses extended instruments in the form of local development strategies, long-term investment programs and plans, budget forecasts, financial engineering of investments, creditworthiness and financial liquidity of the municipality. The essence of the management process lies in making decisions depending on the changing external and internal operating conditions.

Polish local governments are dominated by the administrative model of public finance management, which stems from the current legislation. It is seen as unfavorable from the point of view of effective utilization of resources and achieving intended goals. The second financial management model is used by some local governments on an optional and supplementary basis. Such a situation requires the integration of financial management with other instruments, especially with the municipality's development strategy and long-term investment plans.

3 MODERN CONCEPTS OF LOCAL FINANCE MANAGEMENT

Poland is faced with major challenges, such as an ageing population, low birth rate, decreasing number of persons employed, migrations, which consequently raise concerns about the fiscal sustainability of the state. Challenges for local governments are reflected in the risk of imbalances in the current portion of budgets, which has been growing in recent years. Moreover, local governments are struggling with additional responsibilities and pressures due to the COVID-19 pandemic, the war in Ukraine, rising inflation and interest rates, which have further increased uncertainty and highlighted economic and fiscal challenges.

In order to present a balanced budget and stable debt, local authorities face key challenges of conducting a sound budgetary policy over the medium term. To be effective, strategic, transparent and enjoy the trust of citizens, the budget requires proper management by local government authorities (OECD 2021: 195-200).

The municipality conducts its own financial management on the basis of the budget, the draft of which is prepared by the executive body in accordance with the principles of budgetary law. In line with the principle, current expenditures planned for a financial year cannot be higher than the sum of current revenues, the budget surplus from the previous year, and unallocated funds (Article 243 of the Act of August 27, 2009 on *Public Finance*, Journal of Laws 2022: 1634). Municipalities respect the principle of putting the budget on a sustainable path and strive to achieve an operating surplus; they are also required to keep a reserve (0.1 to 1%). The budget adopted by the council forms part of the management system.

One element of the rationalization of public finance management is the implementation of performance-based budgeting based on a clear division of competences and principles of responsibility as well as transparency and openness of made decisions. It represents a planned statement of revenue and expenditure of LGUs, intended for financing specific public tasks. The management of public funds takes places via particular objectives and priorities, as well as the achievement of specific results, measured by an established system of measures.

The performance-based budgeting system provides essential information that facilitate the preparation of annual and multiannual budgets, including in the field of making decisions regarding the most advantageous allocation or reallocation of limited funds. In Poland, the Public Finance Act does not contain legal provisions obliging the local government to implement a performance-based budget, but it indirectly promotes the use of selected elements, i.e., the obligation to conduct management control, which aims, among others, at ensuring the efficiency and effectiveness of the implementation of public tasks and the obligation to plan long-term programs under the long-term financial forecast (LFF) (Zawadzka-Pąk 2014: 87-103).

Owing to the LFF, local governments have a basis for mid-term budgeting. The LFF encompasses the current financial year and at least three subsequent years; it is part of the draft budget resolution in the annual budget cycle – it specifies revenue and expenditure, deficits and debt, as well as the method of financing debt repayment or allocation of surplus revenues. The LFF is of particular relevance for the financing of long-term contracts and agreements concluded by local authorities (e.g., public-private partnership agreements) (Wołowiec 2013: 72-82).

One effective tool for engaging citizens at the local level is participatory budgeting, which gives residents the opportunity to decide on the implementation of annual public tasks financed from public funds in a given year. Participatory budgeting aims to strengthen public participation and deepen the bond between the government and the citizens. It reflects the willingness of citizens to participate in the formulation and implementation of local policies (Sześciło 2015: 7-15).

The development of participatory budgeting is the most noteworthy innovation in local government in Poland in the recent years. The introduction in 2018 of legislation directly governing the participatory budget for cities with powiat status is a clear incentive for a wider use of the instrument of enhancing the contribution of citizens (Budziarek 2019: 149-158). A related initiative is the Sołecki Fund, which aims to support involvement in rural areas through ring-fencing of funds in the municipal budget, the use of which may be decided by the inhabitants of villages. The presented mechanisms help to strengthen budgetary management and address the challenges faced by local government.

4 REVIEW OF THE MUNICIPAL BUDGET AS A TOOL FOR MANAGING FINANCES IN CONDITIONS OF UNCERTAINTY

Ensuring stable budgetary revenue is a prerequisite for effective and efficient implementation by municipalities of their statutory tasks, allowing for the financing of current expenses, as well as enabling undertaking new investment projects. In connection with the spread of the Covid-19 pandemic in 2020, local government authorities expected a substantial decrease in income in this period, mainly in virtue of taxes and charges.

Meanwhile, as set out in detail in Table 1, individual types of municipalities have not only *not* reduced income, but also maintained a similar dynamic of growth as in 2019. Especially in rural municipalities, the effects of the pandemic did not contribute to the deterioration of the revenue situation. Unfavorable changes concerned the situation of cities with powiat status and urban municipalities. The worsening economic crisis is reflected in the drop in the average increase in income across all types of municipalities in 2021-2022.

The years 2018-2020 saw a downward trend of the share of municipalities' own income in the total amount of budgetary incomes (Table 2). In 2020, all municipalities experienced a significant reduction in the share of personal and corporate income tax in budget revenues compared to the previous year. Undoubtedly, this was the result of the economic crisis caused by restrictions aimed at arresting the spread of coronavirus. A slightly different situation has developed in the case of revenues from fees and taxes directly feeding municipal budgets;

Table 1. Income of municipalities in Poland (thousand PLN).

Specification	Total income in years					Income dynamics (in %)			
	2018	2019	2020	2021	2022	2019/ 2018	2020/ 2019	2021/ 2020	2022/ 2021
Municipalities overall, including:	121 425 598	135 161 459	149 090 471	163 483 715	171 813 486	111,3	110,3	109,7	105,1
urban municipalities	26 908 060	29 818 355	32 467 403	35 204 558	37 386 099	110,8	108,9	108,4	106,2
urban-rural municipalities	41 651 690	46 719 655	51 400 759	56 544 352	59 449 382	112,2	110,0	110,0	105,1
rural municipalities	52 865 848	58 623 449	65 222 309	71 734 805	74 978 005	110,9	111,3	110,0	104,5
Cities with powiat status*	85 507 791	93 894 354	100 314 429	111 045 555	110 217 963	109,8	106,8	110,7	99,3

*including the City of Warsaw
Source: proprietary material based on „*Sprawozdania z działalności regionalnych izb obrachunkowych i wykonania budżetu przez jednostki samorządu terytorialnego w latach 2021-2021*", National Council of the Regional Chambers of Audit, Warsaw 2023 and Information on the budget implementation of LGUs, Budget report 2022, Ministry of Finance (https://www.gov.pl/web/finanse/sprawozdania-budzetowe as of May 10, 2023).

Table 2. Share of own incomes in the overall amount of budgetary revenues (%).

Specification	Own incomes				
	2018	2019	2020	2021	2022
Municipalities overall, including:	40,9	40,0	37,6	39,2	47,2
urban municipalities	49,9	47,9	44,6	46,8	
urban-rural municipalities	42,3	41,3	38,6	40,3	
rural municipalities	35,3	35,1	33,3	34,8	
Cities with powiat status*	61,1	56,5	48,4	58,9	59,9
	shares in PIT and CIT income taxes				
	2018	2019	2020	2021	2022
Municipalities overall, including:	18,0	18,0	16,2	16,8	21,0
urban municipalities	23,4	22,9	20,5	21,4	
urban-rural municipalities	18,4	18,3	16,4	17,1	
rural municipalities	14,9	15,2	13,9	14,4	
Cities with powiat rights	29,3	29,3	24,0	31,0	28,0
	revenues from taxes and fees				
	2018	2019	2020	2021	2022
Municipalities overall, including:	19,0	18,1	17,9	18,3	13,0
urban municipalities	21,2	20,1	19,6	20,2	
urban-rural municipalities	20,2	19,3	19,0	19,4	
rural municipalities	16,8	16,2	16,1	16,4	
Cities with powiat rights	19,4	19,1	17,5	19,1	12,7

*including the City of Warsaw
Source: own compilation, op. cit.

already in 2019, there was a slight decrease in the importance of this source of income, and in 2020 the trend was upheld. This was the result of various types of exemptions granted by municipalities in order to protect business entities from the effects of the lockdown. However, the scale of changes here was much smaller than in the case of income tax shares. Between 2021 and 2022, the share of own revenues in the total amount of municipal revenues increased, which mainly resulted in an increase in the shares of municipalities in income taxes.

Annual external transfers had a similar significance for municipal budgets during the period considered (Table 3), and their largest share was recorded in rural and urban-rural municipalities. Funds from the Local Government Investment Fund (LGIF), established in 2020, were a new source of income; among others they were intended for municipalities to support investments in tourism infrastructure (Resolution of the Council of Ministers No. 6 of January 12, 2021 amending the resolution on support for the implementation of investment tasks by local government units (Monitor Polski, item 26)). This certainly contributed to recording a surplus in 2020-2022 by most municipalities.

Indicators illustrating the level of municipalities' investment activity in the analyzed period and the ratio of liabilities to income (Table 4) give grounds to confirm that the disclosed amounts of budgetary surplus could be caused not only by supporting budgets with funds from the Local Government Investment Fund (PFR), but also a major limitation in the investment activity of municipalities, related to the worsening economic situation and the growing uncertainty as to the implementation of the statement of revenue. On the other hand, the level of municipal indebtedness did not change significantly despite the reduction of the scale of investment.

One can speak of a true tremor in cities with powiat status. The negative result of budgets was probably the result of transformations in the economic situation, PIT regulations and increasing burdens imposed on local governments by the state. Furthermore, the growing

Table 3. Share of external grants in the total amount of budget revenues (%).

	General subvention				
Specification	2018	2019	2020	2021	2022
Municipalities overall, including:	23,4	22,5	21,2	22,6	20,3
urban municipalities	16,7	16,2	15,3	17,9	
urban-rural municipalities	22,5	21,7	20,5	22,0	
rural municipalities	27,4	26,4	24,7	25,3	
Cities with powiat rights	19,5	19,4	19,7	21,7	21,0
	Special purpose grants				
Specification	2018	2019	2020	2021	2022
Municipalities overall, including:	27,7	34,2	30,8	27,5	30,2
urban municipalities	24,3	26,6	29,2	26,4	
urban-rural municipalities	2,7	29,1	31,0	27,7	
rural municipalities	29,4	30,3	31,5	27,8	
Cities with powiat rights	22,7	19,9	22,2	20,1	16,5
	Income from foreign sources				
Specification	2018	2019	2020	2021	2022
Municipalities overall	4,9	5,0	4,1	2,8	4,5
Cities with powiat rights	5,3	5,5	5,1	3,8	5,6

Source: own compilation, op. cit.

Table 4. Capital expenditure vs. debt level and budget outturn.

Specification	Share of investment expenditures in total spending (%)				
	2018	2019	2020	2021	
Municipalities overall, including:	20,3	16,6	14,4	14,3	
urban municipalities	18,9	15,4	13,5	12,6	
urban-rural municipalities	19,6	15,7	13,7	13,8	
rural municipalities	21,6	17,8	15,4	15,5	
Cities with powiat rights	16,4	15,8	14,2	13,8	
	Ratio of labilities to total income (%)				
	2018	2019	2020	2021	2022
Municipalities overall, including:	24,8	23,9	23,0	20,9	20,0
urban municipalities	24,7	24,4	25,0	23,4	
urban-rural municipalities	27,6	26,4	25,2	23,3	
rural municipalities	22,6	21,7	20,2	17,8	
Cities with powiat rights	42,3	43,8	45,7	43,9	41,0
	Budget outturn at the end of the year (million PLN)				
	2018	2019	2020	2021	2022
Municipalities overall, including:	- 5 707,2	- 155,4	5,373,9	10,694,7	- 3,687,1
urban municipalities	- 1,003,4	- 131,8	473,5	1,632,2	
urban-rural municipalities	- 2,064,2	- 90,0	1,702,3	3,163,3	
rural municipalities	- 2,639,6	66,4	3,198,1	5,899,3	
Cities with powiat rights	- 1,506,8	- 2,991,1	- 3,187,8	2,842,0	- 5,541,1

Source: own elaboration, op. cit.

operating costs of local governments, high prices of electricity, gas and building supplies, and pay raises in education, caused most municipalities to record a budget deficit in 2022.

5 CONCLUSION

The assessment of the efficiency of the funds allocation should, in specific socio-economic conditions, demonstrate the optimal selection of tasks and modalities for their financing. It is about counteracting the troublesome phenomenon of lowering the standard of services provided or the inability to finance investment tasks. For this reason, local government authorities should analyze investment priorities and compare them with current expenditure.

The undertaken analysis of financial ratios proves the stated hypothesis. It can be concluded that the events connected with the COVID-19 pandemic and the war in Ukraine have affected the status of local finances and reduced the financial soundness of municipalities. This is evidenced by the decreased significance of tax revenues in the structure of budgetary revenue, as well as the limitation of investment activity, inter alia, in a situation where the vast majority of municipalities closed the years 2020 and 2021 with a budget surplus. The worsening of municipal finances has influenced the decisions of local authorities to economize. An extended local investment co-financing program could be quite helpful. In cutting spendings, local governments should consider organizational optimization of their units, in particular offices and educational institutions, conducting an external audit and reducing the costs of existing debt (e.g., issuing municipal bonds with lower interest rates) (Krawczyk 2021).

Government grants merely allow local officials to finance specific tasks. According to experts, subsidizing local governments not only makes local power centers dependent on the government, but is also conducted according to a political key (Krawczyk 2021). The question of supporting local governments with transfers from the state budget should be the basis for a debate with a view to finding solutions that, by stabilizing the financial economy of municipalities, will strengthen their financial autonomy.

REFERENCES

Act of August 27, 2009 on public finance. *Journal of Laws* 2022.1634.

Budziarek M. 2019. Participatory budgeting in Poland-New legal regulations and rules for implementation. International Journal of Open Governments, Vol. 8.

Filipiak B. 2011. *Finanse samorządowe. Nowe wyzwania bieżące i perspektywiczne*. Difin, Warszawa.

Gwoździcka-Piotrowska M. 2012. Budżet gminy jako element zarządzania jednostką samorządu terytorialnego. *Studia Ekonomiczne i Regionalne*, Vol. V, No. 2, Biała Podlaska.

Jastrzębska M. 1999. *Zarządzanie finansami gmin – aspekty teoretyczne*. Uniwersytet Gdański, Gdańsk.

Kożuch A. 2008. Zmiany w zarządzaniu finansami lokalnymi. Zeszyty Naukowe SGGW w Warszawie. *Ekonomika i Organizacja Gospodarki Żywnościowej*, Warszawa, no. 65.

Krawczyk B. 2021. Pandemia uderza w budżety samorządów. *Przegląd Komunalny* 1 (352).

Król D. 2016. Ocena instrumentów zarządzania finansami samorządu terytorialnego w świetle ewolucji paradygmatu finansów publicznych. *Nauki o Finansach* no. 1 (26).

OECD. 2021. *Lepsze zarządzanie, planowanie i dostarczanie usług w jednostkach samorządu lokalnego w Polsce*. OECD Publishing, Paris.

Resolution of the Council of Ministers No. 6 of January 12, 2021 amending the resolution on support for the implementation of investment tasks by local government units (M.P., item 26).

Sześciło D. 2015. Participatory Budgeting in Poland: Quasi-referendum instead of Deliberation, University of Warsaw.

Wiatrak A.P. 2018. Finansowe uwarunkowania przygotowania i realizacji strategii rozwoju lokalnego. *Nierówności Społeczne a Wzrost Gospodarczy* no. 56 (4).

Wołowiec T. 2013. Multiannual financial perspective as a tool of local government unit development. Financial Internet Quarterly, Vol. 9/3.

Wyrębek H. 2010. Zarządzanie finansami JST na przykładzie gminy. *Polityki Europejskie, Finanse i Marketing* no. 4.

Zawadzka-Pąk U. 2014. Polish Financial Law. Białystok Law Books, Faculty of Law, University of Białystok, Temedia 2, Białystok.

Zioło M. 2013. Instrumenty zarządzania finansami w JST i ich ocena. Wyniki badania ankietowego gmin. Zeszyty Naukowe Uniwersytetu Szczecińskiego, *Ekonomiczne problemy usług* nr 108.

Digital Synergy – El Emary et al. (eds)

Chapter 2
Japanese industry analysis using Cobb–Douglas production function model

Yoshiyuki Yabuuchi
Shimonoseki City University, Japan

Contents

In Japan, the population continues to flow into metropolitan areas. As of 2021, Tokyo's metropolitan area population is expected to be approximately 29% of Japan's total population. In areas where the population flows out, the labor force that supports economic activities is decreasing, placing a burden on these economic activities. Not only is its productivity and economic growth potential declining, it is becoming less attractive as an investment destination. Thus, making it difficult for innovation through human exchanges to occur and falling into a vicious circle of declining birthrates. Therefore, a detailed analysis is required to address this issue. As a steppingstone, this study analyzes Japanese industries using Douglas and possibilistic production functions. We found that the output value of information and communication equipment gradually increased, while the size of the information and communication industry gradually decreased. In addition, the demand for specialists, as well as science, technology, and business support services has increased.

1 INTRODUCTION

There are 47 prefectures in Japan, and the residents of these prefectures move from one location to another for various reasons. The Tokyo metropolitan area comprises of Tokyo (Japan's capital) and four neighboring prefectures. The Tokyo metropolitan area population has an excessive number of in-migrants compared to out-migrants, and this number continues to grow. Conversely, the rest of the region has an excess of out-migrants, with the population declining in many prefectures. The age structure and producer population aged 15 to 64 years has been declining in many prefectures. Furthermore, the Japanese birth rate is declining and the population aging. The number of children under 15 years of age is lower than that of the elderly aged 65 years and older [1]. Consequently, except in urban areas, regional vitality and economic growth potential are declining. Some locations and companies can improve their current situation by developing smart cities through wide-area cooperation. However, to implement such efforts, it is necessary to analyze the economy and industry and understand the current

DOI: 10.1201/9781003440406-2

situation to improve it or create a new business model [2-7]. Under the circumstances of demographic changes and a declining labor force, it is necessary to examine the relationship between capital input and physical output through industrial analysis [8-11]. Therefore, this study conducted an industrial analysis using production functions as steppingstones to solve the problems faced by local Japanese communities [12]. The rest of this paper is organized as follows:

- Section 2 reviews the current situation in Japan using statistical data.
- Section 3 explains the Douglas and possibilistic production functions used in industrial analysis.
- Section 4 analyzes the industries and reviews the current situation in Japan.
- Section 5 summarizes the study.
- Section 6 concludes the paper.

2 JAPAN'S LOCAL AREA ECONOMIC SITUATION

In Japan, municipality mergers were initiated by the government over a period of approximately 10 years, starting in 1999. The purpose was to respond to changes in socioeconomic conditions, such as a declining population, falling birthrates, and an aging population. Municipalities were incorporated into larger areas, and their administrative and financial bases strengthened to become basic municipalities with administrative authority. In other words, they were decentralized.

Japan accepted the Potsdam Declaration on August 14, 1945, which ended World War II. Subsequently, the population flowed into major urban areas, and reconstruction began. In Japan the three major metropolitan areas are Tokyo (i.e., Saitama, Tokyo, Kanagawa, and Chiba), Nagoya (i.e., Gifu, Aichi, and Mie), and Osaka (i.e., Kyoto, Osaka, Hyogo, and Nara). Figure 1 shows the population trends of the three metropolitan areas and other regions [13]. From 1957, the Japanese economy grew by approximately 10% per year for 16 years, due to (among other things) the use of new local school graduates, surplus agricultural labor, coal mine leavers, and government policies. Japan's rapid economic growth continued but ended with the oil crisis triggered by the rise in oil prices following the Fourth Middle East War in 1973, the recession caused by the strong yen following the Plaza Accord in 1985, and the bubble economy in the late 1980s and the early 1990s.

Thus, the situation in Japan has changed drastically since 1945, but the inflow of the population from rural areas to the three major metropolitan areas continues. As the population continues to grow, by 2021, the residents of the Tokyo metropolitan area will account for 29% of Japan's total population. Table 1 shows the results of economic activity in the three metropolitan areas for the year 2019 [14]. From Table 1, the value added calculated for the Tokyo, Nagoya, and Osaka metropolitan areas is 34%, 10%, and 13% of the GDP, respectively [14,15]. The shares of the three metropolitan areas in Japan's primary to tertiary industry output are 7%, 21%, and 38% for the Tokyo metropolitan area; 6%, 15%, and 8% for the Nagoya metropolitan area; and 3%, 13%, and 14% for the Osaka metropolitan area, respectively. The Tokyo metropolitan area has a particularly large economy because it is the country's capital. The secondary industry is the most active of the three industries in the Nagoya area. Osaka has several active secondary and tertiary sectors.

Figure 2 shows the percentages of juvenile, working-age, and elderly populations in Japan and the three metropolitan areas [13]. While juvenile and working-age populations are decreasing, the elderly population continues to increase, a trend that is true for all Japanese regions. The proportion of the population in FY2020 was 12% juvenile, 60% working-age, and 29% elderly. The percentages were 12%, 63%, and 25% for the Tokyo metropolitan area;

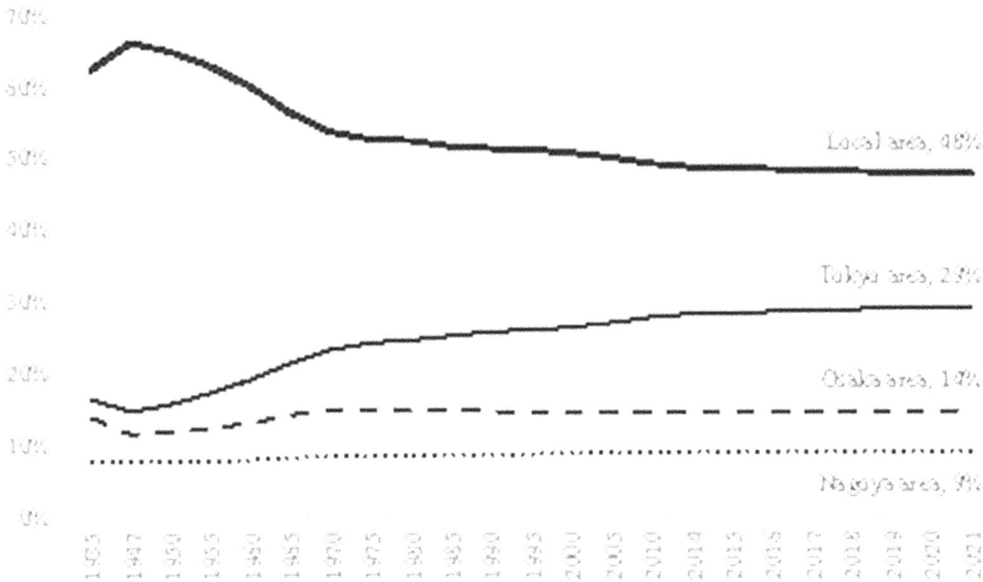

Figure 1. Population trends in major Japanese regions.

Table 1. Contribution of the gross prefectural product of the three major regions to GDP and three industries (as of 2019).

	GPD	Primary industry	Secondary industry	Tertiary industry
Tokyo area	34%	7%	21%	38%
Nagoya area	10%	6%	15%	8%
Osaka area	13%	3%	13%	14%

13%, 60%, and 27% for the Nagoya metropolitan area; and 12%, 60%, and 29% for the Osaka metropolitan area. Table 2 shows the population of the three age groups and their percentages in 2021 [13]. In regions other than the three major metropolitan areas, the proportions of the working-age population is small, and the aged population large (see Table 2). As Figure 2 and Table 2 show, in addition to demographic trends, age structure ratios differ by region. Compared to the three metropolitan areas, rural areas have a larger area, smaller working-age population, and larger elderly population. Therefore, these regions face many challenges in economic activity and growth potential owing to their labor force, financial resources, and geographical conditions.

Table 2. Population and ratios of the three age groups in major regions (as of October 2021).

	Under 15		15 to 64		65 and over		Total
Tokyo area	4,211	(11%)	23,324	(63%)	9,326	(25%)	36,861
Nagoya area	1,412	(13%)	6,769	(60%)	3,054	(27%)	11,235
Osaka area	2,114	(12%)	10,771	(59%)	5,231	(29%)	18,116
Local area	7,047	(12%)	33,640	(57%)	18,603	(31%)	59,290

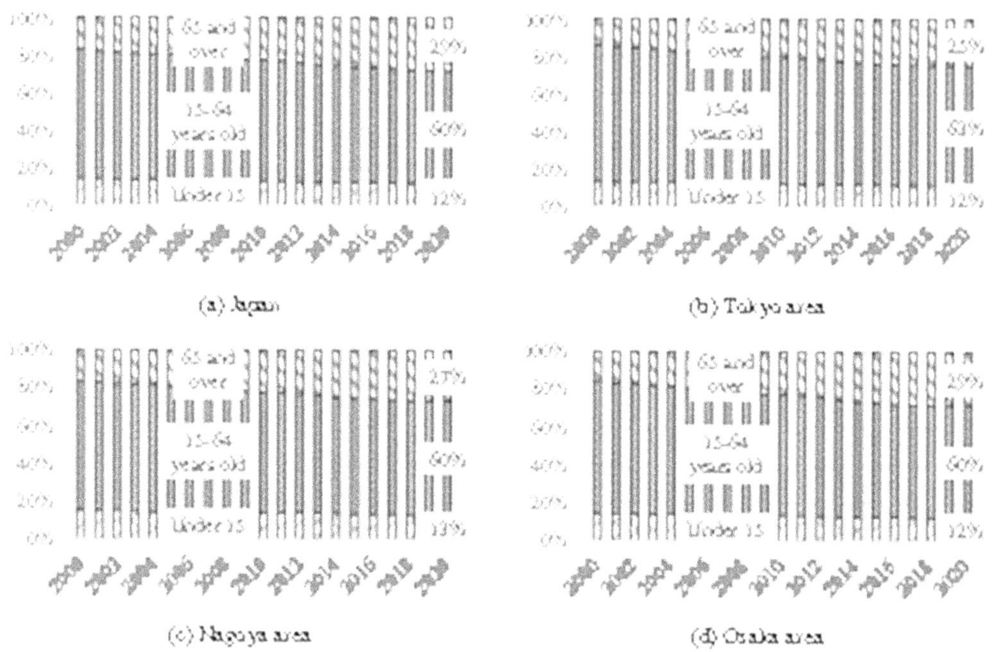

Figure 2. Percentage of three age groups in three major regions, 2000–2020.

3 PRODUCT FUNCTION

In the 1920s, Douglas [16] used statistical data for the entire U.S. manufacturing industry to express the relationship between labor and capital inputs and outputs in a real industry's production function. This production function was expressed using the employment (L), fixed capital stock (C), and physical output (P) indices. The following relationship was established:

$$\log P = \log k + \alpha \log L + (1 - \alpha) \log C \tag{1}$$

where k and α were the coefficients of the above function and α the labor share. The Douglas production function assumes linear homogeneity. Rather than assuming this a priori, it has been refined to discuss whether $\alpha + \beta$ equals one, with 1-α in Equation (1) as β.

$$\log P = \log k + \alpha \log L + \beta \log C \tag{2}$$

Numerous studies have been conducted to prove the validity of the Douglas production function, and although the values of α are scattered between 0.42 and 0.84, the reasons can be explained to some extent, and $\alpha + \beta$ is approximately equal to one. Where α is the coefficient of the employment index, interpreted as the elasticity of employment, and β is the coefficient of the fixed capital stock index, interpreted as the elasticity of capital. The coefficients $\alpha+\beta$ are interpreted as the degree of harvest in the scale of production and have the following meaning regarding their values:

(*i*)	$\alpha + \beta < 1$	*Diminishing returns*
(*ii*)	$\alpha + \beta = 1$	*Constant yield*
(*iii*)	$\alpha + \beta > 1$	*Increasing yield*

In particular, in case (ii), the production function is first-order homogeneous. In general, the Douglas production function assumes the following conditions:

$$\alpha + \beta = 1,\ 0 < \alpha < 1,\ k > 0.$$

Under this assumption, production function (2) is assumed to have the properties of transitory homogeneity and diminishing marginal rates of substitution between factors. The deviation in the coefficients of the production function is attributed to imperfect competition factors in the market. This study describes a possible production function that considers economic phenomena as much as possible and applies a possibilistic regression model to analyze the production function [12].

One possibilistic production function is the Douglas production interval, which uses an interval regression model. We replaced the log-transformed *P*, *L*, and *C* values with *y*, *x1*, and *x2* values, respectively. The regression coefficients *logk*, α, and β were replaced by (*a_0*, *w_0*), (*a_1*, *w_1*), and (*A_2*, *w_2*), respectively. Where *a* is the center of the triangular fuzzy number and *w* is the spread in both directions from center *a*. This allows us to write the possibilistic production function as:

$$y = (a_0, w_0) + (a_1, w_1)x_1 + (a_2, w_2)x_2 \tag{3}$$

Because this possibility production function employs regression coefficients for triangular fuzzy numbers, its output *y* = (*y, s*) is also a triangular fuzzy number. Because the width of the triangular fuzzy numbers is non-negative, the interval outputs of the possibilistic production function are the lower limit *y-s*, center *y*, and upper limit *y+s*. In addition, we sought an interval regression equation that minimized ambiguity when the predicted value *y* encompassed the dependent variable log *P* [17]. Therefore, when constructing the possibilistic production function, a linear programming (LP) problem was solved to minimize *w0+w1+w2* or Σ *s* with the inclusion relation y $\supseteq$ log *P* as a constraint, and the regression coefficients *a* and *w* were obtained. If the data contained ambiguities that rendered the Douglas production function unsuitable for analysis, it could still be considered. In addition, it was possible to interpret the data in a manner that differed from that of a statistical model.

Next, we examined the characteristics of the Douglas and possibilistic production functions using statistical data for the entire U.S. manufacturing industry used by Douglas [18]. First, in the Douglas production function, the coefficient of the employment index *L* is α = 0.766, and the coefficient of the fixed capital stock index *C* is α = 0.245. Because $\alpha+\beta=1.011$, $\alpha+\beta$ is approximately one. Next, when the objective function of the *LP* problem to obtain the coefficients of the model is minimized (*w1+w2+w3*), the coefficients of the employment index *L* in the possibilistic production function (0.748, 0) and employment index *L* (0.294, 0.018) are (1.041, 0.018). This result indicated that the sum of the coefficients of the employment and fixed capital stock indices was [1.024, 1.059].

4 JAPANESE INDUSTRY ANALYSIS

The FY2020 National Accounts published by the Cabinet Office in 2021 include the value of output, gross capital formation, number of workers, and working hours for 30 types of economic activities over 28 years from 1995 to 2021. The number of workers and working hours were converted into the labor force. The output index, labor force, and gross capital formation in 1994 were used as the basis for the log-transformed indices. The output (*P*), employment (*L*), and capital (*C*) indices were then used to analyze the industry through the production function. Only four economic activities were included in the regression analysis. The four activities were:

1. Information and communication equipment and electrical machinery;
2. Two product types in the manufacturing industry;

3. Information and communication technology; and
4. Professional, scientific, technical, and business support services.

Figures 3(a) and 3(b) show the corresponding scatter plots, and Figures 3(b), 4(a), and 5(a) show the distributions, although the sample was not linearly distributed. Table 3 shows the coefficients of the Douglas and possibilistic production function obtained for the four economic activities, with the coefficient of the employment index as α and the coefficient of the capital index as β. The coefficients shown in Table 3 indicated that the elasticity of productivity concerning labor (α) was small for the manufacturing (electromechanical) and information and communication industries, at approximately 0.1. In other words, productivity increased by approximately 10% of the labor input. Conversely, the productivity of the manufacturing industry (information and communication equipment), professional, science and technology, and business support service industries increased by the same amount as labor input. The elasticity of productivity concerning capital (β) was less than one for both the manufacturing industry (information and communication equipment) and the professional, science and technology, and business support service industries, and was approximately 0.5 for the manufacturing industry (information and communication equipment), approximately 0.5 for the manufacturing industry (electromechanical) and information and communication industry, and approximately 0.75% for the professional, science and technology, and the business support service industry was 0.9. The elasticities of the manufacturing (electromechanical) and information and communication industries were approximately 0.75. Similar to the elasticity of labor, the manufacturing (electromechanical) and information and communication industries had α+β values greater than 1.5, indicating increased returns.

(a) scatterplot of log P – log L

(b) scatterplot of log P – log C

Figure 3. Manufacturing industry (Information and communication equipment).

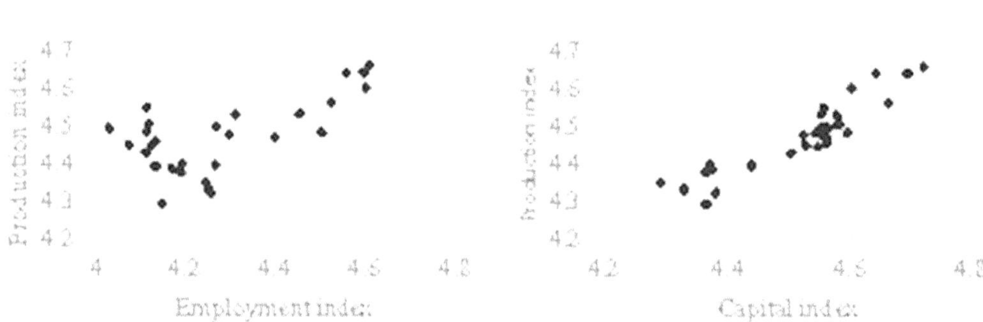

(a) scatterplot of log P – log L

(b) scatterplot of log P – log C

Figure 4. Manufacturing industry (Electromechanical).

Table 3. Production function coefficients.

		Const.	α	β	$\alpha+\beta$
Industry 1	DPF	-2.1720	1.0293	0.4752	1.5045
	PPF	(-2.6610, 0)	(0.9845, 0)	(0.6235, 0.0301)	(1.6080, 0.0301)
Industry 2	DPF	0.7716	0.1086	0.7159	0.8244
	PPF	(0.7111, 0)	(0.0539, 0)	(0.7807, 0.0129)	(0.8347, 0.0129)
Industry 3	DPF	0.5914	0.1257	0.7559	0.8816
	PPF	(0.5756, 0)	(0.1319, 0)	(0.7532, 0.0101)	(0.8851, 0.0101)
Industry 4	DPF	-4.0660	0.9836	0.9028	1.8864
	PPF	(-4.5422, 0)	(0.9494, 0.0093)	(1.0376, 0)	(1.9870, 0.0093)

Note: Abbreviations
DPF: Douglas Production Function, PPF: Possibilistic Product Function,
Industry 1: Manufacturing (Information and communication equipment),
Industry 2: Manufacturing (Electromechanical),
Industry 3: Information and communication,
Industry 4: Professional, science and technology, and business support services.

These results indicated that the Japanese economy had experienced increasing returns. In particular, the relatively high labor force elasticity suggested that the Japanese economy could be revitalized by increasing the labor force's efficiency.

(a) scatterplot of log P – log L (b) scatterplot of log P – log C

Figure 5. Information and communication industry.

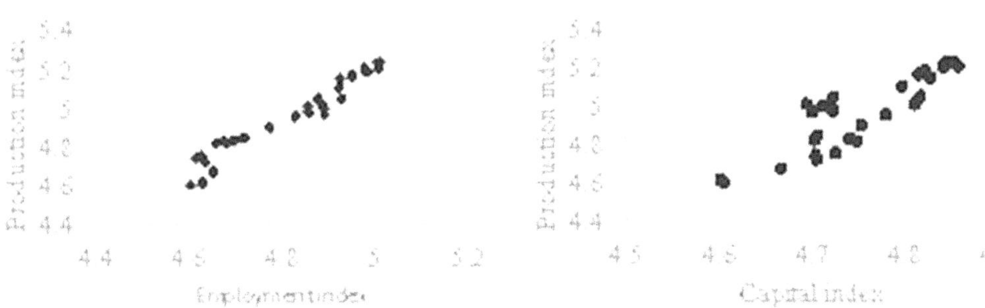

(a) scatterplot of log P – log L (b) scatterplot of log P – log C

Figure 6. Professional, science and technology and business support service industry.

5 CONCLUSION

In Japan, the population continues to flow into the Tokyo area, whereas the rest of the country is experiencing population outflow. Regional vitality is declining, and economies are stagnating. In this study, an industrial analysis was conducted to revitalize a stagnant regional economy. The results showed that the manufacturing (information and communication equipment), professional, science and technology, and business support service industries had relatively high elasticity of production concerning labor. In addition, the elasticity of production concerning capital was high, indicating that both sectors had increased returns. Because this analysis was concerned with economic activity in Japan, the next step is to analyze regional economies.

REFERENCES

[1] Policy Bureau, Ministry of Land, Infrastructure, Transport and Tourism, Japan, "Summary of The White Paper on Land, Infrastructure, Transport And Tourism in Japan, 2020," https://www.mlit.go.jp/statistics/content/001412289.pdf (accessed on 12 June 2023).

[2] O. Bajo-Rubio, "The role of foreign direct investment in growth: Spain, 1964–2013," Applied Economic Analysis, 30(90), 263–276, 2022.

[3] K. Atta Sakyi, "Managerial Economics and Production Functions -Theoretical Review and Practical Applications," International Journal of Research and Innovation in Social Science (IJRISS), IV(IX), 318–321, 2020.

[4] Y. Sidik Pratiknyo, W. Bangun, Z. Hidayah, R. Kambara, "Optimization of Cooperative Production Function in The Philippines And Indonesia," Asean International Journal of Business, 2(1), 49–64, 2023.

[5] L. Samoilova and D. Rodionov, "Production Function Based on Input–Output and Growth Rate Indicators as a Tool for Assessment of Innovation Climate in Russian Regions," Economies, vol.10, Issue 12, 28p, 2022.

[6] R. Pesch and B. Tuck, "Developing a Production Function for Small-Scale Farm Operations in Central Minnesota," Journal of Agriculture, Food Systems, and Community Development, 8(C), 27–36. 2019.

[7] J. Growiec, P. McAdam, and J. Mućk, "R&D Capital and the Idea Production Function." Federal Reserve Bank of Kansas City, Research Working Paper no. 23-05, May 2023. DOI:10.18651/RWP2023-05

[8] I. Domazet, D. Marjanović, D. Ahmetagić, M. Antonijević, "Does the Increase in the Number of Registered Patents Affect Economic Growth? - Evidence from Romania and Bulgaria," Economic Analysis, 55(2), 49–65, 2022.

[9] I. Tziolas & J. Paul Elhorst, "The rise and spread of female labour force participation at the US county level," Spatial Economic Analysis, 18(1), 143–151, 2022.

[10] S. Zhang, W. Gu, "On Nonparametric Estimation for the Frontier Elasticity of Output with DEA Model," Journal of Management Science and Statistical Decision, 7(1), 135–140, 2010.

[11] J. Felipe, F. Gerard Adams, "The Estimation of The Cobb-Douglas Function: A Retrospective View," Eastern Economic Journal, 31(3), 427–445, 2005.

[12] J. Watada, "Possibilistic Production Function and Its Application," In: Proceedings of 5th International Fuzzy Systems Association World Congress'93 at Seoul, Korea, 1, 509–512, 1993.

[13] Statistics Bureau, Ministry of Internal Affairs and Communications, Japan, "Population Estimates," https://www.stat.go.jp/english/data/jinsui/index.html (accessed on 12 June 2023).

[14] Economic and Social Research Institute, Cabinet Office, Government of Japan, "Prefectural economic accounts," https://www.e-stat.go.jp/stat-search/file-download?statInfId=000040019817&fileKind=0 (accessed on 12 June 2023).

[15] Economic and Social Research Institute, Cabinet Office, Government of Japan, "National Accounts for 2020," https://www.esri.cao.go.jp/en/sna/data/kakuhou/files/2020/2020annual_report_e.html (accessed on 12 June 2023).

[16] T. Saepudin, A. Amelia, "Analysis of Rice Production Approach to Cobb Douglas Production Function in Tambakdahan Sub-Didstrict Subang Didstrict," Agricultural Socio-Economics Journal, 22(2), 121–127,2022.

[17] Y. Yabuuchi, J. Watada, "Building Fuzzy Robust Regression Model Based on Granularity And Possibility Distribution," In: Pedrycz, W. and Chen S.-M. (eds), Information Granularity, Big Data, and Computational Intelligence, Springer-Verlag Berlin Heidelberg, 247–272, 2014.

[18] P. H.Douglas, "The Theory of Wages," Reprints of Economic Classics, Augustus M.Kelley, New York, 1964.

Digital Synergy – El Emary et al. (eds)

Chapter 3
Management and image creation in selected local government units

Ibrahiem M.M. El Emary
KAU, Jeddah, Saudi Arabia

Angelika Brzozowska
University of Warsaw, Warsaw, Poland

Agnieszka Kwiatek
Czestochowa University of Technology, Poland

Anna Sawicka & Ewa Witkowska
Regional Development Center Parzęczew sp. z o.o., Parzęczew, Poland

Contents

The trend of creating an image on the Internet as a result of the announced COVID-19 pandemic has intensively embraced government and local government institutions, which have shifted some of their communication with stakeholders to social media profiles. One measure of the effectiveness of ongoing communication on social media is user activity, defined as the behaviour when encountering content. The aim of the article is to identify the determinants influencing users' activity in social media on the official profiles of selected local government units, using an example of the Wielkopolskie Voivodeship. In addition to the effect of promoting content to the target group, local government authorities, through effective activity on official municipal profiles, deepen relations with the region's inhabitants and stakeholders, presenting an attitude of openness, as well as strengthening the user's identification with the brand - in this case, with the selected region. The object of the research is to determine the type, frequency and nature of user activity on local government social media profiles in relation to messages published by the authority, diversified in terms of form and type of content disseminated, taking into account the intensity of the image campaign conducted for the period 2019-2021. The study was carried out using quantitative methods based on statistical data obtained from social media. Observations of communication on local government profiles of the Wielkopolskie Voivodeship were made and a case study of the profile of selected municipalities was performed. In addition, subject scientific articles from the years 2012-2022, public information including development strategies of selected local government units were analysed in order to determine recommendations for local government authorities in the field of model image management of the commune in order to achieve measurable effects in the

DOI: 10.1201/9781003440406-3

form of user activity, including involvement in the discussion of important events or investments for the region.

1 INTRODUCTION

In connection with the announcement in 2020 of the state of the pandemic in Poland (Ministry of Health 2020), the leaders of municipalities faced the challenge of maintaining effective communication with stakeholders, despite new, unprecedented circumstances. The COVID-19 crisis has reduced the ability to communicate directly in public places, including public offices (Hassankhani et al. 2021). Municipalities removed local events from the agendas, including cultural meetings, concerts, exhibitions, celebrations of national and local holidays. The cancellation of each of the events represented a missed opportunity to establish relations with residents and other stakeholders and to provide important information from the point of view of municipal leaders. Despite limited opportunities for direct contact, representatives of municipalities used online channels to maintain continuity of communication with both residents and partners and potential investors (Walle 1996). Despite the difficult economic situation associated with the state of the declared pandemic, local government units fulfilled economic and social objectives, using marketing tools, including social media (Mahdani et al. 2022), to promote ideas, local actions and investments.

2 REVIEW OF THE LITERATURE - TERRITORIAL MARKETING OF LOCAL GOVERNMENT UNITS

Local government units have become entities operating under conditions of market competition as a result of the systemic transformation and introduction of a free market economy (Szwacka-Mokrzycka 2010). In the 1990s, self-government units were established at the commune level (1990) and then at the county and voivodship level (1999), which – as financially autonomous entities – started promotional activities for their products and services, which initiated the separation of territorial marketing (Sekuła 2005). J. Szwacka-Mokrzycka lists the areas in which competition between local government entities is observed as: attracting domestic and foreign investors, access to various sources of financing, particularly public and foreign, maintenance of existing capital, location of administrative, financial and scientific institutions, organization of commercial, cultural and sports events, exhibitions, conferences, political meetings, access to markets, attracting and maintaining tourists, students, residents.

An integral element supporting effective management of these areas is communication, implemented through the marketing strategy of the municipality (Morgan et al. 2019). "Territorial marketing focuses on the policy and strategy of communication of the territorial administration unit with its environment and attracting potential investors or clients" (Jaska and Szczepłek 2010). Local government units present their offers of products and services to various stakeholders: residents, tourists, investors and other public organisations (Selden and Sowa 2011), thanks to which they can pursue strategic objectives and develop the region with a view to the general welfare. For this purpose, they use communication tools, selected in terms of, among others, reach, target group, taking into account media functions depending on the type of intended promotion (Table 1).

In the face of the announced COVID-19 pandemic, the heads of local government units turned their attention to social media (González-Padilla and Tortolero-Blanco 2020). which was one of the tools of territorial marketing understood as "a set of actions of local government units aimed at getting to know and meeting the needs of local communities and stakeholders, determined by efficient communication" (Cichomski 2013). Although there are many definitions of territorial marketing (Kaczorowska-Budek 2014), Cichomski's approach is particularly relevant in the context of the two-year epidemic in Poland and around the world. Unlike other approaches, particular emphasis was placed on understanding the needs of the local community and stakeholders, which was crucial for managing the municipality during the crisis.

Table 1. Types of promotion of municipalities and functions of local and regional media.

Promotion type of municipality	The function of media
Internal economic	– informative, – promotion of local initiatives, – advertising and publicity, – practical
External economic	– informative, – advertising and publicity, – promotion of local initiatives
Internal social	– informative, – integrative, – psychosocial, – controlling, – opinion-forming
External social	– informative, – promotion of local initiatives, – opinion-forming
Internal cultural	– informative, – cultural, – integrative, – entertaining
External cultural	– informative, – psychosocial, – promotion of local initiatives

Source: (own elaboration based on, Jaska 2009: 37).

The main feature that distinguishes social media from other media is the ability to share information found on the portal with other users using the Internet (Osterrieder 2013). Social media enables public administrations to communicate and interact with citizens on a continuous basis. They provide a space for the implementation of part of the tasks related to the communication strategy, the main goal of which is cooperation with the social environment (Gawłowski and Miliszewski 2019). It should be noted that local governments do not have a uniform approach to the role of social media in communicating with the environment (Graham et al. 2015) I. Mergel distinguishes four strategies used by public administrations in this area, in which social media pursues one of the following objectives: informing without waiting for feedback from users, encouraging the audience to be active and comment on the content posted, a customer service element and a place to respond to questions and comments that arise, building cooperation networks with residents (Mergel et al. 2019).

The rulers implement different communication strategies (Floreddu and Cabiddu 2016) to a greater or lesser extent taking into account the activity of the target group. Among unidirectional forms of communication, we distinguish publicity, i. e. publicity and public information, based on facts and figures (Frączek 2012). In both cases, the sender of the message is not interested in receiving feedback. Two-way communication is divided into asymmetric communication, the purpose of which is to obtain benefits for the broadcaster in relation to the published content; and symmetrical, where the parties influence each other in order to obtain mutual benefit from the interaction (Frączek 2012). In the case of communication on social media, it is possible to actively participate in the discussion of portal users, as well as express opinions. Representatives of local governments administering the profiles of the municipality can observe the reactions of users and assess the public mood with regard to the published content on an ongoing basis (Chan and Schofer 2014). Social media offers tools to measure and monitor user behaviour in contact with proposed content, which allows understanding the needs of the audience (Trunfio and Rossi 2021). Social networks, including Facebook, allow you to track the reach of posts, which indicates the number of views of information by users, user activity, understood as the number of interactions by users through reactions (e. g. clicking on a "Like" button), adding a comment, and viewing or sharing information (Facebook 2022). In addition, it is possible to analyse the demographic structure of the audience in terms of age, location in the country or abroad where you come from or use social media. User activity is a measure of engagement, as well as social sentiment with regard to the initiative or idea proposed by the local government (Reddick et al. 2017). The leaders of municipalities can get feedback from the local community, as well as ideas for the implementation of new ones. The behaviour of municipality representatives towards users who express their opinions on official social media profiles builds an image of the municipality (Rudolf and Wæraas 2021), which may encourage or discourage potential tourists to visit the site and potential partners to invest in new ventures. The activity of users and how administrators of social media profiles moderate discussions is therefore an important element of creating the image of a modern municipality.

3 METHODOLOGY

The aim of the study was to examine the communication strategies employed by local government authorities with local stakeholders in response to the announcement of the COVID-19 pandemic. The study focused on exploring the activity and content posted on the official social media profiles of three municipalities in the Wielkopolskie Voivodeship: Chodzież, Lubasz, and Kotlin, specifically on the Facebook platform. The research methodology adopted by the authors involved a combination of quantitative and qualitative approaches. Data for the study were collected from the information posted on the municipalities' official information channels on Facebook. The analysis included examining the number of published posts, COVID-19 related content, and user reactions such as likes, comments, and shares. The research sample comprised the aforementioned three selected rural municipalities from the Wielkopolskie Voivodeship, chosen for comparative purposes. For each municipality, data for specific periods related to the COVID-19 pandemic were analyzed. The study was divided into several stages. The first stage involved the selection of municipalities and analysis periods, which included determining the three rural municipalities from the Wielkopolskie Voivodeship and defining the analysis periods related to the COVID-19 pandemic for each municipality. The subsequent stage focused on data collection from the official municipality profiles on Facebook. This was followed by the analysis of the number of published posts and COVID-19 related content, including quantitative analysis through statistical examination of the number of published posts in each period and comparative analysis of COVID-19 related content against the overall number of posts. Additionally, qualitative data analysis was conducted, involving the examination of post content in terms of user reactions and categorization of posts according to the municipalities' information-promotion functions, such as cultural, social, and economic functions. The final stage of the study encompassed the interpretation of the collected data, analysis of research results, presentation of conclusions regarding the communication strategies employed by local government authorities with local stakeholders during the COVID-19 pandemic, and discussion of potential changes in the communication practices of local authorities in response to the COVID-19 pandemic.

4 RESULTS

The crisis caused by the announced COVID-19 pandemic in 2020 caused local government units to perform promotional functions in a different way. Traditional media such as posters, newsletters or leaflets distributed in public places have been replaced by digital information, placed on social media and on the websites of municipalities.

Pursuant to the Decree of the Minister of National Education, the functioning of schools, kindergartens and universities and other educational institutions was suspended for a period of two weeks from 12 March 2020 to 25 March 2020 (Ministry of Education 2020). The leaders of municipalities and representatives of their educational institutions faced the challenge of crisis management and fulfilling their responsibilities in the new circumstances of limited direct communication. The two-week restrictions on the functioning of educational institutions may indicate that central institutions will quickly deal with the epidemic and that unusual communication solutions will be introduced in the short term. In practice, the revocation of the epidemic occurred more than 2 years later with the announcement of the Regulation of the Minister of Health of 12 May 2022 (Ministry of Health 2022). Due to the fact that local government units were responsible for implementing the crisis management plan related to the declared COVID-19 pandemic, the heads of municipalities introduced a number of changes that permanently changed the way of communication in local government units.

Surveys of the Central Statistical Office show that among households with persons aged 16-74 90. 4% have access to the Internet (GUS 2021) (Figure 1).

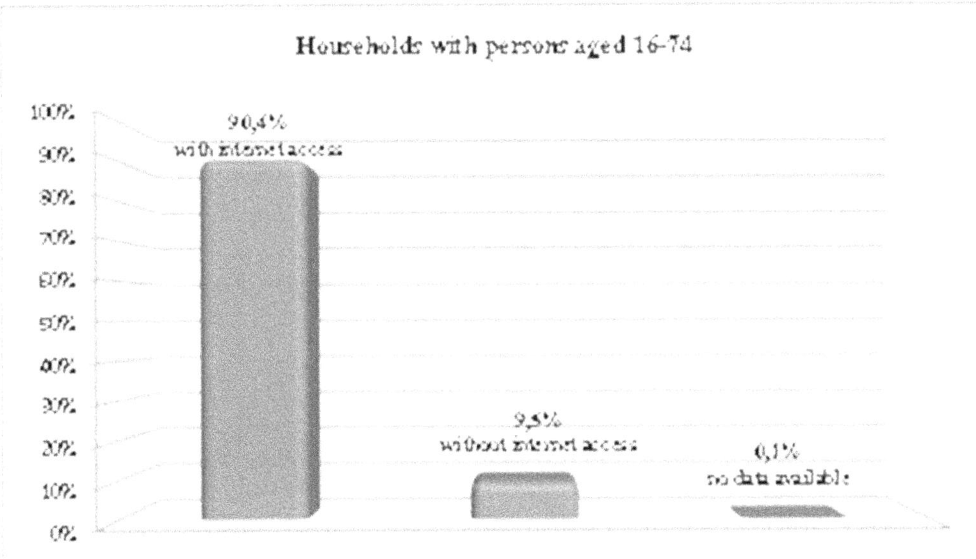

Figure 1. Households with persons aged 16-74.
Source: (own elaboration based on, GUS 2021)

This means that most of the population in Poland could follow the events related to the coronavirus outbreak via online media. During the announced COVID-19 pandemic, websites were an important source of information about the epidemic situation, particularly in the 16-24, 25-34 and 35-44 age groups, where 90. 3%, 86. 9% and 81. 8% of respondents confirmed using this source to obtain information about the coronavirus (GUS 2021) (Figure 2). This means that most of the population in Poland could follow the events related to the coronavirus outbreak via online media. During the announced COVID-19 pandemic, websites were an important source of information about the epidemic situation, particularly in the 16-24, 25-34 and 35-44 age groups, where 90. 3%, 86. 9% and 81. 8% of respondents confirmed using this source to obtain information about the coronavirus (GUS 2021) (Figure 2).

According to the GUS data (Figure 2) social networks were a popular source of information in the 16-24 and 25-34 age groups, where respectively 68% and 59. 4% of respondents confirmed checking information about the COVID-19 epidemic there. People aged 55-64 and 65-74 were least likely to use this source of information, with 16. 4% and 8. 1% respectively indicating social media as a source of information about COVID-19.

In the situation of the announced COVID-19 pandemic, media, including social media, played an important social and cultural function, integrating the local community during the crisis and the shaken sense of security, which "belongs not only to the highest and most important values, but it is one of the most basic and inalienable life needs of man and a sine qua non condition for

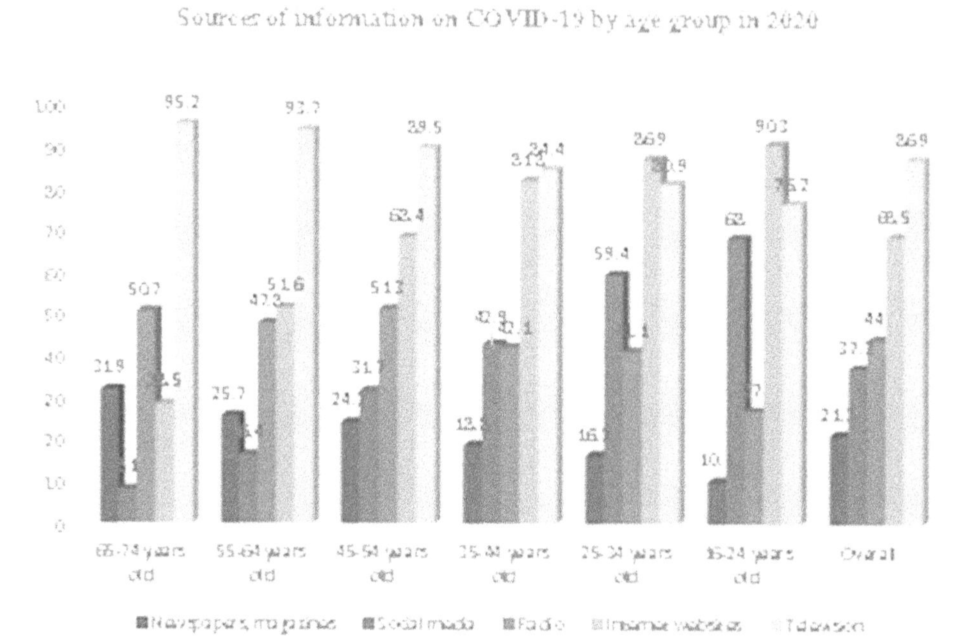

Figure 2. Sources of COVID-19 information by age group in 2020.
Source: (own elaboration based on, GUS 2021)

achieving almost all other values" (Szmyd 2014). In addition, Szmyd points out that "people also – it should be added – expect a thorough and comprehensive knowledge of the current causes and conditions of their endangered security and related anxiety." Informing central and local authorities about the epidemic, as well as the economic and social situation in the region, was therefore a key aspect of maintaining social peace.

5 COMPARISON OF SOCIAL MEDIA COMMUNICATION OF SELECTED MUNICIPALITIES FROM WIELKOPOLSKIE VOIVODSHIP

In order to obtain information about the determinants influencing the activity of users in social media, a study was conducted based on quantitative and qualitative empirical methodology. The study was conducted in 3 municipalities of Wielkopolskie Voivodeship. For comparative purposes, small rural municipalities were selected for the survey, with a population ranging from 6 to 8 thousand inhabitants. The data needed for the survey were collected between 16. 08 and 3. 09. 2022 based on information posted on official information channels of municipalities on the Facebook platform.

Chodzież Municipality

Chodzież Rural Commune in Chodzież County is a small municipality located within the boundaries of Wielkopolskie Voivodeship, surrounding the urban Commune of Chodzież. In 2019 (GUS 2020) the rural commune of Chodzież was inhabited by 6100 people on an area of 211. 90 km2. The Municipality of Chodzież created an official social media profile in 2012 on the Facebook platform, where current information was published (Table 2).

The collected information shows that, despite the creation of an official profile in 2012, social media did not constitute an important communication channel for the municipality's rulers in 2015-2019. The situation began to change in 2020.

Table 2. The number of published posts placed on the official profile of the municipality of Chodzież in the years 2012-2019.

	Municipality of Chodzież									
	2012	2013	2014	2015	2016	2017	2018	2019	2020	2021
The number of published posts	4	16	21	0	0	0	1	1	23	84

Source: own study based on information on the community profile of Chodzież municipality (Facebook 2022).

Ceasure for the following year periods was determined on 11 March 2020, when the Regulation of the Minister of Education on the temporary limitation of the functioning of units of the education system in connection with the prevention, counteracting and combating of COVID-19 was announced (Ministry of Education 2020). The data show that in the first year of the COVID-19 pandemic, there was an increase in the frequency of posting via the official social channel on Facebook to 29 posts, whereas in the previous period between 11. 03. 2019 and 10. 03. 2020 only 1 announcement was published via this medium (Table 3). In the next analogous period, representatives of the rural municipality of Chodzież published 99 posts, which represented an increase of 241% compared to the previous period (Table 2).

Table 3. Number of published posts on the official profile of the municipality of Chodzież in the period 11.03.2019-10.03.2022 on Facebook.

	11.03.2019 - 10.03.2020	11.03.2020 - 10.03.2021	11.03.2021 - 10.03.2022
The number of published posts	1	29	99
The number of posts related to COVID-19	0	1	1

Source: own study based on information on the community profile of Chodzież municipality (Facebook 2022).

According to the data, the community profile of the municipality was not an important source of information about the announced COVID-19 pandemic – posts on this topic were published only twice in 2 years between 11.03.2020 and 10.03.2022.

The greatest activity of users towards announcements published on the municipality's Facebook profile is presented in Table 4.

In the first year of the announced COVID-19 pandemic, users reacted with the largest number of clicks on the "like" button to the coverage of the National Independence Day celebrations. The advertisement served an internal cultural function according to the media classification (Jaska 2010). The largest number of comments were gathered by representatives of the municipality under the announcement concerning Christmas wishes, which also served as an internal cultural function. The vacancy notice was posted 23 times, which was the highest number of posts during that period. The post concerning the job offer was categorized as performing an internal economic function of promotional activities of the local government unit.

In the following period, most users clicked the "like" button under the post about the harvest celebration, while wishes posted before Christmas received the most comments. Both announcements serve an internal cultural function. The announcement that received the largest number of shares related to the collection of donations for refugees from Ukraine. Fasting had an internal social function.

Table 4. Characteristics of posts with the highest activity of users among the ads placed on the official profile of Chodzież in the period 11. 03. 2020-10. 03. 2022 on Facebook.

Period	Publication date	Topic of the post	The number of clicks on the "like" button	The number of comments	The number of shares	The function of media
11.03.2020-10.03.2021	13.11.2020	coverage of National Independence Day celebrations	52	5	5	Internal cultural
	25.11.2020	vacancy announcements	1	0	23	Internal economic
	22.12.2020	Christmas greetings	51	25	3	Internal cultural
11.03.2021-10.03.2022	25.08.2021	coverage of the harvest festival celebrations	49	7	18	Internal cultural
	20.12.2021	Christmas greetings	43	38	8	Internal cultural
	27.02.2022	Collection of donations for Ukrainian refugees	24	0	33	Internal social

Source: own study based on information on the community profile of Chodzież municipality (Facebook 2022).

Lubasz Municipality

Lubasz commune is located in the Czarnkowsko-Trzcianec district on an area of 167 km2. In 2019, the municipality was inhabited by 7701 people (GUS 2020). The leaders of the municipality have maintained a profile on social media since 2012 (Table 5).

Table 5. Number of published posts placed on the official profile of Lubasz municipality in the years 2012-2019.

	2012	2013	2014	2015	2016	2017	2018	2019	2020	2021
The number of published posts	1	5	0	67	164	114	142	110	169	140

Source: own study based on information on the community profile of Lubasz municipality (Facebook 2022).

The information on the municipality's Facebook profile also showed that the municipality had been conducting regular communication with recipients via social media since 2015 (Table 5). In previous years between 2012 and 2013, announcements were published sporadically, but in 2014 no announcements were published.

The data collected show that during the first year of the announced COVID-19 pandemic, representatives of Lubasz municipality regularly informed the recipients of the official social profile about the epidemic situation on Facebook (Table 6).

Table 6. Number of published posts posted on the official profile of Lubasz municipality in the period 11. 03. 2019-10. 03. 2022 on Facebook.

	11.03.2019 - 10.03.2020	11.03.2020 - 10.03.2021	11.03.2021 - 10.03.2022
The number of published posts	102	172	153
The number of posts related to COVID-19	Not applicable	99	29

Source: own study based on information on the community profile of Lubasz municipality (Facebook 2022).

As many as 99 announcements on the official profile were related to the coronavirus outbreak and the vaccination programme, accounting for 56% of all announcements during that period. The total number of published information also increased from 102 to 172, i. e. it increased by about 69% compared to the previous period. In the second year of the announced pandemic, the number of posts related to the coronavirus was much lower, at 29 announcements, and accounted for only 19% of all information published on the municipality's profile page. The number of all announcements during this period amounted to 153 and decreased by about 11% compared to the previous period.

On some of the ads from the surveyed period between 11. 03. 2020 and 10. 03. 2022 users reacted with feedback in the form of clicking on the "Like" button, comment on an advertisement or share it with another user or on an administered profile (Table 7).

Table 7. Characteristics of posts with the highest activity among the ads placed on the official profile of Lubasz municipality in the period 11. 03. 2020-10. 03. 2022 on Facebook.

Period	Publication date	Topic of the post	The number of clicks on the "like" button	The number of comments	The number of shares	The function of media
11.03.2020-10.03.2021	23.12.2020	information about abandoned puppies by the roadside	143	135	1951	Internal social
11.03.2021-10.03.2022	26.02.2022	Collection of donations for Ukrainian refugees	52	5	112	Internal social
	08.03.2022	Women's Day wishes	76	38	1	Internal cultural

Source: own study based on information on the community profile of Lubasz municipality (Facebook 2022).

In the period 11. 03. 2020 - 10. 03. 2021 the most popular information in terms of activity in all three categories was the announcement about puppies abandoned by the road on the day before Christmas Eve. The post received 143 likes, 135 comments and a total of 1951 shares. The information was shared between private individuals, as well as organisations providing assistance to animals, including shelters. According to the classification of types of promotion of municipalities and functions of local and regional media (Jaska 2010), the advertisement was characterized by an internal social function. In the following period appeared two posts with the maximum number of activities in their categories. The most comments received were wishes conveyed by representatives of the municipality on Women's Day, the information served as an internal cultural function. In the category of the highest number of shares and clicks on the "Like" button, he received a post about a charity fundraiser for refugees from Ukraine in connection with the newly started conflict in the East at that time. In this case, the function was assigned as a social internal.

Kotlin Municipality

Kotlin commune is a rural commune in the Jarocin county, inhabited by 7742 people on an area of 84 km2 (GUS 2020). Representatives of the municipality created an official social profile on Facebook in 2019 and have since maintained regular communication with stakeholders, posting 131 ads in 2019, 141 in 2020 and 120 in 2021 (Table 8).

Table 8. Number of published posts placed on the official profile of Kotlin municipality in 2012-2019.

	2012	2013	2014	2015	2016	2017	2018	2019	2020	2021
The number of published posts	No official Facebook profile							131	141	120

Source: own study based on information on the community profile of Lubasz municipality (Facebook 2022).

During the year preceding the announcement of the decree of the Minister of Education (Ministry of Education 2020), representatives of the municipality published 145 announcements, in subsequent periods the number of announcements was similar and amounted to 143 and 137 respectively (Table 9).

Table 9. Number of published posts posted on the official profile of Kotlin commune in the period 11. 03. 2019-10. 03. 2022 on Facebook.

	11.03.2019 - 10.03.2020	11.03.2020 - 10.03.2021	11.03.2021 - 10.03.2022
The number of published posts	145	143	137
The number of posts related to COVID-19	Not applicable	32	1

Source: own study based on information on the social profile of Kotlin commune (Facebook 2022).

In the period 11. 03. 2020-10. 03. 2021 on the profile of the municipality appeared 32 announcements concerning COVID-19. In the following period, only one announcement was placed on the subject. The activity of users on the information published on the profile of the municipality has been collected and categorized in Table 10.

Table 10. Characteristics of posts with the highest activity among the ads placed on the official profile of Kotlin commune in the period 11. 03. 2020-10. 03. 2022 on Facebook.

Period	Publication date	Topic of the post	The number of clicks on the "like" button	The number of comments	The number of shares	The function of media
11.03.2020-10.03.2021	14.04.2020	announcement of the mayor of the commune of Kotlin on the action for free home protection masks	38	9	97	Internal social
	22.04.2020	provision of free protection masks to residents	42	9	3	Internal social
	5.11.2020	completion of renovation of 4 municipal roads	16	15	1	Internal economic
11.03.2021-10.03.2022	14.01.2022	100th birthday of a resident of the municipality	76	15	3	Internal cultural
	30.12.2021	municipal waste collection schedule	5	7	31	Internal economic

Source: own study based on information on the social profile of Kotlin commune (Facebook 2022).

In the first year of the announced COVID-19 pandemic, the ads that received the highest number of shares and "like" clicks related to the distribution by the municipality of free protective masks, which constituted the social function of the medium according to the classification of media functions (Jaska 2010). At the end of the year, the municipality announced the completion of the renovation of 4 municipal roads, which resulted in the most active discussion in the period under review. The function of the announcement was defined as internal economic. In the period 11. 03. 2021-10. 03. 2022 the biggest number of clicks on the "like" button and comments was received by the information about the centenary of the birth of a resident of the municipality (internal cultural announcement function). The waste collection schedule was made available the largest number of times during this period (internal economic function).

6 CONCLUSIONS FROM THE STUDIES CARRIED OUT

Representatives of local government units used social media in various ways to inform the audience about the epidemic situation in the country. One of the municipalities surveyed (the municipality of Chodzież) published information on COVID-19 on the official profile of the municipality only twice in 2 years. However, there is a clear increase in the number of published announcements in the first and second year of the announced COVID-19 pandemic compared to the previous period, which may indicate that the municipality authorities have intensified communication via their Facebook profile as a result of the limited possibility of direct communication with municipal stakeholders.

The other two municipalities surveyed reported more intensively on the epidemic situation and initiatives related to the prevention of the spread of the coronavirus through social media. Lubasz Municipality devoted more than half of its advertisements to this topic during the period under review. Although the issue of COVID-19 was important for the rulers of both municipalities, users showed their greatest commitment mainly to other issues. Among the announcements that elicited the most reaction were occasional events of local celebrations, greetings, including Christmas greetings, as well as information about important social initiatives.

Observations of the surveyed social media profiles show that the greatest activity in the form of "Like" reactions among users is caused by local events and initiatives, close to the inhabitants of the region. Socially important information, including charitable, arousing great emotions, is shared by users. The event in Lubasz municipality, which received a record number of shares in the first year of the ongoing COVID-19 pandemic, was information about abandoned puppies, and in the second year users shared information about the collection of donations for refugees from Ukraine.

7 RECOMMENDATIONS

Social media is based on the possibility of interaction, conversation between the parties. In the case of territorial marketing, they give local governments an insight into the reactions of residents to taking action.

Due to the unregulated situation in Polish law regarding communication of local government units using social media, it is recommended that local governments develop regulations for the use of the medium, taking into account the preservation of the culture of discussion on both sides – administrators and moderators as well as users – residents and other stakeholders. Taking care of the quality of the discussion is in the interest of the municipality and taking care of the image. In addition, it contributes to obtaining constructive opinions that can contribute to initiating projects or making changes to the existing plans of the municipality.

Greater activity of residents on the social profiles of their regions also means greater involvement in local issues and initiatives, which supports building the image of the municipality as acting dynamically and efficiently, with the support of residents who want to implement economic or tourist ventures. Local government units of the municipality should more often encourage users, including residents, to actively participate in creating the image of the region on social media for the general social good and achievement of the municipality's goals. Administrators creating content for community profiles should create a space for two-way symmetrical communication (Frączek 2012), in which residents and users express their opinions and views, as well as create future initiatives in which they can engage.

Moreover, in times of crisis, similar to the epidemic situation, known from the period 2020-2022, the social media profile of the municipality can be not only a showcase of the local government, but also a channel for informing and supporting the local community in recovering the sense of security lost as a result of the crisis. There are many crises to which municipalities are exposed – droughts, storms and related technical problems, health crises, and finally potential military threats – all need to be managed by informing and helping the local community to deal with unexpected situations and preventing the danger of chaos and disruption. In addition, it is recommended to create messages on the social profiles of municipalities emphasizing their local or regional character, which promotes the promotion of places, their unique character. Investors, when deciding on the choice of destination for their investment, outside territorial conditions, check opinions about locations. The first verification of the location for the investment can take place via social media, without the need to physically reach the destination. Similarly, tourists – when choosing a holiday region, they suggest themselves with the recommendations of other users, verify the local accommodation offer, as well as regarding local initiatives, concerts, exhibitions, to spend time in the atmosphere of relaxation.

The activity of users on social profiles of local governments is affected by the publication of content important and exciting for the local community. Users who click the "Like" button on Facebook are guided by the emotions triggered by the content they encounter. At the same time, they show belonging to a community that identifies with similar values and ideas. Information that users willingly share, and thus consciously promote on social media, are ads containing elements of causality, incentives to take action, e. g. charitable aid. Social media users are able to notify their network of contacts about a charity event or the need for intervention, contributing, if not directly, then indirectly to the success of the initiative. A sense of action encourages you to follow the content on your social profile later and to contribute using the available features. Commenting on ads is the result of the need to share your own positive or critical opinion about the content published on the social profile. Although potential criticism from the commentator may be perceived by the rulers as unfavourable, in practice skilful moderation of the discussion based on prepared rules can translate into new ideas, initiatives or investments. Using the potential of social media provides a competitive advantage of the municipality in the competitive battle for investors, partners, tourists, as well as new residents, which directly translates into the financing of the municipality's budget. Currently, social media users are mainly 16-34 year olds, but widespread digitalization is affecting the broadening of the audience available on social media. Bringing discussions about the region's initiatives to the Internet space gives the opportunity to engage residents in local initiatives and helps them identify with the region's brand.

REFERENCES

Chan R. and Schofer J. L. 2014. Role of social media in communicating transit disruptions. *Transportation Research Record*, 2415.1: pp.145–151.

Cichomski W. 2013. Możliwości wykorzystania Internetu w promocji jednostek terytorialnych. In: W. Cichomski and R. Romanowski (eds.), *Marketing terytorialny oparty na wiedzy*, Wydawnictwo Uniwersytetu Ekonomicznego w Poznaniu, Poznań.

Delińska L. and Kęprowska D. 2018. Kreowanie wizerunku polskich miast w mediach społecznościowych. *Zarządzanie i Finanse Journal of Management and Finance* Vol. 16, No. 3/3.

Floreddu P. B. and Cabiddu F. 2016. Social media communication strategies. *Journal of Services Marketing*, 30.5: pp. 490–503.

Frączek A. 2012. Public relations: komunikacja dwukierunkowa. Studia Gdańskie. *Wizje i Rzeczywistość* 9, pp.132–144.

Gawłowski R. and Miliszewski K. 2019. Social media w administracji samorządowej na przykładzie powiatów województwa kujawsko-pomorskiego. *Samorząd Terytorialny* no 5, p. 71.

Gmina Kotlin, 2022. *Facebook*.

Gmina Lubasz, 2022. *Facebook*.

González-Padilla D. A. and Tortolero-Blanco L. 2020, Social media influence in the COVID-19 Pandemic. *International Braz J Urol*, 46: pp.120–124.

Graham M. W., Avery E. J. and Park S. 2015. The role of social media in local government crisis communications. *Public Relations Review*, 41.3: pp.386–394.

Hassankhani M., et al. 2021. Smart city and crisis management: Lessons for the COVID-19 pandemic. *International Journal of Environmental Research and Public Health*, 18.15: pp.7736.

Ibrahim, M., Yusra, Y. and Shah, N. U. 2022. Impact of social media addiction on work engagement and job performance. *Polish Journal of Management Studies*, 25(1), pp.179–192.

Jak korzystamy z Internetu, 2021. *GUS*.

Jaska E. 2009. Media a instrumenty marketingu terytorialnego. In: K. Krzyżanowska (ed.) *Rozwój obszarów wiejskich – wizerunek medialny*. Agencja Reklamowo-Wydawnicza Arkadiusz Grzegorczyk, Warszawa, p. 37.

Jaska E. and Szczepłek A. 2010. *Kształtowanie wizerunku jednostki administracyjnej na przykładzie gminy Legionowo*. In: K. Krzyżanowska (ed.) Szkoła Główna Gospodarstwa Wiejskiego w Warszawie Wydział Nauk Ekonomicznych Katedra Ekonomiki Edukacji, Komunikowania i Doradztwa.

Kaczorowska-Budek A. 2014, *U źródeł marketingu terytorialnego*. Szkoła Główna Handlowa w Warszawie.

Kotler P., Haider D. and Rein I. 1993. *Marketing places: Attracting Investment, Industry and Tourism to Cieties, States and Nations*. The Free Press, New York p. 37

Mergel I., Edelmann N. and Haug N. 2019. Defining digital transformation: Results from expert interviews. *Government Information Quarterly*, 36(4), 101385. DOI: 10.1016/j.giq.2019.06.002.

Miszczuk A., Miszczuk M. and Żuk K. 2007 *Gospodarka samorządu terytorialnego*. Wydawnictwo Naukowe PWN, Warszawa, p. 124.

Morgan N A., et al. 2019. Research in marketing strategy. *Journal of the Academy of Marketing Science*, 47: 4–29.

Osterrieder A. 2013. Wartość i wykorzystanie mediów społecznościowych jako narzędzia komunikacji w naukach o roślinach. *Metody roślinne*, 9, p.1–6.

Reddick Ch. G.; Chatfield A. T. and Ojo A. 2017. A social media text analytics framework for double-loop learning for citizen-centric public services: A case study of a local government Facebook use. *Government Information Quarterly*, 34.1: pp. 110–125.

Rozporządzenie Ministra Edukacji Narodowej z dn. 11 marca 2020 r. w sprawie czasowego ograniczenia funkcjonowania jednostek systemu oświaty w związku z zapobieganiem, przeciwdziałaniem i zwalczaniem COVID-19, Ministerstwo Edukacji Narodowej.

Rozporządzenie Ministra Zdrowia z dn. 12 maja 2022 r. w sprawie odwołania na obszarze Rzeczypospolitej Polskiej stanu epidemii, Ministerstwo Zdrowia.

Rozporządzenie Ministra Zdrowia z dn. 20 marca 2020 r. w sprawie ogłoszenia na obszarze Rzeczypospolitej Polskiej stanu epidemii, Ministerstwo Zdrowia.

Rudolf W. and Wæraas, A. 2021. Municipal Branding and Social Media: Comparing Poland, Norway, and Ukraine. Public Branding and Marketing: *A Global Viewpoint*, pp. 79–115.

Sekuła A. 2005. Marketing Terytorialny. Marketing. Ujęcie systemowe, pod red. M. Daszkowskiej, Wydawnictwo Politechniki Gdańskiej, Gdańsk 2005, pp. 216–237. DOI:10.13140/2.1.3916.8802.

Selden S.; Sowa J. E. 2011. Performance management and appraisal in human service organizations: Management and staff perspectives. *Public Personnel Management*, 40.3: pp. 251–264.

Statystyczne Vademecum Samorządowca, 2020. *GUS*.

Szmyd J. 2014. Poczucie bezpieczeństwa jako wartość społeczna, etyczna i egzystencjalna. Rozważania podstawowe. Państwo i Społeczeństwo. 2014 (XIV) nr 2

Szwacka-Mokrzycka J. 2010. *Rola promocji w strategii gminy*. In: K. Krzyżanowska (Ed.) Szkoła Główna Gospodarstwa Wiejskiego w Warszawie Wydział Nauk Ekonomicznych Katedra Ekonomiki Edukacji, Komunikowania i Doradztwa.

Trunfio M. and Rossi S. 2021. Conceptualising and measuring social media engagement: A systematic literature review. *Italian Journal of Marketing*. 2021(3): pp.267–292

Urząd Gminy Chodzież, 2022. *Facebook*.

Walle A. H. 1996. Tourism and the Internet: opportunities for direct marketing. *Journal of travel research*, 35.1: pp. 72–77.

Wykorzystanie technologii informacyjno-komunikacyjnych w gospodarstwach domowych w 2020 roku. 2021. *GUS*.

Digital Synergy – El Emary et al. (eds)

Chapter 4
Strategic analysis of enterprises and the Avatar model as modern management tools

Piotr Maśloch
War Studies University, Warsaw, Poland

Contents

The rapidly changing socio-economic reality and the challenges of the 21st century resulting from the dynamic development of globalization force modern enterprises to look for new methods of competing on the market. One of the ways to determine the competitive position of an enterprise is its strategic analysis. In this approach, the article is an attempt to present the key methods and tools of strategic analysis of the company, extended by an analysis of the possibility of their use in practice. The article presents the basic issues and results of the implementation of the international Avatar project consisting in developing a method of providing public services and developing customer service standards tailored to the needs of people with special needs. The main objective of the project is to improve the functioning of local government units by developing and implementing an innovative model of support for people with special needs.

The possibilities of increasing local government revenues depend to a large extent on the efficient management of local government units, as well as on macroeconomic conditions and unpredictable events that may significantly disrupt the process of economic and social changes. The appearance of the Covid-19 pandemic in 2020, numerous restrictions related to combating it, and the observed inflationary processes intensified by the war in Ukraine had a negative impact on the activities of local governments in Poland, especially municipalities, which account for over 75% of local government finances.

1 INTRODUCTION

The turn of the 20th and 21st centuries in Europe marked a period of profound political and socio-economic changes. These changes were particularly notable in Eastern European countries characterized by a centrally planned economy. The socio-economic transformation involved systemic changes aimed at multifaceted alterations in the functioning of the state, economy, and society. On one hand, there was a process of democratization of public life, while on the other hand, the economy underwent systemic transformation.

The late 20th and early 21st centuries brought far-reaching changes on a global scale, including the emergence of numerous new and previously unknown phenomena that significantly altered the operating principles of enterprises in the modern world. Although to a lesser

DOI: 10.1201/9781003440406-4

extent, these changes also encompassed military-related phenomena, which had their impact felt. However, in a broader context, uncontrolled economic transformations emerged, exemplified by the demographic crisis, particularly in terms of migration, on an unprecedented scale since World War II. Given the emergence of potential threats and entirely new conditions for the functioning of modern enterprises, the institutional regulation of issues related to strategic building and development planning assumes new significance. Undoubtedly, to ensure a sustainable competitive advantage in the global market, modern enterprises must employ a wide range of available methods of strategic analysis, which must be continuously modified in response to changing international circumstances. The 21st century also signifies the emergence of dynamic changes in the functioning of enterprises, increasingly relying on artificial intelligence and the learning of avatars and bots, representing a visible direction of change in contemporary management.

2 STRATEGIC ANALYSIS OF THE ENTERPRISES – SELECTED METHODS AND ANALYSIS TOOLS

Analyzing the dimensions of global competition in a context understandable in the 21st century, two crucial aspects of contemporary rivalry should be emphasized: economic freedom and positive market outcomes. These conditions can be presented in the form of three theses (Zorska 1998):

1. Economic freedom is guaranteed only when individuals have alternative choices and behavioral possibilities. Competitively organized markets precisely offer such alternatives. Competition is increasingly perceived as a general objective of economic policy. The competition system ensures economic freedom through the existence of alternatives.
2. Information is critical for the ability to choose and decide from an individual point of view. The informational function of competition encompasses two aspects simultaneously: economic freedom and economic efficiency. Market competition ensures, above all, the rapid dissemination of information and, importantly, prevents its concealment, withholding, or distortion.
3. Economic progress in highly developed economies depends significantly on the development and implementation of technological advancements. This encompasses the modernization of production techniques, the organization of plants and enterprises, the utilization of new means of production, and the production of new or improved goods.

The natural state of a company in a market economy necessitates competition in response to environmental pressures. Although the environment is a broad concept encompassing both social and economic forces, the primary environment of a company appears to be the sector(s) in which it competes. The sector's structure strongly influences the definition of competitive rules and the strategies that can be employed (Stankiewicz 2002). The intensity of competition within the sector stems from its economic structure and extends beyond the behavior of current competitors.

The five competitive forces - entry, the threat of substitutes, the bargaining power of customers, the bargaining power of suppliers, and the rivalry among existing competitors - demonstrate that competition within a given sector goes beyond the existing participants in the game. The classic Porter model features (Porter 1996):

1. Strength No. 1: Competition within the sector.
2. Strength No. 2: Bargaining power of buyers.
3. Strength No. 3: Threat of substitutes.
4. Strength No. 4: Bargaining power of suppliers.
5. Strength No. 5: Threat of new entries.

All five forces together determine the intensity of competition in a given sector and its profitability, and the strongest force or forces are decisive for formulating the strategy (Pierścionek

2011). Each of the competitive forces depends on certain economic and technical characteristics of the sector. In today's market economy, competition is the driving force of business activity, presenting both great opportunities and threats for companies. The essence of competition as presented above in the context of Porter's model allows for the analysis of the market environment and, ultimately, the assessment of competition in the sector (Godziszewski 1999). Porter's five forces model serves as an introduction to further in-depth strategic analysis of modern companies competing in the global market. Among the wide range of methods and techniques of strategic analysis, the BCG matrix holds the utmost importance.

The BCG matrix is the most well-known, simplest, and most useful method for presenting a company's product range – it is a portfolio analysis method. The name of the method originates from the American consulting company Boston Consulting Group, which was the first to employ this tool in 1969. Analyzing a company's product portfolio using the BCG matrix enables the assessment of the company's development opportunities and determination of its strategic position. Through the application of the BCG method, company management can ascertain which products generate the highest profits, where to invest, and identify the assortment that should be phased out. The structure of the BCG matrix is as follows:

1. Question marks.
2. Stars.
3. Cash cows.
4. Difficult children (dogs).

Question marks - also known as dilemmas, these are scarce products with difficult-to-determine possibilities. They have a low market share in a rapidly growing market.

Stars - these are products that require relatively large funding and typically do not generate surplus. Investing in stars is highly profitable because of the high market growth rate and the product's competitiveness and development.

Cash cows - these are products that form the basis of the company's operations. The market growth is slow, but due to a large market share, they hold a strong and stable position. These products generate high profits for the company.

Difficult children (dogs) – these are products that do not bring significant surplus and have no prospects for development. For these products, the possibility of withdrawing from a specific market sector should be considered as they consume excessive financial resources while providing minimal income.

The presented BCG matrix should be associated with the product life cycle curve. The classic product life cycle consists of 4 phases:

1. Phase 1. Market Introduction. In the market introduction phase, sales are low and grow slowly. Profit is zero. Both the product and the company are relatively unknown in the market, which is why sales are growing slowly. Significant expenditures are required, which will only pay off in later stages of product development. The company's profitability is very low, sometimes even negative.
2. Phase 2. Sales Growth. The sales growth phase is characterized by a rapid increase in sales and profit, resulting from product acceptance and an increase in the number of customers. Due to growing competition, product improvement is necessary.
3. Phase 3. Market Maturity. In the market maturity phase, sales reach a peak, followed by a slowdown caused by market saturation or displacement by another product. This is the period when the product is purchased by loyal customers, and the company maximizes its profits.
4. Phase 4. Decline. The final phase is the declining popularity of the product. It is characterized by a significant decrease in sales and company profits as the product declines.

This situation arises from the fact that the product becomes less attractive over time, and new or improved substitutes for the product appear in the market.

However, the concept of the product life cycle curve, which is well-known and widely used in the analysis of modern enterprises, is rarely combined with the BCG matrix concept. Therefore, the introduction phase corresponds to the group of products referred to as question marks. In practice, there is rarely certainty whether and when a particular product will achieve market success, especially in conditions of increased market competition. On the other hand, the second phase - the growth of popularity - corresponds to the stage of the product life cycle curve dedicated to stars. Therefore, stars are products that are worth investing in, as it will result in an increase in their market popularity. The third phase - maturity - reflects the group of products referred to as cash cows. Cash cows are products that maximize the company's profit and are clearly in the maturity phase. The last stage is the decline in popularity. The natural situation in the market is the "aging" of the product due to natural market processes. The consequence of product aging is a decline in popularity and, consequently, withdrawal from the market - hence these products are referred to as question marks.

3 RESOURCE APPROACH TO MANAGEMENT

According to the resource-based approach, the source of a company's success is the possession and appropriate use of valuable resources and skills, including knowledge and competence (Hamel 1994). Representatives of the resource theory of the enterprise focus on explaining which of the resources owned by enterprises have the potential to provide them with a competitive advantage and, consequently, enable them to achieve better economic results. Strategic resources should be (Lockett, Thompson, Morgernstern 2009:9-28):

1. valuable,
2. rare,
3. inimitable,
4. properly organized.

In order for resources to be treated as the basis for an effective strategy, they should be (Collis, Montgomery 2008:140-150):

1. hard to copy,
2. durable (long-lasting value),
3. controlled by the company, not its employees or suppliers,
4. difficult to replace with other resources,
5. better than analogous resources held by competitors

The resource competitive advantage of companies can also be described using the concept M. Peteraf pointed four basic sources (Peteraf 1993:179-191):

1. diversity of organization,
2. limited mobility of resources in the market,
3. ex ante competition restrictions,
4. ex post competition restrictions.

The diversity of organizations is a consequence of the availability of resources and the ability to use them. The limited mobility of resources on the market results from:

1. physical constraints related to the location of resources,
2. the nature of the market that restricts the free movement of resources,
3. high costs of transporting resources,
4. decisions made by resource owners, including legal protection of intangible resources.

Limitations of ex ante competition mean that companies do not have equal access to knowledge about which resources will be the most valuable on the market. They result from the low accuracy of forecasts and the selective sharing of information used for forecasting. Because the knowledge of different companies-competitors is diverse, there are unequal opportunities in access to resources, which affects the ability of some of them to gain a competitive advantage. The last source of competitive advantage is the limitation of competition ex post, i.e. difficulty imitation and substitution of the resources of the best organizations by other entities.

4 METHODOLOGY OF THE AVATAR MODEL: RESEARCH METHODS AND RESULTS OF THE RESEARCH

In connection with the implementation of the international scientific project "Innovative assistance model avatar for the carer of the elderly", a pilot survey was conducted at the beginning of 2020 (Maśloch 2022).

The survey questionnaire consisted of a main part comprising 23 questions and a metric with 4 questions. The main questions of the survey concerned two main areas. The first was related to the assessment of respondents in the operation and service of applicants at public administration offices. The second area concerned the expectations and requirements of clients regarding their service at public administration offices. The respondents' habits were also examined here, mainly in relation to computer skills and functioning on the Internet.

The pilot purpose was to verify the correctness (elimination of defects) of the assumed research procedure: selection of the examined people and the research tool used (survey). It was not used to verify hypotheses, but to provide information enabling the construction of a good research plan.

The study was qualitative (questionnaire test) and was carried out in the form of a meeting of people from a deliberately selected sample with the number N = 120. The pilot survey was carried out using the conventional method (verification, among others, whether the examined persons correctly understand all of the questions asked? Is the instruction attached to the survey clear for the examined persons? Are there any missing answers in the survey?), Supplemented with cognitive interview (suggestions for changes)/supplementing the scope and type of questions, analysis of the target group of respondents). The avatar tool used is presented in Figure 1.

Legend: 1 - [illegible]; 2 - touch screen; 3 - Avatar; 4 - voice synthesizer.

Figure 1. Avatar tool.
Source: P. Maśloch, *The New Age of Management*, Shineeks, Las Vegas, 2023, p. 107.

The research sample, due to the subject matter, was mostly elderly: 45% between 56 and 65 years old, 35% over 65 years old and the remaining 20% under 55 years old; 65% of the research sample were women and 35% men; 60% of respondents had higher education, 20% vocational, 15% secondary and 5% primary and 45% of the respondents are retired, 40% are working, 10% are pensioners, 5% are unemployed. The sample size ensured statistical significance of the results.

Statistical analysis showed that all study participants have ever used public administration offices, but most of them (85%) used the services of a city, municipality or district office. The remaining part used the services of the poviat eldership. In most cases (50%), the respondents handle official matters several times a year (50%) or once every few years (25%); 10% of respondents could not accurately determine the frequency, while 5% of respondents admitted that they use several times a month, once a month or once a year. Next 10% of respondents had a problem determining the frequency of using public administration offices. In addition, 40% of respondents said they had been in charge of official affairs in the last six months to three years, 20% two months ago, 15% each month or last month, and 5% last week.

Then the respondents were asked about the type of matters they usually handle in public administration offices. It was a multiple choice question: 40% of respondents said that they handle matters related to waste management, location of landfills in the Department of Environmental Protection and replace the old ID card or produce an ID card in the Department of Civil Affairs. About 20% of the respondents take care of matters related to social assistance - allowances and other benefits in the Municipal or Municipal Social Assistance Center; tax matters - tax payment, tax discontinuation etc. In the Tax Department and exchange of the registration certificate, production of the proof - vehicle registration/deregistration of the vehicle in the Communication Department; 15% of those surveyed deal with registration issues - permanent check-in, check-out, etc. In the Department of Civil Affairs; cases related to the issue of death and birth records, changes in civil status files in the Civil Registry Office and matters related to obtaining water and legal permits at the Department of Environmental Protection. 10% of the respondents arrange exchange of driving licenses, obtaining a driving license at the Department of Communication and obtaining maps for agricultural subsidies, obtaining information on spatial development plans, etc. at the Department of Geodesy and Cartography; 5% of respondents arrange obtaining building permits at the Faculty of Architecture and Construction. None of the surveyed group indicated dealing with job search or obtaining unemployment benefits at the Labor Office or registering a company at the Economic Development Department.

5 CONCLUSION

Contemporary enterprises operating in the dynamic global landscape are compelled to prioritize their activities based on two fundamental aspects:

1. Implementing traditional, time-tested management strategies.
2. Exploring novel approaches in enterprise management and operations by harnessing the latest technological advancements in the field.

Among the diverse array of solutions, the avatar tool stands out as a noteworthy example, having undergone testing at two regional sites. Concurrently with the testing, surveys were conducted to gather feedback on the project. Looking back, it can be asserted that this innovative solution, known as the Avatar, was warmly received by local communities.

REFERENCES

Collis, D.J., Montgomery, C.A., 2008, Competing on resources, *Harvard Business Review*, 86(7–8).

Godziszewski B., 1999, *Potencjał konkurencyjności przedsiębiorstwa jako źródło przewag konkurencyjnych i podstawa stosowania instrumentów konkurowania*, [in:] M.J. Stankiewicz, *Budowanie potencjału konkurencyjności przedsiębiorstwa*, TNOiK, Toruń.

Hamel, G., Prahalad, C. K., 1998, Competing for the future, MA: *Harvard Business Press*, Boston.

Lockett, A., Thompson, S., Morgenstern U., The development of the resource-based view of the firm: A critical appraisal, *International Journal of Management Reviews*, No. 11(1).

Maśloch P, 2022, The concept of using artificial intelligence in the process of building a marketing communication strategy (avatar model), *Scientific Papers of Silesian University of Technology. Organization and Management Series*, No. 167.

Maśloch P., 2023, *The New Age of Management*, Shineeks, Las Vegas.

Peteraf M. A., 1993, The cornerstones of competitive advantage: A resource-based view, *Strategic Management Journal*, 14(3).

Pierścionek Z., 2011, *Zarządzanie strategiczne w przedsiębiorstwie*, PWN, Warszawa.

Porter M. E., 1996, *Strategia konkurencji. Metody analizy sektorów i konkurentów*, PWE, Warszawa.

Stankiewicz M.J., 2002, *Determinanty konkurencyjności polskich przedsiębiorstw. Sposoby i warunki umacniania konkurencyjności przedsiębiorstw w perspektywie globalizacji gospodarki*, UMK Toruń.
Zorska A, 1998, *Ku globalizacji. Przemiany w korporacjach transnarodowych i gospodarce światowej*, Wyd. Naukowe PWN, Warszawa.

WEBSITE

https://www.business-to-you.com/, 10.03.2023.
https://www.professionalacademy.com/, 18.04.2023.
https/brandequity.economictimes.indiatimes.com/, 20.04.2023.

Digital Synergy – El Emary et al. (eds)

Chapter 5
The digital transformation of financial services

Nouhayla Boutaleb & Laarbi Tamnine
Encg Fes, Morocco

Contents

The analysis confirms the impact of events related to the COVID-19 pandemic and the war in Ukraine on the state of local finances and reduced financial stability of municipalities. This is evidenced, among other things, by the reduced importance of tax revenues in the structure of budget revenues and reduced investment activity.

However, trust is crucial for success, and financial institutions must prioritize data privacy, security, transparency, and ethical conduct to build and maintain customer trust.

1 INTRODUCTION

Financial services organizations are at a transformational tipping point. Faced with fierce market pressures throughout the industry nimble disruptors, complex regulations, digital native customers, and the fallout of a global pandemic technology transformation is no longer merely a competitive advantage, but an absolute necessity. The importance of digital transformation in financial services cannot be overstated. The rise of digital technologies has fundamentally altered how consumers interact with financial institutions, and has created new opportunities and challenges for financial institutions themselves. Digital transformation enables financial institutions to improve operational efficiency, enhance the customer experience, and create new revenue streams through innovative products and services. Additionally, digital transformation allows financial institutions to compete more effectively in an increasingly crowded and competitive market, and to stay ahead of disruptive new entrants such as fintech startups.

Overall, digital transformation is a critical component of success for financial institutions in the modern era. It allows them to stay relevant and competitive in a rapidly evolving landscape, and to better serve the needs of their customers in an increasingly digital world.

Digital transformation in financial services refers to the process of leveraging technology and digital capabilities to improve business processes, enhance customer experiences, and

DOI: 10.1201/9781003440406-5

create new revenue opportunities for financial institutions. It involves the adoption of digital technologies such as cloud computing, artificial intelligence, and blockchain to automate processes, provide real-time insights, and enable more personalized customer interactions. Digital transformation is essential for financial institutions to remain competitive in a rapidly evolving market and to meet the changing expectations of customers who increasingly expect seamless, convenient, and secure digital experiences when interacting with financial services.

In this perspective, we question ourselves:

What are the challenges and opportunities of digital transformation in the financial services sector, and how does it impact businesses, consumers, and the economy in general?

To address this question, the study will be structured as follows: The first part presents the literature review that allowed us to assess the existing knowledge and develop hypotheses; and it will conclude with a final section.

2 LITERATURE REVIEW AND HYPOTHESIS DEVELOPMENT

2.1 *The importance of activities in the digital transformation of financial services*

Financial services are essentially mechanisms that enable individuals and businesses to access and utilize financial assets in order to achieve certain benefits or preserve the value of their assets. These services are legally sanctioned and typically involve various types of financial transactions that are carried out in the best interests of the consumers. Some common examples of such transactions include lending, insurance, capital management, pension savings, securities trading, and money transfers. These operations are facilitated by various financial institutions, such as banks and other financial organizations that operate in the financial markets. These institutions play a critical role in facilitating financial transactions and ensuring the smooth functioning of financial systems, thereby contributing to the overall economic development of a country.

2.2 *Types of digital transformation in financial services*

Digital transformation in financial services has resulted in significant changes to the industry. There are several types of digital transformation in financial services, including process automation, data analytics, cloud computing, and artificial intelligence. Process automation involves the use of digital technologies to streamline business processes, reduce costs, and improve efficiency. Data analytics involves the use of data and analytics tools to gain insights into customer behavior and preferences, as well as to improve risk management and fraud detection. Cloud computing enables financial institutions to store and process data in a scalable and cost-effective way, while artificial intelligence is being used to automate customer service and create personalized experiences. The impact of digital transformation on financial services has been significant, with online banking and mobile payments becoming increasingly popular as consumers demand more convenient and accessible services.

Additionally, digital currencies such as cryptocurrency are becoming more widely accepted as a means of payment, while blockchain technology is being used to streamline cross-border transactions and reduce costs.

Overall, The impact of digital transformation on finance has been profound, and has fundamentally altered the way in which financial services are delivered and consumed. One of the key impacts of digital transformation has been the shift towards online and mobile banking, which has enabled consumers to manage their finances more conveniently and easily than ever before. The ability to check account balances, transfer money, and pay bills from a smartphone or computer has made banking more accessible and convenient, particularly for younger consumers who are comfortable with technology.

In addition to online and mobile banking, digital transformation has also led to the development of new financial products and services. For example, the rise of fintech startups has led to the creation of innovative new products such as peer-to-peer lending, robo-advisors, and mobile payments. These products have disrupted traditional financial institutions, challenging their dominance and forcing them to adapt to changing customer preferences.

Digital transformation has also had a significant impact on financial operations and back-office functions. The adoption of cloud computing has enabled financial institutions to store and process data more efficiently, reducing costs and improving scalability. Additionally, the use of data analytics and artificial intelligence has enabled financial institutions to gain insights into customer behavior and preferences, as well as to improve risk management and fraud detection.

Perhaps one of the most significant impacts of digital transformation on finance has been the rise of cryptocurrency and blockchain technology. Cryptocurrency, such as Bitcoin, has emerged as a viable alternative to traditional currencies, and is increasingly being accepted by merchants and consumers as a means of payment. Blockchain technology, which underpins cryptocurrency, is being used to streamline cross-border transactions and reduce costs, and is also being explored as a means of improving transparency and security in financial operations.

Overall, digital transformation has had a significant impact on the finance industry, enabling financial institutions to improve operational efficiency, enhance customer experiences, and create new revenue streams. While these changes have created new opportunities for financial institutions, they have also created new challenges, particularly in the areas of cybersecurity and data privacy. Nonetheless, it is clear that digital transformation will continue to play a key role in the future of finance, shaping the industry in new and innovative ways.

2.3 *Challenges of digital transformation in financial services*

While digital transformation has opened up new opportunities for financial institutions, it has also presented significant challenges.

Legacy systems are a challenge for financial institutions during digital transformation. Many financial institutions rely on outdated technology systems, which can be difficult to integrate with new digital systems. Financial institutions must carefully manage the transition from legacy systems to digital systems, to ensure that the transition is smooth and that there are no disruptions to business operations.

Another challenge that financial institutions face during digital transformation is a shortage of talent with the necessary skills to implement and manage digital systems. As the demand for digital skills in the finance industry grows, financial institutions must compete with other industries to attract and retain talent.

In addition to these challenges, financial institutions also face challenges related to regulatory compliance, vendor management, and customer adoption of new digital products and services.

But the biggest challenges of all faced by financial institutions during digital transformation is cybersecurity. As financial services increasingly rely on technology to deliver services, they become more vulnerable to cyber attacks. Financial institutions must ensure that their systems are secure, and that they have robust cybersecurity measures in place to protect against data breaches and other security threats.

Data privacy is another key challenge that financial institutions face during digital transformation. As financial institutions collect more data on their customers, there is a growing risk that this data could be compromised or misused. Financial institutions must ensure that they comply with data privacy regulations, such as the General Data Protection Regulation (GDPR) in the European Union, and that they have measures in place to protect customer data.

Which lead us to talk about the trust of the users

In the digital world, trust is essential to establishing and maintaining relationships between financial service providers and their customers. Customers must be able to trust that their data and money are safe and secure when using digital finance services. They need to have confidence that the financial institutions they are dealing with are trustworthy and reliable.

Moreover, trust is crucial in the adoption of new digital financial products and services. Consumers are often hesitant to try new technologies or products without first establishing trust in the provider. All these aspects affect the level of the digital trust, raising questions related to the transparency and confidentiality of data, the validity and controllability of the use of algorithms, and the impact of robots on job opportunities and employment.

Trust is considered to be able to minimize perceived risk thereby increasing consumer commitment to service providers

2.3.1 *Customer trust affects competitive advantage*

Competitive advantage is a crucial aspect that businesses strive to achieve to remain relevant and successful in their respective industries. The concept of competitive advantage revolves around the idea of possessing unique capabilities, resources, and human assets that provide a company with a superior position in the market. These unique capabilities or resources can range from advanced technology, skilled labor, cost leadership, brand reputation, or intellectual property rights, among others.

Achieving competitive advantage requires a strategic approach that aligns the company's internal strengths with external environmental opportunities. This entails a continuous evaluation of the company's capabilities, resources, and human assets, as well as monitoring the external environment for potential opportunities or threats. Companies must also be willing to invest in research and development, innovation, and talent development to enhance their competitive advantage continually.

In conclusion, competitive advantage is a vital component of business success, and companies must continuously strive to achieve it. The concept of competitive advantage involves leveraging internal strengths to respond to external environmental opportunities. As such, companies must have a strategic approach that aligns their internal capabilities with external opportunities to achieve sustainable competitive advantage.

2.4 *The necessary strategies to enhance trust in an increasingly digital financial environment*

In an increasingly digital financial landscape, building and maintaining trust is crucial. Several strategies can be employed to enhance trust in this environment. First, ensuring robust cybersecurity measures is essential to protect customer data and prevent unauthorized access. Implementing encryption protocols, multi-factor authentication, and regular security audits can instill confidence in the security of digital transactions.

Second, transparent communication and clear disclosure of terms and conditions are vital. Financial institutions should provide comprehensive information about their digital services, including privacy policies, data handling practices, and any potential risks involved. Transparent communication helps to establish trust and ensures customers have a clear understanding of how their information is used and protected.

Third, regulatory frameworks play a significant role in fostering trust. Governments and regulatory bodies should establish and enforce strong data protection and privacy regulations specific to the digital financial sector. Clear guidelines and standards can enhance consumer trust by demonstrating that industry practices are regulated and monitored.

Fourth, investing in customer education is important. Providing educational resources on safe online financial practices, such as recognizing phishing attempts, creating strong passwords, and being vigilant against scams, can empower customers to protect themselves in the digital realm. Increased financial literacy can build confidence and reduce vulnerability to fraud.

Lastly, actively addressing customer concerns and feedback is crucial. Establishing responsive customer support channels and promptly resolving any issues or complaints contributes to a positive customer experience. Open dialogue and responsiveness demonstrate a commitment to customer satisfaction and help build trust over time.

By implementing these strategies, financial institutions can reinforce trust in an evolving digital financial landscape, providing customers with a secure and reliable experience while fostering long-term relationships based on confidence and peace of mind.

3 CONCLUSIONS

This article analyzes the set of forces driving the global financial system toward a period of radical transformation and explores the transformational challenges that lie ahead for global financial intermediaries. It is explained how these challenges derive from the newly emerging post-crisis structure of the market and from shadow and digital players across all operations.

The successful integration of digital technologies necessitates a comprehensive change management strategy, ensuring that employees are equipped with the necessary skills to navigate the evolving landscape and deliver exceptional customer experiences.

Above all, nurturing trust is paramount. By prioritizing data security, transparent communication, and exceptional customer experiences, financial institutions can cultivate trust in the digital realm. Only by establishing and maintaining trust can financial services truly harness the full potential of digital transformation, fostering lasting customer relationships and propelling the industry toward a more prosperous future.

REFERENCES

Book: Digital Transformation in Financial Services, by Claudio Scardovi, edition number 1.

Deloitte. https://www2.deloitte.com/us/en/insights/topics/digital-transformation/building-long-term-trust-in-digital-technology.html

Ernst & Young: https://www.ey.com/en_us/nextwave-financial-services/how-financial-institutions-can-win-the-battle-for-trust

Haddad, C., & Hornuf, L. (2019). The emergence of the global fintech market: economic and technological determinants. Small Business Economics, 53, 81–105.

Manta, O. (2018). Financial Technologies (Fintech), Instruments, Mechanisms and Financial Products. Internal Auditing & Risk Management, 4, 78–102

The Financial Brand. (n.d.). Digital Transformation in Banking – 2021 and Beyond. Retrieved from https://thefinancialbrand.com/78780/digital-banking-transformation-trends/

World Economic Forum. (2018). The New Physics of Financial Services: How Artificial Intelligence Is Transforming the Financial Ecosystem. Retrieved from https://www.weforum.org/reports/the-new-physics-of-financial-services-how-artificial-intelligence-is-transforming-the-financial-ecosystem

Digital Synergy – El Emary et al. (eds)

Chapter 6
The digital banking evolution: An opportunity or a pitfall?

Houda Mahboub & Hicham Sadok
Mohammed V University in Rabat, Rabat, Morocco

Contents

Over the past two decades, banks have intensified their digital transformation and investment. Between the metamorphoses of bank branches and the development of new digital services, projects to improve their profession and the customer experience are multiplying. The digital transformation of banks is not just a trend, it responds to the new structural and strategic challenges facing the sector. However, on this transformation path, the bank still faces competition from shadow banking and digital transformation obstacles. This article aims to present a brief synthesis of the literature on the main developments induced by digital technology in the banking sector. We outline this ongoing transformation in the analysis of the case of the Fintech Lenddo which introduces an innovative banking paradigm based on the analysis of big data and the application of artificial intelligence allowing more banking inclusion. It can serve as a roadmap for banks interested by the implementation of the psychometric approach. It also allows a better understanding of digital transformation and its impacts from an organizational perspective.

1 INTRODUCTION

In an ever-changing environment, each company is constantly competing to ensure its survival. With the emergence of digital transformation (DT), this challenge is even greater. Shaking all industries, digital transformation induces significant changes in processes, organizational culture, workflows, and core businesses, nearly all organizational aspects (Mahboub and Sadok, 2023).

Digital transformation describes the changes and developments that affect the activities, processes, skills, and especially the organizational culture of companies through digital technologies (Mahboub and Sadok, 2022: 203–214). It affects five stages according to the level of maturity: products and services, technologies and innovation, people, organization, and the environment (Capgemini and MIT, 2023). The latter organizes companies into five categories based on their digital status: waiters, impressionists, outsourcers, integrators, and transformers. The first category sees digital as an abstract concept, resulting in late action as they are always in wait-and-see mode. Impressionists, on the other hand, have a misconception of digital leading to ineffective choices. The Outsourcers category includes companies that choose to focus on their core business and therefore delegate the digital implementation mission to an intermediary, while the Integrators include new methods and knowledge into the company

DOI: 10.1201/9781003440406-6

structure without managerial or cultural development. Transformers represent the highest level of digital maturity, as these companies apply the five levers to achieve optimization. The MIT and Capgemini model presents a further classification of companies' digital maturity by industry: Beginners with an immature digital culture and a reduced application; Fashionistas, applying digital in silos but with an underdeveloped culture and organization while the Conservators have a clear vision and master the use of digital. Finally, the Digirati category has centralized governance and an advanced application of digital guarantying high added value (Capgemini and MIT, 2023).

As one of the most digitally impacted industries, the banking sector continues to invest and transform using digital to succeed in this endeavor. However, this transformation has advantages and disadvantages. Among the banking tasks most impacted by digital transformation, the method of risk assessment and analysis is undergoing a major revolution thanks to big data and the applications of artificial intelligence. This practice remains of great importance for banks given its impact on performance, canvassing, and customer knowledge (Fishelson-Holstine, 2004; Hermes and Lensink, 2007; Ibtissem and Bouri, 2013; Sharma and Zeller, 1997). In addition, this new banking approach to valuation optimizes the decision-making process by reducing human biases impacting the loan decision (De Cnudde et al., 2019), reduces the cost of recovery, minimizes losses and insolvency risks, and improves the quality of the loan information (Min and Jeong, 2009; Han et al., 2020: 2874–2878). However, this change of process in the core business of the bank also has limits and biases (Han et al., 2020: 2874–2878).

Despite the important advance in research on digital transformation (DT), its impacts in practice and definition remain fuzzy (Verina and Titko, 2019). Moreover, research on behavioral credit scoring are limited (Muñoz-Cancino et al., 2023).

Thus, this article aims to contribute to a better understanding of the impact of digital transformation by analyzing two points: the first one deals with the main impacts of digital transformation on the banking sector, and the second allows us to conclude whether this transformation is more of an opportunity or a peril. In addition, it provides an overview of the main application of psychometric analysis approach on several levels, which can serve as a guide for future research and applications.

To answer these two important questions, this work will first present an overall analysis of the changes induced by digital technology. In a second step, it will be a question of deepening one of the essential points in the banking digital transformation which is the process of credit evaluation and analysis. Finally, we will end with a case study on the fintech Lenddo and its applications to illustrate the benefits and mistrust of this ongoing digital revolution. In this sense, our work remains among the rare works outlying the state of art of both theoretical and empirical research, especially in terms of psychometric scoring models.

2 FROM TRADITIONAL BANKING TO ITS DIGITAL FORM: THE BANKING DIGITAL TRANSFORMATION

The emergence of new fully digital banking competitors is pushing traditional banks to reinvent themselves, to completely rethink the user experience, and to deliver new digital offers more quickly while controlling their costs (Benkhayat, Manouar and Sadok, 2015, 172–178). These changes led to the appearance of a new form of banking: digital banking. It is the process of "enabling banking transactions by the realization or presentation of information via the Internet, mobile, ATM, and similar technology-based channels through digitizing information using technology" (Bozkuş Kahyaoğlu, 2021).

Determined to maintain the relationship with the customer in the face of neo-banks, fintech, and Bigtechs, banking establishments are forced to review their strategic positioning and reconfigure their operational processes by increasingly resorting to digital technology.

However, this change in the business process of banks has the advantage of making the customer relationship closer with faster and easier access to operations, simplification of tasks, reduction of costs, and refocusing on the core business since account opening, transfer, and other operations have been automated. But on the other hand, this digital paradigm also presents a threat given the security constraints and rapid and unlimited access to information allowing comparison and banking transhumance. All these changes require investments and therefore additional financial costs. In addition, the DT of the banking industry requires organizational development focused on greater openness, strengthening training, recruitment and motivation of strategic skills, and responding to new IT needs and risks (El Alami, Sadok, Elhaoud, 2015: 1–5).

These challenges that traditional banks must overcome represent a major threat taking into consideration the breakthrough of Fintechs and GAFAM in the banking sector (Fayon, 2018: 309). These new competitors have immense advantages such as access to massive data, the scalability of their model, and the competitive cost price (Philippon, 2017: 173–205). These levers allow them to distinguish themselves by quality, speed of file processing (Fuster et al., 2019: 1854–1899) as well as the transparency and convenience of the process. The development potential of this competition between this new technological version of banks and traditional banking is measured in the literature by two key criteria (Weill, 2019: 181–192,): the H statistic and the Lerner index providing information on the market power of a company compared to its competitors, or a sector compared to another tending to replace it.

However, this ongoing change in the banking business process is not the first of its kind; the banking sector is renowned for being one of the first to invest in technology each time an innovation emerges: the implementation of ATMs, smart cards, software, and information systems, traditional banks were always at the forefront of innovation and technological implementation. Except for the one currently underway, it is radical in the sense that it introduces competitors likely to take the lead if they manage to produce secure services (Casalo, Flavián, and M. Guinalíu, 2007: 1–17; Yoon and Barker Steege, 2013: 1133–1141), practical, of quality (Broderick and Vachirapornpuk, 2002: 327–335.), cheaper (Gerrard et al., 2006: 160–168), more ergonomic (Mallat, 2007: pp. 413–432), more accessible (Estrella-Ramon, Sánchez-Pérez, and G. Swinnen, 2016: 1072–1092; Kesharwani, 2020; Luo et al., 2010: 222–234; Xue, Hitt and Chen, 2011: 291–307), and generating added financial value (Veríssimo, 2016: 5456–5460).

Based on these elements identified in the literature, this digital transition in progress within the banking sector is succeeding in reforming its most profound aspects: its functioning, its organization, its interactions, and its products. All the components of the banking profession have undergone modifications. But it does not stop there, because the banking professions are also evolving.

A total and exhaustive prediction of future banking professions is certainly not easy to predict in light of the emergence of artificial intelligence. However, two main categories of professions will be strongly impacted by digital transformation: administrative management operations and professions related to customer services.

As one of the most obvious impacts observed on banking services, digital transformation is changing the core business of banking, namely the process of credit analysis and risk assessment.

To decide whether or not to allow credit, banks rely on the rating approach. Traditionally, the scoring method consists of a judgment approach relying on banking analysis of financial ratios taken from customer experience (Van Gool,et al., 2009; Sadok, 2021: 21). The literature abounds in the analysis of this method of the loan based on the historical relations of the customer (De Cnudde et al., 2019: 353–363) to reveal its advantages and its disadvantages. Among the major disadvantages of this method is that it benefits those who already have a favorable financial history (Sadok, 2021: 21), contrary to Potential customers with no financial history or beginners who are often discriminated against (Schreiner, 2003). Moreover, the sort of client depends on the loan officer's point of view which may be negative, not due to the eligibility of the client but only due to the borrower's bad mood! This method leads therefore to an increase in the unbanked population and therefore excludes many clients, reducing the performance and the bank's outcomes (Goel and Rastogi, 2021). Another type of lending is the group—based lending in which social capital is used to base the final decision (Sharma and Zeller, 1997: 1731–1742). This social capital represents "features of social organization such as networks, norms, and social trust that facilitate cooperation and coordination" (Putnam, 1995: 65–78). The loan officer uses this social capital as peer pressure to detect any sort of asymmetric information or moral hazard (Hermes and Lensink, 2007: F1–F10. However, this method is limited since it doesn't allow the use of statistical scoring due to the lack of individual risk data (De Cnudde et al.,2019: 353–363).

Due to these limitations of traditional scoring, and with the raising development of technologies and digital transformation, some modern approaches to scoring emerged. This modern approach doesn't rely only on balance sheets (Min and Jeong, 2009: 5256–5263) or sociodemographic factors (Hand, Sohn and Kim, 2005: 684–690), but integrates "alternative data" to overcome the limits of the traditional method with the help of artificial intelligence and Big data, through a psychometric approach. For a better understanding of this new paradigm, the next section exposes Lenddo's method of using psychometric analysis, with the help of artificial intelligence, for loan decisions.

3 THE NEW SCORING APPROACH: LENDDO CASE STUDY

Nowadays, we can see the emergence of many interesting technologies. Among the latter, artificial intelligence (AI) remains one of the most powerful tools shaking all industries and life aspects in the worldwide area. In this sense, the financial sector seems to be a hard-hit industry but has also made a significant investment in this direction. Indeed, the emergence of digital transformation and Robotic Process Automation (RPA) highly impacted the banking industry, which led to new trends such as GAB, Fintechs, and artificial intelligence. The shifting pace of change resulting from this digital adventure and its technologies is more illuminating in the area of credit analysis (Figure 1), which will be the core point of our coming analysis.

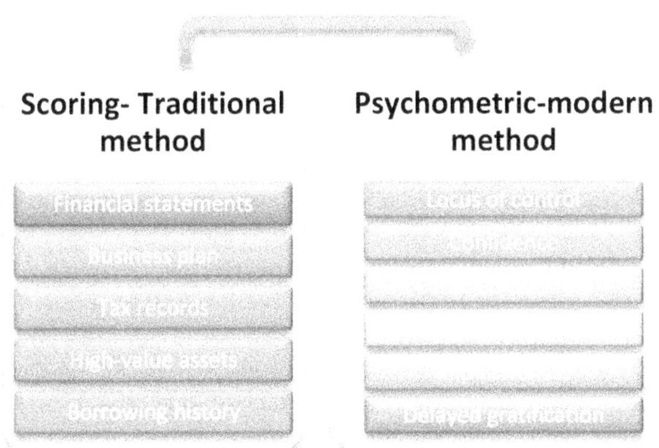

Figure 1. The scoring logic shift in the era of digital transformation.
Source: author's contribution based on several scientific papers

Traditionally, allowing or not credit is based on qualitative variables (income, nature of the activity, assets, and customer bank relations) supplemented by statistical risk assessment models. Thus, the decision is made based on a technical approach through the scoring. The latter discriminates against many companies by describing them as eligible for loans. However, the AI emergence increases financial inclusion through a big data enrichment analysis which improves the allocation of credit. Additionally, it allows significant productivity gains, in data pre-processing, data management, and modeling for decision-making (Sadok, Sakka and El Maknouzi, 2022; McCanless, 2023). The modern AI credit allocation approach integrates information derived from social media networks into its analysis database, allowing a good default prediction, reaches out to more clients, reduces default rates, and optimizes organizational performance (Muñoz-Cancino et al., 2022.; Björkegren and Grissen, 2020: 618–634).

If banks base their decisions merely on scoring and risk assessment methods, they will surely miss a valuable customer portfolio: the "missing middle" segment. This segment contains clients with credit needs higher than microfinance and lower than the minimum required by commercial banks. As an example of the scoring's financial exclusion, influencers may not have genuine assets or a fixed income, but they can certainly be creditworthy customers and repay their loans. For example, influencers may not have genuine assets or a fixed income, but they can certainly be creditworthy customers and repay their loans. Additionally, inadequate loans represent another limit of traditional banking since the latter offer credits with discriminatory conditions or too small loans insufficient to fuel business growth (Alibhai, Buehren and Papineni, 2018). It is these kinds of limitations of banking institutions that FinTech capitalize on to develop their strengths. These new institutes are crossing the limits of banks to develop their competitive advantages, thus offering high-quality and lower-expensive financial products.

To overcome this limitation with support from digital investment, a new approach to credit distribution is arising. Lenddo Entrepreneurial Finance Lab (LenddoEFL) developed a modern method that is based on psychometric tools rather than business plans or traditional financial statements. This method judges the client's attributes based on the locus of control, impulsiveness, fluid intelligence, confidence, conscientiousness, and delayed gratification. The Lenddo method is based on a self-administered test (duration of 45 minutes) to judge the client's ability to get a loan.

The psychometric credit scoring method improves financial inclusion and performance through the integration of alternative data (Azma et al., 2019: 188–200), mostly unused by the banking industry. These alternative data include additional information derived from social media (De Cnudde et al., 2019: 353–363; Hendricks and Budree, 2019: 157–169), web browsers, mobile phones (Agarwal et al., 2019), point-of-sale transaction devices, and utility payments. These specific data provide the loaner (mostly Fintech) with a better understanding of the client's character traits, networks, and creditworthiness, but also reduce information scarcity through their integration in the decision-making analysis. Additionally, these alternative data have strong predictive power and availability (Alibhai et al., 2018). In general, these alternative data are divided into three categories: the broader/mobile footprint data that involves downloaded applications and their number, and the mobile operating system type, the social footprint including social applications, number of contacts, number of calls and SMS and their length, the preferred social network for logging in the lender's apps, and deep social footprint data that captures information derived from call logs pattern (Agarwal et al., 2019).

Since the borrower's character remains a determinant of loan repayment, several researchers took the adventure to understand the client's personality and proved that the latter is translated into measurable traits such as locus of control, impulsiveness, confidence, delayed gratification, fluid intelligence, and conscientiousness (Schreiner, 2003; Ogeisia et al., 2014). However, banks have already understood the impact of the client's character on creditworthiness but were unable to translate the personality side into a clear set of information to assess risks (Van Gool et al., 2012: 103–123). Thus, fintech and especially Lenddo's team have successfully resolved this limitation through their proposal.

Lenddo applied the psychometric approach in the Ethiopian context. Their experience showed the major role of psychometric assessment in credit prediction and risk management (Alibhai et al., 2018).

The psychometric credit scoring method (Figure 2) is based on a test on a mobile device or a tablet. The results are uploaded by the lender who receives the client's score and relative risk after data processing. If the client goes beyond the bare minimum score, he can use his/her score as collateral to obtain a loan and even qualify for a larger credit.

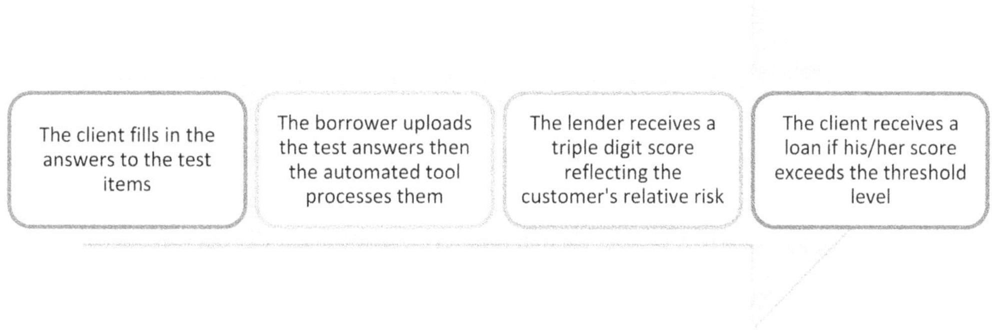

Figure 2. The psychometric approach process.
Source: (Alibhai et al., 2018).

After collecting all the required data, artificial intelligence processes these data to provide the borrower with predictive information to implement and justify the decision made. The data collection and processing stage relies on advanced machine-learning tools that support predictive algorithms. These algorithms back on rich databases pulled from Twitter, LinkedIn, Facebook, Instagram, Android, Gmail, and other databases.

4 THE PSYCHOMETRIC CREDIT APPROACH: EMPIRICAL EVIDENCE

Given its important added value, some researchers took the adventure to implement Lenddo's innovative approach in several contexts. Agarwal and al (Agarwal et al., 2019) used alternative data collected from the applicant's mobile phone (social footprint). These data concern social connections, the number and types of applications downloaded, and call logs. Their idea was to verify if this new approach can replace the traditional scoring method, and its impact on financial inclusion. After testing the psychometric approach in India, their results show that the alternative data improve default prediction, and outperform the credit score. In addition, this method increases access to a large wide of clients, especially those with low income, improving thus financial inclusion.

Other researchers went further than a simple application of the psychometric approach by proposing their own model. For example, Hendricks and Budree (Hendricks and Budree, 2019: 157–169) focus more on the presence of collateral and its substitutes in South Africa to develop a best practice conceptual model credit scorecard. Their model relies also on the client's credit score, social media, psychometric score, and mobile credit score.

Wei and al (Wei et al., 2014) analyzed the impact of network use on customer score accuracy and tie formation. The authors propose several series of models for different cases. Their findings show that fewer ties with similar partners improve the individual's score. It shows also the impact of the social network change on credit scores. However, social exclusion improves the low-type members' creditworthiness. Additionally, the authors investigate the performance of this shift and find that "*when people have an above-average chance of interacting with others of similar creditworthiness, then network ties provide additional reliable signals about a consumer's true creditworthiness*".

In 2022, Munoz-Cancino and al (Muñoz-Cancino et al., 2022) used data extracted from a Latin American bank. They create 12 datasets on a period of 12 months that were analyzed with the help of Big Data. Their study aims to understand the creditworthiness assessment performance each month after obtaining the first credit for a year. Their results show the contribution of borrower's history, social interactions, and loan repayment factures in credit scoring performance enhancement.

Based on the current review of theoretical and empirical works, the psychometric credit approach shows its great importance. The latter allows access to financial services and loans to underprivileged recipients, especially the underbanked and especially low-tech and low-literacy clients. Therefore, their contextual conditions don't serve as an exclusion criterion as is the case for the traditional approach, but rather a strength for their application. The integration of this new method in the banking industry will improve its competitiveness and provide solutions for traditional scoring limitations. Despite these interesting findings, the psychometric method seems far from being an alternative approach to the traditional credit scoring approach in the few coming years, but rather a completion due to its limits.

Indeed, its opacity does not allow us to understand or control the variables or the process behind it. This obscurity threatens the quality of predictions and banking regulation. The second risk is in terms of liability in case of harm in a self-managed financial system. Moreover, by using private data from social networks, does not AI exceed the privacy limits of customers? In addition, the psychometric test can be manipulated (Bernards, 2019: 815–838), but impacts also employment. Moreover, this method is hard to apply in countries with a high level of resistance and lack of confidence in technology such as Morocco. Also, if the bank uses social media data as the basis for its final decision, it can therefore support a big risk since these data change rapidly (the decrease of followers or a cybercriminal attack on an Instagram account for example). Greenfield is beneficial in this sense since it will allow to get rid of all the constraints and start all over again based on an innovative approach in a new environment or the adoption of white-label banking machines to choose a local branch between several banks.

5 CONCLUSIONS

With the evolution of the fourth industrial revolution, and the emergence of strong competitors such as Fintech, the banking sector finds itself in a hard situation. Between the necessity to adapt to continuously-changing customer needs, to adopt recent technologies, and to conduct radical organizational changes, banks are faced with huge investments and efforts to make. Indeed, digital transformation has impacted also the core business of banks, on several levels. As an example, an important shift in the scoring approach arises, moving therefore from the traditional method based on risk assessment and guarantee logic to psychometric analysis. The latter uses alternative data for better predictions and the improvement of the decision-making process. By introducing these new data, more clients are served and become eligible for loans. It improves, therefore, organizational performance, increases financial inclusion, and reduces the unbanking category. However, the latter has some limitations such as privacy concerns, and opacity. In general, we can say that this new scoring trend has a double facet and must be considered by the banking industry with careful attention. In addition, investing in the application of this new method requires interesting investment in terms of infrastructure and technologies, employee training, resistance reduction, cultural change, and organizational adaptation. Digital transformation represents therefore an opportunity for the banking sector, but only to those who master it and have enough resources to invest in it. Otherwise, this paradigm will be a pitfall if the company isn't agile enough to convert this adventure into her interest.

Generally, digital-induced investment is considered beneficial if it improves the company's positioning and market share through a strong focus on customer loyalty, increases the company's overall performance, facilitates tasks, and results in a better working climate... However, each bank has its unique picture of the success of digital-induced investment according to its specificities, context, resources, efforts deployed, and others.

To obtain the best results from the digital transformation of the baking sector, it is important to opt for partnerships, especially with FinTechs. This is beneficial since banks can take advantage of FinTech's expertise and mastery of niches and other areas while ensuring a win-win relationship. Moreover, the phenomenon of the digital divide, representing the disparities in access to ICT, either because of age, incompetence in terms of internet usage, lack of tools, or culture, especially for women and seniors, must be taken into consideration as it represents a part of the untapped consumers to whom an explanation and motivation for digital are required. Optimizing the use of chatbots through a reinforcement learning approach is also interesting as well as the use of ghost codes allowing to get money by using Self-service Banking with the help of the application which is an ideal solution for the case of bank card loss or environmental insecurity.

REFERENCES

Agarwal S., S. Alok, P. Ghosh, and S. Gupta, 'Fintech and Credit Scoring for the Millennials: Evidence using Mobile and Social Footprints', SSRN Journal, 2019, doi: 10.2139/ssrn.3507827.

Alibhai S., N. Buehren, and S. Papineni, 'Better Loans or Better Borrowers? Impact of Meso-Credit on Female-Owned Enterprises in Ethiopia'. Rochester, NY, Jul. 10, 2018. Accessed: May 10, 2023. [Online]. Available: https://papers.ssrn.com/abstract=3238351

Alibhai S., N. Buehren, R. Coleman, M. Goldstein, and F. Strobbe, Disruptive Finance: Using Psychometrics to Overcome Collateral Constraints in Ethiopia. 2018. doi: 10.1596/29746.

Azma N., M. Rahman, A. A. Adeyemi, and M. K. Rahman, 'Propensity toward indebtedness: evidence from Malaysia', Review of Behavioral Finance, vol. 11, no. 2, pp. 188–200, Jan. 2019, doi: 10.1108/RBF-05-2017-0046.

Benkhayat A., A. E. Manouar, and H. Sadok, 'Firm business strategy and IT strategy alignment: A proposal of a new model', in 2015 Xth International Scientific and Technical Conference 'Computer Sciences and Information Technologies' (CSIT), Lviv, Ukraine: IEEE, Sep. 2015, pp. 172–178. doi: 10.1109/STC-CSIT.2015.7325460.

Bernards N., 'The poverty of fintech? Psychometrics, credit infrastructures, and the limits of financialization', Review of International Political Economy, vol. 26, no. 5, pp. 815–838, Sep. 2019, doi: 10.1080/09692290.2019.1597753.

Björkegren D. and D. Grissen, 'Behavior Revealed in Mobile Phone Usage Predicts Credit Repayment', World Bank Economic Review, vol. 34, no. 3, pp. 618–634, Oct. 2020, doi: 10.1093/wber/lhz006.

Bozkuş Kahyaoğlu S., Ed., The Impact of Artificial Intelligence on Governance, Economics and Finance, Volume I. in Accounting, Finance, Sustainability, Governance & Fraud: Theory and Application. Singapore: Springer Nature Singapore, 2021. doi: 10.1007/978-981-33-6811-8.

Broderick A.J. and S. Vachirapornpuk, 'Service quality in Internet banking: the importance of customer role', Marketing Intelligence & Planning, vol. 20, no. 6, pp. 327–335, Nov. 2002, doi: 10.1108/02634500210445383.

Capgemini and MIT, 'The Digital Advantage: How digital leaders outperform their peers in every industry', 2017. Accessed: May 12, 2023. [Online]. Available: https://www.capgemini.com/wp-content/uploads/2017/07/The_Digital_Advantage__How_Digital_Leaders_Outperform_their_Peers_in_Every_Industry.pdf

Casalo L.V., C. Flavián, and M. Guinalíu, 'The Influence of Satisfaction, Perceived Reputation and Trust on a Consumer's Commitment to a Website', Journal of Marketing Communications, vol. 13, no. 1, pp. 1–17, Mar. 2007, doi: 10.1080/13527260600951633.

De Cnudde S., J. Moeyersoms, M. Stankova, E. Tobback, V. Javaly, and D. Martens, 'What does your Facebook profile reveal about your creditworthiness? Using alternative data for microfinance', Journal of the Operational Research Society, vol. 70, no. 3, pp. 353–363, Mar. 2019, doi: 10.1080/01605682.2018.1434402.

El Alami A., H. Sadok, and N. Elhaoud, 'Cloud computing & the organizational performance different approach of assessment', in 2015 International Conference on Cloud Technologies and Applications (CloudTech), Marrakech, Morocco: IEEE, Jun. 2015, pp. 1–5. doi: 10.1109/CloudTech.2015.7337007.

Estrella-Ramon A., M. Sánchez-Pérez, and G. Swinnen, 'How customers' offline experience affects the adoption of online banking', Internet Research, vol. 26, no. 5, pp. 1072–1092, Jan. 2016, doi: 10.1108/IntR-03-2015-0092.

Fayon D., 'Mesure de la maturité numérique des acteurs du secteur bancaire, dans une perspective de transformation digitale', p. 309, 2018.

Fishelson-Holstine H., 'The role of credit scoring in increasing homeownership for underserved populations', 2004.

Fuster A., M. Plosser, P. Schnabl, and J. Vickery, 'The Role of Technology in Mortgage Lending', The Review of Financial Studies, vol. 32, no. 5, pp. 1854–1899, May 2019, doi: 10.1093/rfs/hhz018.

Gerrard P., J. Barton Cunningham, and J. F. Devlin, 'Why consumers are not using internet banking: a qualitative study', Journal of Services Marketing, vol. 20, no. 3, pp. 160–168, Jan. 2006, doi: 10.1108/08876040610665616.

Goel A. and S. Rastogi, 'Understanding the impact of borrowers' behavioural and psychological traits on credit default: review and conceptual model', Review of Behavioral Finance, vol. ahead-of-print, Dec. 2021, doi: 10.1108/RBF-03-2021-0051.

Han S. et al., 'Profit evaluation for virtual power plant in power load response: From the perspective of power grid', in 2020 IEEE 4th Conference on Energy Internet and Energy System Integration: Connecting the Grids Towards a Low-Carbon High-Efficiency Energy System, EI2 2020, 2020, pp. 2874–2878. doi: 10.1109/EI250167.2020.9347338.

Hand D.J., S. Y. Sohn, and Y. Kim, 'Optimal bipartite scorecards', Expert Systems with Applications, vol. 29, no. 3, pp. 684–690, Oct. 2005, doi: 10.1016/j.eswa.2005.04.032.

Hendricks M.K. and A. Budree, 'Can a mobile credit-scoring model provide better accessibility to South African citizens requiring micro-lending?', Int. J. Electron. Financ., vol. 9, no. 3, pp. 157–169, Jan. 2019, doi: 10.1504/ijef.2019.099001.

Hermes N. and R. Lensink, 'The Empirics of Microfinance: What Do We Know?', The Economic Journal, vol. 117, no. 517, pp. F1–F10, 2007, Accessed: May 19, 2023. [Online]. Available: https://www.jstor.org/stable/4625473

Ibtissem B. and A. Bouri, 'Credit risk management in microfinance: the conceptual framework', vol. 2, no. 1, 2013.

Kesharwani A., 'Do (how) digital natives adopt a new technology differently than digital immigrants? A longitudinal study', Information & Management, vol. 57, no. 2, p. 103170, Mar. 2020, doi: 10.1016/j.im.2019.103170.

Luo X., H. Li, J. Zhang, and J. P. Shim, 'Examining multi-dimensional trust and multi-faceted risk in initial acceptance of emerging technologies: An empirical study of mobile banking services', Decision Support Systems, vol. 49, no. 2, pp. 222–234, May 2010, doi: 10.1016/j.dss.2010.02.008.

Mahboub H. and H. Sadok, 'Implementing enterprise digital transformation: a contribution to conceptual framework design', NBRI, vol. 14, no. 1, pp. 35–50, Mar. 2023, doi: 10.1108/NBRI-06-2022-0067.

Mahboub H. and H. Sadok, 'Towards a Better Digital Transformation: Learning from the Experience of a Digital Transformation Project', in Digital Economy. Emerging Technologies and Business Innovation, M. A. Bach Tobji, R. Jallouli, V. A. Strat, A. M. Soares, and A. A. Davidescu, Eds., in Lecture Notes in Business Information Processing, vol. 461. Cham: Springer International Publishing, 2022, pp. 203–214. doi: 10.1007/978-3-031-17037-9_15.

Mallat N., 'Exploring consumer adoption of mobile payments – A qualitative study', The Journal of Strategic Information Systems, vol. 16, no. 4, pp. 413–432, Dec. 2007, doi: 10.1016/j.jsis.2007.08.001.

McCanless M., 'Banking on alternative credit scores: Auditing the calculative infrastructure of U.-S. consumer lending', Environ Plan A, p. 0308518X2311740, May 2023, doi: 10.1177/0308518X231174026.

Min J.H. and C. Jeong, 'A binary classification method for bankruptcy prediction', Expert Systems with Applications, vol. 36, no. 3, Part 1, pp. 5256–5263, Apr. 2009, doi: 10.1016/j.eswa.2008.06.073.

Muñoz-Cancino R., C. Bravo, S. A. Ríos, and M. Graña, 'On the dynamics of credit history and social interaction features, and their impact on creditworthiness assessment performance'. arXiv, Apr. 12, 2022. Accessed: Jun. 14, 2023. [Online]. Available: http://arxiv.org/abs/2204.06122

Ogeisia S.K., D. O. Alala, D. D. Musiega, and G. W. Manase, 'Impact of borrower character on loan repayment in commercial banks within Kakamega Town', vol. 1, no. 2, 2014.

Philippon T., 'L'opportunité de la FinTech', Revue d'économie financière, no. 127, pp. 173–205, 2017, Accessed: May 12, 2023. [Online]. Available: https://www.jstor.org/stable/44649735

Putnam R.D., 'Bowling Alone: America's Declining Social Capital', Journal of Democracy, vol. 6, no. 1, pp. 65–78, 1995, doi: 10.1353/jod.1995.0002.

Sadok H., 'How can inclusive growth be enabled from financial technology?', p. 21, 2021.

Sadok H., F. Sakka, and M. E. H. El Maknouzi, 'Artificial intelligence and bank credit analysis: A review', Cogent Economics & Finance, vol. 10, no. 1, p. 2023262, Dec. 2022, doi: 10.1080/23322039.2021.2023262.

Schreiner M., 'Scoring: The Next Breakthrough in Microcredit?', no. 7, 2003.

Sharma M. and M. Zeller, 'Repayment performance in group-based credit programs in Bangladesh: An empirical analysis', World Development, vol. 25, no. 10, pp. 1731–1742, Oct. 1997, doi: 10.1016/S0305-750X(97)00063-6.

Van Gool J.V., B. Baesens, P. Sercu, and W. Verbeke, 'An Analysis of the Applicability of Credit Scoring for Microfinance', 2009.

Van Gool J., W. Verbeke, P. Sercu, and B. Baesens, 'Credit scoring for microfinance: is it worth it?', International Journal of Finance & Economics, vol. 17, no. 2, pp. 103–123, 2012, doi: 10.1002/ijfe.444.

Verina N. and J. Titko, 'Digital transformation: conceptual framework', in Proceedings of 6th International Scientific Conference Contemporary Issues in Business, Management and Economics

Engineering '2019, Vilnius Gediminas Technical University: Vilnius Gediminas Technical University, May 2019. doi: 10.3846/cibmee.2019.073.
Veríssimo J. M.C., 'Enablers and restrictors of mobile banking app use: A fuzzy set qualitative comparative analysis (fsQCA)', Journal of Business Research, vol. 69, no. 11, pp. 5456–5460, Nov. 2016, doi: 10.1016/j.jbusres.2016.04.155.
Wei Y. 'Max', P. Yildirim, C. Van den Bulte, and C. Dellarocas, 'Credit Scoring with Social Network Data'. Rochester, NY, Jul. 01, 2014. doi: 10.2139/ssrn.2475265.
Weill L., 'L'impact des Fintech sur la structure des marchés bancaires', Revue d'économie financière, vol. 135, no. 3, pp. 181–192, 2019, doi: 10.3917/ecofi.135.0181.
Xue M., L. M. Hitt, and P. Chen, 'Determinants and Outcomes of Internet Banking Adoption', Management Science, vol. 57, no. 2, pp. 291–307, Feb. 2011, doi: 10.1287/mnsc.1100.1187.
Yoon H.S. and L. M. Barker Steege, 'Development of a quantitative model of the impact of customers' personality and perceptions on Internet banking use', Computers in Human Behavior, vol. 29, no. 3, pp. 1133–1141, May 2013, doi: 10.1016/j.chb.2012.10.005.

SECTION 2
Global Trends and Challenges in Management

Digital Synergy – El Emary et al. (eds)

Chapter 7
A redefinition of determinants defining the potential for further development and management of modern global maritime containerized shipping after the Covid-19 pandemic

Ryszard K. Miler
WSB Merito University Gdańsk, Poland

Małgorzata Wach-Kloskowska
Merito WSB University in Gdansk, Poland

Akram Al Mouhamad Akoel
Briese Shipping, Germany

Tomasz Nowosielski
University of Gdansk, Poland

Contents

Maritime containerized shipping have been recently challenged by stochastic shocks, such as the Covid -19 pandemic clearly indicating shortfalls and weaknesses of global maritime containerization flows. The aim of the paper is to present a holistic analysis of factors that globally affect the potential for further development of containerized shipping. The entire research design comes as an attempt made at identifying the main determinants, building and testing a new tool for development comparison. The results are presented as a combined matrix of the eight main determinants, key factors and indices and a radar chart for a better comparison and synthesis. Moreover, there is a potential for further utilization of the presented matrix and adopted methodology as a universal tool that will support management in the field of the expected architecture of global containerized shipping after absorption of any global shocks, that can be expected in the years to come.

1 INTRODUCTION

Containerized transport comes as a fundamental sector in almost every country in the world, thus containerized shipping is a global sector and a part of a global supply chain to most industries (Review of Maritime Transport 2019). Identified in contemporary literature, the key factors (determinants) of development of containerization in maritime transport are: the dynamically changing market and geopolitical environment (illustrated by the relations between North America, Asia and Europe, referred to as "the triad regions") (Jackson, n.d.),

DOI: 10.1201/9781003440406-7

advancing internationalization and standardization of trade relations (based on such standards as Incoterms or ISO for containerization) (Becha et al. 2020), globalization of international trade (measured by the growth of the foreign trade volumes) (Ghosh 2020; Papava and Chkuaseli 2021; WTO 2020), the specific role of maritime transport in international trade (accounting for 90% of the volume of transported cargo) (Notteboom et al. 2021; Madhav et al. 2017; Menhat et al. 2021; Danelia 2021), universality of information technology (IT), information and communication technology (ICT) in telematics systems (Kim et al. 2022; Matczak 2013) and pressure to protect natural environment, including the concern about zero emission transportation processes (decarbonization of shipping and port/terminal operations) (Cullinane and Yang 2022; Lindstad et al. 2021; Cullinane and Haralambides 2021).

All these factors had been monitored separately and controlled against potential risks and till the end of the year 2019 nothing suggested an incoming catastrophe. In 2019 the development of containerized cargo transport free from any significant risk was dramatically interrupted by the risk factors of stochastic nature, such as the Covid-19 pandemic (Millefiori et al. 2021; Yazir et al. 2020).

The main objective of this study is to evaluate the largest possible set of determinants that can affect global containerized shipping in the light of deep shocks that have recently occurred to the global economy and also to elaborate on the eight main determinants by synthesis. This research study has been particularly aimed at verifying whether a holistic analysis and systematic identification of the key factors can help in the comprehensive analysis of the condition of containerized shipping. The entire research has been also conducted in order to test and verify a working hypothesis stating that it is possible to assess the condition of development of maritime containerization and its current status and also to identify trends that can occur in the future with the use of a tool specifically dedicated to this purpose.

Taking the presented hypothesis into account, another aim of the research has been to evaluate if the originally constructed and developed matrix of determinants/factors, including its graphical presentation (a radar chart), can be a useful tool for the assessment of developmental capabilities of containerized shipping and also a tool for predicting its future potential. This study is distinct from the previous ones as it examines widely all the aspects and determinants identified as a whole (one matrix) in much more a holistic approach, focusing not just on one selected factor but on a set of factors combined into one tool. In addition, it clarifies and introduces a methodology for the calculation of each factor describing the eight main determinants. Through this, in the future it may be possible to evaluate the status of the potential of maritime containerized transport as a whole on a yearly, quarterly or even monthly basis.

Taking the entire structure of the presented paper into account, Section 2 presents the main tools applied during the research that refer to the analysis and synthesis, the concept of applying indices based on the LPI, Delphi methods applied to assess weights and a radar chart as one of graphical methods used for presenting study results. Section 3 comes as a presentation of all the stages of the entire research, by providing a synthesis of the existing trends and challenges. In Section 3 the main determinants are identified (presented as Det 1-8) and subsequently two main factors (F1, F2) are assessed, clearly indicating the nature of the particular determinants; Subsequently, a matrix of determinants (Det 1-8) is presented, the factor volumes (F1-F2) are introduced and the Indices are calculated according to the formulas adopted for the years 2018-2020 (2018=100). Finally, Section 3 provides the results of the entire research study in a graphical form (a radar chart), allowing the Authors to point out that Det 8 (the capabilities for further digitalization and computerization of maritime and container operations) becomes one of the most important and most promising determinants of further development of maritime containerized transport. The research findings have also proved that the presented analysis - utilizing (Det 1-8) - comes as an original and promising research tool for providing a holistic analysis of determinants driving the development of containerized shipping.

2 AN OVERVIEW OF THE LITERATURE

Since the outbreak of the Covid-19 pandemic in China, global economy and logistics supply chains have been seriously disrupted (Al-Mansour and Al-Ajmi 2020). The Covid-19 pandemic has considerably affected global economy in terms of the global economic growth (Jackson n. d.; Mishra 2020), world trade (Global Trade Rebound, n.d.; Report on G20 Trade Measures 2020), economic development (The World Bank 2022; Naseer et al. 2023) and new challenges to economic/financial/protectionism policy (Global Financial Stability…n.d.; Jackson, n.d.; Annual Economic Report 2020). This crisis also caused various ramifications in the container market, however, this time the situation was very different from the previous one, since it involved an external shock that rapidly impacted all the elements of global supply chains approximately at the same time (Notteboom et al. 2021), exposing all the weaknesses of maritime containerized cargo transport so far hidden from the global audience (Miler et al. 2022). Notteboom et. al (2021) proves that the impact of the shock caused by the Covid-19 pandemic on ports and the shipping industry was mitigated by strategic operation of shipping companies that quickly responded to a decrease in demand and implemented the means of throughput control. Those means became specifically important from April to June 2020, when carriers withdrew up to 20% of their transport capacities along the main trade routes because of empty sailings and cancellation of services. Millefiori L.M. et al. (2021) also confirm that in their research, indicating an unprecedented decrease in maritime mobility observed in all the categories of merchant shipping during the initial period of the pandemic and subsequently its increase.

In the field of services offered by container ports, after the stagnation during the first half of 2020, a spectacular revival in demand for port services was observed in the second half of 2020. Numerous ports reported record volumes of cargo handling in September, October and November 2020 (Cullinane and Haralambides 2021). The research presented by Guerero at al. (2022) indicate that very large ports and also smaller ones that are provided with numerous feeder connections handled the crisis better than other ports. It seems that smaller cargo handling hubs have suffered most. The situation in the market of containerized transport has already improved in the post-pandemic period, as it is indicated by the fact that ship owners have been expressing higher demand for container vessels and for production of new containers (Youd 2021).

It should be emphasized that the results of scientific research (Notteboom et al. 2021; Pelagidis, Haralambides 2020) indicate high resilience of shipping companies and of terminal and port operators to the effects of the Covid-19 pandemic in a short time. Nevertheless, it has been also possible to observe negative effects of the pandemic on the developmental capabilities of containerized shipping in a short time.

As identified in literature, the most significant weaknesses involve delays observed at sea ports (Merk et al. 2022; Beškovnik et al. 2022; Mańkowska et al., 2021), shortage of empty containers (repositioning problems) (Youd 2021; Abdelshafie et al. 2022), inflexible management of the capabilities of the container vessel fleet, especially during the initial stage of the pandemic (Notteboom et al. 2021; Cullinane and Haralambides 2021; Millefiori et al. 2021), low coefficients of automation, robotization and digitalization of processes in maritime containerized transport (Kim et al. 2022; Xu et al. 2021; Choi 2020).

During the post-pandemic period, the first research studies of a more comprehensive character started to appear to discuss the necessity of changes to be done to the organization of logistics supply chains based on containerized shipping. They present suggestions referring to rethinking, redefinition and reconstruction (Raj et al. 2022). However, so far there have not been any research studies presenting a concept of a holistic methodology for assessing the condition of maritime containerized transport, its developmental capabilities and possibilities to provide a systematic evaluation of emerging trends and threats (including external risks). Hence, it is advisable to undertake scientific research referring to the cognitive gap that has been already identified.

3 RESEARCH METHODS

After the exposition to a number of stochastic shocks, such as the pandemic, the Authors believe that it is necessary to provide a tool for a comprehensive analysis of the condition of containerized transport – a tool that will present the entire specificity of the industry in a holistic way (Song 2021; Bentaleb et al. 2021) in order to manage its developmental capabilities and to prepare the sector for absorbing other shocks that will certainly occur in the future.

The contemporary scientific achievements and literature do not provide any tools comprising such a wide scope of assessing developmental capabilities of containerized shipping (Wang et al. 2022), integrated under one research methodology, as it is in the case of the determinant matrix discussed here. Hence, both the scope of the tool presented in the paper and the methodology for identifying the description factors, including the originally developed methodology of calculating Indices (Gorajek 2021; Handbook on Constructing Composite Indicators. Methodology and user guide 2008), are of innovative nature. The methods applied in the research include the analysis of available literature (Onwuegbuzie et al. 2015) and the synthesis (Paré et al. 2015) that come as tools allowing the Authors to identify the determinants (Det 1-8). The next part of the research refers to the methodology based on the LPI concept (Logistics Performance Index) (Arvis et al. 2018), applied to design and conduct processes of factor weighting (F1, F2) and the Delphi methods (such as brainstorm, expert evaluation) (Grisham 2009; Skulmoski et al. 2007), in order to establish the proper weights. A radar chart comes as a graphical presentation of the results of the research (Benedito 2018; Hugh and Antje 1999).

The final pragmatic aim of the research has been to provide a new tool that can be applied by analysts of the discussed sector. Using the originally developed methodology for assessing determinants (through the factors and their indices) and developmental capabilities of containerized shipping (a comparative analysis provided with the use of superimposed radar charts), it has been initially possible to prove that the discussed matrix is useful for further analysis and risk/change management in the sector of containerized shipping.

The entire research is divided into five stages:

- the first stage includes identification of the main determinants (presented as Det 1-8) through a synthesis of the existing trends and challenges, (stage 1 end state: all the determinants are identified and clearly described);
- the second stage provides an assessment of the two main factors (F1, F2) clearly indicating the nature of the particular determinants Det 1-8, (stage 2 end state: all the determinants are ascribed with the defined specific factors F1/F2 and Index formulas, in a form of a matrix of determinants);
- the third stage operates on the matrix of determinants that is challenged with real data in order to calculate all the associated Indices (stage 3 end state: all the Indices are calculated and synthetically presented);
- the fourth stage introduces a weighted formula (equation 1) for the assessment of a synthetic value of each determinant (Det 1-8) (stage 4 end state: all the determinants are presented with the single values for further presentation and comparison);
- the fifth stage presents graphically all the calculated values for Det 1-8 on a radar chart, allowing the Authors to provide a comparison and further assessment (stage 5 end state: all the determinants are graphically presented on a radar chart and the results are discussed).

4 RESULTS OF THE RESEARCH

Stage 1 Results – Identification of Determinants

In order to provide a synthetic approach toward all the potential for further development of containerization processes in maritime transport, the following key/driving determinants (indicating the growth limits), should be stated:

- capabilities for further growth of international trade volumes (in the context of economic and geopolitical relations, implemented terms of trade and disturbances caused by the pandemic) – limits to international trade;
- capabilities for further development of container vessels (in relation to their size given in TEU and the limits to the economics of their use) – limits to container ship capacity;
- capabilities for the supply of new containers (in relation to the capabilities of the industry responsible for container construction) – limits to the container volume;

- capabilities for further development of terminal infrastructure (in relation to the size, expansion, levels of competitiveness and operational efficiency of container terminals) – limits to container terminal capacity;
- capabilities for further development and capacity of maritime transport infrastructure (in relation to navigation sea routes and canals, especially the Suez Canal and the Panama Canal) – limits to the capacity of sea communication routes;
- the level of safety and security of maritime and terminal/port operations (including both these aspects: safety and security and also safe container turnover) – limits to maritime (container) safety and security;
- capabilities for further lowering of maritime transport anthropopressure (in relation to a decrease in emission of greenhouse gases – GHG, CO_2 and the general lowering of external effects) – limits to the internal costs of container transport;
- capabilities for further digitalization and computerization of maritime and container operations (in relation to automation, robotization, autonomation, implementation of IT systems supporting management, the use of database systems, artificial, virtual and augmented reality) – limits to information management.

Stage 2 Results – Construction of the Matrix of Determinants

At this stage of the research, each identified determinant is described by two key factors. According to the assumed methodology, the selected factors that are presented in terms of their quantity or quality, have been also ascribed with originally prepared calculation and each factor is presented as an Index. The scope of the proposed matrix is depicted in Table 1.

Table 1. The original matrix of containerized maritime transport development determinants.

Determinant (Det)	Factor (F)	Short description	Index	Calculation
Det 1 (capabilities for further growth of international trade volume)	F1	Total global trade	Index of Global Trade $I_{(GT)}$	initially in USD billion, then compared with the basic year, basic year=100; $I_{(GT)}$= 1.0,
	F2	Implemented terms of trade	Index of Trade Freedom $I_{(TF)}$	calculated as the % of freedom "volume", lower $I_{(TF)}$ the higher restrictions to the global trade imposed (e.g. restrictions, lockdowns etc.), [vary between 0.00-1.00]
Det 2 (capabilities for further development of container vessels)	F1	Global container vessel fleet	Index of Container Vessel Fleet $I_{(CV)}$	TEU [thousands], then compared with the basic year, basic year=100; $I_{(CV)}$= 1.0
	F2	The capacity of the largest container vessel commissioned in the particular year	Index of Container Vessel Capacity $I_{(VC)}$	TEU [thousands], then compared with the basic year, basic year=100; $I_{(VC)}$= 1.0
Det 3 (capabilities for the supply of new containers)	F1	Production/supply of new containers in the world	Index of Container Supply $I_{(CS)}$	items [thousands], then compared with the basic year, basic year=100; $I_{(VC)}$= 1.0
	F2	The general number of containers in the international trade	Index of General Number of Containers $I_{(NC)}$	items [thousands], then compared with the basic year, basic year=100; $I_{(VC)}$= 1.0

(*Continued*)

Table 1. (*Continued*)

Determinant (Det)	Factor (F)	Short description	Index	Calculation
Det 4 (capabilities for further development of terminal infrastructure)	F1	The number of containers handled at container ports	Index of General Number of Containers Handled $I_{(CH)}$	TEU [thousands], then compared with the basic year, basic year=100; $I_{(VC)}$= 1.0
	F2	The number of container terminals at sea ports	Index of General Number of Maritime Terminals $I_{(MT)}$	TEU [thousands], then compared with the basic year, basic year=100; $I_{(VC)}$= 1.0
Det 5 (capabilities for further development and capacity of maritime transport infrastructure)	F1	The number of vessels handled at the Suez Canal	Index of Vessels Handled @SC $I_{(SC)}$	[vessels], then compared with the basic year, basic year=100; $I_{(SC)}$= 1.0
	F2	The number of vessels handled at the Panama Canal	Index of Vessels Handled @PC $I_{(PC)}$	[vessels], then compared with the basic year, basic year=100; $I_{(PC)}$= 1.0
Det 6 (the level of safety and security of maritime and terminal/port operations)	F1	The number of maritime/port collisions and accidents (including those that involve container vessels)	Index of Maritime Collisions $I_{(MC)}$	[reported incidents], then compared with the basic year, basic year=100; $I_{(MC)}$= 1.0
	F2	The number of terrorist and pirate attacks	Index of Maritime Piracy $I_{(MP)}$	[reported incidents], then compared with the basic year, basic year=100; $I_{(MP)}$= 1.0
Det 7 (capabilities for further lowering of maritime transport anthropopressure)	F1	The total CO_2 emission generated by maritime shipping	Index of Maritime Emission $I_{(ME)}$	total CO_2 emission [million tonnes], then compared with the basic year, basic year=100; $I_{(ME)}$= 1.0
	F2	The number of ECA (Emission Control Areas) with limitations to shipping in terms of marine fuel specification	Index of ECA $I_{(ECA)}$	the $I_{(ECA)}$ for absolutely free shipping without considering emission control is assumed as 1.0 and with the subsequent restrictions it will strive to achieve 0.0 in the years 2030/2050.
Det 8 (capabilities for further digitalization and computerization of maritime and container operations) in relation to automation, robotization, autonomation, implementation of IT systems supporting management, the use of database systems, artificial, virtual and augmented reality)	F1	The number of automated terminals	Index of Automation of Maritime Container Terminals $I_{(AUTER)}$	Index $I_{(AUTER)}$ =automated maritime terminals/total maritime terminals x 100%, [0.00-1.00]
	F2	The number of e-documents applied in maritime container trade and transportation	Index of Digitalization of Documents in Maritime Container Transport $I_{(e\text{-}doc)}$	Index $I_{(e\text{-}doc)}$ =e-doc/total doc x 100% [0.00-1.00]

Source: author's work.

Stage 3 Results – Calculation of Indices

In the next stage of the research, the determinants of further development of maritime containerized transport (Det), their factor volumes (F1-F2) and Indices calculated according to the Table 1 formulas, are presented for the years 2018-2020 (2018=100) with real data:

1/ Determinant 1 (Det 1) - capabilities for further growth of international trade volume (in the context of economic and geopolitical relations, implemented terms of trade and disturbances caused by the pandemic) – limits to international trade – for the purpose of the research are described by two factors:

- factor 1 (Det1/F1): total global trade [in USD billion] represented by the Index of Global Trade $I_{(GT)}$
- factor 2 (Det1/F2): implemented terms of trade represented by the Index of Trade Freedom $I_{(TF)}$

The foreign trade volume in the analysed years with the changes compared to the basic year (2018) and the Index of Global Trade $I_{(GT)}$ are presented in Table 2 (Worldwide Export Trade Volume 1950-2018, n.d.).

Table 2. The foreign trade volume and the Index of Global Trade $I_{(GT)}$.

Year	Total global trade [in USD billion]	Change [in USD billion]	Change [%]	Synthetically Index $I_{(GT)}$
2018	19,549,335	2018=100	2018=100	1.00
2019	19,014,315	-539,020	-2.30	0.98
2020	17,648,468	-1,900,865	-9.72	0.90

Source: author's work.

The second factor of the assessment (Det1/F2) comes as the implemented terms of trade represented by the $I_{(TF)}$ Index of Trade Freedom. The basic factor that liberalizes terms of international trade is the General Agreement on Tariffs and Trade (GATT) which is intended to eliminate trade barriers (rounds in 1947, 1950, 1956, 1960, 1964, 1973, 1986 and 2021) (WTO, 2018). The GATT regulations in their unchanged formula were applied in the years 2018-2020, hence in order to calculate the value of the $I_{(TF)}$ indicator, this factor is considered as constant. In 2019 regulations referring to the trade war between the USA and China became particularly significant to (containerized) shipping. Furthermore, in 2019, after the *vacatio legis* period, regulations referring to green shipping were implemented. In 2020 other very severe restrictions were implemented in relation to the lockdown and they were strictly followed (especially in the People's Republic of China). In the methodology assumed for the discussed research it is assumed that $I_{(TF)}$ for free and absolutely unrestricted international trade and maritime transport of containerized cargo is 1.0. Considering the above-mentioned trade and transport restrictions, the values of $I_{(TF)}$ are assumed for the particular years as follows:

2018 – $I_{(TF)}$ =0.75 – the local regulations, GATT remain in force; 2018 is assumed as the base year, the indicator reaches the level of 0.75 which means that the restrictions accounted for only 25% of the total capabilities of free trade.

2019 - $I_{(TF)}$ =0.65 – the local regulations, GATT, regulations additionally implemented in relation to the trade war between the USA and China, green shipping regulations; hence the value of the indicator should be decreased by the estimated influence exerted by the trade war between the USA and China on free maritime containerized trade at the level of 5%, green shipping regulations and their estimated influence on free maritime containerized trade at the level of 5%, which allows us to calculate the aggregated $I_{(TF)}$ at the level of 0.65.

2020 - $I_{(TF)}$ =0.45 – the local regulations, GATT, regulations additionally implemented in relation to the trade war between the USA and China, green shipping regulations, restrictions additionally implemented in relation to the global lockdown; hence the value of the indicator should be additionally decreased by the value of the consequences of the lockdown with the influence on free maritime containerized trade at the level of 20%, which allows us to calculated the aggregated $I_{(TF)}$ at the level of 0.45.

2/ Determinant 2 (Det 2): capabilities for further development of container vessels (in relation to their size given in TEU, the global fleet of container vessels and the limits to the economics of their use) – limits to container ship capacity – for the purpose of this research are described by two factors:

- factor 1 (Det2/F1): global container vessel fleet in TEU [thousands] represented by the Index of Container Vessel Fleet $I_{(CV)}$
- factor 2 (Det2/F2): the capacity of the largest container vessel given in TEU in the particular year represented by the Index of Container Vessel Capacity $I_{(VC)}$

The volume of the global container vessel fleet in the years 2018-2020 and the Index of Container Vessel Fleet $I_{(CV)}$ are presented in Table 3 (Container Ship Fleet Data 2023).

Table 3. The Global Container Vessel Fleet [TEU thousands], Index of Container Vessel Fleet $I_{(CV)}$.

Year	Global Container Vessel Fleet [in TEU thousand]	Change [in TEU thousand]	Change [%]	Synthetically Index $I_{(CV)}$
2018	22,012	2018=100	2018=100	1.00
2019	22,596	584	2.65	1.03
2020	23,632	1620	7.36	1.07

Source: author's work.

The other factor of the Det2 assessment is Det2/F2 that indicates the capacity of the largest container vessel which operated along one of the shipping routes in the particular year during the analysed period of 2018-2020. The operational parameters of the largest container vessels in the research time frame and Index of Container Vessel Capacity $I_{(VC)}$ are presented in Table 4.

Table 4. The largest container vessels 2018-2020 and Index of Container Vessel Capacity $I_{(VC)}$.

Year	Capacity [in TEU]	Change [in TEU]	Change [%]	Synthetically Index $I_{(VC)}$
Commissioned 2018; OOCL Hong Kong, G-Class, flag Panama, length 399.9 m	21,413	2018=100	2018=100	1.00
Commissioned 2019; MSC Gülsün, MSC Megamax-24 Class, flag Panama, length 400 m	23,756	2,343	10.94	1.11
Commissioned 2020; HMM Algeciras, Megamax-Class, flag Panama, length 400 m	23,964	2,551	11.92	1.12

Source: author's work.

3/ Determinant 3 (Det 3): capabilities for the supply of new containers (in relation to the capabilities of the industry responsible for container construction) – limits to the container volume – for purpose of this research are described by two factors:

- factor 1 (Det3/F1): production/supply of new containers in the world represented by the Index of Container Supply $I_{(CS)}$
- factor 2 (Det3/F2): the general number of containers in the international trade represented by the Index of General Number of Containers $I_{(NC)}$

It is estimated that the total number of containers used for transport reaches an approximate level of TEU 65 - 73 million, including TEU 23 – 38.5 million in the current use, TEU 14 – 23.3 million not used and TEU 6 – 10 million (Shipping Container Quick Facts 2020; Higson, 2018) newly purchased. The numbers of registered maritime ISO containers (newly manufactured and in use) represented by the Index of Container Supply $I_{(CS)}$ and by the Index of General Number of Containers $I_{(NC)}$ are presented in Table 5 and 6 (ITCO International Tank Container Organisation, n.d.).

Table 5. The numbers of containers that have been produced 2018-2020, the Index of Container Supply $I_{(CS)}$.

Year	Global Container Production [in thousand]	Change [in thousand]	Change [%]	Synthetically Index $I_{(CS)}$
2018	59700	2018=100	2018=100	1.00
2019	54650	-5050	- 8.46	0.92
2020	35800	-23900	- 40.03	0.60

Source: author's work.

Table 6. The numbers of global container fleet 2018-2020, the Index of General Number of Containers $I_{(NC)}$.

Year	Global Container Fleet [in thousand]	Change [in thousand]	Change [%]	Synthetically Index $I_{(NC)}$
2018	552500	2018=100	2018=100	1.00
2019	604700	52200	9.45	1.09
2020	652350	99850	18.07	1.18

Source: author's work.

4/ Determinant 4 (Det 4): capabilities for further development of terminal infrastructure (in relation to the size, expansion, levels of competitiveness and operational efficiency of container terminals) – limits to container terminal capacity – for the purpose of the research are described by two factors:

- factor 1 (Det4/F1): the number of container (TEU) handled at ports represented by the Index of General Number of Containers Handled $I_{(CH)}$
- factor 2 (Det4/F2): the number of container terminals at sea ports represented by the Index of General Number of Maritime Terminals $I_{(MT)}$

The global container port throughput (in TEU million) and the Index of General Number of Containers Handled $I_{(CH)}$ are presented in Table 7 (UNCTADStat, 2023).

The number of container terminals at sea ports and calculated the Index of General Number of Maritime Terminals $I_{(MT)}$ are presented in Table 8 (UNCTAD, 2022).

5/ Determinant 5 (Det 5): capabilities for further development and capacity of maritime transport infrastructure (in relation to navigation sea routes and canals, especially the Suez Canal and the Panama Canal) – limits to the capacity of sea communication routes – for the purpose of the research are described by two factors:

Table 7. The global container port throughput (in TEU million) and $I_{(CH)}$.

Year	Container port throughput [in TEU million]	Change [in TEU million]	Change [%]	Synthetically Index $I_{(CH)}$
2018	792	2018=100	2018=100	1.00
2019	807	15	1.89	1.02
2020	799	7	0.88	1.01

Source: author's work.

Table 8. The number of container terminals (2018 – 2020) at container ports that handle regular shipping lines and $I_{(MT)}$.

Year	Container port throughput [in TEU million]	Change [in TEU million]	Change [%]	Synthetically Index $I_{(MT)}$
2018	975	2018=100	2018=100	1.00
2019	962	-13	-1.33	0.99
2020	942	-33	-3.38	0.97

Source: author's work.

- factor 1 (Det5/F1): the number of vessels handled at the Suez Canal represented by the Index of Vessels Handled @SC $I_{(SC)}$
- factor 2 (Det5/F2): the number of vessels handled at the Panama Canal Index of Vessels Handled @PC $I_{(PC)}$

The Suez Canal and the Panama Canal are of the highest significance to container shipping. The Suez Canal is a key shipping route to maritime trade between Europe and Asia, whereas the Panama Canal is a maritime route for vessels providing connections between Asia, Oceania, North, South and Central Americas and the Caribbean.

The traffic of container vessels that sail through the Suez Canal and Panama Canal and the adequate Indices are presented in Table 9 and 10 (*SCA - Home*, n.d.; UNCTAD, 2021).

Table 9. The traffic of container vessels that sail through the Suez Canal and the Index of Vessels Handled @SC $I_{(SC)}$.

Year	The number of vessels handled at the Suez Canal	Change	Change [%]	Synthetically Index $I_{(SC)}$
2018	5,663	2018=100	2018=100	1.00
2019	5,321	-342	-6.04	0.94
2020	835	-4828	-93.96	0.15

Source: author's work.

6/ Determinant 6 (Det 6): the level of safety and security of maritime and terminal/port operations (including both these aspects: safety and security and also safe container turnover) – limits to maritime (container) safety and security - for the purpose of the research are described by two factors:

- factor 1 (Det6/F1): the number of maritime/port collisions and accidents (including those that involve container vessels) is represented by the Index of Maritime Collisions $I_{(MC)}$

Table 10. The traffic of container vessels that sail through the Panama Canal and the Index of Vessels Handled @PC $I_{(PC)}$.

Year	The number of vessels handled at the Panama Canal	Change	Change [%]	Synthetically Index $I_{(PC)}$
2018	13795	2018=100	2018=100	1.00
2019	13785	-10	-0.07	1.0
2020	13369	-426	-3.09	0.97

Source: author's work.

- factor 2 (Det6/F2): the number of terrorist and pirate attacks is represented by the Index of Maritime Piracy $I_{(MP)}$

The number of maritime accidents (including those that involve container vessels, containers and port failures) and the number of piracy attacks (including container vessels) with the adequate Indices are presented in Table 11 and 12 (European Maritime Safety Agency 2022; Statista 2022).

Table 11. Maritime accidents and the Index of Maritime Collisions $I_{(MC)}$.

Year	The number of maritime accidents	Change	Change [%]	Synthetically Index $I_{(MC)}$
2018	2,667	2018=100	2018=100	1.00
2019	2,756	89	3.34	1.03
2020	2,547	-120	-4.50	0.96

Source: author's work.

Table 12. The number of pirate attacks (including container vessels) and the Index of Maritime Piracy $I_{(MP)}$.

Year	The number of pirate attacks against vessels	Change	Change [%]	Synthetically Index $I_{(MP)}$
2018	201	2018=100	2018=100	1.00
2019	162	-39	-19.40	0.81
2020	195	-6	-2.99	0.97

Source: author's work.

7/ Determinant 7 (Det 7): capabilities for the further lowering of maritime transport anthropopressure (in relation to a decrease in emission of greenhouse gases – GHG, CO_2 and the general lowering of external effects) – limits to the internal costs of container transport – limits to container terminal capacity – for the purpose of the research are described by two factors:

- factor 1 (Det7/F1): CO_2 emission (equivalent) generated by maritime shipping [million tonnes] is represented by the Index of Maritime Emission $I_{(ME)}$
- factor 2 (Det7/F2): the number of ECA areas with limitations to shipping in terms of marine fuel is represented by the Index of ECA $I_{(ECA)}$

CO_2 emission generated by international shipping in the adopted Net Zero Scenario (as a part of Green Deal) and the adequate Index are presented in Table 13 (International Shipping – Analysis, n.d.).

Table 13. CO_2 emission generated by international shipping and the calculated Index of Maritime Emission $I_{(ME)}$.

Year	CO2 emission (equivalent) [million tonnes]	Change	Change [%]	Synthetically Index $I_{(ME)}$
2018	740	2018=100	2018=100	1.00
2019	692	-48	-6.49	0.94
2020	635	-105	-14.19	0.86

Source: author's work.

The other assessment factor (Det7/F2) is the number of ECAs represented by the $I_{(ECA)}$ Index of ECA. The main factor that limits the free movement of vessels propelled by heavy fuel is the implementation of the areas with restrictions to SOx, PM, NOx emission (Akoel and Miler 2019). They are aimed at putting systematic pressure on the lowering of emission generated by maritime shipping to achieve the ultimate zero-emission goal (2030/2050). Over the analysed period of time, in the years 2018-2020 the ECA regulations were implemented in four key areas. In the methodology assumed for the research, the $I_{(ECA)}$ for absolutely free shipping without considering emission is 1.0 and with the subsequent restrictions it will strive to achieve 0.0 in the years 2030/2050. In the research the $I_{(ECA)}$ for the particular years is assumed as follows:

2018 – $I_{(ECA)}$ =0.85 – the current legal regulations included ECAs of North America, the United States, Caribbean Sea, the Baltic Sea and North Sea. 2018 was assumed as the base year, the indicator was 0.85 which means that restrictions accounted only for 15% of the total capabilities of free shipping propelled by heavy fuel.

2019 - $I_{(ECA)}$ =0.75 – further stricter restrictions were added to the basic regulations in the ECAs at the Baltic Sea and the North Sea, which allows us to calculate the aggregated $I_{(TF)}$ at the level of 0.75.

2020 - $I_{(ECA)}$ =0.75 – no new regulations and new ECAs were implemented; the indicator remained at the same level.

8/ Determinant 8 (Det 8): capabilities for further digitalization and computerization of maritime and container operations (in relation to automation, robotization, autonomation, implementation of IT systems supporting management, the use of database systems, artificial, virtual and augmented reality) – limits to information management – for the purpose of the research are described by two factors:

- factor 1 (Det8/F1): the number of automated terminals - the Index of Automation of Maritime Container Terminals $I_{(AUTER)}$,
- factor 2 (Det8/F2): the number of e-documents applied in trade - the Index of Digitalization of Documents in Maritime Container Transport $I_{(e\text{-}doc)}$

An inventory of terminal automation reveals a rapidly evolving situation. Although the information is likely to be partial and incomplete, 55 container terminals around the world were either fully or partially automated as of mid-2020; this represents 7.3% of all the main container terminals, but 12.2% of the total global footprint in terms of hectares. While the average container terminal size was 51.7 hectares, it was 85.5 hectares for fully automated terminals and 69.9 hectares for semi-automated terminals, underlining the scale propensity for automation (Notteboom 2022). The fully and semi-automated terminals as a part of entire volume of terminals within the timeframe of the research associated with the Index of Automation of Maritime Container Terminals $I_{(AUTER)}$ are presented in Table 14 (Fully and Semi Automated Container Terminals, Total Hectares 2019 | Port Economics, Management and Policy 2020).

Table 14. An inventory of terminal automation with calculated Index $I_{(AUTER)}$.

Year	The number of Container terminals	Fully and semi-automated terminals	Index [%]	Synthetically Index $I_{(AUTER)}$
2018	975	42	4.31	0.04
2019	962	44	4.57	0.05
2020	942	49	5.20	0.05

Source: author's work.

Global trade involves several processes with up to 20+ documents being interchanged for a single shipment between various stakeholders in the chain e.g. a booking contract and a booking list, a sea waybill, a bill of lading (B/L), direct (through), multimodal and FIATA bills of lading, a slot-hire agreement, a commercial invoice, an arrival notice, an import/export custom declaration, a packing list/stow plan, a mate receipt, an import/export license, a letter of credit, a certificate of origin (Shipping Documents You Need When Transporting Your Cargo, n.d.). At present, there are several types of software and technology available for digitalization of trade documentation, so the legal aspect in implementing and using electronic trade documentation over physical paper documentation must be clearly decided. Digitalizing trade documentation has come as an important step to reduce costs, save time, and enhance trade transactions, also improving supply-chain resilience and helping to mitigate future disruptions. According to the analysis and research by McKinsey, physical B/L costs account for between 10-30% of total trade documentation costs. Although the work on electronic bills of lading (e-B/L) started in the late 1990s with many companies working with different systems to ensure the originality and uniqueness of the documents, as of today, approximately only 2% of all bills of lading issued have been electronic [66]. Due to the unavailability of detailed information about e-docs, the progress of implementing digitalization in this field is presented only by the e-B/L (Table 15) (Digitizing Trade Documentation and the Bill of Lading | McKinsey n.d.; DCSA n.d.).

Table 15. Digitalization of documentation and the associated $I_{(e\text{-}B/L)}$; for $I_{(e\text{-}doc)}$ data are not available (n/a).

Year	Number of Main Docs Applied in Maritime Containerization	E-docs [in potential use; feasible for digitalization]	Index I(e-doc)	Subindex I(e-B/L) = e-B/L/total B/L x 100 [%]	Synthetically Index I (e-B/L)
2018	18	12	n/a	0.14	0.01
2019	20	19	n/a	0.18	0.02
2020	22	20	n/a	0.20	0.02

Source: author's work.

Identified above, the determinants of further development of maritime containerized transport (Det) and the synthetic indicators (F1-F2) calculated for the years 2018-2020 are presented in a synthetic way in Table 16.

Stage 4 Results – Calculation of Weighted Formulas for Determinants Det 1-8

In order to prepare synthetic data for further comparison, a graphical presentation (radar charts) and evaluation, the weighted results for the particular determinants Det 1-$8_{(w)}$ are calculated in accordance with the following equation:

$$Det_{w(n;n=1-8)} = \left[Det_{(n;n=1-8)}F1xW\right] + \left[Det_{(n;n=1-8)}F2xW\right] \tag{1}$$

where:

Table 16. Determinants of further development of maritime containerized transport (Det) and the synthetic indicators (F1-F2) [2018-2020].

	Det 1		Det 2		Det 3		Det 4		Det 5		Det 6		Det 7		Det 8	
Year	F1	F2	F1	F2	F1	F2	F1	F2	F1	F2	F1	F2	F1	F2	F1	F2
2018	1.0	0.75	1.0	1.0	1.0	1.0	1.0	1.0	1.0	1.0	1.0	1.0	1.0	0.85	0.04	0.01
2019	0.98	0.65	1.03	1.11	0.92	1.09	1.02	0.99	0.94	1.0	1.03	0.81	0.94	0.75	0.05	0.02
2020	0.90	0.45	1.07	1.12	0.60	1.18	1.01	0.97	0.15	0.97	0.96	0.97	0.86	0.75	0.05	0.02

Source: author's work.

Det $_{w\ (n;\ n=1\text{-}8)}$ - weighted determinants for Det 1-8
Det$_{(n;\ n=1\text{-}8)}$ F1 - factor 1 for the n determinant
Det$_{(n;\ n=1\text{-}8)}$ F2 - factor 2 for the n determinant
W - weight of each determinant (may assume the values from 0.0 to1.0; the weights of F1 and F2 for each Det must sum up to 1.0).

The weights are assigned by the use of Delphi method: a panel of experts consists of the representatives of the shipowner/ship operator, master mariner, superintendent, terminal operation department, academic staff – professors in maritime transportation and supply chain management, for Det 1weight were assessed as follows: F1 – 0.6; F2 – 0.4, all the rest of Dets were assessed accordingly to the panel findings and are presented in subsequent equations (2)-(25). Hence, Det 1$_{(w)}$ in the subsequent years of the analysed period of time is calculated as follows:

$$\text{Det } 1_{(w)}\text{in2018} = 1.0\text{x}0.6 + 0.75\text{x}0.4 = 0.60 + 0.30 = 0.90, \tag{2}$$

$$\text{Det } 1_{(w)}\text{in2019} = 0.98\text{x}0.6 + 0.65\text{x}0.4 = 0.59 + 0.26 = 0.85, \tag{3}$$

$$\text{Det } 1_{(w)}\text{in2020} = 0.90\text{x}0.6 + 0.45\text{x}0.4 = 0.54 + 0.18 = 0.72. \tag{4}$$

Similarly, Det 2$_{(w)}$ in the subsequent years of the analysed period of time is calculated as follows:

$$\text{Det } 2_{(w)}\text{in2018} = 1.0\text{x}0.7 + 1.0\text{x}0.3 = 0.7 + 0.30 = 1.00, \tag{5}$$

$$\text{Det } 2_{(w)}\text{in2019} = 1.03\text{x}0.7 + 1.11\text{x}0.3 = 0.72 + 0.33 = 1.05, \tag{6}$$

$$\text{Det } 2_{(w)}\text{in2020} = 1.07\text{x}0.7 + 1.12\text{x}0.3 = 0.75 + 0.34 = 1.09. \tag{7}$$

Det 3$_{(w)}$ in the subsequent years of the analysed period of time is calculated as follows:

$$\text{Det } 3_{(w)}\text{in2018} = 1.0\text{x}0.4 + 1.0\text{x}0.6 = 0.7 + 0.30 = 1.00, \tag{8}$$

$$\text{Det } 3_{(w)}\text{in2019} = 0.92\text{x}0.4 + 1.09\text{x}0.6 = 0.37 + 0.65 = 1.02, \tag{9}$$

$$\text{Det } 3_{(w)}\text{in2020} = 0.60\text{x}0.4 + 1.18\text{x}0.6 = 0.24 + 0.71 = 0.95. \tag{10}$$

Det 4$_{(w)}$ in the subsequent years of the analysed period of time is calculated as follows:

$$\text{Det } 4_{(w)}\text{in2018} = 1.0\text{x}0.6 + 1.0\text{x}0.4 = 0.70 + 0.30 = 1.00, \tag{11}$$

$$\text{Det } 4_{(w)}\text{in2019} = 1.02\text{x}0.6 + 0.99\text{x}0.4 = 0.61 + 0.39 = 1.00, \tag{12}$$

$$\text{Det } 4_{(w)}\text{in2020} = 1.01\text{x}0.6 + 0.97\text{x}0.4 = 0.60 + 0.38 = 0.98. \tag{13}$$

Det 5$_{(w)}$ in the subsequent years of the analysed period of time is calculated as follows:

$$\text{Det } 5_{(w)}\text{in2018} = 1.0\text{x}0.6 + 1.0\text{x}0.4 = 0.7 + 0.30 = 1.00, \tag{14}$$

$$\text{Det } 5_{(w)}\text{in2019} = 0.94\text{x}0.6 + 1.0\text{x}0.4 = 0.56 + 0.40 = 0.96, \tag{15}$$

$$\text{Det } 5_{(w)}\text{in2020} = 0.15\text{x}0.6 + 0.97\text{x}0.4 = 0.09 + 0.39 = 0.48. \tag{16}$$

Det $6_{(w)}$ in the subsequent years of the analysed period of time is calculated as follows:

$$\text{Det } 6_{(w)}\text{in2018} = 1.0\text{x}0.7 + 1.0\text{x}0.3 = 0.7 + 0.30 = 1.00, \tag{17}$$

$$\text{Det } 6_{w)}\text{in2019} = 1.03\text{x}0.7 + 0.81\text{x}0.3 = 0.72 + 0.24 = 0.96, \tag{18}$$

$$\text{Det } 6_{(w)}\text{in2020} = 0.96\text{x}0.7 + 0.97\text{x}0.3 = 0.67 + 0.29 = 0.96. \tag{19}$$

Det $7_{(w)}$ in the subsequent years of the analysed period of time is calculated as follows:

$$\text{Det } 7_{(w)}\text{in2018} = 1.0\text{x}0.7 + 0.85\text{x}0.3 = 0.70 + 0.26 = 0.96, \tag{20}$$

$$\text{Det } 7_{w)}\text{in2019} = 0.94\text{x}0.7 + 0.75\text{x}0.3 = 0.66 + 0.23 = 0.89, \tag{21}$$

$$\text{Det } 7_{(w)}\text{in2020} = 0.86\text{x}0.7 + 0.75\text{x}0.3 = 0.60 + 0.23 = 0.83. \tag{22}$$

Det $8_{(w)}$ in the subsequent years of the analysed period of time is calculated as follows:

$$\text{Det } 8_{(w)}\text{in2018} = 0.04\text{x}0.6 + 0.01\text{x}0.7 = 0.02 + 0.01 = 0.03, \tag{23}$$

$$\text{Det } 8_{(w)}\text{in2019} = 0.05\text{x}0.6 + 0.02\text{x}0.7 = 0.03 + 0.01 = 0.04, \tag{24}$$

$$\text{Det } 8_{(w)}\text{in2020} = 0.05\text{x}0.6 + 0.02\text{x}0.7 = 0.03 + 0.01 = 0.04. \tag{25}$$

The weighted results defined for the particular determinants Det 1-$8_{(w)}$ are presented in Table 17.

Table 17. The weighted results defined for the particular determinants Det 1-$8_{(w)}$.

Year	Det 1(w)	Det 2(w)	Det 3(w)	Det 4(w)	Det 5(w)	Det 6(w)	Det 7(w)	Det 8(w)
2018	0.90	1.00	1.00	1.00	1.00	1.00	0.96	0.03
2019	0.85	1.05	1.02	1.00	0.96	0.96	0.89	0.04
2020	0.72	1.09	0.95	0.98	0.48	0.96	0.83	0.04

Source: author's work.

Stage 5 Results – a Radar Chart as a Graphical Presentation of the Weighted Det 1-8

The summary table presenting the weighted results defined for the determinants Det 1-$8_{(w)}$ allows the Authors to provide a radar chart in order to compare the factors determining the capabilities for the development of maritime containerized transport in the years 2018 – 2020 (with the consideration of the pandemic consequences). The radar chart is presented in Figure 1.

5 DISCUSSION/LIMITATION AND FUTURE RESEARCH

Presented in the paper, the research indicates the multi-aspect and multi-disciplinary character of the determinants that shape and drive modern maritime transport of containerized cargo

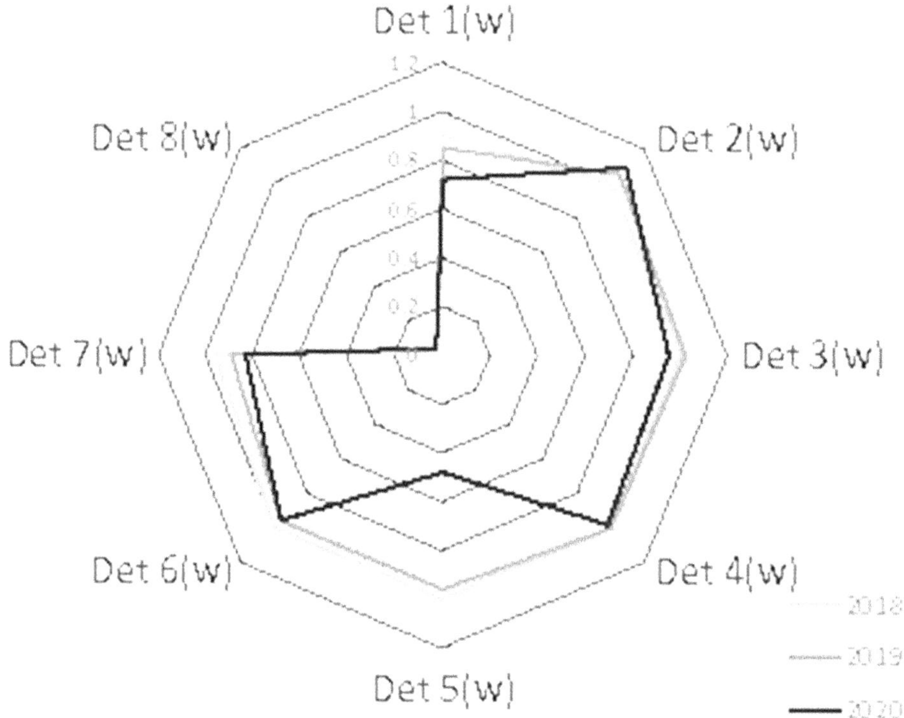

Figure 1. Radar chart of weighted values for Det 1-8.
Source: author's work.

on the scale which has not been represented in any contemporary research studies. The factors analysed (Factors 1, 2) for Determinant 1 (Det 1) clearly indicate a negative influence exerted by the pandemic on the volume of containerized cargo transport, particularly in the first half of 2020. The main reason for that involved formal changes to the terms of trade and transport regulations (first of all – the lockdown as a F2 representation). As far as Det 2 is concerned, in a short time the pandemic neither affected the reduction of the container vessel fleet nor influenced the processes of increasing the loading capacities of container vessels F2 (in order to achieve the effect of the economies of scale in the global maritime transport). During the analysed period of time the loading capacity increased by almost TEU600; however, at the beginning of 2023 it exceeded the level of TEU 24K. A more serious crisis that concerns the number of container vessels appears to be expected in a long-term perspective (not included in the research analysis). Some serious consequences of the pandemic are observed for Det3 where the data indicate a 40% decrease in the production of new containers (2020, in comparison to the period of time before the pandemic). However, also in 2020 there was an increase by 18% approximately, recorded in the general volume of containers in trade (mostly caused by reintroducing containers that had been temporarily withdrawn, into trade and some increased pressure on repositioning). As far as Det 4 is concerned, the research indicates the resilience of the system applied to terminal productivity control against the stress caused by the pandemic (a slight increase by approximately 2% in the volume of cargo handled at ports with an inconsiderable decrease in the number of terminals at the same time). The pandemic exerted some significant influence in terms of Det 5 (correlated with Det 1) that involves the number of vessels handled at the Suez Canal (F1), where a decrease in relation to the base year was over 85%; a significantly smaller decrease was recorded for the Panama Canal (only 3%); it indicates a total collapse of logistic supply chains in 2020 between Asia and Europe. Det 6 (both F1 and F2) indicates that the pandemic did not affect the number of maritime accidents and the number of pirate attacks. These numbers have been decreasing (however, its correlation with the pandemic cannot be proved at this stage of the research). Det 7 indicates a successive decrease in the CO_2 emission (Det 7/F1) which comes as a result of the policy pursued in order to achieve zero-emission and does not indicate any correlation with the consequences of the pandemic – similarly to F2, the value of which presents the implementation of the subsequent ECAs that decrease emission. The last determinant (Det 8) is indisputably related to the consequences of the pandemic as it determines the necessity of applying solutions that pertain to automation at maritime container terminals (F1). It comes as an antidote to the shortage of workforce and restrictions following the lockdown. An indirect relation to the pandemic can be observed in the necessity of implementing e-documents to trade (considering remote work/home office implemented during the pandemic on an unprecedented scale and often applied at present). Unfortunately, the research also indicates very low coefficients of terminal automation (at the level of 5%) and documentation digitalization (at the level of 2% for e-B/Ls). At the same time, Det 8 becomes one of the most important and most promising determinants of further development of capabilities of maritime containerized transport. Utilizing the presented matrix, the capabilities for the development of maritime containerized transport $P_{(CS)}$ may be calculated (for further comparisons) with the equation as follows:

$$P_{(CS)} = f\left(Det_{(n;n=1-8)}F1, F2\right), \tag{26}$$

where:
$Det_{(n;\ n=1\text{-}8)}$ - determinants for Det1-8
F1 - factor 1 for the *n* determinant
F2 - factor 2 for the *n* determinant

At this stage of the research, it is also possible to state that the discussed matrix that involves eight determinants (Det 1-8) comes as an original and promising research tool (that obviously requires further specification and improvement) for providing a holistic analysis of determinants of development of containerized shipping, with the consideration of challenges characteristic to the era of sustainable development, digitalization, automation and frequent turbulences (stochastic occurrences, global shocks such as the pandemic or the present war in Ukraine). It also allows the Authors to state that the working hypothesis has been initially proved.

Considering the stochastic character of economic phenomena and shocks, the discussed research indicates the practicality of applying a holistic analysis of factors that determine capabilities for the development of containerized shipping. In the light of specialist literature (Notteboom et al. 2021; Madhav et al. 2017; Cullinane and Haralambides 2021; Song 2021; Bentaleb et al. 2021), such an analysis has not been currently provided on such a comprehensive scale. The Authors will continue their research studies, focusing on a more adequate selection of the factors F1 and F2 applied to describe determinants, also on a more detailed source query in search of relevant information. So far, the most discouraging factor in the research has been the lack of specific information on containerized shipping referring to numerous processes of the modern era (digitalization, automation, sustainable development). This fact has considerably limited an adequate selection of indicators at this stage of the research. A more adequate dimension of the research will be possible by adding the data of 2021 and 2022 to the analysis. This will allow the Authors to indicate more precisely the fields for the potential development of containerized shipping and to present the usefulness of the discussed tool in a much more elaborated way.

6 CONCLUSION

The Covid-19 pandemic will have short- and long-term impact on the global container shipping industry with a necessity to adapt to some possible changes in the global supply chain system. Intensified inspections of containerized cargo transported by sea, including delays at border checkpoints and complex procedures have already increased costs of global logistics services. Considering temporary trade barriers and export restrictions, some possibilities have appeared to increase alternative logistics solutions, such as intercontinental railway services that can streamline trade between the East and the West. Unfortunately, because of the Russian military operations in Ukraine, those solutions have proved to be of temporary nature. After a long time, in the market of containerized cargo transport it is possible to expect some acceleration of digitalization development, increased investment in new technologies supporting automation trends in this sector (Raza et al. 2023). An increase in the levels of containerization and global capacity will be possible in the sector of container shipping. However, it is expected that larger vessels will be commissioned along with more efficient loading and unloading systems at port terminals. Considering the experience acquired during the pandemic related to limited production and shipping, the models of production and implementation of logistics services may be changed from the Just-in-Time to Just-in-Case (Danelia 2021). The maritime industry, including the container shipping sector, will have to adapt itself to the upcoming changes. It will be necessary to consider the development of shorter supply chains, increased implementation of alternative logistics solutions such as intercontinental railway services (Choi 2021) or multi-functionality of warehouses in the vicinity of markets that will be required to shorten the transit time to various destinations.

However, it should be also remembered that during the implementation of the above-mentioned development scenario, it is necessary to consider factors that determine the discussed development, e.g., geopolitical challenges (the war in Ukraine), economic challenges (the trade war between the USA and China), environmental and health limitations (related to the Covid-19), volatility of fuel prices or changes to trade policies pursued by various countries after the pandemic (increased protectionism) (World Trade Report 2022).

Considering the above-mentioned arguments, issues related to the development of the geopolitical situation and global trade conditions, it is possible to draw only three general conclusions that determine future governance in the field of international (global) supply chains, directly affecting the shape of international maritime transport of containerized cargo:

- it is highly probable that a re-configuration of supply chains and international exchange will take place, considering tension between China and the USA, the expansive policy of China in the development of the New Silk Road, the search of new locations for production and distribution, based on the re-orientation of trade policy pursued by the "triad" entities (PRC, USA, EU). This will result in shortening and making current supply chains more flexible (a new "geography" of connections);
- it is highly probable that production locations will be moved closer to potential sales markets. This will result in a re-configuration of current production locations which have been so far dominated by the strong economy of China (a new "structure" of production networks);
- it is highly probable that new guidelines concerning the amounts of reserves and flexibility of production and supply chains will be issued by the "triad" entities and countries directly affected by the war in Ukraine. This will result in an increase in reserves at the particular stages of logistics processes, in a change in the attitude toward obligatory (strategic) reserves and also in a necessity of increasing national reserves (which, in turn, will increase pressure on storage area, warehouse surface, cargo handling capacities of port terminals, etc.) (a new "architecture" of supply chains).

REFERENCES

Abdelshafie A., Salah M., Kramberger T. and Dragan D. 2022. Repositioning and Optimal Re-Allocation of Empty Containers: *A Review of Methods, Models, and Applications. Sustainability*, 14(11), 6655. https://doi.org/10.3390/su14116655.

Akoel A. and Miler R. K. 2019. Economic and operational impact of the MRV implementation on maritime transport processes. *WSB Journal of Business and Finance*, 53(1), 133–143. https://doi.org/10.2478/wsbjbf-2019-0013.

Al-Mansour J. F. and Al-Ajmi 2020. Coronavirus "COVID-19" – Supply Chain Disruption and Implications for Strategy, Economy, and Management. *The Journal of Asian Finance, Economics and Business*, 7(9), 659–672. https://doi.org/10.13106/jafeb.2020.vol7.no9.659.
Annual Economic Report 2020 Bank for International Settlements. (n.d.). Bank for International Settlements.
Annual Overview of Marine Casualties and Incidents 2022, European Maritime Safety Agency.
Arvis J.F., Ojala L., Wiederer C., Shepherd B., Raj A., Dairabayeva K., Kiiski T. 2018. Connecting to Compete 2018 Trade Logistics in the Global Economy. The Logistics Performance Index and Its Indicators, The International Bank for Reconstruction and Development/The World Bank, Washington 2018, https://lpi.worldbank.org/report.
Becha H., Lind M., Bottin F., Larsen S.E. 2020. Standarisation in container shipping is key to boosting economies of scale - importance of data collaboration between shipping lines, Smart Maritime Network. DOI:10.13140/RG.2.2.17623.91043.
Benedito M. A. P. 2018. The applying accounting methodology of radar chart for textile production activity in Great *Britain. Archives of Business Research*, 6(10). https://doi.org/10.14738/abr.610.5491.
Bentaleb O., Belloum A. S. Z., Sebaa A. and El-Maouhab A. 2021. Containerization technologies: taxonomies, applications and challenges. *The Journal of Supercomputing*. https://doi.org/10.1007/s11227-021-03914-1.
Beškovnik B., Zanne M. and Golnar M. 2022. Dynamic Changes in Port Logistics Caused by the COVID-19 Pandemic. *Journal of Marine Science and Engineering*, 10(10), 1473. https://doi.org/10.3390/jmse10101473.
Choi K.-S. 2021. The Current Status and Challenges of China Railway Express (CRE) as a Key Sustainability Policy Component of the Belt and Road Initiative. *Sustainability*, 13(9), 5017. https://doi.org/10.3390/su13095017.
Choi T.-M. 2020. Risk Analysis in Logistics Systems: A Research Agenda During and After the COVID-19 Pandemic. Transportation Research Part E: Logistics and Transportation Review, 145, 102190. https://doi.org/10.1016/j.tre.2020.102190.
Container Ship Fleet Data. (2023, February 24). https://agtransport.usda.gov/stories/s/Ocean-Container-Fleet-Dashboard/pjaw-nxa9.
Cullinane K. and Haralambides H. 2021. Global trends in maritime and port economics: the COVID-19 pandemic and beyond. *Maritime Economics & Logistics*, 23(3), 369–380. https://doi.org/10.1057/s41278-021-00196-5.
Cullinane K. and Yang J. 2022. Evaluating the Costs of Decarbonizing the Shipping Industry: A Review of the Literature. *Journal of Marine Science and Engineering*, 10(7), 946. https://doi.org/10.3390/jmse10070946.
Danelia I. 2021. Impact of COVID-19 on Global Container Shipping Industry. *European Scientific Journal*, ESJ, 17(27), 5. https://doi.org/10.19044/esj.2021.
DCSA. (n.d.). DCSA's member carriers commit to a fully standardised, electronic bill of lading by 2030. DCSA. Retrieved May 7, 2023, from https://dcsa.org/newsroom/resources/dcsas-member-carriers-commit-to-a-fully-standardised-electronic-bill-of-lading-by-2030/.
Digitizing trade documentation and the bill of lading | McKinsey. (n.d.). Www.mckinsey.com. https://www.mckinsey.com/industries/travel-logistics-and-infrastructure/our-insights/the-multi-billion-dollar-paper-jam-unlocking-trade-by-digitalizing-documentation.
Fully and Semi Automated Container Terminals, Total Hectares, 2019 | Port Economics, Management and Policy. (2020, January 6). https://porteconomicsmanagement.org/pemp/contents/part3/terminal-automation/fully-semi-automated-container-terminals-total-hectares.
GATT disputes: 1948-1995 volume 1: Overview and one-page case summaries, WTO, Geneva 2018, https://www.wto.org/english/res_e/booksp_e/gatt4895vol1_e.pdf
Ghosh J. 2020. The Pandemic and the Global Economy. https://council.science/current/blog/the-pan demic-and-the-globaleconomy/.
Global Financial Stability Report. (n.d.). International Monetary Fund.
Global Trade Rebound Beast Expectations But Marked by Regional Divergences. (n.d.). World Trade Organisation.
Gorajek A. 2021 Econometric Interpretations of Index Numbers, Comparing Income and Price Levels and International Income Inequality, IARIW Virtual General Conference, 23-27 August, 2021, https://iariw.org/wp-content/uploads/2021/08/gorajek_paper.pdf.
Grisham T. 2009. The Delphi technique: a method for testing complex and multifaceted topics. *International Journal of Managing Projects in Business*, 2(1), 112–130. https://doi.org/10.1108/17538370910930545.

Guerrero D., Letrouit L. and Pais-Montes C. 2022. The container transport system during Covid-19: An analysis through the prism of complex networks. *Transport Policy*, 115, 113–125. https://doi.org/10.1016/j.tranpol.2021.10.021.
Handbook on Constructing Composite Indicators. Methodology and user guide, OECD Publications, Paris 2008.
Higson D. 2018 (July 9). How Many Shipping Containers are Out There? Porta-Stor. https://porta-stor.com/many-shipping-containers
Hugh M., Antje M. 1999. Benchmarking national labour market performance: A radar chart approach. WZB Discussion Paper, No. FS I 99-202, https://www.econstor.eu/handle/10419/43952.
International Shipping – Analysis. (n.d.). IEA. https://www.iea.org/reports/international-shipping.
ITCO International Tank Container Organisation. 2023. February 15. http://www.itco.org
Jackson J. n.d. Global Economic Effects of COVID-19. Congressional Research Service
Kim B., Kim G. and Kang, M. 2022. Study on Comparing the Performance of Fully Automated Container Terminals during the COVID-19 Pandemic. *Sustainability*, 14(15), 9415. https://doi.org/10.3390/su14159415.
Lindstad E., Lagemann B., Rialland A., Gamlem G. M. and Valland A. 2021. Reduction of maritime GHG emissions and the potential role of E-fuels. Transportation Research Part D: *Transport and Environment*, 101, 103075. https://doi.org/10.1016/j.trd.2021.103075.
Madhav N., Oppenheim B., Gallivan M., Prime Mulembakani, Rubin E. and Wolfe N. (2017). Pandemics: Risks, Impacts, and Mitigation. Nih.gov, 17. https://doi.org/10.1596/978-1-4648-0527-1/pt5.ch17.
Mańkowska M., Pluciński M., Kotowska I. and Filina-Dawidowicz L. 2021. Seaports during the COVID-19 Pandemic: The Terminal Operators' Tactical Responses to Disruptions in Maritime Supply Chains. *Energies*, 14(14), 4339. https://doi.org/10.3390/en14144339.
Matczak M. 2013. Intelligent container terminals – ITS solutions for seaports, Archives of Transport System Telematics, Vol. 6, Issue 2.
Menhat M., Mohd Zaideen I. M., Yusuf Y., Salleh N. H. M., Zamri M. A. and Jeevan. 2021. The impact of Covid-19 pandemic: A review on maritime sectors in Malaysia. *Ocean & Coastal Management*, 209(1), 105638. https://doi.org/10.1016/j.ocecoaman.2021.105638.
Merk O., Hoffmann J. and Haralambides H. 2022. Post-COVID-19 scenarios for the governance of maritime transport and ports. *Maritime Economics & Logistics*. https://doi.org/10.1057/s41278-022-00228-8.
Miler R. K., Gostomski E. and Nowosielski T. 2022. *Containerization in Maritime Transport. Contemporary Trends and Challenges*, 1st ed.; CRC Press, Taylor and Francis Group.
Millefiori L. M., Braca P., Zissis D., Spiliopoulos G., Marano S., Willett P. K. and Carniel S. 2021. COVID-19 impact on global maritime mobility. *Scientific Reports*, 11(1), 18039. https://doi.org/10.1038/s41598-021-97461-7
Mishra M. K. 2020. *The World after COVID-19 and its impact on Global Economy*. Www.econstor.eu. http://hdl.handle.net/10419/215931.
Naseer S., Khalid S., Parveen S., Abbass K., Song H. and Achim M. V. 2023. COVID-19 outbreak: Impact on global economy. *Frontiers in Public Health*, 10. https://doi.org/10.3389/fpubh.2022.1009393.
Notteboom T., Pallis A., Rodrigue J.P. 2022. *Port Economics, Management and Policy*, New York: Routledge.
Notteboom T., Pallis T. and Rodrigue J.-P. 2021. Disruptions and resilience in global container shipping and ports: the COVID-19 pandemic versus the 2008–2009 financial crisis. *Maritime Economics & Logistics*, 23(2), 179–210. https://doi.org/10.1057/s41278-020-00180-5.
Onwuegbuzie A., Leech N. and Collins K. 2015. *Qualitative Analysis Techniques for the Review of the Literature*. The Qualitative Report, 17(28). https://doi.org/10.46743/2160-3715/2012.1754.
Papava V. and Chkuaseli M. 2021. Economic Consequences of the COVID-19 Pandemic and the Economic Ability of a Government as a Factor of Production. *International Business & Economics Studies*, 3(2), p67. https://doi.org/10.22158/ibes.v3n2p67.
Paré G., Trudel M.-C., Jaana M. and Kitsiou S. 2015. Synthesizing information systems knowledge: A typology of literature reviews. *Information & Management*, 52(2), 183–199. https://doi.org/10.1016/j.im.2014.08.008.
Pelagidis T., Haralambides H. 2020. What Shipping Can Tell Us About Europe's Efforts to Face the Risk of COVID-19-Induced 'Japanification'. *World Economics*, 21 (3): 29–39.
Raj A., Mukherjee A. A., Jabbour A. B. L. de S. and Srivastava S. K. 2022. Supply Chain Management during and post-COVID-19 pandemic: Mitigation Strategies and Practical Lessons Learned. *Journal of Business Research*, 142(1), 1125–1139. NCBI. https://doi.org/10.1016/j.jbusres.2022.01.037.

Raza Z., Woxenius J., Vural C. A. and Lind M. 2023. Digital transformation of maritime logistics: Exploring trends in the liner shipping segment. Computers in Industry, 145, 103811. https://doi.org/10.1016/j.compind.2022.103811.

Report on G20 Trade Measures (Mid-October 2019 to Mid-May 2020). (n.d.) World Trade Organisation.

Review of Maritime Transport 2019. (n.d.) United Nations Publications.

SCA - Home. n.d. Www.suezcanal.gov.eg. https://www.suezcanal.gov.eg.

Shipping Container Quick Facts. (2020, November 3). Norman Global Logistics. https://www.normanglobal.com/shipping-container-quick-facts.

Shipping documents you need when transporting your cargo. (n.d.) Www.twill.net. https://www.twill.net/knowledge-hub/logistics-know-how/important-shipping-documents.

Skulmoski G.J., Hartman F. T., and Krahn J. 2007. The Delphi Method for Graduate Research. *Journal of Information Technology Education: Research*, 6, 001–021. https://doi.org/10.28945/199.

Song D.-P. 2021. *Container Logistics and Maritime Transport*. DOI:10.4324/9780429320996.

Statista. 2022. The number of pirate attacks against ships worldwide from 2010 to 2021. https://www.statista.com.

The World Bank. 2022. WDR 2022 Chapter 1. Introduction. World Bank. https://www.worldbank.org/en/publication/wdr2022/brief/chapter-1-introduction-the-economic-impacts-of-the-covid-19-crisis.

UNCTAD. 2021. Beyond 20/20 WDS - Table view. Unctad.org. https://unctadstat.unctad.org/wds/TableViewer/tableView.aspx.

UNCTAD. Review of Maritime Transport 2022. (2023, February 23). https://unctad.org/publication/review-maritime-transport-2022.

UNCTADStat. Container port throughput. (2023, February 15). https://unctadstat.unctad.org/wds/TableViewer/tableView.aspx?ReportId=13321.

Wang C.-N., Dang T.-T., Nguyen N.-A.-T., Chou C.-C., Hsu H.-P. and Dang L.-T.-H. 2022. Evaluating Global Container Shipping Companies: A Novel Approach to Investigating Both Qualitative and Quantitative Criteria for Sustainable Development. *Axioms*, 11(11), 610. https://doi.org/10.3390/.

World Trade Report 2022. (n.d.) World Trade Organisation.

Worldwide export trade volume 1950-2018. (n.d.) Statista. https://www.statista.com/statistics/264682/worldwide-export-volume-in-the-trade-since-1950

WTO. 2020. Second Quarter 2020 Merchandise Trade. https://www.wto.org/english/res_e/statis_e/daily_update_e/merch_latest.pdf.

Xu L., Yang S., Chen J. and Shi J. 2021. The effect of COVID-19 pandemic on port performance: Evidence from China. *Ocean & Coastal Management*, 209, 105660. https://doi.org/10.1016/j.ocecoaman.2021.105660.

Yazir D., Şahin B., Yip T. L. and Tseng P.-H. 2020. Effects of COVID-19 on maritime industry: a review. *International Maritime Health*, 71(4), 253–264. https://doi.org/10.5603/IMH.2020.0044.

Youd F. 2021. April 29. *Global shipping container shortage: the story so far. Ship Technology*. https://www.ship-technology.com/features/global-shipping-container-shortage-the-story-so-far.

Digital Synergy – El Emary et al. (eds)

Chapter 8
Last chance tourism in the light of challenges for sustainable management

Barbara Pabian
University of Economics, Katowice, Poland

Contents

This article is the result of my own research. They are motivated by the hitherto failures in mitigating climate change, as well as the progressive degradation of ecosystems and the loss of biodiversity on a global scale, which has social and economic consequences. Its aim is to discover how and to what extent mass tourism of "last chance" (LCT), motivated by the desire to see a given place or area before it disappears, aggravates these threats, as well as to indicate the need to introduce specific solutions in the field of sustainable management that will contribute to mitigating these threats. These actions should be systemic. Due to the exploratory study and the need to use a wide range of materials in the undertaken research, which concerns various places and areas on an international scale, it was decided to use the desk research method, participant observation and descriptive analysis. The research was based on an interpretative paradigm related to inductive reasoning. The most important results achieved include the identification and classification of places threatened by the development of mass tourism, as well as the determination of the main directions of activities in the field of sustainable management, serving pro-ecological goals, after which the quality of a specific element of the environment should be improved or its current satisfactory condition should be maintained. So far, there have been many studies from the perspective of tourism management, but there is no research on "tourism of last resort" (LCT) in the context of challenges for management, referring to the concept of sustainable development. The article partly fills this gap, it contains conclusions and recommendations regarding activities in the field of sustainable management in tourism of last resort (LCT), resulting from the conducted research.

1 INTRODUCTION

The World Economic Forum (WEF) recently published the 18th edition of the Global Risks Report 2023, which indicated, among others, the most serious threats to the world in the decade ahead. These are: "Failure to Mitigate Climate Change ", "Failure of Climate Change Adaptation", followed by "Natural Disasters and Extreme Weather Events", and "Biodiversity Loss and Ecosystem Collapse". Currently, atmospheric levels of carbon dioxide, methane and nitrous oxide have all reached record highs. It is also very unlikely that global warming will be limited to 1.5°C. (PTSprint 2023:18).

DOI: 10.1201/9781003440406-8

In connection with the progressive degradation of nature and negative changes in the anthropogenic environment, many places in the world, which researchers write about as "humanized space" (Tuan 1987: 158), and are also marked on the map, have their own name and distinguished from others by their materiality and identity (Grésillon 2010: 21), are at risk of partial or complete destruction. The process of destruction concerns not only tourist attractions but also entire natural and cultural landscapes, i.e. areas and their appearances saturated with meanings (Baldwin et al. 2007: 169). The situation is not improved by the spontaneous development of mass tourism, which is defined by the formula 3xS (sun, see, sand). Massive traveling changes to the disadvantage of many specific places, tourist attractions, and areas in the world, e.g. hitherto paradise corners, known for their beautiful beaches and coral reefs, and even Antarctica. The Independent calculates that over the past 15 years, the number of tourists in the Maldives has increased by 68 per cent, in the Galapagos by 38 per cent, and in Glacier Park by 15 per cent (Hare 2018). As research shows, some tour operators are able to use this situation to their financial advantage, preying on this type of threat. They offer "last chance trips" to places whose existence is threatened. In this way, tourism of last resort (LCT) develops, which can be defined as trips to places or areas of tourist reception at risk of destruction due to ongoing climate change or other factors, also of a socio-cultural nature, such as terrorism, armed conflicts. Promotional activities and alarming statements from experts become a factor that motivates tourists to take advantage of such an offer. Tourists want to be able to visit endangered places or landscapes in time and see with their own eyes those that may soon cease to exist. They often do not realise that by traveling en masse and in an unsustainable way, they themselves are driving a spiral of destruction. As research shows, tourism slowed down during the Covid-19 pandemic, which was caused by the lockdown and the lack of freedom to travel around the world. The tourism, catering, cultural, hotel and transport sectors suffered the most during this time (Bilińska et al. 2023: 3). After this stagnation, with the advent of Covid passports certifying vaccination, there was a revival in tourism. Airlines have resumed connections to both leisure and business destinations. The problem of "last chance tourism" has returned.

Although there are numerous studies on tourism management, no research has been conducted on "tourism of last resort" (LCT) in the context of management strictly referring to the idea of sustainable development. The article partly fills this gap, presenting specific conclusions and solutions regarding this issue resulting from the analysis of the existing data. It consists of the following parts. After the introduction, a literature review thematically related to the issues discussed in this article was reviewed. It was obtained from information on places and areas saturated with meanings as well as motivations for traveling as a result of climate change and the development of mass tourism. Then, the adopted research methodology was discussed. The next part of the work contains the identification of particularly endangered places and areas. The final part of the work consists of conclusions and recommendations regarding activities in the field of sustainable management in "tourism of last resort" (LCT), resulting from the conducted research. The Discussion section contains references to the findings of other researchers, he points out. It also indicates the limitations of the research and further possible directions of its development.

2 LITERATURE OVERVIEW

Last chance tourism (LCT), which is the result of the motivation to see a place before it disappears from the face of the Earth, is increasingly becoming the subject of interest for researchers. The issues related to this phenomenon are analyzed from various research perspectives and with the use of multiple methods depending on the represented scientific discipline. However, there are no studies on the use of the new concept of sustainable management and the implementation of specific solutions in the field of sustainable management. Researchers agree that there is an urgent need to adopt transformative methods of tourism management approaches in order to avoid an eventual industry collapse (Fumagalli et al. 2022; Cave and Dredge 2020; Pacheco et al. 2021).

So far, there have been many papers on the motivation of undertaking last-chance tourism (LCT) trips, e.g. the role of environmental awareness in determining motivation and the impact of such motivational elements on satisfaction and place recommendation. As it turns out, environmental awareness has a significant impact on all motivation elements (Kucukergin and Gürlek 2020).

Among the areas popular for tourism of last resort (LCT), Antarctica and Antarctica are most often indicated, where the motive for embarking on a trip is the chance to see the "permafrost" before the ice sheets melt. Tour operators hope that polar tourism will fulfill the desired educational functions in the field of ecology. This positive effect is referred to as "ambassadorship" and was coined by Lars-Eric Linbald in his Antarctic tourism trips. However, as scientific research from 2018 shows, while a trip to Antarctica modifies the opinions of tourists, such changes in perspective are not always conducive to ecological practices (Vila et al. 2016). In addition, most last chance tourists (LCTs) are not willing to offset carbon emissions produced during their trip (Groulx et al. 2019). In this respect, it seems reasonable to ask researchers what will happen to Arctic tourism after the last chances to see these things have gone, and what would this resulting "post-Arctic" tourism be? Alix Varnajot, Jarkko Saarinen stress that these aspects are important to study before glaciers and other key attractions disappear, as this would help the Arctic tourism industry and tourism-dependent communities to adapt to a looming apocalyptic turn (Varnajot and Saarinen 2021: 1-2).

Research also shows that tourists are not aware of the paradox that mass travel to see pristine and raw landscapes or experience the beauty of wild nature paradoxically leads to its degradation. This finding was confirmed by a survey of cruise passengers in Antarctica, which showed that 59 per cent of the respondents felt that their travels did not affect climate change, and less than 7% stated that their emissions have been or may be offset as a result of their experience (Zając 2018). However, as recent research shows, the situation is starting to change for the better. Currently, an increasing number of people are aware of the dysfunctions brought about by the spontaneous development of mass tourism. In August 2022, the European Investment Bank (EIB), which is the European Union's lender and the world's largest multilateral lender for climate action, conducted a survey of over 28,000 people. respondents, with a representative panel of people aged 15 and over from 30 countries, about their views on climate change. They concern individual human behavior and actions taken to combat climate change. As many as 72% of the respondents expressed the view that their own behavior can be important in the fight against the climate crisis. As far as Poles are concerned, as many as 79%, i.e. 7 percentage points more than the EU average, are convinced that their behavior may be important in counteracting the climate crisis. The impact of personal behavior on climate action is more likely to be believed by women (82%) than men (69%) (EBI).

The search for solutions in the field of tourism of last resort (LCT) continues and does not lose its relevance. In their latest research, experts deal with its various segments. Watching whales in their natural habitat, which is now popular among tourists, is the best example of this. It is postulated, for example, to pay attention to reconciling tourists' interests and operators' behaviors with more responsible practices;, new technologies, co-creation process and business responsibility, collective involvement of various stakeholders in the decision-making process, with particular emphasis on the vision of women and their caring attitudes and animal rights ethics. (Suárez-Rojas et. al. 2023). This article fits these assumptions.

3 RESEARCH METHODS

This article focuses on the development of tourism of last resort (LCT) and the risks associated with it, discussed in the context of challenges for sustainable management. The main problem of the research was expressed in the form of a question: What are the effects of the development of mass last chance tourism and will they take the form of permanent trends? The main problem was made more specific by issues that took the form of the following detailed questions:

Are there and what the connections are between climate threats and the development of last chance tourism?

- How do places, areas and their appearance change under the influence of last resort mass tourism?
- Is mass tourism of last resort showing a growing trend and will it become a permanent trend in the global economy?
- Are tourists aware of the negative consequences of uncontrolled and mass travel to places/areas whose existence is at risk?
- What effective management mechanisms should be applied so that tourism of last resort can develop in a sustainable way?

The desk research method was chosen for the research. A critical analysis of the literature and specialized press was carried out, and the method of descriptive analysis was used. The research procedure consisted of searching for information, collecting, and analyzing secondary data. Secondary data analysis "has a rich intellectual tradition in the social sciences" (Frankfort-Nachmias 2001). This method was chosen due to the exploratory study and the need to use a wide range of materials that concern various places and areas around the world. Thanks to this, the scope and depth of the analysis are much greater than they would be when using primary data obtained in a single research project. In addition, the analysis of data from different time periods, related to similar topics, has contributed to the fact that the description and explanation of changes are more accurate. The currently obtained secondary data will be used for comparison purposes in the next research period. Further, in-depth research on this issue is planned. The content of the documents supplemented on an ongoing basis was compared with the previously obtained materials. The query was of a library and Internet nature. Domestic and foreign literature on the subject was used in the research. Information provided by various types of institutions monitoring ecological threats and/or the development of mass tourism as the last resort was obtained, as well as materials of companies using social media to communicate these threats. The analysis was carried out through compilation, mutual verification, comparison, and processing of existing data.

The supplementary method and autopsy were also used, i.e. participant observation and experiences gained from traveling to significant tourist destinations such as Singapore, Japan, China, Middle East countries (United Arab Emirates), Mediterranean countries (Italy, France, Malta, Portugal, Spain, Greece, Turkey, Tunisia, Egypt) and other destinations (e.g. Norway, Sweden, Czech Republic, Slovakia, Poland). A complementary method of observation was chosen because the literature emphasizes that it is "the basis of all research methods in the social and behavioral sciences" (Angrosino 2010). This observation was hidden. The idea was to capture the natural behavior of tourists and tour operators so that the fact of observing would not affect them. The observation was uncontrolled because although the disadvantage of this type of method is a certain degree of subjectivity, its advantage is its flexibility, and sensitivity to unplanned, unexpected events that take place during the observation.

Since the research was not conclusive, but only explanatory, its sequence and direction were determined from beginning to end by the formulated research problem and the accompanying research questions. The research was based on an interpretative paradigm related to inductive reasoning. It was assumed that the research conducted will in the future be an introduction to quantitative research, giving the basis for formulating research hypotheses that will be verified at further stages of research.

4 EMPIRICAL RESULTS - IDENTIFICATION OF PLACES/AREAS MOST AT RISK DUE TO MASS TOURISM

Regions of coral reefs - (Red Sea, Australia, Micronesia and Polynesia, Caribbean). The largest reef in the world, visible even from space, is considered to be the reef stretching along the northeastern coast of Australia to Papua New Guinea. It is about 20 million years old! As a result of global warming, environmental pollution, sea acidification, and soil erosion that silts up coastal waters, the reef is under serious threat. The immediate effect is coral bleaching and polyp death. Tourists applying sunscreen before swimming and/or trying to remove elements of the reef as souvenirs contribute significantly to the destruction of this natural potential. It is worth noting that, as research shows, bringing natural souvenirs from holidays (e.g. sand, gravel, stones, shells, fragments of volcanic rocks, parts of plants, and even small animals) has become a permanent practice. Not all tourists are aware that it is illegal, punishable, and causes environmental damage (Pabian et al. 2020).

Beaches and islands –an example is the Philippine island of Boracay, which has suffered from an overabundance of tourists and shoreline wastewater discharge. Similarly, Thailand's Maya Bay beach on Phi Phi Island in the Andaman Sea, which became famous for the Leonardo di Caprio film "The Beach", was closed for 3 years to allow the ecosystem to recover (Kunz). The problem with the ever-higher water level is noted by the paradise Maldives. As much as 80 per cent surface is located just 1 meter above sea level. Maldives could disappear from the face of the Earth in 100 years, scientists alarm. Also in Europe, reports concerning the Balearic Islands (Ibiza, Mallorca, Minorca) are worrying. Experts argue that the islands could permanently lose up to 65 per cent of their land. amphibian (Zając 2022).

National parks – Glacier National Park in the USA, which Americans call the Crown of the Continent, is one of the most interesting tourist attractions in the world. However, it is predicted that by 2030 the glaciers, on whose existence the life of the local fauna and flora depends, will disappear. A similar situation is in the Los Graciales National Park in Argentina. In 2022, the Perito Moreno glacier collapsed.

Metropolises and big cities – urban centers are also suffering as a result of climate change. An example is Bangkok, which is only 2 meters above sea level and is particularly vulnerable during the monsoon season. The metropolis suffers from the weight of skyscrapers, the coverage of a part of the natural drainage system, i.e. canals, with a network of roads, the pumping out of groundwater, and others. Another example is Venice, Italy. Research carried out by a team of Italian and French geophysicists and volcanologists, published in the scientific journal "Quaternary International", shows that the rise in the sea level could definitively flood the city as early as 2100. (wp.turystyka).

Historic cultural objects and wonders of the world – an example is the Taj Mahal, existing since 1654. It is located in Agra, which is the 8th most polluted city in the world. Dirty air, garbage, a polluted river, and insects cause the marble from which the mausoleum was built to turn green-yellow. As a result, the Indian government has decided to limit the number of Indian tourists to 40,000. per day, while the visit time was limited to 3 hours (Zając 2018).

5 EMPIRICAL RESULTS - CONCLUSIONS FOR SUSTAINABLE MANAGEMENT

Tourism consists of the following main actors: 1) the community of the area receiving tourists, 2) the tourism industry (firms directly and indirectly related to tourism), 3) tourists. In the search for systemic solutions for these entities from the perspective of the concept of sustainable management, one must first refer to the Corporate Social Responsibility (CSR) strategy, according to which organizations, including those in the tourism industry, should voluntarily take into account social and environmental good in their business activities and take care of proper relations with various stakeholder groups, starting with employees. Social responsibility means accepting and implementing various elements of sustainable management into practice. It means investing not only in the protection of the natural environment, but also in the social environment, in human resources and in relations with the company's environment. With regard to tourism (LCT), basic tools (CSR) can be used, in particular:

- Actions for the benefit of the local community - cooperation and support at the local level for the well-being of residents and indigenous peoples in the areas of tourist reception and companies operating there.
- Pro-ecological activities – implementation of pro-ecological tourist products and services. Conventional resources that should undergo pro-ecological transformation in the first

place are: 1) human resources (managers and executive employees who must have knowledge in the field of sustainability, as well as social and ecological sensitivity, openness to new solutions, personal creativity and innovation) 2) construction infrastructure (locating tour operators, including hotels and gastronomy in energy-saving buildings, preferably autonomous, which were erected in the clean production process based on natural, renewable and healthy materials of local origin), 3) equipment of tourist facilities (it should consist of from durable, safe and health products, e.g. ecological furniture), 4) tourist transport (tourists should be transported by means of transport that have a less harmful impact on the environment, and at the same time ensure the availability of communication destinations in a safe and non-threatening way, moreover, they function in accordance with the trend of chances for long duration), 5) input goods (all durable and non-durable products that the producer of tourist services purchases in order to conduct current activity should come from those producers and suppliers who are characterized by high ecological and social sensitivity, and their products have been manufactured in accordance with the principles of sustainable development and awarded with ecological certificates).

- Social campaigns – organizing and supporting pro-social and pro-ecological campaigns through the media, eg transferring part of the profits from the sale of tourist events to support people in need.
- Programs for employees – equal opportunities for people with disabilities and people over 50, investing in training programs, integration and flexible forms of work, using the intellectual potential of women.
- Social reports - preparing systematic and transparent publications on sustainable management, taking into account the interests of various stakeholders.
- Management systems – building credibility by introducing transparent quality, environmental management and social responsibility systems, such as: Quality Management System ISO 9000, Environmental Management System ISO 14000, Social Accountability SA 8000 (PARP).
- Employee volunteering – voluntary provision of help by employees of tourist companies (eg residents, guides, pilots, officials, drivers) without remuneration in order to support prosocial and proecological initiatives.
- Supply chain management - applying the principles of corporate social responsibility at all six stages of the tourist product supply chain, i.e.: 1) second-tier suppliers (e.g. food producers), 2) first-tier suppliers (e.g. accommodation providers), 3) intermediaries/ 2nd tier organizers (receiving agencies), 4) 1st tier intermediaries/organizers (tour operators assembling a tourist product and selling it directly to tourists, 5) intermediaries/sellers ("travel shops" intermediating between tour operators and clients), 6) tourist (purchaser of the product tourism) (Kusa 2009).
- Labeling of products - ecolabeling of a tourist product (eg agritourism).

It should be emphasized that CSR is no longer enough today. A more recent trend is the Environmental, Social, and Corporate Governance (ESG) formula. It includes factors based on which ratings and non-financial assessments of the organization are created. Taking into account social and environmental goals in the development of the company must take place already at the level of the company's strategy and be reflected in the business justification. Social responsibility is not only taking care of employees, legal regulations, ensuring working conditions, but also providing products of appropriate quality to the customer (Sobocińska 2021). It is also the selection of suppliers, appropriate rules for recruiting employees, confirmation of material legality certificates, waste management policy, transparency of the organization for its shareholders, as well as appropriate communication with them (Body 2022). Researchers are right that extensive social activity is needed already at the planning stage. Whether planning for tourism must also consider a number of universal principles. These include a focus on the present, a perspective that goes beyond economic development, the incorporation of all three tourism sectors (business, non-profit organizations and governments), an interactive approach, and integration of three planning scales (community, destination and region). All these principles are equally relevant to ecotourism planning **(Backman 2001).**

In general, this is not about sporadic or apparent activities for sustainable development, aimed at improving their own image, but about a comprehensive, systemic transformation that will make all resources and activities of the tourism service provider contribute to balancing intergenerational needs and the development of sustainable tourism.

6 DISCUSSION

The conclusions of the research conducted at the end of the second decade of the 21st century (Vila et al. 2016) were pessimistic. The researchers emphasized that tourists are not aware of the dangers of their mass travel. Currently, it is worth repeating the research, because the latest discoveries show that tourists' awareness of the threats posed by mass and uncontrolled tourist traffic is clearly increasing. Therefore, it is a positive change in the attitude of tourists to ecological problems. It is necessary to examine the attitude of the young generation to the problem of tourism to places and areas that may cease to exist in the near future. However, it should be agreed that in terms of management it is important to develop an approach to visitor segmentation (Groulx et al. 2019). It should be added that tourism segmentation should be an activity undertaken by both tourist companies and institutions responsible for the development of tourism in tourist destinations. Recognizing the needs of tourists and then dividing the market into segments is also the key to defining a marketing strategy.

In conclusion, it is worth noting the limitations of this study. Due to the fact that the conducted research was only explanatory and non-conclusive, it did not allow for making generalizations regarding the research problem (e.g. in relation to some places, areas in all countries of the world). Further directions of research may concern such aspects as the power of place, politics, locality, as well as philosophy and critical understanding of the place, the impact of culture and the sense of national identity on the perception of the importance of last resort tourism (LCT), as well as the attitude of representatives of different generations to the need to monitor this form of tourism and implementation of sustainable management principles in business practice. Further research should take into account the potential role of various actors: scientists, governments, business practitioners of local communities in striving to improve the condition of the natural environment and social well-being, also for future generations.

REFERENCES

Angrosino M. V. 2010. *Ethnographic and observational studies*. PWN. Warszawa.

Backman K. F. 2001. *Planning, management and institutions*. In: D.B. Weaver (ed.). *The encyclopedia of ecotourism*. CABI Publishing, London, pp. 447–450.

Baldwin E., Longhurst B., Mccracken S., Ogborn M. and Smith G. 2007. *Introduction to cultural studies*. Zysk i S-ka. Poznań.

Bilińska K., Pabian B., Pabian A. and Reformat B. 2023. Development Trends and Potential in the Field of Virtual Tourism After the COVID-19 Pandemic: Generation Z Example. *Sustainability* 2023, 15/3, pp. 1–13, https://doi.org/10.3390/su15031889.

Bodych M. 2022. Sustainable project management - fashion or necessity?, *Strefa PMI* 2022, nr 37 https://strefapmi.pl/strefa-wiedzy/zrownowazone-zarzadzanie-projektami-moda-czy-koniecznosc/ (2023, January 05).

Cave J. and Dredge D. 2020. Regenerative tourism needs diverse economic practices, *Tourism Geographies*, 22 (3), pp. 503–513, https://doi.org/10.1080/14616688.2020.1768434.

Frankfort-Nachmias C. and Nachmias D. 2001. *Research methods in social sciences*. Poznań.

Fumagalli M., Guerra M., Brough T., Carome W., Constantine R., Higham J., Rayment W., Slooten E., Stockin K. and Dawson S. 2021. Looking back to move forward: Lessons from three decades of research and management of Cetacean Tourism in New Zealand, *Frontiers in Marine Science* 8, p. 7, https://doi.org/10.3389/fmars.2021.624448.

Groulx M., Boluk K., Lemieux C.J. and Dawson J. 2019. Place stewardship among last chance tourists, *Annals of Tourism Research* 75, pp. 202–212 https://doi.org/10.1016/j.annals.2019.01.008.
Kucukergin K.G., Gürlek M. 2020. What if this is my last chance?: Developing a last-chance tourism motivation model. *Journal of Destination Marketing & Management*, 18. https://doi.org/10.1016/j.jdmm.2020.100491.
Kunz P. 2023. *Koniec raju? Jedno z najpiękniejszych miejsc świata przegrywa w starciu z turystami i hotelarzami*, https://www.fly4free.pl/zamkniecie-boracay/ (2023, March 14).
Kusa R. 2009. *Analysis of the tourist product supply chain*. In: J. Pyka (ed.), *Competition and cooperation in organizational management strategies*, TNOiK Oddział w Katowicach. Katowice, pp. 129–139.
Official website of the European Investment Bank (EBI) https://www.eib.org/en/surveys/climate-survey/5th-climate-survey/climate-impact-important-factor-for-jobseekers (2023, May 05).
Pabian A., Pabian A., Brzeziński A. 2020. Young People Collecting Natural Souvenirs: A Perspective of Sustainability and Marketing, *Sustainability*, 12(2), pp. 1–12 https://doi.org/10.3390/su12020514.
Pacheco A.S., Sepúlveda M., Corkeron P. 2021. Whale-watching impacts: Science, human dimensions and management, *Frontiers in Marine Science*, 1126, https://doi.org/10.3389/fmars.2021.737352.
PARP. Grupa PFR. CSR – Corporate Social Responsibility https://www.parp.gov.pl/csr#narzedzia [2023, June 01].
PTSprint 2023 Environment and Ecology, March 2022-2023 https://www.drishtiias.com/pdf/1680513506_PT%20Sprint%202023%20Environment_Final.pdf (2023, May 20).
Sobocińska M. 2021. Customer value management in the context of digital development. Impact Lower Silesia. *Review of the Think Tank of the Wrocław University of Economics*, 2021, 1, pp. 8–10.
Suárez-Rojas C., González Hernández M.M. and León C.J. 2023. Sustainability in whale-watching: A literature review and future research directions based on regenerative tourism, *Tourism Management Perspectives* 47, p. 1–13 https://doi.org/10.1016/j.tmp.2023.101120.
Tuan Y.-F. 1987. *Przestrzeń i miejsce*. PIW. Warszawa.
Varnajot A. and Saarinen J. 2021. 'After glaciers?' Towards post-Arctic tourism. *Annals of Tourism Research*, 91, pp. 1–3 https://doi.org/10.1016/j.annals.2021.103205.
Vila M., Costa G., Angulo-Preckler C., Sarda R. and Avila C. 2016. Contrasting views on Antarctic tourism: 'last chance tourism' or 'ambassadorship' in the last of the wild. *Journal of Cleaner Production*, 111, pp. 451–460 https://doi.org/10.1016/j.jclepro.2014.12.061.
Wp.turystyka. *Six cities that will disappear from the face of the Earth* https://turystyka.wp.pl/6-miast-ktore-znikna-z-powierzchni-ziemi-6402200460527745a (2023, May 26).
Zając A. 2018. *See before it disappears. Tourism of last resort does more harm than good?* https://www.fly4free.pl/miejsca-ktore-znikna/ (2023, January 05).
Zając A. 2022. *Ibiza will lose 2/3 of its beaches, the symbol of Zakynthos disappears. Should we hurry up with our travels?* https://www.fly4free.pl/turystyka-ostatniej-szansy/ (2023, January 05).

Digital Synergy – El Emary et al. (eds)

Chapter 9
Foreign direct investment and economic growth: A systematic literature review

Oumaima Bouarfa & Mohammed Abdellaoui
University Sidi Mohammed Ben Abdellah Fès, Morocco

Contents

Objective: The objective of this article is to test scientific production regarding the behaviour of economic growth and international direct investment, in English and French.

Methods: A bibliometric study using a mixed approach was carried out using the SCOPUS platform for research. Although much research is available, this paper bases exclusively on the studies of the behaviour of economic progress and direct foreign investment, making it a systematic literature review. In order to encourage researchers interested in studying these behaviours, this research has compiled a summary table of the main findings and gaps identified in the literature on this topic. Results: From the results obtained, it was observed that the majority of work focuses mainly on problems linked to economic inequality, as well as on tools to promote increased business opportunities and the dissemination of knowledge and technology. In conclusion, this study highlights the importance attached to these aspects and points to further research opportunities in this field. Other research opportunities worth highlighting include the empirical validation of theoretical studies. The use of different research methodologies would also help to encourage and channel investments that promote, rather than degrade, sustainable development.

1 INTRODUCTION

Attracting foreign direct investment (FDI) holds pivotal importance for both developed and developing economies. Empirical evidence underscores that in host nations, FDI plays a vital role in economic expansion, contributing directly through capital infusion and indirectly by fostering job creation, as well as facilitating the transfer of knowledge and technology. Publications commonly acknowledge that the influence of incoming FDI on economic development may be constrained by the host country's limited absorptive capacity. Factors such as human capital, institutional quality, macroeconomic stability, financial development, and effective governance stand out as key determinants for attracting FDI and leveraging its benefits. [1] To what extent can current scientific production be used to understand the impact of foreign direct investment on economic growth? To answer our research question,

DOI: 10.1201/9781003440406-9

and given its relevance in the field of organizational studies, we consulted the SCOPUS database. The structure of this study includes an introduction, a theoretical section addressing the main aspects of FDI behaviour and economic progress, research methods, presentation and analysis of findings and conclusions.

2 REVIEW OF LITERATURE

A significant amount of theoretical and empirical research exists on FDI's relationship with economic growth. The theoretical foundations of literature suggest that an influx of foreign capital constitutes a net addition to the resources available for investment. The paper draws on the theoretical framework of endogenous growth theory, in particular from the work of Paul Romer, who studies the factors conducive to long-term economic growth. In addition, total factor productivity models explore the impact of foreign direct investment on productivity and growth. Furthermore, the study uses the theory of dependence on natural resources to understand the effects of FDI in resource-rich contexts. Beyond their impact on the capital stock in host country, FDI is known to have a positive impact on the economy by enhancing the general productivity of factors through transferring technology and managerial know-how that accompanies them [2]. Furthermore, FDI can make easier to access export markets and helping to improve the competitiveness of local businesses. However, several conditions need to be met for these spillover effects to be effective, including sufficient absorptive capacity in the host country, allowing local firms to benefit from technological, informational, or organizational spillovers. [3] Macroeconomic stability is also a crucial determinant of the influence of FDI on the host nation's economic expansion.[4] Political stability and good governance are important for attracting FDI. The risk of political instability creates an unfavourable environment for both domestic and foreign investments due to the increased uncertainty it brings. Ultimately, the repercussion of FDI on economic progress undeniably hinge on the unique characteristics by individual countries and the differentiated effects according to the sector of activity of the invested subsidiary. However, it is essential to ponder the limitations related with econometric issues inherent in the specifications upon which more empirical studies on the subject are based [1].

3 METHODOLOGY

The search strategy used was a combination of a bibliometric study and a systematic literature review, using the methods of Denyer et al. and Tranfield et al. offering a transparent and scientific approach. To do this, we consulted the recognized SCOPUS Portal database, which indexes national and international journals. The keywords used for the search were "foreign direct investment" and "economic growth", the twain separately and jointly. We applied several filters during the search, such as peer-reviewed articles in French or English, as well as scientific articles exclusively. The approach adopted in this study is considered a mixed method, since it includes both quantitative and qualitative studies. The quantitative analysis was performed with the IBM SPSS Statistics 25 software. The purpose behind this approach is to provide a description of the data using frequency tables and univariate statistics, enabling the characteristics of the articles studied to be identified. A breakdown of the articles by type of document, year of publication and number of citations was carried out, as well as an analysis of the temporal evolution of the themes covered. The quantitative part of our study was completed by a qualitative analysis using Nvivo software. The 3 main objective was to carry out a lexical analysis based on word frequency, in order to identify the key concepts addressed in the scientific research. This analysis generated a scatterplot highlighting the most frequent concepts, and provided an initial overview of general trends in research topics.

4 PRESENTATION AND ANALYSIS OF RESULTS

We have undertaken a research of scientific articles on the Scopus scientific portal to collect data regarding this following concepts: economic growth, foreign direct investment. This research provided this following data:

Table 1. Keywords used in the research.

Key words	Total found	Total after reading titles and abstracts
Economic growth	378	60
Foreign direct investment	404	37
EG & FDI	25	19

Source: ourselves.

After searching for articles on the concepts related to our research topic, we organized and sorted the themes according to their relevance. This approach allowed us to identify 116 articles published between 2020 and 2023, the characteristics of which are presented in the table below.

Table 2. Annual publication percentage.

		Frequency	Percent	Valid Percent	Cumulative Percent
Valid	2020	25	32,1	32,1	32,1
	2021	28	35,9	35,9	67,9
	2022	21	26,9	26,9	94,9
	2023	4	5,1	5,1	100,0
	Total	78	100,0	100,0	

Source: produced under IBM SPSS Statistics 27.

The selected papers are mainly full scientific papers, published as indexed articles on the Scopus portal. These articles focus on themes that incorporate concepts such as economic growth, foreign direct investment. They were mainly published in 2020, with 32.1% of articles, followed by 35.9% in 2021, 26.9% in 2022 and finally 5.1% in 2023.

Table 3. Number of citations of articles.

	Mean	Count	Median	Standard Deviation	Minimum	Maximum
CITED BY	10	78	4	17	1	89

Source: produced under IBM SPSS Statistics 27.

The majority of the papers reviewed were referenced in at least 10 scientific papers. The descriptive analysis of the number of citations per article reveals a median of 4, indicating that 50% of the articles analysed were cited in more than 4 scientific works published on Scopus.

The histogram represents the results of the table regarding the number of citations previously presented. It is clear that more than 30 articles have been cited in more than 30 scientific papers, and that some articles exceed 81 citations.

The selected papers are grouped under three research themes: "economic growth", "foreign direct investment", "economic growth and foreign direct investment".

Our article base includes 48 percent of documents correlated to the theme of economic expansion, as well as 19 percent of articles dealing with foreign direct investment. Finally,

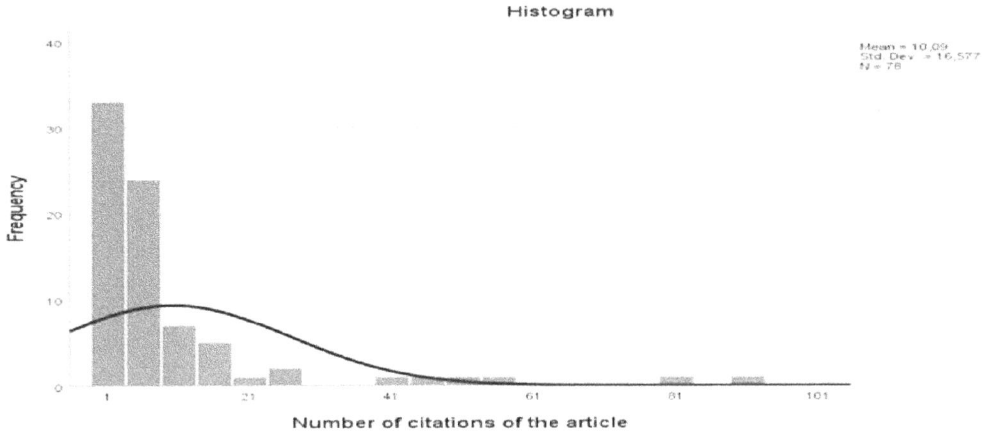

Figure 1. Number of citations of articles.
Source: produced under IBM SPSS Statistics 27.

Table 4. Distribution of articles by theme.

		Frequency	Percent	Valid Percent	Cumulative Percent
Valid	FDI	1 9	24,4	24,4	24,4
	IDE & RIB	1 1	1 4,1	1 4,1	38,5
	EG	48	61,5	61,5	1 00,0
	Total	78	1 00,0	1 00,0	

Source: produced under IBM SPSS Statistics 27.

there are 11 percent of clauses dealing with economic advancement and inward investment. A lot of the research was done in 2021 and 2022, but after that period there was a significant decrease in research on these themes.

Through the analysis of the content of the abstracts of the 116 papers, we were able to highlight the concepts frequently used in these papers, as well as the overall context of the research.

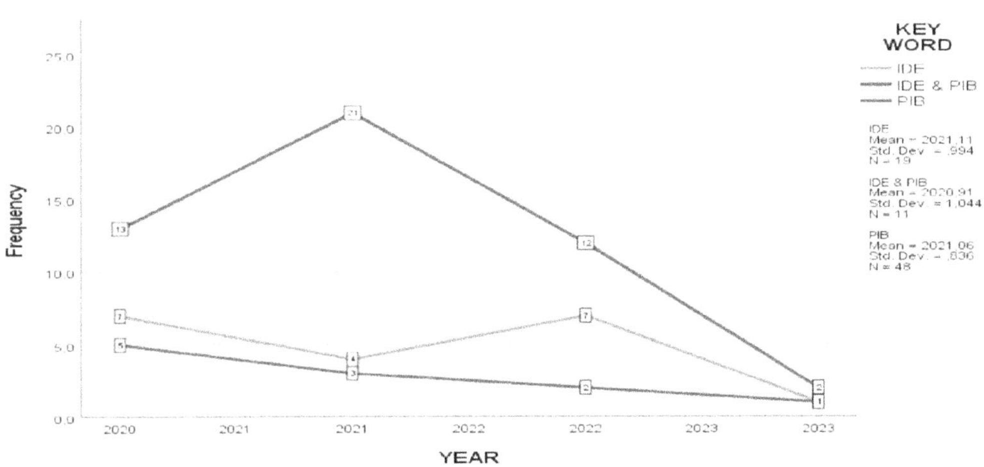

Figure 2. Temporal evaluation of the theme.
Source: Produced under IBM SPSS Statistics 27.

The comparative analysis of the temporal evolution of the articles dealing with different concepts reveals that 2021 was the most prolific year in terms of publications on the themes of economic growth and foreign direct investment.

Using the time curves, we observed that the 13 articles on the theme of economic growth were all published in 2020, with 21 publications on this theme in 2021, 12 publications in 2022 and 7 publications published in 2023.

On the FDI theme, we identified 19 articles, 7 of which were published in 2020, 4 in 2021, 7 in 2022 and one published in 2023.

As for the themes related to economic growth and FDI, we identified a total of 11 articles, divided as follows: 5 articles in 2020, 3 in 2021, 2 in 2022 and one publication in 2023.

This change over time shows that research in these three fields slowed down from 2022.

Figure 3. Keywords Cloud.
Source: produced under NVivo 12.

Analysis of the keyword cloud reveals that the terms "economic ","growth", "countrie", "investment" are the most frequently cited in the various documents examined. This finding highlights the importance attached to the concepts of the economy, growth and investment in the papers analysed, making it a dynamic area of research for work related to economics and management.

Looking at the most commonly used keywords, economic growth is more studied than FDI.

Table 5. Word frequency in abstracts.

Word	Length	Number	Weighted percentage (%)
growth	6	9301	0,99
economic	8	9177	0,98
countries	9	6345	0,68
development	11	4795	0,51
investment	10	4029	0,43
foreign	7	3586	0,38
financial	9	2801	0,30
model	5	2770	0,30
capital	7	2697	0,29
country	7	2651	0,28

Source: produced under NVivo 12.

Based on the analysis of the most frequently used keywords, it can be observed that economic growth receives more attention in research compared to FDI.

5 PRESENTATION OF RESULTS

There is a noticeable academic development regarding the factors influencing FDI and economic progress have been the subject of this research. While some studies indicate a positive correlation between the two, others do not find supporting evidence.

Most items have found a strong beneficial long-term correlation between economic expansion and international investment.

The results demonstrate that among the conditions for foreign direct investment to enhance economic progress, macroeconomic stability, characterized by inflation control, is a crucial necessity for FDI to have a beneficial influence on growth.

Wherefrom, foreign direct investment has a positive effect on economic growth in the regions examined. A summary of the findings is provided in Table 6.

Table 6. Bibliographic summary of articles consulted.

Author/Year/Paper	Country/ Region	Research aim	Methodology	Results
Seefat-E-Rabbi Khan, Dimitrios Asteriou and Claudia Jefferies. (2023). *Economic Modelling*	BRICs (Brazil, Russia, India, and China)	The objective is to elucidate divergence in economic progress from four prominent rising economies commonly referred to as BRIC and the countries outside the BRIC group.	Quantitative method: They employed a balanced panel data collection comprising BRIC countries and an additional 50 developing countries in the period 19802020.	The research results strongly support the significance of FDI, gross capital training, human capital and infrastructure. in driving economic growth.
Kusairi, S., Wong Z. Y., Wahyuningtyas, R. and Sukemi, M. N. 2023. *Journal of International Studies*	Developed countries	The article aimed to study the impact of digitalization and FDI on economic advancement in developing economies.	Panel data analysis was utilized on a dataset comprising 16 advanced country, covering the period from 2006 to 2019.	The results indicate that both digitalization and foreign direct investment exerts a positive influence on economic growth, making significant contributions to the advancement of the economy and the enhancement of welfare.
Tanaya O. and Suyanto S. 2022. *Periodica Polytechnica Social and Management Sciences.*	Indonesia	This present study addresses the research disparity by investigating the responsible relationship between FDI and economic expansion in Indonesia from 1970 to 2018.	In this article, a modern temporal data methodology is utilized, which incorporates various unit- root tests like Augmented Dickey-Fuller. Additionally, an AutoRegressive Distributed Lag (ARDL).	The issue from the Granger causality test support the findings obtained from the ARDL analysis, suggesting a one-way causal relationship from GDP to FDI.
Vlatka Bilas and Sanja Franc. 2022. *Ekonomski horizonti.*	Bulgarie, Croatie, Chypre, Estonie, Hongrie, Lettonie, Lituanie, Malte, Pologne,	The aim is to examine the extent to which foreign direct investment and exports	Quantitative method: to explore the correlation and causal connection between the three recorded data, several statistical	Findings suggest that the beneficial impacts of international investment and exports are not mechanical or

(*Continued*)

Table 6. (*Continued*)

Author/Year/Paper	Country/ Region	Research aim	Methodology	Results
	Roumanie, Slovaquie, Slovenie	contribute to the economic growth of the thirteen European Union new member states.over the period from 2005 to 2020.	evaluations were conducted.	uniform across all economies. Instead, they depend on various determinants that the governments of the chosen territories have to take into account when devising policy interventions to attract FDI and stimulate exports.
Haggai Chibale Chibalamula, Yeboah Evans, Mukuka Kachelo and Dastan Bamwesigye. 2023. *Economics and Informatics*	Ghana, Morocco, Kenya, Uganda, and Zambia.	This research paper explores the significance of foreign direct investment (FDI) and the degree of free trade in five African countries.	The study utilized longitudinal data analysis to analyze statistics from the World Bank spanning Between 1994 and 2019 for the five African countries selected.	According to the findings of the Random Intercept model employed, the results demonstrate that FDI has a positive effect on economic progress in the selected African countries.
Heppi Millia, Pasrun Adam, Abd Azis Muthalib, Tajuddin, Yuwanda Purnamasari Pasrun. 2022. *Periodica Polytechnica Social and Management Sciences*	Indonesia	The main objective of the paper is to investigate the effect of direct and indirect inward, on the GDP growth of Indonesia.	The data was analyzed by Autoregressive Distributed Lag in this study.	The findings revealed significant impacts of short-range and long-range inward FDI on the economic advancement of Indonesia.
Emre Gökçeli, Jan Fidrmuc and Sugata Ghosh. 2022. European Journal of Business Science and Technology,	OECD countries	The aim of this study is to evaluate the influence of FDI inflows on both economic progess and domestic investment in a group of countries belonging to OECD during the time span from 1990 to 2017.	The researchers employed the fixed-effects methodology along with the system generalized method of moments (GMM) to evaluate the data.	The results indicate a statistically significant and positive correlation between the inflow of foreign direct investment and the growth of the economy in the recipient country.

Source: ourselves.

6 CONCLUSION

The aim of this article was to study scientific production in the fields of foreign direct investment and economic growth, focusing on articles written in English and French. To achieve this objective, a bibliometric approach was adopted, involving searches of the SCOPUS database. After selecting the relevant results, a final sample of 116 articles was selected, and these were used for the analyses presented in this study.

The aim of this work was to analyze the evolution of scientific publications on the subject and to identify opportunities for improvement in this field of research. From the results obtained, it was observed that the majority of work focuses mainly on problems linked to economic inequality, as well as on tools to promote increased business opportunities and the dissemination of knowledge and technology.

In conclusion, this study highlights the importance attached to these aspects and points to further research opportunities in this field. Other research opportunities worth highlighting include the empirical validation of theoretical studies. The use of different research methodologies would also help to encourage and channel investments that promote, rather than degrade, sustainable development. It should be noted that this article is limited to works available in English and French. However, it would be beneficial to include other languages in future research in order to enrich the results obtained here.

REFERENCES

Selenge B.M. and Kasongo M.M. 2022. Investissements directs etrangers et croissance economique: une analyse empirique des donnees de l'Afrique des Grands Lacs, Revue *Reperes et Perspectives Economiques* [En ligne], Vol. 6, N 2/septembre 2022, mis en ligne le 30 septembre 2022.

Djepang K.M. and Adamou M. H. 2019. *Les investissements directs etrangers comme facteur de croissance economique au Cameroun: Quelle est la realite?* 27, no 1.

Nurbel, Alain, et Ibrahim Ahamada. 2008. Investissements directs etrangers entrants et developpement: l'enjeu de la capacite d'absorption. *Mondes en developpement* n° 143, no 3 (1 octobre 2008): 79–96.

Abdelmalki, Lahsen, Monnet Benoit Patrick Gbakou, Mustapha Sadni Jallab, et Rene Sandretto. 2012. La stabilite macroeconomique conditionne-t-elle l'impact des IDE sur la croissance economique et l'emergence?: Une etude empirique sur des pays d'Afrique, d'Amerique latine, des Caraibes et d'Asie. *Mondes en developpement* n°158, no 2 (18 juillet 2012): 101–14.

Ayenew, Belesity Bekalu. 2022. «The Effect of Foreign Direct Investment on the Economic Growth of Sub-Saharan African Countries: An Empirical Approach». Cogent Economics & Finance 10, no 1 (31 decembre 2022): 2038862.

Boudohay Y. and Sadik A. 2023. Les organisations de l'economie sociale et solidaire et le developpement local: Une revue de litterature systematique par la methode PRISMA, 31 janvier 2023. https://doi.org/10.5281/ZENODO.7581842.

Bajraktari, Kaltrina, Roberta Bajrami, et Medain Hashani. 2023. «The Impact of International Trade Freedom on Economic Growth: Empirical Evidence of the Western Balkans Countries». Corporate and Business Strategy Review 4, no 2: 132–42.

Wehncke, Francois Cornelius, Godfrey Marozva, et Patricia Lindelwa Makoni. 2022. Economic Growth, Foreign Direct Investments and Official Development Assistance Nexus: Panel ARDL Approach. *Economies* 11, no 1 (21 decembre 2022): 4.

Wehncke, Francois Cornelius, Godfrey Marozva, et Patricia Lindelwa Makoni. 2022. Economic Growth, Foreign Direct Investments and Official Development Assistance Nexus: Panel ARDL Approach. *Economies* 11, no 1 (21 decembre 2022): 4.

Gökçeli, Emre, Jan Fidrmuc, et Sugata Ghosh. 2022. Effect of Foreign Direct Investment on Economic Growth and Domestic Investment: Evidence from OECD Countries. *European Journal of Business Science and Technology* 8, no 2 (31 decembre 2022): 190–216. https://doi.org/10.m18/ejobsat.2022.012.

Kusairi, Suhal, Zun Yuan Wong, Ratri Wahyuningtyas, et Muhammad Najit Sukemi. 2023.Impact of Digitalisation and Foreign Direct Investment on Economic Growth: Learning from Developed Countries. Journal of International Studies 16, no 1: 98–111.

Rahman, Preethu, Zhihe Zhang, et Mohammad Musa. 2023. Do Technological Innovation, Foreign Investment, Trade and Human Capital Have a Symmetric Effect on Economic Growth? Novel Dynamic ARDL Simulation Study on Bangladesh. *Economic Change and Restructuring* 56, no 2: 1327–66.

Sokhanvar, Amin. 2022. THE ROLE OF TOURISM AND FDI IN THE ECONOMIC GROWTH OF EU11 COUNTRIES. *Tourism and Hospitality Management* 28, no 2: 343–59.

The Effect of Trade, Foreign Direct Investment, Expenditure, and Inflation on Economic Growth: Evidence from Members of The G20. *Quality - Access to Success* 24, no 194 (1 janvier 2023). https://doi.org/10.47750/QAS/24.194.28.

Vilutiene, Laura, et Daiva Dumciuviene. 2020. The Impact of International Capital Flows on Central and Eastern European Countries' Investments, Savings, Consumption, and Current Accounts. *Engineering Economics* 31, no 4 (29 octobre 2020): 450–60.

Digital Synergy – El Emary et al. (eds)

Chapter 10
Trust in Artificial Intelligence and the 5.0 leadership

Dorota Balcerzyk & Katarzyna Czainska
Land Forces University, Wrocław, Poland

Content

On the horizon of the future, technology leaders look to the fifth industrial revolution. Its main assumption is to be the synergy between artificial intelligence, autonomous machines and humans. Both in the literature dealing with the issue of artificial intelligence, as well as in organizational reality and in social awareness, there are certain theories that inspire respect for artificial intelligence. AI which, as a developing technology, causes an undefined dose of distrust. When discussing the subject of leadership of the new generation 5.0, and in particular the issue of leadership competences, the following question was posed: can a leader who does not trust artificial intelligence effectively fulfill the role of a leader in the modern reality?

1 INTRODUCTION

While Industry 4.0 is not well developed yet, many technology leaders are looking ahead to the fifth industrial revolution. While the main goal of Industry 4.0 is automation, the goal of Industry 5.0 will be the synergy between people and autonomous machines. This implies new challenges and creates new opportunities for the next generation of leadership. According to researchers (Nahavandi 2019), it will be appropriate to talk about Industry 5.0 when its three basic elements: intelligent devices, intelligent systems and intelligent automation, connect with the physical world in cooperation with human intelligence. So, following questions appears: what role will the new reality determine for the leadership of the next generation; what will be the determinants of leadership 5.0?

Leadership understanding and practice must be updated to meet the challenges and remain effective. The competencies and roles of the leader should be verified. In view of the above, researchers put forward the thesis that trust in the relationship between a human and the other party, which will be artificial intelligence, will be one of the determinants of leadership 5.0.

2 AN OVERVIEW OF THE LITERATURE

The beginnings of defining artificial intelligence date back to the 1950s. When Turing, also known as the “father of computer science”, asked the following question: “Can machines

DOI: 10.1201/9781003440406-10

think?" (Turing 1950: 433). In his work, a journey through many controversial theses can be noted. One of them is that "the consequences of machine thinking would be too terrible. Let us hope and believe that they cannot do that" (Turing 1950: 442). Turing justifies this with man's fear of losing decision-making ability. It is amazing how relevant this theses is today.

Artificial intelligence is a term coined by John McCarthy in 1955. It was defined by him as the engineering of creating intelligent machines that use language, create abstractions and concepts, and solve problems currently reserved for humans (McCarthy et al. 1955).

Nowadays, John McCarthy (2007b: 2-3) describes artificial intelligence as the science and engineering of creating intelligent machines, especially intelligent computer programs. McCarthy's modern thought boldly moves towards the possibility of comparing AI to human intelligence. This result can be achieved by directing the efforts of researchers to create computer programs to achieve goals and solve the problems of the world. However, is it possible to simulate human intelligence without fully knowing how the human intellect works (Copertari 2016: 1-11; McCarthy 2007a: 1175; Sejnowski 2018: 3-27).

Nowadays, artificial intelligence is not so much a concept as a subject of consideration and research of various disciplines of science, from computer science through psychology, sociology and philosophy.

A literature search reveals a wealth of definitions of the term artificial intelligence. In the Dictionary of the Polish Language (SJP 2023), the term artificial intelligence is defined as "a branch of computer science that studies the rules governing human mental behavior and creates computer programs or systems that simulate human thinking. The Cambridge Dictionary (CD 2023) describes AI as the science of creating machines that possess some of the characteristics of the human mind, such as the ability to understand language, recognize images, solve problems and learn. The Cambridge Business English Dictionary compares AI to computer technology that allows you to do something in a way that is similar to the way a human would do it. In other words, artificial intelligence is "the ability of machines to exhibit human skills such as reasoning, learning, planning and creativity" (EPN 2023). In its broadest sense, artificial intelligence has been described as "the study of the computations that enable perception, reasoning and action" (Winston 1992: 8).

In summary, AI can be defined as non-human intelligence as measured by the ability to replicate human mental skills such as pattern recognition, natural language understanding (NLP), adaptive learning from experience, strategy development or reasoning.

3 ARTIFICIAL INTELLIGENCE AND TRUST

Such a rapid development of technology as it is today has not been noticed throughout history. The modern world is faced with modern technologies. Social awareness and moral norms do not keep up with the use of artificial intelligence. In the literature on the subject, there are various approaches to artificial intelligence depending on the perspective. Russell and Norvig (2016: 2-5) propose two approaches to AI that distinguish computer systems based on rationality and thinking as opposed to acting:

1. The human approach: systems that think like people, systems that act like people;
2. The ideal approach: systems thinking rationally, systems acting rationally.

In computer science, there is a division into two types of artificial intelligence. The first is weak artificial intelligence, also known as narrow AI. It is trained and used to perform specific tasks. The second type of artificial intelligence is strong artificial intelligence. Thanks to strong artificial intelligence, the machine exhibits all the behaviors you would expect from a person. Some computer scientists define strong AI as general AI - broad intelligence that is not applicable to just one narrow task (Rose 2020: 11-14). It consists of: Artificial General Intelligence (AGI) and Artificial Super Intelligence (ASI). It is worth noting that strong artificial intelligence is still only theoretical, and its examples can be found in the sphere of science fiction (Gurkaynak et al. 2016: 3-5).

On the one hand, strong artificial intelligence is still relegated to the world of science fiction, and on the other hand, we are dealing with examples of weak artificial intelligence tools, such as expert systems that, based on databases, can propose and present to the patient the most probable diagnosis, or the revolutionary Blue brain. The Blue Brain project, which uses a reverse engineering technique to reconstruct the structure and function of the brain in detail, biologically. It is based on brain simulations and representations [BBP 2023].

There are many applications of artificial intelligence in everyday life. Among the leading spheres in the application of artificial intelligence, the following should be mentioned: military, economic, information, health, socio-cultural, educational, legal (Ako-Nai et al. 2022; Fast et al. 2017; Kanari et al. 2022; Rudd 2018, Sejnowski 2018, Yu et al. 2018).

Trust begins where anticipation ends (Lewis and Weigert 1985: 1978). So, can we trust the development of technology, can we trust artificial intelligence? The unquestionable development of artificial intelligence raises concerns among some researchers (Cellan-Jones 2014,Fast et al. 2017). Hawkins expresses a fear of creating something equal to or even superior to humans. The limitation of humans is their slow biological evolution. Among the threats, he also notes ethical problems that may be caused by the consequences of the use of artificial intelligence, issues related to limiting freedom and privacy. A key role in counteracting these difficulties is attributed to Internet companies (Cellan-Jones 2014). Researchers also point to the threat of maintaining significant human control over very general and capable artificial intelligence systems operating autonomously to perform a task (Bostrom 2012, Shanahan 2015, Fast et al. 2017).

Researchers put forward the thesis that the modern development of artificial intelligence and the prospect of Industry 5.0 forces trust in it. The thesis is based on the assumption that trust is treated as the most universal social fact, inextricably linked to the existence of relationships and marked by the need to take risks (Luhmann 2000: 94-107).

4 RESEARCH METHODS

In order to implement the undertaken research problem, the position of combining theoretical methods aimed at determining the current state and empirical methods was used. A critical analysis of the literature on the subject of research allowed to build theoretical foundations. Contemporary trends in the approach to leadership 5.0 and the use of artificial intelligence were identified. This prompted the researchers to use the diagnostic survey method. In the survey studies, a questionnaire was used to obtain answers to the research questions, which were verified during the pilot studies. This paper presents a fragment of broader research on trust in artificial intelligence.

Empirical research was conducted at the beginning of 2023. 320 respondents took part in the survey. Representatives of various levels of management in organizations. Senior management accounted for 1.88%, middle management 21.88%, lower management 11.88%, and employees 64.38%. Women accounted for 66.67% of the respondents, the remaining 33.33% were men. Among them, employees with seniority over 20 years are 7.50%, employees with 16-20 years of service 5.63%, 11-15 years 13.13%, 6-10 years 20% and the largest percentage of 53.75% were employees with internship 0-5 years. It was decided that the education of the respondents would also be an important indicator in the analysis of research problems. The largest percentage of respondents - 77.50%, are people with first-cycle higher education with a bachelor's degree, then 13.75% have secondary education, and the smallest percentage - 8.75% - are people with second-cycle higher education with a master's degree.

5 RESULTS OF THE RESEARCH

Pilot studies conducted among Generation Z have shown that young people use artificial intelligence without realizing it. Therefore, the role of one of the questions in the survey was to suggest to the respondents what artificial intelligence is. For this purpose, a cafeteria of five definitions of artificial intelligence was proposed, developed on the basis of an analysis of the literature on the problem. Respondents were asked to choose the one definition of artificial intelligence that they thought was most accurate. The results from the responses are presented in Table 1.

Table 1. The most accurate definition of artificial intelligence in the opinion of respondents.

No.	Response categories	n	%
1.	Computer technology that allows you to do something in a way similar to the way a human would do it.	76	23.75
2.	The study of the computations that enable perception, reasoning, and action.	2	0.63
3.	The science of creating machines that possess some of the characteristics of the human mind, such as the ability to understand language, recognize images, solve problems, and learn.	36	11.25
4.	A branch of computer science that studies the rules that govern human mental behavior and creates computer programs or systems that simulate human thinking.	24	7.50
5.	Non-human intelligence as measured by the ability to duplicate human mental skills such as pattern recognition, natural language.	182	56.88
	Total	320	100

Source: own compilation

The research results indicate that in the opinion of the largest percentage of respondents, i.e. 56.88%, artificial intelligence is "non-human intelligence measured by the ability to duplicate human mental skills, such as pattern recognition, understanding natural language (NLP), adaptive learning based on experience, developing strategy or reasoning." This definition was proposed by the authors after a critical analysis of the literature on the subject. The second of the definitions indicated by 23.75% of the respondents was the one proposed in the first item of table No. 1 - the definition from the Cambridge Dictionary (CD 2023). Then, 11.25% of the respondents pointed to the definition from the third position of Table 1, a definition based on the Cambridge Business English Dictionary (EPN 2023). A slightly smaller percentage of respondents - 7.50% chose the definition from the fourth position of Table 1, proposed from the Dictionary of the Polish Language (2023). Only 0.63% of the respondents pointed to Winston's definition (1992: 8).

One of the questions addressed to the respondents was the issue of using artificial intelligence. The respondents were asked in what spheres of life they use artificial intelligence? The data obtained from the respondents' answers are presented in Table 2.

Table 2. Spheres in which respondents use artificial intelligence.

No.	Response categories	n	%
1.	Private	112	35.00
2.	Private and professional	98	30,63
3.	Professional	30	9,38
4.	None	80	25.00
	Total	320	100

Source: own compilation.

The results indicate that the largest percentage of respondents, as 35%, use artificial intelligence only in the private sphere. A slightly lower percentage of 30.63% of respondents use AI both in the private and professional spheres. Only in the professional sphere, 9.38% use AI. On the other hand, 25% of respondents stated that they do not use artificial intelligence in any of the spheres. The last answer is puzzling, especially since recognizing the widespread use of artificial intelligence, it seems difficult not to use it at all. This gives rise to the assumption that the respondents are not aware that they use artificial intelligence. Despite the use of pre-questions in the questionnaire that could awaken their knowledge of AI applications, still a quarter of respondents marked a negative answer. The context of Industry 5.0 entering the social consciousness makes the data obtained from the respondents' opinions unsatisfactory. Moreover, these results do not raise hopes for introducing the assumptions of Industry 5.0 to the organizational and social reality in Poland.

Both in the literature examining the issue of artificial intelligence, as well as in organizational reality and in social awareness, there are certain theories that inspire respect for artificial intelligence. AI which, as a new sphere, is not fully known, causes an undefined dose of distrust. When discussing the subject of the leadership ecosystem 5.0, and in particular the issue of the leader's competence, one should consider whether a person who does not trust artificial intelligence can fully use it. Moreover, whether a leader who does not trust artificial intelligence can play the role of a leader in modern reality. In order to find out the level of respondents' trust in artificial intelligence, a five-point Likert scale was used. In the questionnaire, respondents were asked to mark their level of trust in artificial intelligence on a scale, where 1 meant "no trust" and 5 meant "full trust". The data obtained from the respondents' answers are presented in Figure 1.

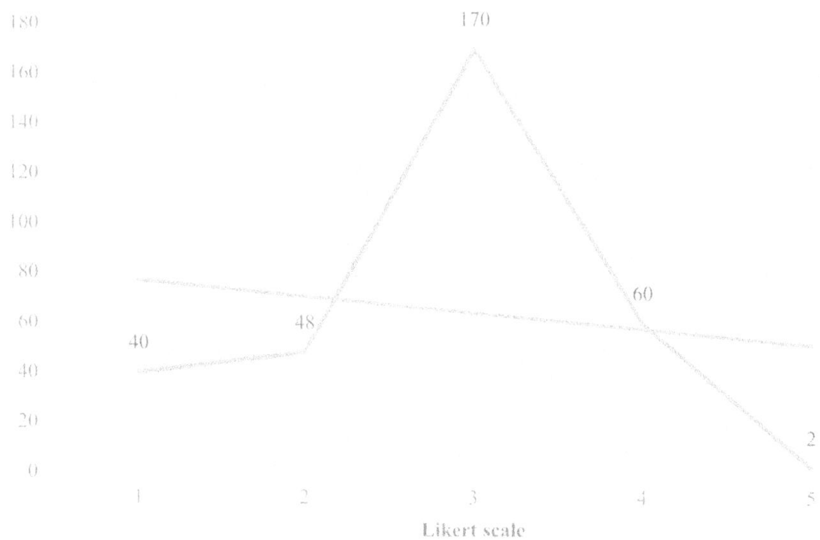

Figure 1. Level of trust in artificial intelligence (n=320).
Source: own compilation

The research results clearly show that the vast majority of respondents, i.e. 170 people, defined their level of trust in artificial intelligence as 3, i.e. medium. Then, 48 people defined their level of trust as low, indicating 2. Lack of trust in artificial intelligence was declared by as many as 40 people. Guided by the increase in the level of trust, it should be noted that 60 people rated their trust level at 4. However, only two people declared full trust in artificial intelligence, assessing it at 5. When analyzing the data in terms of trust level trends, more opinions tending to distrust towards to artificial intelligence.

6 CONCLUSION. LIMITATION AND FUTURE RESEARCH

The on the verge of Industry 5.0, nearly a third of respondents use artificial intelligence only in the private sphere, and a quarter in none of the spheres. On the other hand, trust in artificial intelligence is at an average level with a trend towards distrust. These results are not optimistic in the context of the development of new generation leadership relationships.

When discussing the subject of leadership of the new generation 5.0, and in particular the issue of leadership competences, the following question was posed: can a leader who does not trust artificial intelligence effectively fulfill the role of a leader in the modern reality? Juxtaposing the previously conducted research (Balcerzyk 2020; Balcerzyk 2021; Czainska 2022) in the field of the addressed issues with the obtained results allows to obtain a certain perspective. The review of the literature and the results of the surveys indicate certain limitations in terms of trust in artificial intelligence. They most likely result from the fact that the social and organizational reality is not keeping up with the development of technology. The key limitations include:

- Cognitive - afraid of the unknown;
- Normative - no rules or customs for using artificial intelligence;
- Legislative - the law does not keep up with technical solutions, does not regulate responsibility for decisions made by artificial intelligence;
- Psycho-social - fear of losing jobs, being guided by conspiracy theories, etc.

Undoubtedly, the above limitations contribute to problems with trust in artificial intelligence. The conducted research confirms that the society is not yet ready for Industry 5.0. This study does not allow to describe all the research carried out. Its goal was to speak in the discourse on the leadership of the new generation. Undoubtedly, research needs to be continued. At the moment, we cannot talk about effective leadership 5.0, its barriers lie in competence and contextual limitations.

However, the presented research can be a guideline for leaders who think about effectiveness. Priority directions for improving the leader's workshop can be identified. Attention should be paid to: leadership best practices, high flexibility, competency matching, and considering and updating contexts.

REFERENCES

Ako-Nai F., de la Cal Marin E. & Tan Q. 2022. *Artificial Intelligence Decision and Validation Powered Smart Contract for Open Learning Content Creation*, In: Prieto, J., Partida, A., Leitão, P., Pinto, A. (eds) *Blockchain and Applications*. BLOCKCHAIN 2021. Lecture Notes in Networks and Systems, Vol 320. Springer, Cham. doi: 10.1007/978-3-030-86162-9_37.

Balcerzyk D. 2021. The Role of a Leader in Contemporary Organizations. *European Research Studies Journal*, Vol. 24, Issue 1, 226–240, doi:10.35808/ersj/1959.

Balcerzyk R. 2020. Knowledge Management in Small and Medium-Sized Enterprises, *European Research Studies Journal*, Vol. 23, Special Issue 3, 529–544. doi:10.35808/ersj/1943.

Bostrom N. 2012. The Superintelligent Will: Motivation and Instrumental Rationality in Advanced Artifcial Agents. *Minds and Machines*. Vol.22, No 2, 71–85, dx.doi.org/10.1007/s11023-012-9281-3.

Cellan-Jones R. 2014. Stephen Hawking warns artificial intelligence could end mankind, *BBC News*, 2 December 2014, https://christusliberat.org/wp-content/uploads/2017/10/Stephen-Hawking-warns-artificial-intelligence-could-end-mankind-BBC-News.pdf, 23.02.2023.

Copertari L. 2016. Free Will for Artificial Machines with Natural Intelligence. *Open Access Library Journal*, 3, 1–11. doi: 10.4236/oalib.1102355.

Czainska K. 2022. *Benefits and threats of knowledge management supported with artificial intelligence algorithms from the end user's perspective*, in: Stor M. (ed.) *Human Capital Management in the Wandering Context of Events – Challenges for the Managerial Staff*, Publishing House of Wroclaw University of Economics and Business, Wroclaw, 68–76, https://dx.doi.org/10.15611/2022.988.7.

Fast E. & Horvitz E. 2017. Long-Term Trends in the Public Perception of Artificial Intelligence. *Proceedings of the AAAI Conference on Artificial Intelligence*, Vol.31, No 1. https://doi.org/10.1609/aaai.v31i1.10635

Gurkaynak G., Yilmaz I. & Haksever G. 2016. Stifling artificial intelligence: Human perils. *Computer Law & Security Review: The International Journal of Technology Law and Practice*. Vol. 32, Issue 5, October, 749–758, https://doi.org/10.1016/j.clsr.2016.05.003.
Kanari L., Dictus H., Chalimourda A., Arnaudon A., Van Geit W., Coste B., Shillcock J., Hess K. & Markram H. 2022. Computational synthesis of cortical dendritic morphologies, *Cell Reports*, Vol. 39, Issue 1, 110586, https://doi.org/10.1016/j.celrep.2022.110586.
Luhmann N. 2000. *Familiarity, Confidence, Trust: Problems and Alternatives*, in: Gambetta D. (ed.) *Trust: Making and Breaking Cooperative Relations*, electronic edition, Department of Sociology, University of Oxford, Chapter 6, 94–107, http://www.sociology.ox.ac.uk/papers/luhmann94-107.pdf. 20.01.2020.
Lewis, J. D., & Weigert, A. 1985. Trust as a social reality. *Social Forces*, Vol. 63, No 4, 967–985.
McCarthy J. 2007a. From here to human-level AI. *Artificial Intelligence* 171, 1174–1182.
McCarthy J., 2007b. What is Artificial Intelligence? *Computer Science Department Stanford University Stanford*. November 12, 1–15. https://www-formal.stanford.edu/jmc/whatisai.pdf. 21.01.2023.
McCarthy J., Minsky M.L., Rochester L. & Shannon C.E. 1955. A Proposal for the Dartmouth Summer Research Project on Artificial Intelligence. August 31, https://cse-robotics.engr.tamu.edu/dshell/cs625/2014-09-02.pdf. 10.02.2023.
Nahavandi S. 2019. Industry 5.0—A Human-Centric Solution. *Sustainability*, Vol.11, No 16, 4371; https://doi.org/10.3390/su11164371.
Rose D. 2020. *Artificial Intelligence for Business: What You Need to Know about Machine Learning and Neural Networks*. Chicago Lakeshore Press.
Rudd J. 2018. Building the Blue Brain Nexus. https://www.technologynetworks.com/informatics/articles/building-the-blue-brain-nexus-295851. 20.02.23.
Russell S., Norvig N. 2016. *Artificial Intelligence: A Modern Approach*. Global Edition, Pearson Education.
Sejnowski T. J. 2018. *The deep learning revolution. Artificial Intelligence Meets Human Intelligence*. The MIT Press.
Shanahan M. 2015. *The Technological Singularity*. The MIT Press Essential Knowledge series. MA: The MIT Pres.
Turing A. M. 1950. Computing Machinery and Intelligence. *Mind*. Vol. 49, No 236. 433–460. https://redirect.cs.umbc.edu/courses/471/papers/turing.pdf, 11.02.2023.
Winston P. H. 1992. Artificial Intelligence. 3rd ed., Addison-Wesley Pub. Co.
Yu K. H., Beam A. L. & Kohane, I. S. 2018. Artificial intelligence in healthcare. *Nature Biomedical Engineering 2*, (10), 719–731. doi:10.1038/s41551-018-0305-z.
BBP 2023. The Blue Brain Project [online]. https://www.epfl.ch/research/domains/bluebrain/. 23.02.2023.
CD 2023. *Cambridge Dictionary* [online]. https://dictionary.cambridge.org/pl/dictionary/english/artificial-intelligence. 11.02.2023.
EPN 2023. *European Parliament News* [online]. https://www.europarl.europa.eu/news/en/headlines/society/20200827STO85804/what-is-artificial-intelligence-and-how-is-it-used. 12.02.2023.
SJP 2023. *Słownik Języka Polskiego*. PWN [online]. https://sjp.pwn.pl/szukaj/sztuczna%20inteligencja.html. 20.01.2023.

Digital Synergy – El Emary et al. (eds)

Chapter 11
Agile marketing at R&D organizations

Beata Poteralska
Jan Kochanowski University of Kielce, Poland

Marzena Walasik
Łukasiewicz Institute for Sustainable Technologies, Radom, Poland

Piotr Maśloch
War Studies University, Warsaw, Poland

Barbara Grześ
WSB Merito University Warsaw, Poland

Agnieszka Thier
Cracow University of Economics, Cracow, Poland

Contents

Agility is necessary in different areas of functioning of organisations. It is also of growing importance in marketing, where agility is the foundation that allows organisations to respond and adapt quickly to the changing market conditions, customer expectations, and dynamic trends. This is also important for research organisations, as market changes and the focus on commercialisation of research results force them to improve their competitiveness and adopt a business-like way of managing and marketing their activity. Therefore, the purpose of the article is to recognise the benefits of introducing agile marketing in R&D organisations that want to maintain their competitive advantage and actively market their innovations.

For the needs of the paper, the state of the art analysis was conducted to identify the benefits of agile marketing, and expert surveys were conducted with a view to identifying benefits of agile marketing that are of critical importance to R&D organisations. The novelty lies in the recognition of the potential benefits of and the possibility to adopt agile marketing in independent R&D organisations and not in enterprises or corporate R&D centres where such measures are already taken.

For an R&D organisation to successfully implement agile marketing, its agile readiness in the future must first be analysed and assessed. Additionally, the scope of expert surveys should be extended. Those conducted and presented by the authors were limited by the number of the respondents. The findings are treated by the authors as a pilot study only.

1 INTRODUCTION

Contemporary organisations must respond to new challenges posed by the social, economic, and political changes as well as globalisation and technological developments. Nowadays, it

DOI: 10.1201/9781003440406-11

seems that change is the only constant. The ability to adapt quickly to changes is defined as agility. Agile management depends on numerous internal and external factors.

In the first half of the 21st century, organisations have undoubtedly been verifying their ability to respond rapidly and flexibly to everyday challenges. The organisational courage, commitment, determination, readiness and openness to change, treating changes as a constant occurrence, but also as a driver of innovation and development, as well as the ability to adapt to change are make-or-break factors for all types of organisations.

Agile management is growing in importance under the influence of numerous external factors, including, among other things, constant technological developments, growing market needs, and socio-political changes. Given the above, traditional organisational structure is no longer efficient and precludes organisations from adapting quickly to the ever-changing environment.

In the literature and in business the concept of agility has been known and used for years and the interest in the topic is still growing. The first mention of agility dates back to 1920s and in 1960s management scholars worked on the concept that would illustrate how organisations coped with the ever-changing and unpredictable external environment. The concept of agility has evolved over decades – researchers at the Lehigh University in Pennsylvania introduced the concept of agile manufacturing; the concept was also used with reference to supply chains and information technologies, with the latter becoming the area in which the concept of agility is currently mentioned and used most frequently. Such agile methods as Design Thinking, Scrum or Kanban are widely known and important. It is also a fact that the topic of agility has become one of the main business concepts of the 21st century (Włodarkiewicz-Klimek 2018: 148).

McKinsey conducted a very interesting study on organisational transformation to achieve organisational agility (Salo 2017). In McKinsey Global Survey 'How to create an agile organisation,' organisational agility is defined as the ability to quickly reconfigure strategy, structure, processes, people, and technology toward value-creating and value-protecting opportunities. The survey shows that agile organisations report better performance than companies that have not yet fully implemented agile ways of working. For many respondents transformation towards organisational agility ranks as a strategic priority. However, according to the survey, organisation-wide agile transformations were rare and only 4 percent of all respondents said their companies had fully implemented one.

Agility is required in many parts of organisation and areas of its operation. It is also catching fire in marketing, where agility is the foundation that allows organisations to respond and adapt quickly to the changing market conditions, customer expectations, and dynamic trends. Marketing agility refers to a company's ability to adapt its marketing strategy and activity to the changing environment in a rapid and flexible manner. It is an approach that assumes that change is a standard and that an organisation should be ready to adapt to it (Smith, Brown 2018: 145–162).

Agile marketing processes allow companies to stay competitive in a dynamically changing environment. All organisations must be able to adapt their marketing strategies in real time to meet the evolving trends and customer preferences. This calls for agile marketing, which makes such adaptation quick and effective and at the same time allows better understanding of and response to changing customers' needs (Davis, Wilson 2015: 55–68). By using data analytics and monitoring customer behaviours, organisations may personalise their marketing messages and offers, which boosts their effectiveness, as well as source promising opportunities, develop innovations, and stay competitive (Johnson 2016: 201–215).

The concept of marketing agility is still in its infancy (Alghamdi & Agag 2024). This is all the more important for research organisations, as market changes and the focus on commercialisation of research results force them to improve their competitiveness and adopt a business-like way of managing and marketing their activity, which means higher marketing spending and calls for improved customer service.

Therefore, the purpose of the article is to recognise the benefits of introducing agile marketing in R&D organisations that want to maintain their competitive advantage and actively and continuously market their innovations. If agile marketing is properly implemented, R&D organisations may disseminate their research results in a better planned, more efficient, and highly customised manner, build better relationships with businesses, and win and implement business projects, which, in turn, streamlines technology transfer processes (Poteralska, Walasik 2022).

2 METHODS

The study involved desk research (analysis of the state of the art) and an expert panel. The desk research was conducted to identify the benefits of agile marketing. To this end, articles in the Web of Science database were searched and analysed by the following keywords: 'agile marketing' and 'marketing agility' (Table 1). The authors also analysed up-to-date reports on agile marketing performance in business (AgileSherpas 2023, Ascend 2022).

Table 1. Selection of articles in the Web of Science database.

Search criteria	No. of documents found	Database after reading abstracts	Final database (after reading whole papers)	Final database
'Agile Marketing'	12	8	6	13
'Marketing agility'	22	16	7	

Source: own study.

Through desk research the authors were able to identify a set of critical benefits of agile marketing, which was then assessed by the managers of marketing and/or commercialisation departments/teams at 20 Polish R&D organisations, including institutes in the Łukasiewicz Research Network. The survey was conducted with a view to identifying benefits of agile marketing that are of critical importance to R&D organisations.

3 RESULTS

Through desk research the authors were able to collect information on the benefits agile marketing may bring companies, including SMEs and multinational corporations (Table 2).

Table 2. Benefits of agile marketing.

BENEFITS OF AGILE MARKETING	AUTHORS
Helps the organisation respond quickly to the dynamically changing and highly uncertain environment (e.g. technological developments and ever-changing customer expectations)	Alghamdi & Agag, 2024; Ascend2, 2022; Moi & Cabiddu, 2022; Lubowiecki-Vikuk, et al., 2022; Sachdeva & Kumar, 2022; Hughes, N and Chandy, R, 2021; Kalaignanam et al., 2021; Moi & Cabiddu, 2021; Hagen et al., 2019; Zhou et al., 2019
Facilitates organisational ability to rapidly scan the external environment for threats, opportunities, emerging customer demands, and competition	Alghamdi & Agag, 2024; AgileSherpas, 2023; Tarn & Wang, 2023
Enables quick response to changing customer needs	Tarakçi & Aslan, 2023; Khan et al., 2022; Sachdeva & Kumar, 2022; Moi & Cabiddu, 2021
Provides greater customer engagement, including constant and updated communication with customers	Moi & Cabiddu, 2022; Moi & Cabiddu, 2021; Poolton, et al., 2006
Enables reconfiguration of a marketing approach at short notice	Sachdeva & Kumar, 2022; Poolton, et al., 2006
Enables fast-paced work and fast decision making	AgileSherpas, 2023; Moi & Cabiddu, 2022; Kalaignanam et al., 2021; Moi & Cabiddu, 2021
Gives competitive advantage	Alghamdi & Agag, 2024; Poolton, et al., 2006
Improves work organisation	AgileSherpas, 2023
Improves team performance	Ascend2, 2022; Sachdeva & Kumar, 2022
Improves communication within an organisation	Tarakçi & Aslan, 2023

(Continued)

Table 2. (*Continued*)

BENEFITS OF AGILE MARKETING	AUTHORS
Enhances firm's capacity to prevent, address, and cope with crisis events	Moi & Cabiddu, 2022
Contributes to the organisation's performance and its long-term success	AgileSherpas, 2023; Khan et al., 2022; Kalaignanam et al., 2021
Connects daily activities and organisation's strategy	AgileSherpas, 2023
Brings a change in habits and fosters innovation thanks to learning from failing and learning from mistakes	Sachdeva & Kumar; 2022
Supports change processes	Tarakçi & Aslan, 2023
Enables different forms of work (e.g. office and remote)	AgileSherpas, 2023
Enables more effective use of assets	Tarakçi & Aslan; 2023, Ascend2, 2022; Zhou et al., 2019

Source: own study.

The indicated benefits concern two areas in particular, i.e. improving the effectiveness and flexibility of relationships with customers and competitors (external) and streamlining organisation's operations (internal).

Based on the respondents' assessment of the importance of the 17 benefits found in the literature the authors compiled a list of six (6) benefits that were found to be critically important to R&D organisations (critical benefits of agile marketing, CBAMs).

They include:

External:

- Facilitates organisational ability to rapidly scan the external environment for threats, opportunities, emerging customer demands, and competition.
- Enables quick response to changing customer needs.
- Provides greater customer engagement, including constant and updated communication with customers.

Internal:

- Improves team performance.
- Contributes to the organisation's performance and its long-term success.
- Connects daily activities and organisation's strategy.

The respondents identified both external and internal benefits of agile marketing important to R&D organisations. External – not to keep up with, but to stay ahead of the changing world and make science-business communication more efficient; and internal – to improve the effectiveness of R&D organisation activity, particularly in the area of internal communication. The obtained results also confirm the paramount importance of the organisational, planning, and strategic activities to be taken at the initial stage of agile marketing implementation. Additionally, the identified CBAMs (especially internal) depend highly on top managers who are responsible for designing and implementing the strategy, formulating the communication policy (both external and internal), and overseeing brand building activities.

CBAMs identified by the experts appear to be model because they are independent of the specifics of a given sector, industry, or environment in which an R&D organisation operates. This means that organisations can acquire certain universal skills with reference to the identification and creation of conditions conducive to successful implementation of an agile approach. The analysis allowed the authors to conclude that organisational transformation towards agility depends on the competences of managers as well as on the ability of teams to verify, create, and implement agile marketing.

4 DISCUSSION

Effective marketing of R&D organisations is hampered by many factors. The authors' analyses indicate the benefits of agile marketing for R&D organisations, which should operate similarly to agile enterprises. The literature review did not allow the identification of independent R&D organisations that use agile marketing. However, the agile approach and agile marketing are to some extent used by R&D units at SMEs and large enterprises (Meier & Kock 2023, Riesener et al. 2019) or in R&D projects they implement (Paasivaara et al. 2018).

The benefits indicated in the literature in the context of the corporate R&D activity coincide with the benefits indicated by scholars and practitioners with regard to agile marketing in companies without the particular consideration of this area of activity. The literature on the benefits of adopting an agile approach in the R&D activity is scarce.

The benefits presented in the literature coincide with the benefits indicated by the experts. The external benefits indicated in expert surveys presented in the article, that is the organisational ability to (I) quickly scan the external environment, (II) engage customers, and (III) respond rapidly to changing customer needs were found to be important also in the case of the activity run by R&D units within enterprises. In this case the following were stressed: the ability to quickly adapt to external changes in the market environment (Riesener et al. 2019), better cope with highly turbulent, uncertain and complex environment (Meier & Kock 2023), and rapidly respond to changing customer requirement (Paasivaara et al. 2018). As for the internal benefits, the experts mainly named the improved performance of individual teams and the whole organisation, which is reflected in the benefits discussed in the literature with reference to the R&D activity that include better performance of cross-functional, cross-component teams (Paasivaara et al. 2018), and a constant improvement of the organisation (Riesener et al. 2019). The authors did not find any reference to the connection between the daily activities and organisation's strategy in the literature dealing with the topic of research and development activity.

The expert panel identified the unequivocal benefits that R&D organisations can achieve from using agile marketing. Another point for discussion are the features and characteristics of the organisation that are conducive to obtaining these benefits. Kalaignanam et al. (2021) are of the opinion that "a marketing activity is best suited for agility when the market response is highly unpredictable, activity can be broken down into smaller components, it is plausible to get customer validation, and there is less need to involve external partners."

The criteria identified by Kalaignanam et al. (2021), which enable the assessment whether a given marketing activity will be more effective as a result of adopting an agile approach, can certainly be implemented to evaluate the validity of using agile marketing by R&D organisations, as they perfectly reflect the changing conditions under which they operate:

- The market response is highly unpredictable – R&D results – particularly breakthroughs, are characterised by high unpredictability of the market response. By using foresight methods, R&D organisations have the ability to cope with uncertainty and unpredictability.
- Activity can be broken down into smaller components – projects implemented by R&D organisations are divided into stages (increments), which is in line with agile marketing. Agile principles help reduce the risk by iterating through 'smaller bets.' A good example, and one that is often used in practice, is the concept of milestones which help in making one of the three key decisions with regard to project implementation (regardless of the source of its funding), i.e. the decision whether to (I) continue the tasks planned; (II) repeat a given stage of project implementation; or (III) cease further implementation of the project.
- It is plausible to get customer validation – R&D organisations for which the development and implementation of innovations should be the core activity should not do so in isolation from the market. Those products or services that are created in close cooperation with entrepreneurs (potential customers) or at least validated with them at critical levels of the product/service development, i.e. technology readiness levels, e.g. 1, 5, 8, are more likely to

be commercialised. In fact, R&D organisations implement some projects in this way, however, such an approach is not possible in all areas of their activity; nevertheless, the awareness of this need is unquestionable.

- There is less need to involve external partners – if an activity requires the involvement and participation of the marketing ecosystem, the benefits of agility need to be balanced with the increased need for coordination. In some situations, external partners, understood as other R&D organisations, might be unable to match the clock speed (i.e., short iterative cycles) of firms, making it difficult to complete a task in an agile manner.

To compete in the market, R&D organisations must be in constant contact with customers to learn what their present and future needs are. R&D organisations employ creators and innovators who guarantee high level of innovativeness. They are always interested in acquiring information from the external environment. It is possible to conclude that the introduction of agile marketing will help organisations adapt to the changing environment in a more agile way and that, above all, it will translate into the creation of customised innovations sought by customers. Such an innovative approach is beneficial to R&D organisations and their customers, thereby influencing the development of market economies.

5 SUMMARY

The organisational courage, commitment, determination, readiness and openness to change, treating changes as a constant occurrence, but also as a driver of innovation and development, as well as the ability to adapt to change will be make-or-break factors for all types of organisations. Agile management is growing in importance under the influence of numerous external factors, including, among other things, continuous technological development and progress, ever-growing market needs, and socio-political changes. Hence, organisational agility is a broad concept that requires multidimensional consideration, both in terms of an organisation's ability to deal with external and internal challenges. At the same time, organisation's ability to adapt quickly to changes should be analysed in terms of its operational, organisational, technological, and competence agility. Only such approach gives a complete image of agility (Grześ 2023: 271–288), also in terms of marketing processes.

The specificity of R&D organisations' operations means that the marketing activities undertaken are primarily aimed at presenting the R&D work they carry out and at continuously developing and improving R&D results by transforming them into products and services sought by the market. R&D organisations should have the ability to create the demand for R&D results, especially breakthroughs, by using BTL marketing tools. This is in line with the concept of agile marketing. Digital marketing (primarily using social media) is another direction marketing efforts at R&D organisations should take. To sum up, R&D organisations that pursue a policy of short sales cycles and undertake the above-mentioned marketing activities to market their R&D results are among those entities that should benefit the most from the introduction of agile marketing.

The expert panel allowed the identification of the critical benefits of agile marketing for R&D organisations.

The next stage of the research should be an assessment of organisations' agile readiness, which could employ indicators based on fuzzy logic and fuzzy calculus enabling the determination of the agile readiness level and, consequently, the identification of the agility gap or competence in need of improvement. Agility is a strategy that enables organisations operate in a turbulent environment in a way that ensures sustainability through continuous improvement.

Moreover, it would be interesting for future research to consider how an agile culture originating at the level of individual teams or projects could subsequently spread outwards to other (relevant) parts of the R&D organisation. Such a process would not negate the importance of top management in fostering culture, but it might suggest a different process through which organisational transformation might occur.

REFERENCES

AgileSherpas 2023. Report: State of Agile Marketing, Agile Marketing Alliance.

Alghamdi O.A., Agag G. 2024. Competitive advantage: A longitudinal analysis of the roles of data-driven innovation capabilities, marketing agility, and market turbulence. Journal of Retailing and Consumer Services, 76, 103547, multhttps://doi.org/10.1016/j.jretconser.2023.103547.

Ascend2 2022. Report: The Impact of Agile Marketing. Research Created for Marketers, Ascend2 Research-Based Marketing.

Davis M., Wilson S. 2015. The Impact of Market Dynamism on Marketing Strategies. Journal of International Marketing, 30(4), pp. 55–68.

Grześ B. 2023. Managing an Agile Organization – Key Determinants of Organizational Agilty. Scientific Papers of Silesian University of Technology. Organization & Management/Zeszyty Naukowe Politechniki Slaskiej. Organizacja i Zarządzanie, (172), pp. 271–288.

Hagen B., Zucchella A. and Ghauri P.N. 2019. From fragile to agile: marketing as a key driver of entrepreneurial internationalization. International Marketing Review, 36(2), pp. 260–288. https://doi.org/10.1108/IMR-01-2018-0023.

Hughes N., Chandy R. 2021. Trajectories and twists: perspectives on marketing agility from emerging markets. Journal of Marketing, 85(1), pp. 59–63. DOI: https://doi.org/10.1177/00222429209730372021.

Johnson C. 2016. Agile Marketing: Adapting to a Fast-Changing Landscape. International Journal of Marketing and Innovation, 35(3), pp. 201–215.

Kalaignanam K., Tuli K.R., Kushwaha T., Lee L., Gal D. 2021. Marketing Agility: The Concept, Antecedents, and a Research Agenda. Journal of Marketing, 85(1)pp. 35–58.

Lubowiecki-Vikuk A., Budzanowska-Drzewiecka M., Borzyszkowski J., Taher B. 2022. Critical reflection on VUCA in tourism and hospitality marketing activities. International Journal of Contemporary Hospitality Management, 35(8), pp. 2983–3005, DOI 10.1108/IJCHM-04-2022-0479.

Meier A., Kock A. 2023. Agile R&D units' organisation and its relationship with innovation performance. R&D Management, https://doi.org/10.1111/radm.12655.

Moi L., Cabiddu F. 2021. Leading digital transformation through an Agile Marketing Capability: the case of Spotahome, Journal of Management and Governance, 25, pp. 1145–1177.

Moi L. and Cabiddu F. 2022. Navigating a global pandemic crisis through marketing agility: evidence from Italian B2B firms. Journal of Business & Industrial Marketing, 37(10), pp. 2022–2035. https://doi.org/10.1108/JBIM-01-2021-0034.

Paasivaara M., Behm B., Lassenius C., Hallikainen M. 2018. Large-scale agile transformation at Ericsson: a case study. Empir Software Eng, 23, pp. 2550–2596.

Digital Synergy – El Emary et al. (eds)

Chapter 12
Determinants of the effectiveness of virtual teams management

Barbara Grześ
WSB Merito University Warsaw, Poland

Contents

The issue of virtual team functioning is perceived as an important area in the contemporary business environment, and virtual teams themselves provide a significant competitive advantage to organizations. Virtual teams are characterized by the use of information and communication technologies to connect and perform daily tasks, communicate, and achieve common goals. These teams can consist of members from the same organization or individuals from different organizations working together on a specific project or task. In this article, the author conducts a multifaceted analysis of virtual teams and defines the dilemmas associated with remote work and the virtual environment. Based on existing literature and secondary research, both at the national and international levels, which illustrate the perceptions of work in a virtual environment by employees and employers, the author synthesizes the key opportunities and threats to ultimately provide a definition of a virtual team, taking into account the crucial aspects of its functioning as a team.

1 INTRODUCTION

Virtual teams are increasingly becoming a significant force in the contemporary business environment. Their characteristic element is the utilization of information and communication technologies in daily work. The growing role and importance of virtual teams necessitate breakthrough changes in the design of their activities and the allocation of a multicultural workforce within organizations (Gilson et al. 2014).

When analysing this area, it is important to note that significant differences can exist within the structures of virtual teams. These can include teams composed of members from the same organization who work in a virtual environment for the benefit of that organization.

This paper conducts an analysis of the main dilemmas related to managing a virtual team, where employees perform their work remotely. Common characteristics among different virtual team structures are identified, as well as areas that differentiate them from the perspectives of team members, managers, and organizations. Based on this analysis, a definition of a virtual team will be presented. The emergence of remote work as a viable option marked the starting point for building virtual teams. Consequently, the initial focus of this analysis will be on remote work and the utilization of communication technologies.

DOI: 10.1201/9781003440406-12

2 DEFINITION OF VIRTUAL TEAMS

Remote work is sometimes referred to as telework, virtual work, or the commonly used term in Polish organizations - home office. Remote work, as well as functioning in teams referred to as virtual, is not a new area. A precursor in this field was F International, a company from the United Kingdom that employed women to work from home as early as 1962 in order to reduce staff turnover in the field of programming services (Wyrzykowska, 2014). In the following years, this trend became increasingly widespread, although it was primarily utilized in technology and IT companies.

Jarvenpaa and Leidner defined a virtual team as follows: “A virtual team is a group of individuals functioning as a unified entity but not located in one physical location, communicating and collaborating through communication technologies” (Jarvenpaa & Leidner 1999).

Powell, Piccoli, and Ives point out that “A virtual team is a group of individuals who use communication technologies to coordinate and accomplish common tasks, even though team members may be geographically dispersed” (Powell, Piccoli, & Ives 2004).

Similar views on the definition of a virtual team are held by Hertel, Geister, and Konradt, defining a virtual team as “a group of individuals who utilize communication and information technologies to work on a common project or task, regardless of their geographic location” (Hertel, Geister, & Konradt 2005).

The common denominator of the above-mentioned definitions of virtual teams is a group of people collaborating to accomplish a common endeavor, dispersed in terms of physical work location, and communicating through communication technologies. The key aspect is the ability to communicate remotely.

The rapid development of the technological aspects of remote communication, especially driven by the outbreak of the COVID-19 pandemic, has widely opened the doors for remote work and the establishment of entire teams operating in this form. There has also been an improvement in the attitudes of employers and employees towards this form of work, as shown in the ‘Remote Work 2.0′ report (2021) prepared by Pracodawcy RP (Employers of Poland), which will be further discussed in the subsequent part of the study.

In recent years, the term “virtual” has been used differently in various management concepts. For example, Goldman, Nagel, and Preiss define a virtual organization as an alliance of key competencies distributed among a series of distinct operational units within a single large company or a group of companies (Goldman et al. 1994). There is also a perspective that excludes the presence of central coordination or supervision in virtual teams, often contradicting traditional hierarchy and vertical integration (Chiesa & Manzini 1997).

The multitude of similar definitions and the omission of aspects related to building relationships among members of virtual teams provide a stimulus for reflection and analysis of the topic in terms of the factors underlying the effectiveness of managing virtual teams. Importantly, the key aspects related to the perception of virtual teams, as derived from the presented definitions, remain relevant and constitute the foundation of their functioning.

3 PERSPECTIVES OF THE FUNCTIONING OF VIRTUAL TEAMS – BENEFITS & RISKS

Despite many challenges caused by the COVID-19 pandemic - and partially because of it innovations and digitalization are advancing rapidly. A McKinsey survey among global executives revealed that companies have expedited the digitization of customer interactions, supply chains, and internal operations by an average of three years (McKinsey Survey 2020).

However, it is important to note that these advancements have significantly increased remote collaboration, leveraging technology for innovation, automation, and digitalization more boldly than ever.

The functioning of virtual teams can offer numerous benefits to an organization. McKinsey conducts quarterly surveys showing, among other things, how major companies view remote work in virtual environments (McKinsey Survey 2020). The 2020 surveys highlighted that the shift to remote work offers an opportunity to improve it as a long-term practice. Some of the main benefits include expanded reach, access to a larger talent pool, reduced commuting time, optimization of fixed costs, and normalization of virtual interactions.

However, it is equally important to consider the associated risks of virtual work environments. These risks, as identified in the 'Virtually Possible' report (Hamlin et al. 2021), include the breakdown of organizational culture, burnout, challenging adaptation processes, skill limitations, and inadequate technological conditions.

Moreover, the 'Remote Work 2.0: Solution for the Pandemic or a Lasting Change?' report (Raport Praca zdalna 2.0. 2021) provides insights into the perception of remote work in Poland. Notable benefits include time savings and reduced expenses, while negative aspects such as blurred boundaries between personal life and work, difficulty focusing, and increased personal infrastructure costs are also highlighted.

Flexibility in virtual environments is beneficial for both employees and employers. Research by Employers of Poland underscores the advantages and challenges perceived by employers, including cost savings and decreased sick leaves, balanced against additional expenses for equipment and software, and reduced employee control (Raport Praca zdalna 2.0. 2021).

4 MANAGING A VIRTUAL TEAM

The organizational changes implemented regarding team functioning and workplace virtualization pose a challenge for individuals building virtual teams. The lack of direct contact, reliance on IT tools for communication, limited access to traditional communication support areas, and notably diminished nonverbal cues contribute to a sense of disconnection among virtual team members. Building relationships not only becomes difficult but, in some cases, even impossible. This situation can lead to tension within teams, resulting in misunderstandings and conflicts. The decision-making process may also be disrupted.

This situation requires virtual team leaders to exercise special vigilance and respond promptly when the situation is still manageable and can be resolved. These accumulating communication problems and, in many cases, the perceived anonymity of virtual team members negatively impact mutual cooperation and hinder knowledge sharing among team members. It is important to remember that one of the key aspects of virtual team effectiveness is precisely the ability to leverage the synergy of team members' knowledge.

Functioning and working in a remote environment and the need for effective management of virtual teams have influenced the way leaders operate. Much attention is now focused on the "soft" aspects of leadership. Leaders have had to change management models, reshape the way employees work, and adapt to a different way of monitoring their performance. Pre-established relationships, if leaders had the opportunity to work with employees in a traditional model, are of enormous importance.

Trust, building a culture of responsibility, self-organization, self-discipline, and engagement are crucial factors without which the effectiveness of remote work significantly declines. It is stated that remote work is not just about communication but also about the ability to use remote work tools, which were previously more auxiliary tools until they became the primary means of daily work and communication.

In addition to ensuring the necessary equipment for work, leaders' tasks also include supporting employees in their daily struggles with new technology and ensuring their training in this area and its proper utilization for task accomplishment and team goals achievement.

Changing one's thinking about oneself also entails a change in perception of the leader's role in a virtual team, where hierarchy loses value and practically has no place. Instead, partnership emerges. The leader is one of the team members, and the roles of each member are determined by the scope of shared tasks. As research conducted by D. Shwartz-Asher, N. Ahituv indicates, it is also worth noting that a distinguishing feature of virtual teams compared to teams working in a traditional office setting is the fact that in the former, informal leaders often emerge among team members who take charge of team tasks. (Shwartz-Asher, Ahituv 2019)

Working in a virtual team also hampers the socialization of its members and can result in a sense of isolation. The feeling of isolation can lead to a lack of identification as a team member, which translates into inconsistency in team functioning, a disruption of unity, and limited trust among team members. Considering that trust is the foundation for the effective functioning of any team, especially those working in a virtual environment, addressing this area appears to be a key task for the leader of such a team, as well as one of the goals for each team member. (Chhay, Kleiner 2013).

Multinational teams will encounter significantly more communication barriers. Not only is there a language barrier, which is often difficult to overcome, but the aspect of cultural differences proves to be an even greater challenge. Time differences and the associated barriers resulting from asynchronous communication are also significant factors to consider. (Chang et al. 2011)

The development of virtual teams in a dynamic business environment presents many organizations with various organizational challenges, including: formalizing processes and strategies for virtual team work (Carter et al. 2015), communication issues in virtual teams (Cramton, Orvis, 2003), creating appropriate organizational structures for virtual team operations (Bryant et al. 2009), interaction among virtual team members, adapting leaders' competencies to the changing needs of virtual teams management, building relationships between the organization and virtual team members, understanding and addressing challenges arising from cultural difference, the necessity to change existing team management models, reduced control over employees - collaboration based on trust, overcoming communication barriers resulting from the loss of direct communication.

5 OPPORTUNITIES AND THREATS DETERMINED BY WORKING IN VIRTUAL TEAMS

Based on market experiences, research findings, and analysis, as well as the author's ownexperiences, a compilation was made of the most significant factors identified as opportunities and threats determined by working in virtual teams, from both the organizational and employee perspectives - members of virtual teams (Table 1). Many of the benefits listed inthis compilation also reflect potential risks - the absence of geographical limitations associated with working in dispersed virtual teams located in different parts of the world can lead to the risk of lacking direct contact and, consequently, the inability to build relationships among employees.

6 SUMMARY/CONCLUSION

Analysing the aspects related to managing virtual teams presented in this study and considering the complexity of the identified opportunities and challenges, it can be concluded that these are just some of the dilemmas faced by organizations and leaders managing virtual teams.

Considering the mentioned risks and negative effects of remote work implementation for organizations, it is believed that in the long term, they will transform into benefits and strengthen the competitive advantage of those organizations that have made efforts, invested in technical infrastructure, developed new competencies in their teams, and transformed their organizational culture into a culture based on collaboration and trust.

The author states that regardless of whether we are talking about an organization working with virtual teams or a traditional model of work organization, in the organizations of the future, the aspect of control should be replaced with trust, building engagement, and forming teams of the right people who are focused on striving towards and achieving common goals and carrying out tasks that are important for the organization and for themselves. In such organizations, control will be merely an unnecessary formality included as one of the elements of the manager's role. Communication within and with the remote team is the foundation and guarantee that this "virtual mission" can succeed.

Table 1. Compilation of opportunities and threats arising from working in virtual teams in an Organization.

Opportunities	Threats
• Lack of geographical limitations in recruiting employees. • Cost savings resulting from the elimination of commuting to the workplace. • Cost savings on office space for employers. • Flexible working hours. • Reduced employee turnover and sick leave. • Shortened task completion time. • Increased team productivity. • Increased independence and autonomy of employees. • Innovation resulting from team diversity. • High organizational flexibility. • Agile and quick adaptation to changing market conditions. • Increased job opportunities for specific groups of workers, such as people with disabilities. • Reduction in environmental pollution due to reduced employee transportation. • Flexibility in increasing or decreasing employment without incurring additional space costs. • Access to job opportunities worldwide. • Using the technology for global business development. • Ability to work from anywhere in the world	• Lack of direct contact with employees. • Impaired communication and information flow. • Misunderstandings that may arise from cultural differences. • Possibility of losing important aspects of building employer-employee relationships. • Difficulty in managing a remote team without direct contact. • Challenges associated with asynchronous communication due to different time zones. • Insufficient managerial skills for remote team leadership. • Insufficient digital skills of team members and managers. • Concerns about data security. • Reliability issues with information technology. • Reduced control over employees. • Need for employees to use their own workspace. • Difficulty in separating work from personal life. • Impaired knowledge sharing process. • Reduced opportunity to observe others' work and learn from their experiences. • Difficulty in maintaining work efficiency.

Source: own elaboration based on the literature of the subject.

The author of this study poses the question:

What is the way to achieve effective collaboration and management of virtual teams?

When searching for answers to the aforementioned question, it should be emphasized that the key aspect of effective collaboration in a virtual team is primarily the maturity and mutual respect among its members, along with a high level of responsibility and autonomy in organizing work and completing tasks. The attitude of the leader will play a significant role, including their openness and ability to listen to the team's needs, as well as their attentiveness at every stage of the team's operations.

In summary, the author defines a virtual team as follows:

"A virtual team is a group of people working in a virtual environment - dispersed in terms of their work location - connected by a common goal that is important to each member of the group. They collaborate collectively to achieve this goal, fostering trust and respect, taking responsibility for their actions, supporting and complementing each other, and drawing upon the potential that lies within each team member. These individuals share a special bond, centred around a common idea, values, and mission that they identify with."

The elements underlined in the above definition form the foundation for asserting that it is a team, rather than just a group of people organized functionally to achieve a specific goal.

The leader in a virtual team, while being one of the members, plays a crucial supportive role in building the team's identity and fostering cohesion around a shared vision.

REFERENCES

Bryant, S.M., Albring, S.M., Murthy, U. (2009) The effects of reward structure, media richness and gender on virtual teams. International Journal of Accounting Information Systems, 10.

Carter D.R., Seely, P.W., Dagosta, J., De Church, L.A., Zaccaro, S.J. (2015) Leadership for global virtual teams: Facilitating teamwork processes. In Wildman, J.L, Griffith, R.L. (Eds) Leading Global Teams, Springer, New York.
Chang, H.H., Chuang, S.S, Chao, S.H., (2011) Determinants of cultural adaptation, communication quality, and trust in virtual teams' performance. Total Quality Management.
Chhay, R., Kleiner, B.H. (2013) Effective communication in virtual teams. Industrial Management, 7/6.
Chiesa, V.; Manzini, R., (1997) Managing virtual R&D organisations: lessons from the pharmaceutical industry, in: International Journal of Technology Management, vol. 13, n. 5/6.
Cramton, C.D., Orvis, K.L., (2003) Overcoming barriers to information sharing in virtual teams. In: Gibson, C.B., Cohen, S.G. (Eds.), Virtual Teams that work: Creating conditions for virtual team effectiveness, Jossey-Bass, San Francisco.
Gilson, L.L., Maynard, M.T., Young, N.C.J., Vartiainen, M., Hakonen, M. (2014) Virtual Teams Research 10 Years, 10 Themes, and 10 Opportunities. Journal of Management.
Goldman, S.L., Nagel, R.N.; Preiss, K. (1994): Agile competitors and virtual organizations: strategies for enriching the customer.
Hamlin R., Shirali A., Singh S., Woodcock E. (14 May 2021) Virtually possible: Getting remote work right for G&A functions; https://www.mckinsey.com/business-functions/operations/our-insights/virtually-possible-getting-remote-work-right-for-g-and-a-functions#
Hertel, G., Geister, S., Konradt, U. (2005). Managing virtual teams: A review of current empirical research. Human resource management review, 15(1), 69–95. https://doi.org/10.1016/j.hrmr.2005.01.002
Jarvenpaa, S. L., Leidner, D. E. (1999). Communication and trust in global virtual teams. Organization science, 10(6), 791–815, https://doi.org/10.1287/orsc.10.6.791
McKinsey Survey (2020) "How COVID-19 has pushed companies over the technology tipping point—and transformed business forever", https://www.mckinsey.com/business-functions/strategy-and-corporate-finance/our-insights/how-covid-19-has-pushed-companies-over-the-technology-tipping-point-and-transformed-business-forever
Powell, A., Piccoli, G., Ives, B. (2004) Virtual Teams: A Review of Current Literature and Directions for Future Research. Database for Advances in Information Systems, 35, 6–37, https://doi.org/10.1145/968464.968467
Praca zdalna 2.0 (2021) Rozwiązanie na czas pandemii czy trwała zmiana, Księga rekomendacji oraz ekspertyzy; https://pracodawcyrp.pl/upload/files/2021/03/praca-zdalna-2-0-rekomendacje-i-ekspertyzy-v2.pdf
Shwartz-Asher D., Ahituv N., (2019) Comparison between Face-to-Face Teams and Virtual Teams with Respect to Compliance with Directives, Journal of Service Science and Management, Vol.12 No.4, June 2019, https://doi.org/10.4236/jssm.2019.12438
Wyrzykowska, B. (2014) Przedsiębiorstwo bez pracowników-telepraca. Logistyka, Tom 4, Sieć Badawcza Łukasiewicz – Instytut Logistyki i Magazynowania.

Digital Synergy – El Emary et al. (eds)
© 2025 The Author(s), ISBN 978-1-032-57658-9

Chapter 13
Energy policy instruments supporting the development of energy communities

Grzegorz Maśloch
Warsaw School of Economics, Warsaw, Poland

Contents

Energy communities are new organizational and legal forms that enable the construction of energy structures at the local level, which in turn will enable local communities to achieve energy autonomy. The development of energy communities depends to a large extent on the available energy policy instruments. This chapter explores the role of energy policy instruments for energy communities and identifies key lessons to guide the adoption or advancement of the most appropriate instruments.

1 INTRODUCTION

Achieving international climate goals and switching to low-emission, sustainable energy requires an energy transformation in which renewable energy plays a key role. Renewable energy offers the potential that is the basis for a fair and rational energy transformation. It determines, among others, its zero-emission impact on the natural environment, modularity, and ability to generate energy at the local level. As a consequence of the widespread use of renewable energy, it becomes necessary to reorganize central energy systems and develop new organizational forms based on local, democratic, and participatory initiatives.

The possibility of using the potential of renewable energy within individual prosumer forms or through organized organizational forms based on the concepts of energy communities creates new opportunities for socio-economic development. It should be emphasized here that the benefits of community initiatives in the field of renewable energy go far beyond technological solutions. Significant social and economic benefits can be achieved by consolidating local capital and potentials and adjusting them to real needs and expectations.

Taking the initiative to transform the conventional system into a distributed energy system using renewable energy sources requires the initiators to make an effort to cover the financial, economic, social, and cultural costs. A special role in this respect is played by the public sector, which is responsible both for formulating and implementing strategic goals, as well as for organizing the very process of change based on regulation or public investments. The scope, pace, and effects of the ongoing energy transformation depend to a large extent on a properly selected system of energy policy instruments affecting social and economic entities.

This chapter explores the role of energy policy instruments for energy communities and identifies key lessons to guide the adoption or advancement of the most appropriate instruments.

DOI: 10.1201/9781003440406-13

2 ENERGY POLICY INSTRUMENTS

In order to build an effective energy system, the public sector uses a variety of energy policy instruments. The use of selected instruments or their use in a hybrid way also serves the implementation of various functions, among which the most common are controlling, stimulating, initiating or mediating functions (Rotmans et al. 2001).

In the literature on the subject, there has been a discussion for years about the role and importance of energy policy instruments for energy transformation processes (Rogge & Reichardt 2016; Rosenow et al. 2017). The set of available energy policy instruments can be divided into tools of the following nature (Egmond, et al. 2006):

- regulatory (laws, standards, regulations, prices, taxes, etc.),
- supporting motivation for action (subsidies, tax reliefs and other incentives),
- public investment (investments by public sector entities in energy infrastructure),
- communication (informing and communicating about adopted policies, support programs, education, etc.).

There is general agreement among researchers that energy policy instruments play a key role in enabling or constraining the energy transition and are essential for its course (Belain et al. 2021; Grashof 2021).

Each country or region creates its own incentive policy and currently, there is no textbook recipe for universal solutions in this matter. As a rule, the instruments are usually targeted at all stakeholders involved in energy processes - i.e. energy producers, producers of energy-supplied equipment, and consumers. Having appropriate political instruments is one of the determinants of a country's ability to mitigate anthropogenic greenhouse gas emissions. Without these tools, it is impossible to fully use various resources (technical, capital, human, institutional, etc.) (Winkler et al. 2007).

The use of any instrument entails the adoption of certain legal acts. Legal instruments may also contain economic elements, e.g. fines and fines for breaking the law, tax reliefs. In practice, energy policy instruments are usually a mixture of legal, economic and persuasive elements.

In the existing literature on the subject, policy instruments that are used to develop energy communities are widely discussed (Brzozowska et al. 2023; Leonhardt et. al. 2022). Bearing in mind that energy communities are based on renewable energy resources, it can be assumed that the instruments stimulating the development of RES and energy communities are the same.

It should be unequivocally stated that the political will of decision-makers acting as regulators is largely dependent on society. This means that the energy policy of a given country and the instruments used in it are shaped by citizens on three levels (Łucki & Misiak 2010):

- macro (citizens choose a specific political option and express their views on energy policy in referenda and public opinion polls),
- meso (citizens choose local authorities and influence their decisions, and directly, they have a large impact on energy consumption by entities in which they operate, e.g. enterprises, farms),
- micro (citizens, as consumers, buy and operate energy-using devices, and also buy a variety of products and services that require a certain amount of energy to produce (food, clothes, etc.).

The effectiveness of energy policy instruments used in a given region or country depends to a large extent on the society's approach to energy issues, environmental protection, cooperation skills, trust in public authority, wealth, and entrepreneurship. Large differences between individual societies in this respect are caused by the following conditions:

- environmental (richness in energy sources, climate, etc.),
- economic (level of economic development, business culture, human capital, the structure of industry and trade, etc.),
- social (history, culture, social model, lifestyle, level of development of civil society, division of powers (federal, national, local).

3 ENERGY COMMUNITIES

An efficient, innovative, and safe energy system should be built with the use of endogenous conditions. Therefore, it means full mobilization of local material and human resources in order to achieve common, local benefits. The organizational and legal forms enabling the mobilization of the aforementioned local resources are energy communities.

Energy communities are local, small-scale producers of energy from renewable sources. Its advantages include equal access to energy for all citizens, improvement of household energy efficiency, and development of distributed renewable energy sources throughout the region/country.

There are many definitions of an energy community. Even in the legal acts of the EU, there is no uniform definition of energy community (see Table 1).

Table 1. Definitions of energy community in EU law.

Concept	Legal act	Definition
Renewable Energy Community	Article 2(16) Recast Renewable Energy Directive	"A legal entity: (a) which, in accordance with the applicable national law, is based on open and voluntary participation, is autonomous, and is effectively controlled by shareholders or members that are located in the proximity of the renewable energy projects that are owned and developed by that legal entity; (b) the shareholders or members of which are natural persons, SMEs or local authorities, including municipalities; (c) the primary purpose of which is to provide environmental, economic or social community benefits for its shareholders or members or for the local areas where it operates, rather than financial profits"
Citizen Energy Community	Article 2(11) Recast Internal Electricity Market Directive	"A legal entity that: (a) is based on voluntary and open participation and is effectively controlled by members or shareholders that are natural persons, local authorities, including municipalities, or small enterprises; (b) has for its primary purpose to provide environmental, economic or social community benefits to its members or shareholders or to the local areas where it operates rather than to generate financial profits; (c) may engage in generation, including from renewable sources, distribution, supply, consumption, aggregation, energy storage, energy efficiency services or charging services for electric vehicles or provide other energy services to its members or shareholders";
Citizen Energy Community	Article 2(70) Proposal Recast Internal Gas Market Directive	"A legal entity that: (a) is based on voluntary and open participation and is effectively controlled by members or shareholders that are natural persons, local authorities, including municipalities, or small enterprises; (b) has for its primary purpose to provide environmental, economic or social community benefits to its members or shareholders or to the local areas where it operates rather than to generate financial profits; and (c) engages in production, distribution, supply, consumption, or storage of renewable gas in the natural gas system, or provides energy efficiency services or maintenance services to its members or shareholders";

Source: author's work based on https://rural-energy-community-hub.ec.europa.eu/ [25-05-2023].

As can be seen from the analysis of the energy community definitions presented in Table 1, there are some interpretation discrepancies. They mainly come down to the area of activity, the role of RES and the possibility of cooperation with conventional energy, or the participation of various stakeholders.

Undoubtedly, however, the main goal of energy communities is to produce clean and safe energy for the own needs of community members (Bielig et al. 2022). The goal of activity understood in this way is to generate social and environmental benefits, and not to focus on financial profits.

The main areas of interest and activity of the energy communities therefore include:

- generation of energy from RES,
- voluntary and open membership,
- participation and effective control of citizens, local authorities, and enterprises whose main economic activity is not in the energy sector,
- provision of electric mobility or other energy services.

Energy Communities are therefore a new organizational and legal formula in the energy sector. Energy communities also enable the participation of local communities in larger energy projects, which in turn may lead to the creation of autonomous energy regions. Collective ownership in energy communities allows democratization of access to capital (or means of production) and thus has the potential to contribute to the energy transition in a socially deeper way than a mere technological solution (Johanisova & Wolf 2012). All members actively participate in and control the energy community. Production should not exceed consumption, and communities cannot operate in markets that could be considered speculative.

As extensive scientific research has shown, energy communities can contribute to many positive environmental, financial, and social benefits (Bielig et al. 2022, Koirala et al. 2016, Young & Brans 2017). The environmental and socio-economic benefits resulting from the operation of the energy communities are presented in Table 2.

Table 2. Environmental and socio-economic benefits.

Environmental benefits	Benefits for society	Economic benefits
• increased use of renewable energy, • access to local, sustainable energy sources and mobility services, • reduction of environmental pollution, • lower energy transmission losses.	• democratic control over energy investments and the energy system, • creating local jobs, • development of local business, • building a civil society, • public education.	• savings for the end consumer, • investment opportunities for residents and local businesses, • a chance to generate income that stays for the local community, • building local economic potential based on local and regional resources.

Source: own study

4 KEY ENERGY POLICY INSTRUMENTS SUPPORTING THE DEVELOPMENT OF ENERGY COMMUNITIES

Making a change in the energy sector in a direction consistent with the concept of sustainable development is a complex process. This is a challenge that requires financial and organizational expenditures by public authorities, enterprises, and entire societies. In order to make the right choice between alternative organizational and legal solutions or energy technologies, it is necessary to properly consider all costs and benefits. This is of particular importance in the process of creating energy communities in a given area, where energy policy instruments determine the attractiveness and competitiveness of the adopted solutions.

Often in the early stages of the energy transition, the public sector acts as a brake. It usually seeks to improve existing technologies and uses its regulatory and often ownership role to limit or reduce the attractiveness of new solutions. Later, however, when a new technological system comes into force, the public sector can play a supporting role through the use of large capital and organizational resources. This does not mean, however, that individual stakeholders (individuals, companies, local government) cannot be the initiator of the process of transformation and construction of an energy community. With the spread of initiatives, supporting instruments appear. (Rotmans et al. 2001). There are many instruments, which can directly or indirectly support energy communities. The most frequently used in economic practice include: financial support, feed-in tariff, grid services and fiscal incentives (Ackermann et al. 2001, Leonhardt et. al. 2022).

When choosing an instrument and the scope of application, many criteria should be considered that allow minimizing the adverse effects resulting from the introduction of given solutions. These include criteria such as:

- ecological efficiency,
- economic efficiency,
- the possibility of implementing the system,
- social acceptability,
- political acceptability,
- compliance with the public finance system,
- compliance with competition rules,
- public and energy security,
- compliance with accepted international obligations.

5 SUMMARY

The transition of local and regional communities, currently dependent on conventional energy (based on source material from fossil fuels or nuclear energy), will be possible thanks to transformation, then at the level of energy investment, but also in human capital.

The public sector plays an important role in the process of organizing, programming, and managing the energy transformation, including in particular in creating conditions for the creation and effective functioning of energy communities. For this purpose, the public sector, both at the central and regional or local level, can use a wide range of instruments, the application of which determines the directions and possibilities of development of energy communities. The use of individual instruments is also an expression of the role and importance that energy communities play and will play in the energy mixes of individual countries.

The issues of the limits and scope of public intervention and the strength of the intervention of individual instruments in socio-economic processes remain debatable issues. One of the areas of intervention that should undoubtedly be of interest to the public sector is the implementation of adopted policies (e.g. implementation of climate policy) or the issue of ensuring energy security (e.g. ensuring the functioning of critical infrastructure).

REFERENCES

Ackermann, T., Andersson, G. Söder, L. (2001). Overview of government and market driven programs for the promotion of renewable power generation. Renewable Energy, 22(1), 197–204. https://doi.org/10.1016/S0960-1481(00)00015-X.

Belaid, F., Dagher, L., Filis, G. (2021). Revisiting the resource curse in the MENA region. Resources Policy, 73, 2021. https://doi.org/10.1016/j.resourpol.2021.102225.

Bielig, M., Kacperski, C., Kutzner, F., Klingert, S. (2022). Evidence behind the narrative: Critically reviewing the social impact of energy communities in Europe. Energy Research & Social Science, 94, https://doi.org/10.1016/j.erss.2022.102859.

Brzozowska, A., Maśloch, P., Maśloch, G. (2023). Management of Civic Energy and the Green Transformation: A Case Study of Poland. CRC Press. https://doi.org/10.1201/9781003370352.

Egmond, C., Jonkers, R., Kok, G., (2006). One size fits all? Policy instruments should fit the segments of targets groups. Energy Policy, 34, 3464–3474. https://doi.org/10.1016/j.enpol.2005.07.017.
Grashof, K. (2021). Who put the hammer in the toolbox? Explaining the emergence of renewable energy auctions as a globally dominant policy instrument. Energy Research & Social Science, 73. https://doi.org/10.1016/j.erss.2021.101917.
Johanisova, N., Wolf, S. (2012). Economic democracy: A path for the future?. Futures, 44(6) 562–570. https://doi.org/10.1016/j.futures.2012.03.017.
Koirala, B.P., Koliou, E., Friege, J., Hakvoort, R.A., Herder, P.M. (2016). Energetic communities for community energy: A review of key issues and trends shaping integrated community energy systems. Renewable and Sustainable Energy Reviews, 56, 722–744. https://doi.org/10.1016/j.rser.2015.11.080.
Leonhardt, R., Noble, B., Poelzer, G., Fitzpatrick, P., Belcher, K., Holdmann, G. (2022). Advancing local energy transitions: A global review of government instruments supporting community energy. Energy Research & Social Science, 83. https://doi.org/10.1016/j.erss.2021.102350.
Łucki, Z., Misiak, W. (2010). Energetyka a społeczeństwo. Warszawa: PWN.
Polzin, F., Migendt, M., Täube, F. A., von Flotow, P. (2015). Public policy influence on renewable energy investments - A panel data study across OECD countries. Energy Policy, 80, 98–111. https://doi.org/10.1016/j.enpol.2015.01.026.
Rogge, K.S., Reichardt, K. (2016). Policy mixes for sustainability transitions: An extended concept and framework for analysis. Research Policy, 45(8), 1620–1635. https://doi.org/10.1016/j.respol.2019.103832.
Rosenow, J., Kern, F., Rogge, K. (2017). The need for comprehensive and well targeted instrument mixes to stimulate energy transitions: The case of energy efficiency policy. Energy Research & Social Science, 33, 95–104. https://doi.org/10.1016/j.erss.2017.09.013.
Rotmans, J., Kemp, R., van Asselt, M. (2001). More evolution than revolution: transition management in public policy. Foresight, 3(1), 15–31. https://doi.org/10.1108/14636680110803003.
Young, J., Brans, M. (2017). Analysis of factors affecting a shift in a local energy system towards 100% renewable energy community. Journal of Cleaner Production, 169, 117–124, https://doi.org/10.1016/j.jclepro.2017.08.023.
Winkler, H., Baumert, K., Blanchard, O., Burch, S., Robinson, J. (2007). What factors influence mitigative capacity? Energy Policy, 35(1), 692–703. https://doi.org/10.1016/j.enpol.2006.01.009.

Digital Synergy – El Emary et al. (eds)

Chapter 14
Female leaders in times of (post) COVID

Piotr Olaf Żylicz
WSB Merito University Warsaw, Poland

Contents

The COVID-19 pandemic has caused significant disruptions worldwide, with far-reaching implications for women. Women have experienced disproportionate impacts on employment, caregiving responsibilities, and mental well-being. They have faced higher job losses, reduced work hours, and increased work-family conflict. The pandemic has also adversely affected women's mental health, leading to increased anxiety, depression, and stress. However, female leaders have demonstrated remarkable success in crisis management, in both politics and business. They have exhibited strong leadership skills, resilience, and adaptability. Despite these achievements, women leaders often face imposter syndrome, which has been amplified during the pandemic. Supporting female leaders is crucial for women's personal development and also for societies and business organizations in general. Future trends in leadership are expected to embrace more collaborative and inclusive styles, aligning with traditionally feminine leadership attributes.

1 INTRODUCTION

The COVID-19 is a unique point in human history. It has been compared to other historical plagues, such as the Plague of Justinian, the Bubonic Plague, and the Spanish Flu, but it has its own distinct characteristics due to its high transmission efficiency, asymptomatic carrier transmission, and global impact. The pandemic has caused significant disruptions to daily life, including economic, social, and psychological trauma. The pandemic has resulted in unprecedented significant global health, social and economic problems. As of 2022, there have been over 70 million confirmed cases and 1.5 million casualties worldwide due to COVID-19.

It has created a global health crisis, leading to various social and psychological problems (Harutyunyan et al. 2021). The emergence of COVID-19 has posed significant threats to public health systems and exacerbated national economic conditions worldwide (Ghecham 2022). Especially since it had an adverse impact on countries with lower income inequality. The International Monetary Fund (World Economic Outlook 2021) estimates that the global economy contracted by 3.5% in 2020, representing the worst economic downturn since the Great Depression.

Moreover, the pandemic has led to widespread job losses, business closures, and increased levels of poverty and inequality. The World Bank (2021), in turn, reports that the pandemic has pushed millions of people into extreme poverty, reversing years of progress in poverty reduction.

DOI: 10.1201/9781003440406-14

2 WOMEN IN COVID-19

In Poland Heidtman and Zylicz (2020) conducted an online anonymous survey devoted to the personal experience of Poles between May and July 2020. It was a convenience group, widely diversified on demographic variables. Two figures below present answers to critical questions in a female subpopulation.

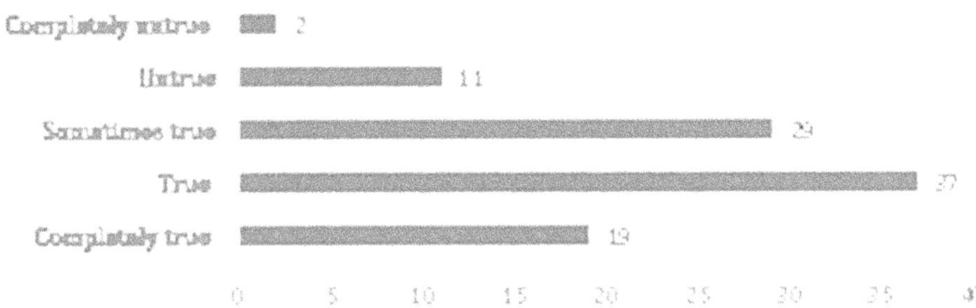

Figure 1. Answers (%) on the question: „*It feels that almost everything changed around me.*" (N= 529).
Source: own study

As Figure 1 shows as many as 85% of women under investigation at least occasionally experienced a sense of fundamental change in their lives. At the same time, close to 80% of the female respondents reported that the situation they found themselves in is perceived by them as personally difficult (answers 'completely true', 'true', and 'sometimes true') - see Figure 2.

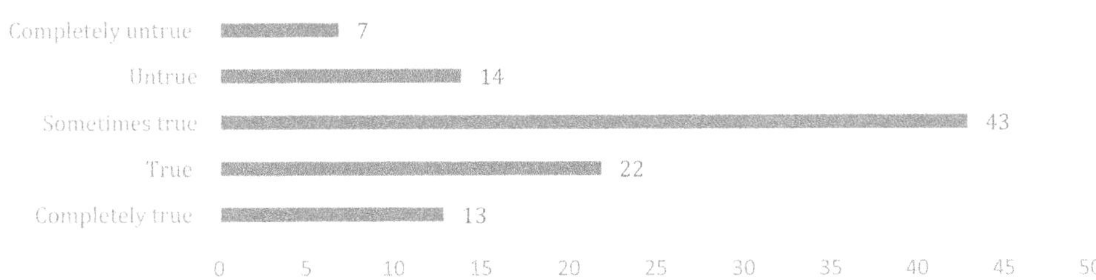

Figure 2. Answers (%) on the question: „*Current situation is very difficult to me.*" (N= 529).
Source: own study

Under all geographies, the COVID-19 pandemic has had significant implications for women, affecting various aspects of their lives. Research has highlighted specific challenges faced by women during this crisis, including the disproportionate impact on their employment, caregiving responsibilities, and mental well-being. Studies have shown that women have experienced higher levels of job loss and reduced work hours compared to men, with those in low-wage jobs being particularly vulnerable (Alon et al. 2020, Yavorsky et al. 2022, Lotta et al. 2021). Furthermore, the closure of schools and the shift to remote learning have placed an increased burden of caregiving on women, leading to heightened work-family conflict and the need to juggle multiple responsibilities (Collins et al. 2021, Frank et al. 2021, Mendolia et al. 2021).

These challenges have resulted in women reducing their work hours or leaving the labour force altogether, which can have long-term implications for their career progression and economic well-being. In addition to employment-related impacts, the pandemic has taken a toll on women's mental health. Women have reported increased levels of anxiety, depression, and stress during this crisis (Avery 2021, Broche-Pérez et al. 2021, Khademian 2021). The unique challenges of balancing work, caregiving, and household responsibilities have contributed to heightened levels of stress and burnout among women. The closure of support networks and limited access to mental health services have further compounded these issues, highlighting the need for targeted support and resources to address the mental well-being of women during the pandemic (Pierce et al. 2020, Zhang and Ma 2020). Recent research has also highlighted the gendered impacts of the pandemic on children's mental well-being, with girls being particularly vulnerable to negative mental health outcomes (Christner et al. 2021).

3 MALES VS FEMALES AS LEADERS

Generally, there are relatively small differences between male and female leaders in terms of transformational, transactional, and laissez-faire leadership styles (Ergle 2015). However, females tend to have the highest frequency in terms of transformational style of management, while males have the highest frequency in terms of transactional leadership style in an organization (Jallow, 2020).

Congruently, Khan, Abdullah, & Zada (2023) found that in transactional and laissez-faire styles of leadership, male leaders have an edge over female leaders. Following the prevailing stereotypical expectations, women leaders were found to tend to display a more participative and inclusive leadership style, while men leaders often lean towards a directive and assertive style (Eagly, Johannesen-Schmidt & van Engen 2003).

Male leadership is often symbolized by an ego-driven form of direction-giving, while female leadership entails more listening and cooperation (Manzoor & Abrar 2011). Female leaders may over time be perceived as effective as male leaders if the present shift in definitions of effective leadership styles continues to align with female gender roles and organizational cultures embrace collective practices (Cundiff 2022).

4 FEMALE LEADERS IN COVID

COVID for obvious reasons has been a globally exceptionally challenging time, especially for women as presented above. Such times favor glass cliff phenomenon to surface. It refers to the tendency for women to be appointed to leadership positions that are risky and precarious, particularly during times of crisis or when organizations are failing (Ryan et al. 2016).

Studies have shown that glass cliff appointments are associated with beliefs that they suit the distinctive leadership abilities of women, provide women with good leadership opportunities, and are particularly stressful for women (Haslam & Ryan 2008). The glass cliff effect may contribute to gender inequity in professions such as local government management, where women are more likely to be hired during difficult times, increasing the likelihood of failure (Yang, Connolly, & Connolly 2022).

In times of COVID, the phenomenon has been particularly visible. Women have been more often entrusted with leading organizations and countries through the challenges posed by the crisis (Appelbaum & Emadi-Mahabadi 2022, Smith 2021). Two domains will be dealt with in more detail: politics and business.

4a. Politics. Female political leaders have played a significant role in responding to the COVID-19 pandemic, showcasing their leadership skills in various countries and contexts. For instance, Jacinda Ardern, the Prime Minister of New Zealand, implemented strict border controls, implemented a nationwide lockdown, and emphasized clear communication to effectively manage the crisis (Chowdhury 2021). Angela Merkel, the Chancellor of Germany, took a scientific approach by consulting with experts, implementing widespread testing, and implementing a cautious reopening strategy (Cluver et al. 2021). Tsai Ing-Wen, the President of Taiwan, implemented early and aggressive measures such as border controls, contact tracing, and mass production of masks to effectively control the spread of the virus (Brouwer & Hessels 2021).

These examples demonstrate the strong leadership exhibited by female political leaders during the COVID-19 pandemic, emphasizing decisive action, reliance on scientific evidence, and effective communication to protect the health and well-being of their citizens.

During the COVID-19 pandemic, women in political leadership positions have been praised for their empathic approach and successful management of the crisis (eg., Tatum, Thompson, Yates 2022, Dimitrova-Grajzl, Gornick, & Obasanjo 2022). Evidence from previous research shows that countries with female leaders were more successful in dealing with COVID-19 (Wulandari, Nurhaeni, Suharto 2022).

However, women in political leadership positions have also faced challenges, including underrepresentation in decision-making roles (Brooks, & Saad, 2020) and criticism for emphasizing the maternal aspect of femininity in their COVID-19 response (Lak & Husein 2022).

4b. Business. On the effectiveness of female business leaders in times of COVID we can foremost learn from extensive research by Zenger and Folkman. The authors already previously in a large (over 60000 leaders), multinational research (Zenger & Folkman 2019) proved that women prevail in most leadership skills. In times of COVID (Zenger & Folkman 2020) they found that women appeared to be on average way more effective leaders than their male counterparts in handling the COVID-19 crisis. As compared with pre-pandemic times the overall assessment of leadership effectiveness based on data from multisource assessment (known as '360′) showed that the gap between women and men only increased! Women were rated significantly more positively on 13 of the 19 leader's competencies. Of course, we would not have the same results for every industry or geographical context, but the basic message is clear: very often women manage and lead more effectively than men, particularly in times of crisis. In COVID- as shown above – they usually had to face more adversities.

Interestingly, women experience more often than men imposter syndrome. Although imposter syndrome affects both men and women, studies have found that women are more likely to experience it (Women with imposter syndrome fear that their perceived incompetence will be discovered by those around them, leading to exposure as a fraud or imposter (Baumann et al. 2020).

Imposter syndrome covers feelings of inadequacy, self-doubt, and fear of being exposed as a fraud or imposter despite having the necessary qualifications and objective accomplishments. First described in 1978 by psychologists Clance and Imes, they noted that many highly successful women did not feel internal recognition of their success and instead believed their accomplishments were due to chance or luck (Baumann et al. 2020, Feigofsky 2022, Mainali 2020, Mullangi and Jagsi 2019).

In addition, research has shown that women are more disproportionately impacted by the syndrome (Belcher et al. 2022, Grossman 2020, Ivie et al. 2016, KPMG 2023). Moreover, the pandemic has amplified societal expectations and pressures on women, particularly in terms of career progression and balancing work and family life. Women in leadership positions, in particular, may easily face imposter feelings as they navigate these complex demands.

6 SUMMARY AND CONCLUSION

However, the outbreak of COVID-19 has exacerbated existing gender differences in the labour market, with women being more vulnerable workers than men and bearing most of the burden of domestic tasks and childcare during the lockdown. Despite these challenges, female leaders have shown good and sometimes extraordinary performance in crisis management during the pandemic, and pretty often female leaders both in politics and business were significantly more effective than males. At the same time, many successful women under diverse geographies do not appreciate enough their own contributions and accomplishments.

Future trends in leadership are likely to continue to shift towards more collaborative and inclusive styles, which may align more closely with traditionally feminine leadership styles. As organizations become more diverse and global, leaders will need to be able to navigate cultural differences and work effectively with people from different backgrounds, which may require a more collaborative and inclusive approach. Therefore, supporting female leaders is appropriate for the sake of women themselves but also will be beneficial for business and social communities alike.

REFERENCES

Alon, T., Doepke, M., Olmstead-Rumsey, J., & Tertilt, M. (2020). The impact of COVID-19 on gender equality (No. w26947). National Bureau of Economic Research.

Appelbaum, S. H., & Emadi-Mahabadi, S. (2022). Gender Parity in The Workplace: How COVID-19 Has Affected Women. European Journal of Business and Management Research, 7 (1),.

Avery, A. R., Tsang, S., Seto, E. Y., & Duncan, G. E. (2021). Differences in stress and anxiety among women with and without children in the household during the early months of the COVID-19 pandemic. Frontiers in Public Health, 9, 688462.

Baumann, N., Faulk, C., Vanderlan, J., Chen, J., Bhayani, R. K. (2020). Small-group Discussion Sessions On Imposter Syndrome. Retrieved from https://www.mededportal.org/

Belcher, H. M. E., Copeland-Linder, N., Stone, J., Waters, C. R., Kuo, A. A., Moerchen, V. A., … & Reddy, M. (2022). Mch Pipeline Training Program: Connecting With Academia To Build Capacity Through Mentoring. Matern Child Health J, S1(26).

Broche-Pérez, Y., Fernández-Fleites, Z., Jiménez-Puig, E., Fernández-Castillo, E., & Rodríguez-Martin, B. C. (2021). Anxiety, Health Self-Perception, and Worry About the Resurgence of COVID-19 Predict Fear Reactions Among Genders in the Cuban Population. Frontiers in Global Women's Health, 2, 634088.

Brooks, D. J., & Saad, L. (2020). Double whammy: Why the underrepresentation of women among workplace and political decision makers matters in pandemic times. Politics & Gender, 16(4).

Brouwer, A. M., & Hessels, J. (2021). Female leaders' crisis communication during COVID-19: A comparative study. Plos one, 16 (4), e0248693.

Chowdhury, A. (2021). Female political leadership and COVID-19 pandemic: A comparative study of New Zealand and Bangladesh. Journal of Asian and African Studies, 56 (1).

Christner, N., Essler, S., Hazzam, A., & Paulus, M. (2021). Children's psychological well-being and problem behavior during the COVID-19 pandemic: An online study during the lockdown period in Germany. Plos one, 16(6), e0253473.

Cluver, L., Lachman, J. M., Sherr, L., Wessels, I., Krug, E., Rakotomalala, S., & McDonald, K. (2021). Parenting in a time of COVID-19. The Lancet, 397(10280).

Collins, C., Landivar, L. C., Ruppanner, L., & Scarborough, W. J. (2021). COVID-19 and the gender gap in work hours. Gender, Work & Organization, 28(S1).

Cundiff (2022). Gender and Organizational Culture: Perceptions of Leadership Style and Effectiveness. AWLJ, 1(41).

Dimitrova-Grajzl, V., Gornick, J., & Obasanjo, I. (2022). Leader gender, country culture, and the management of COVID-19. World Medical & Health Policy, 14(4).

Eagly, A. H., Johannesen-Schmidt, M. C., & van Engen, M. L. (2003). Transformational, transactional, and laissez-faire leadership styles: A meta-analysis comparing women and men. Psychological Bulletin, 129(4).

Ergle (2015). Perceived feminine vs masculine leadership qualities in corporate boardrooms. MOSR, (74).

Feigofsky, S. (2022). Imposter Syndrome. Heart Rhythm Case Reports, 12(8).

Frank, E., Zhao, Z., Fang, Y., Rotenstein, L. S., Sen, S., & Guille, C. (2021). Experiences of work-family conflict and mental health symptoms by gender among physician parents during the COVID-19 pandemic. JAMA network open, 4(11), e2134315–e2134315.

Ghecham, M. A. (2022). The impact of COVID-19 on economic growth of countries: What role has income inequality in it?. Economies, 10(7).

Grossman, R. C. (2020). The Imposter Phenomenon In the Medical Profession. Gender Equity in the Medical Profession.

Harutyunyan, H., Mukhaelyan, A., Hertelendy, A. J., Voskanyan, A., Benham, T., Issa, F., … & Ciottone, G. R. (2021). The psychosocial impact of compounding humanitarian crises caused by war and CoViD-19 informing future disaster response. Prehospital and Disaster Medicine, 36(5).
Haslam, S. A., & Ryan, M. K. (2008). The road to the glass cliff: Differences in the perceived suitability of men and women for leadership positions in succeeding and failing organizations. The Leadership Quarterly, 19(5).
Heidtman, J., Żylicz, P.O. (2020). O Polakach w trudnych czasach. [Poles in Difficult Times]. Unpublished research report.
Ivie, R., White, S. W., Chu, R. Y. (2016). Women's and Men's Career Choices In Astronomy And Astrophysics. Phys. Rev. Phys. Educ. Res., 2 (12).
Jallow (2020). Gender Differences in Managerial Behavior and Their Leadership Styles. IJISRT, 9(5), 6–10.
Khademian, F., Delavari, S., Koohjani, Z., & Khademian, Z. (2021). An investigation of depression, anxiety, and stress and its relating factors during COVID-19 pandemic in Iran. BMC Public Health, 21(1).
Khan, S. I., Abdullah, N. N., & Zada, R. S. E. (2023). Transformational, Transactional & Laissez-Faire Leadership Styles: A Gender Analysis. Qalaai Zanist Journal, 8(1).
KPMG (2023). Facing the Future of Women in Business: A KPMG Women's Leadership Summit Report. Retrieved from https://www://info.kpmg.us/news-perspectives/people-culture/.
Lak, A. S., & Hussain, T. (2022). Hegemonic Masculinity and Leadership Response to Covid-19: Critical Discourse Analysis of President Trump's Political Rhetoric in the Global Pandemic. Pakistan Journal of American Studies, 40(1).
Lotta, G., Wenham, C., Nunes, J., Pimenta, D. N., & de Oliveira, W. K. (2021). Gender, race, and health workers in the COVID-19 pandemic. The Lancet, 397(10280).
Mainali, S. (2020). Being An Imposter: Growing Out Of Impostership. J Nepal Med Assoc, 232(58).
Manzoor, Abrar (2011). The Difference Between Female And Male Leadership. PJGS, 1(5).
Mendolia, S., Suziedelyte, A., & Zhu, A. (2022). Have girls been left behind during the COVID-19 pandemic? Gender differences in pandemic effects on children's mental wellbeing. Economics Letters, 214, 110458.
Mullangi, S., Jagsi, R. (2019). Imposter Syndrome. JAMA, 5(322).
Pierce, M., Hope, H., Ford, T., Hatch, S., Hotopf, M., John, A., … & Abel, K. M. (2020). Mental health before and during the COVID-19 pandemic: a longitudinal probability sample survey of the UK population. The Lancet Psychiatry, 7(10).
Ryan, M. K., Haslam, S. A., Morgenroth, T., Rink, F., Stoker, J., & Peters, K. (2016). Getting on top of the glass cliff: Reviewing a decade of evidence, explanations, and impact. The Leadership Quarterly, 27(3).
Smith, J. (2021). The glass cliff in COVID-19: Women's leadership during times of crisis. Journal of Gender Studies, 10(2).
Tatum, A., Thompson, S., & Yates, C. (2022). Perceptions of women as political leaders at a time of crisis – a psychosocial study. Journal of Psychosocial Studies, 15(3).
World Bank. (2021). The Global Economic Outlook during the COVID-19 Pandemic: A Changed World. Retrieved from https://www.worldbank.org/en/news/feature/2021/01/05/global-economic-prospects-january-2021
World Economic Outlook, April 2021: Managing Divergent Recoveries. International Monetary Fund. Retrieved from www.imf.org/en/Publications/WEO/Issues/2021/03/23/world-economic-outlook-april-2021.
Wulandari, S., Nurhaeni, I. D. A., & Suharto, D. G. (2022, December). Transformation of Women's Leadership Styles in Post-Pandemic Crisis Recovery. In 7th International Conference on Social and Political Sciences (ICoSaPS 2022) (pp. 115–122). Atlantis Press.
Yang, L. K., Connolly, L., & Connolly, J. M. (2022). Is there a glass cliff in local government management? Examining the hiring and departure of women. Public Administration Review, 82(3).
Yavorsky, J. E., Qian, Y., & Sargent, A. C. (2022). The gendered pandemic: The implications of COVID-19 for work and family. In Working in America. Routledge.
Zenger, J., & Folkman, J. (2019). Women score higher than men in most leadership skills. Harvard Business Review, 92(10).
Zenger, J., & Folkman, J. (2020). Research: Women are better leaders during a crisis. Harvard Business Review, 30.
Zhang and Ma (2020). Impact of COVID-19 on mental health and quality of life among local residents in Liaoning province, China: A cross-sectional study. International Journal of Environmental Research and Public Health, 17(7).

Digital Synergy – El Emary et al. (eds)

Chapter 15
The extent to which Saudi business schools meet the standards of the global sustainability tracking and evaluation system "STARS" case study: Princess Noura bint Abdul Rahman University

Norah bint Fahd Al-Riqabi
Administrative Assistant to the Vice Dean, Princess Noura Bint Abdul Rahman University for Academic Support and Student Services, Saudi Arabia

Asma bint Abdul Rahman Al-Ghamdi
Lecturer in the Department of Administrative Sciences at the Applied College, Princess Noura bint Abdul Rahman University, Saudi Arabia

Najlaa bint Mohammed Al-Khalaf
Department of Public Administration, College of Business Administration, King Saud University, Saudi Arabia

Nevin bint Saeed Irfan
Department of Administrative Sciences, College of Applied Sciences, Princess Noura bint Abdul Rahman University, Saudi Arabia

Al-Hanouf bint Ahmad Kadasa
Lecturer in the Department of Administrative Sciences at the Applied College, Princess Noura bint Abdul Rahman University, Saudi Arabia

Contents

This study seeks to introduce the Global Sustainability Tracking and Evaluation System "STARS" and measure the extent to which the College of Business and Administration at Princess Nourah bint Abdul Rahman University meets its standards, hoping to reach supportive recommendations for adopting the concept of sustainability in the college. To achieve this, a questionnaire was designed consisting of two parts, the first of which has four questions related to personal variables, while the second part consists of (43) statements under five basic axes measuring academic aspects, participation in sustainability issues, planning and management, measuring operational impact, and leadership and innovation.

The study community, as the source of data, consisted of the faculty members of the college during the second semester of the year 1444 AH, amounting to (98) members, using the simple random sampling method. The questionnaires were distributed among the (80) individuals in the sample, and the number of valid responses for statistical analysis was (35) questionnaires, with a response rate of (44%).

The study found that its hypotheses were proven correct, except for the hypothesis that "the College of Business and Administration links its administrative aspects to sustainability".

DOI: 10.1201/9781003440406-15

The most important reached results were that the college allows its faculty members to cooperate with different sectors to conduct research in the field of sustainability and employs assistive technologies to create sustainable ideas. In addition, it was concluded that there is an emergent need to exert more efforts in raising awareness and education in the field of sustainability, as well as in activities supporting the adoption of the concept. It was also noticed that there was an absence of an administrative unit specialized in sustainability affairs.

According to these results, the study recommended most notably the development of academic programs in the field of sustainability, the creation of an administrative unit concerned with sustainability affairs, the construction of a special index to measure sustainability at the college level similar to the international indicators, and the development of a guide to sustainability in business and higher education institutions and their concepts.

1 INTRODUCTION

Universities contribute to the preparation of human cadres for the labor market in light of their three main functions that are education, scientific research, and community service. To achieve this, they deplete a lot of resources in all forms (human, material, and technical). This makes it imperative for these universities to create a balance between achieving their goals and the responsibility of protecting the resources of their societies and preserving their natural environment.

From this standpoint, the trend towards sustainability concepts in higher education emerged, such as the concept of green universities that do not have a negative impact on the environment, economy, and society in general. These universities, as defined by the United Nations Environment Program (UNEP), integrate the environment and various aspects of sustainability into education, training strategies, and its campus operations (United Nation Environment Program, 2022). From another perspective, these practices have been called the concept of sustainable universities, which refers to the universities that provide visions to their employees and society on how to overcome societal challenges, and show solutions to problems related to the environment, climate, insufficient available resources, and how to preserve them (UNEP, 2022).

At the local level, sustainability in the Kingdom of Saudi Arabia has been given importance and priority in its ambitious Vision 2030, as the vision stipulates that "the sustainability of our success is only by sustaining the elements of this success mainly in relation to the environmental sustainability, the financial sustainability, and the social sustainability through several initiatives including the announcement of the National Renewable Energy Program, the establishment of the Saudi Investment Company for Recycling "Sirc", the launching of the National Environment Strategy, joining the International Solar Alliance (Vision 2030, 2023) and many other projects and initiatives of Vision 2030 based on sustainability in their basis.

From the foregoing, it has become imperative for universities to move towards adopting sustainability practices. In view of the prominent role of Princess Nourah Bint Abdul Rahman University as one of the targeted universities for preparing women leaders and human cadres who are responsible and aware of sustainability; It has become imperative to adopt the concept of sustainability in its practices, raise awareness among its students and employees, benefit from its many advantages, follow up on this implementation and measure its results in the light of the international indicators in the field of sustainability.

2 RESEARCH JUSTIFICATIONS

Many international universities are engaged in sustainability as a contribution to the protection of the resources and the natural environment. In fact, the Global Sustainability Assessment System registered 1126 higher education institutions to use the STARS Reporting Tool, 580 universities and colleges globally were monitored as sustainable (The Sustainability Tracking, Assessment & Rating System, 2022). Whereas, in this context, the STARS tool has proven its worth as the most effective tool for assessing and tracking sustainability in all fields within the university campus according to (Kamal and Asmuss, 2012). Their study examined the most used measurement tools in the United States of America and Canada namely SAQ, CSAF, CSRC, and STARS. It showed that the Sustainability Report Card (CSRC) is ineffective for addressing sustainability in the context of education and research despite its preference for addressing governance and operations, as well as the inadequacy of the Sustainability Assessment Questionnaire (SAQ) and Campus Sustainability Assessment Framework (CSAF) to address sustainability issues in campus operations. This conclusion is supported by one of the five findings of the study of (Urbanski and Filho, 2015), which showed the emergence of an increased interest and participation in STARS within higher education institutions and the high participation rate of universities awarding master's and doctoral degrees in STARS.

At the local level, the trend towards sustainability in higher education was evident in the future plan for university education in the Kingdom of Saudi Arabia 1450 AH 2029 AD "Horizons 2029", which in turn focuses on achieving sustainability with its social, economic, and financial pillars in higher education institutions (Ministry of Higher Education, 2011). This led to the trend towards Saudi universities adopting the concept of sustainability. This approach is supported by the evaluation of (Alshuwaikhat et al., 2016) in their study of sustainability within higher education institutions in the Kingdom of Saudi Arabia. Their study results showed that less than half of Saudi universities include sustainability issues and challenges in their curricula, and projects related to sustainability do not link the various departments and other stakeholders inside and outside the universities with each other. Al-Omari, 2019, in his study to design his proposed vision for the role of Saudi university administrations in the transition towards sustainability, concluded that the role of university administrations towards the transition to sustainability is an average role that needs more effort and development.

Princess Nourah Bint Abdul Rahman University has shown a clear interest in this trend through its vision of promoting sustainability values and its great interest in environmental sustainability issues. This interest was indicated by the establishment of the environmental sustainability administration with the aim of supporting visions of the environmental sustainability, the rationalization of resources and their optimal utilization, health promotion, and waste management in the university environment. As well, it obtained the (Leadership in Energy and Environmental) or (LEED) gold global system certification for leadership in energy and environmental design, which contributed to its presence in the 138th rank among 780 universities around the world, and the second rank at the local level in the UI Green Metric University Rankings for the year 2019, and then it jumped to the 79th place for the year 2020 AD and the 71st place for the year 2021 AD (UI Green Metric, 2022). University colleges have a fundamental role in achieving the concept of sustainability in a comprehensive manner. In this regard, the College of Business and Administration is one of the major colleges that made great contributions. Accordingly, the research problem is summarized in examining the following basic hypothesis: The College of Business Administration at Princess Noura bint Abdul Rahman University meets the standards of the global system for tracking and evaluating sustainability STARS. The following hypotheses are derived from this main hypothesis:

- The College of Business and Administration has academic curricula and research that address sustainability issues.
- The College of Business and Administration shares with students and society issues of sustainability.
- The College of Business and Administration measures the impact of its administrative operations on sustainability.
- The College of Business and Administration links its administrative aspects with sustainability.
- The College of Business and Administration seeks to find innovative solutions to the challenges of sustainability.

3 METHODOLOGY

To achieve the objectives of the study, the descriptive survey method was used to access accurate and adequate data, and the current members of the teaching staff at the College of Business and Administration at Princess Noura bint Abdul Rahman University - who are 98 members - constituted the study community. (Princess Noura Bint Abdul Rahman University, December 2022).

4 THE STUDY TOOL

To achieve the objectives of the study, a special questionnaire was developed based on the Global Sustainability Tracking and Assessment System (STARS) indicator in version 2.2. The study tool comes in its final form in two main parts: the first of which is the main data of the sample: (the educational department, the practice of leadership work, the rank, the number of years of academic experience), while the second part is concerned with 43 statements that measure the point of view on the five criteria of the system, which are: Sustainability issues in curricula and academic research, sharing sustainability issues with students and society, the impact of operations on sustainability, planning and management, leadership and innovation. The questionnaire was presented to specialized academics in order to ascertain the apparent truthfulness, which is related to the structure of the phrases, their objectivity, and their linguistic structures, as well as the extent of their suitability for the individuals targeted by the study, so that, according to their opinions, the necessary adjustments are made. Finally, the approval of the Scientific Research Ethics Committee at Princess Noura University was issued to publish the questionnaire for the targeted sample.

5 RESULTS

To determine the method of response, the statements were constructed gradually based on the five-point Likert scale, for the purpose of informative enrichment and providing the opportunity to easily review what is related to the concept in design or use alike. And in order to adopt the criterion for judging, the response was given a degree at each gradual point in an ascending order. The following table illustrates this concept.

Degree	1	2	3	4	5
Gradation	Strongly disagree	Disagree	Agree to some extent	Agree	Strongly agree
Criterion	1=<1.80	1.81=<2.60	2.61=<3.40	3.41=<4.20	4.21=<5
Agreement Level	Very low	Low	Medium	High	Very high

In order to check the validity of the hypotheses of the study, the necessary tests were used by analysing the criterion phrases which results are explained (One Sample T-Test), so that the phrase is judged positive in the sense that the sample members agree on its content if the calculated (t) value is greater than the tabular (t) value or The level of significance is less than (0.05) and the relative weight is greater than (60%), while the expression is negative in the sense that the sample members refuse to agree on its content if the calculated (t) value is less than the tabular (t) value or the level of significance is greater than (0.05) and the relative weight is less than (60%).According to all of the above, the results are arranged as follows:

The first hypothesis: The College of Business and Administration has academic curricula and research that address sustainability issues

	T-Value	Significance Level	Arithmetic Mean	Standard Deviation	Relative Weight	Agreement Degree
The general arithmetic mean of (8) statements that measure the first sub-hypothesis	3.26	0.01	3.34	0.61	66.8	Agree to some extent

It is noted from the foregoing that the arithmetic mean of all the criterion statements is equal to (3.34), which is greater than the default mean of the study (3), and that the average effect ratio for all the criterion statements was (66.8%), in excess of the estimated relative weight of 60%, and the calculated (T) value (3.26), when its significance level is equal to (0.01), which is less than the calculated significance level of 0.05. Thus, the hypothesis of "The College of Business and Administration has curricula and academic research that addresses sustainability issues" is proven.

The second hypothesis: The College of Business and Administration shares with the students and the community issues of sustainability

	T-Value	Significance Level	Arithmetic Mean	Standard Deviation	Relative Weight	Agreement Degree
The general arithmetic mean of (9) statements that measure the second sub-hypothesis	3.00	0.01	3.30	0.59	66.0	Agree to some extent

It is noted from the foregoing that the arithmetic mean of all the criterion statements is equal to (3.30), which is greater than the default mean of the study (3), and that the average effect ratio for all the criterion statements was (66.0%), in excess of the estimated relative weight of 60%, and the calculated T value is (3.00), while the significance level is equal to (0.01), which is less than the calculated significance level of 0.05. Thus, the validity of the hypothesis that says, "The College of Business and Administration participates with students and society in issues of sustainability" is proven.

The third hypothesis: The College of Business and Administration measures the impact of its administrative operations on sustainability

	T-Value	Significance Level	Arithmetic Mean	Standard Deviation	Relative Weight	Agreement Degree
The general arithmetic mean of (10) statements that measure the third sub-hypothesis	3.33	0.00	3.37	0.67	67.4	Agree to some extent

It is noted from the foregoing that the arithmetic mean of all the criterion statements is equal to (3.37), which is greater than the default mean of the study (3), and that the average effect ratio for all the criterion statements was 67.4%, in excess of the estimated relative weight of 60%, and the calculated (T) value is (3.33), at a level of significance equal to (0.01), which is less than the calculated significance level of 0.05. Thus, the hypothesis that "the College of Business and Administration measures the impact of its administrative operations on sustainability" is valid.

The fourth hypothesis: The College of Business and Administration links its administrative aspects with sustainability

	T-Value	Significance Level	Arithmetic Mean	Standard Deviation	Relative Weight	Agreement Degree
The general arithmetic mean of (8) statements that measure the fourth sub-hypothesis	0.06-	0.95	2.99	0.72	59.8	Agree to some extent

It is noted from the foregoing that the arithmetic mean of all the criterion statements is equal to (2.99), which is close to the hypothetical mean of the study (3), and that the average effect ratio for all the criterion statements was (59.8%), not exceeding the estimated relative weight of 60%, and the calculated value of (T) is (0.06), which is less than the tabular (T) value and the significance level was (0.95), greater than the calculated significance level (0.05). Thus, the hypothesis that "the College of Business and Administration links its administrative aspects to sustainability" is rejected.

The fifth hypothesis: The College of Business and Administration seeks to find innovative solutions to the challenges of sustainability

	T-Value	Significance Level	Arithmetic Mean	Standard Deviation	Relative Weight	Agreement Degree
The general arithmetic mean of (8) statements that measure the fifth sub-hypothesis	4.10	0.00	3.52	0.75	70.4	Agree

It is noted from the foregoing that the arithmetic mean of all the criterion statements is equal to (3.52), which is greater than the default mean of the study (3), and that the average effect ratio for all the criterion statements was (70.4%), in excess of the estimated relative weight of 60%, and the calculated value of (T) is 4.10, at a level of significance equal to (0.01), which is less than the level of significance calculated at 0.05, thus proving the validity of the hypothesis of "The College of Business and Administration seeks to find innovative solutions to the challenges of sustainability."

The study reached a number of conclusions, the most important of which are:

- The members of the (administration) department represent the largest share of the study sample by (40%), and that (40%) of the faculty members in the college currently occupy leadership positions, and more than (57%) of them hold the academic rank of (assistant professor). While the results show that most of the study individuals have academic experience between (5-10) years, at a rate of (45.7%).
- The College of Business and Administration has academic curricula and research that address sustainability issues to some extent, according to the arithmetic mean of (3.34%). The highest extent is represented in several practices, including the facts that the college allows faculty members to cooperate with the public and private sectors to conduct research in the field of

sustainability, motivates them to include sustainability concepts in current academic courses, and encourages its postgraduate students to research in the areas of sustainability. While the shortcomings came in the same axis of (lack of a research chair specialized in sustainability, not granting different scientific degrees in an academic discipline related to sustainability, such as financial or organizational sustainability). The results of the hypothesis test (One Sample T-Test) for the axis show the calculated (T) value of 3.26, at a level of significance equal to (0.01), which is less than the calculated significance level of 0.05. Henceforth, it is clear that the hypothesis stating that "The College of Business and Administration has academic curricula and research that address sustainability issues" is correct.

- The results of the study revealed that the college engages students and the community to a moderate degree in sustainability issues with an arithmetic mean of (3.30), and that the most prominent forms of participation are that the college organizes conferences, scientific seminars, forums, and general educational lectures in the areas of sustainability. Its topics are included in the plans of its extracurricular activities. Moreover, the college has community partnerships with government and civil agencies in the field of sustainability. While there is still a need to make more efforts in the field of issuing publications that promote sustainable learning and knowledge, periodic evaluation of female students and educational staff about their awareness of sustainability issues and challenges, and conducting awareness competitions in the field of sustainability and its practices. The results of the hypothesis test (One Sample T-Test) for the axis show the calculated (T) value of 3.00, at a level of significance equal to (0.01), which is less than the calculated significance level of 0.05. Thus, it is clear that the hypothesis stating that "The College of Business and Administration participates with female students and society in issues of sustainability" is correct.
- The study showed the approval of the members of the teaching staff of the college to measure the impact of its administrative operations on sustainability with an arithmetic average of (3.37) with several practices, including adopting mechanisms to reduce the volume of waste, and smart technologies to save energy such as turning on and off lights automatically. While the college did not adequately adopt the most sustainable means of transportation, and the activities supporting the adoption of the concept of sustainability in food systems and avoiding waste in it. The results of the hypothesis validity test (One Sample T-Test) for the axis show the calculated (T) value of 3.33, at a level of significance equal to (0.01), which is less than the calculated significance level of 0.05. From the foregoing, it is clear that the hypothesis stating that "The College of Business and Administration measures the impact of its administrative operations on sustainability" is correct.
- With regard to the extent to which the college links its administrative aspects to sustainability, the results showed varying degrees of approval of the study respondents regarding the standard statements, as the approval rates ranged to some extent between 3.49% and 2.51% on all the phrases of the axis except (the structure of the college includes an administrative unit for sustainability). The results of the hypothesis test (One Sample T-Test) for the axis show the calculated T value of (0.06), which is less than the tabular (T) value, and the level of significance reached (0.95), which is greater than the calculated level of significance (0.05). Thus, rejecting the hypothesis that states that "The College of Business and Administration links its administrative aspects to sustainability."
- The members of the teaching staff unanimously agree that the college seeks to find innovative solutions to the challenges of sustainability, with an arithmetic mean of (3.52) in several practices, most notably the presence of encouragement and motivation from the college leaders for its employees to innovate and invent in work performance, employing assistive technologies to create sustainable ideas, and targeting them to achieve a competitive advantage than any other business school. College leaders allocate enough time to study new ideas. The results of the hypothesis test (One Sample T-Test) for the axis show the calculated value of (T) as 4.10, at a level of significance equal to (0.01), which is less than the level of significance calculated at 0.05. Sustainability."

The study recommendations:

Based on the previous results, the study recommends the following:

- Seeking help from experts, academics and specialists to develop academic programs in the field of sustainability.
- Including the concept of sustainability in the curricula of cooperative projects, small businesses and entrepreneurship, and activating sustainable thinking in commercial and social projects.
- Activating more partnerships and research cooperation with other business schools locally and globally, as well as research centres in the field of sustainability.
- Addressing the concept of sustainability in research from an Islamic perspective and highlighting the similarity between the ethical values of Islam and the foundations of sustainability.
- Educating and training college employees by holding courses and workshops and signing agreements with local and international institutes for training in the field of sustainability.
- Inclusion of voluntary initiatives and movements serving sustainability issues in the annual activity plan.
- Preparing the Sustainability Experts Program at the College of Business and Administration, SESPM, which contributes to achieving the goals of the United Nations for sustainable development.
- Establishing the Green Administrative Sciences Award, emphasizing the importance of sustainability science in the business world.
- Launching the Confront Sustainability competition by monitoring cases that impede the adoption of sustainability and proposing solutions to confront them.
- Creating an executive administrative unit that deals with sustainability affairs and requirements at the college level, in coordination with the Sustainability Department of the Agency for Facilities and Operation, so that the latter assumes the tasks of supervision and follow-up.
- Building a special index to measure sustainability (Sustainability Index) at the college level, similar to the international indicators in the same context, with the aim of periodic evaluation of the mechanism of the transformation towards a sustainable college.
- Creating an integrated guide dealing with sustainability in business, sustainability in higher education, and its most important concepts such as defining the concept, types, areas of application, measuring the impact of application as part of spreading the culture of sustainability to the faculty and its external community.
- Adopting policies and regulations for sustainability practices and the mechanism of adherence to them and following up on that commitment.
- Adopting the Green Assessment - by granting part of the evaluation of the employee's performance or the student's academic achievement - on the basis of responding to environmental issues, community services, or sustainability growth initiatives.
- Applying the study to other faculties at Princess Noura bint Abdul Rahman University to consider the extent to which they meet the STARS global system requirements on campus.
- Carrying out more future studies in organizational and financial sustainability, and at the level of business schools, as it is a modern and fertile field for research.

The theoretical and applied contributions of this study

Despite the availability of research and studies that dealt with measuring the degree of university transformation towards sustainability in various countries of the world, to the best of the researchers' knowledge, there are no studies that fill the research gap in this context in the Arab region. Therefore, this study constitutes a contribution to the enrichment of Arab libraries in general and Saudi libraries in particular, by adding a qualitative study of sustainability in the field of higher education and business.

This study also contributes to the consolidation of the concept of sustainability in universities through the actual measurement of sustainability in the light of an international standard for its evaluation. It also measures sustainability in business colleges, unlike its predecessor, which measures the orientation of university systems as a whole towards sustainability. It is expected that the results of this measurement and the implementation of the recommendations of the study will contribute to motivating decision-makers to transform Saudi universities from a traditional university to a sustainable one in order to achieve its efficiency and contribute to achieving the Kingdom's Vision 2030, in which the concept of sustainability is its most prominent goal and the basis for many of its programs and initiatives. The study is also based on a supportive guide for universities shifting from the traditional to the sustainable approach, issued by an organization with a legal personality (Association for the Advancement of Sustainability in Higher Education AASHE). In addition to shedding light on the study of the STARS system in the universities of the Kingdom of Saudi Arabia, unlike the previously targeted studies in the United States of America and Canada, in conjunction with the scarcity of studies in the Arab region in the same matter, especially Saudi Arabia, where the STARS 2022 system included the two local universities of KAUST and Prince Sultan bin Abdelaziz on the lists of international universities without any data on the category or version of the system.(STARS, 2023).

In addition, it is worth mentioning the possibility of identifying the reality of adopting the concept of sustainability from the point of view of faculty members through this study, as some studies indicated a lack of awareness of the importance of institutionalizing sustainability within the university campus and applying it in colleges, and the method of setting and controlling it is not known as in the study of (Lidstone et al., 2015), in addition to the fact that the researchers did not find any studies dealing with the role of leadership and faculty members in spreading a culture of sustainability within higher education institutions.

Finally, the study is comprehensive as it was built according to a five evaluation criteria for the STARS system, which dealt with all dimensions of higher education institutions related to sustainability (research and curricula, participation, operations, planning and management, leadership, and innovation), while the previous studies measured sustainability in investment, in operations, and in research and educational curricula separately as well as allocating the College of Administration and Business at Princess Noura bint Abdul Rahman University as a research community for measuring and analysing sustainability, as it was not allocated in this way in previous studies in the same field, which came with many measures with different results according to the type of colleges and their specializations.

REFERENCES

Al-Omari, Majid (2019). A proposed vision for the transformation of university administrations towards sustainability in the light of the experiences of international universities: The International Journal of Specialized Education, Volume (8), Issue 2.

Ministry of Higher Education. (2011). The future plan for university education in the Kingdom of Saudi Arabia. Retrieved from https://www.moe.gov.sa/ar/aboutus/aboutministry/Documents/StrategyArciveHE001.pdfAlshuwaikhat

Adenle Y., H., & Saghir B., (2016). Sustainability Assessment of Higher Education Institutions in Saudi Arabia: Sustainability 2016, 8, 750; doi:10.3390/su8080750.

The Sustainability Tracking, Assessment & Rating System. (2022). (STARS) is a transparent, self- reporting framework for colleges and universities to measure their sustainability performance. Available: https://reports.aashe.org/institutions/participants-and-reports/?sort=rating.

UI Green Metric (2022), Overall Rankings 2021 https://greenmetric.ui.ac.id/rankings/overall-rankings-2021

UI Green Metric (2022), Overall Rankings 2019 https://greenmetric.ui.ac.id/rankings/overall-rankings-2019

UI Green Metric (2022), Overall Rankings 2020 https://greenmetric.ui.ac.id/rankings/overall-rankings-2020

United Nation Environment Programme. (2022). About UN Environment Programme. Available: https://www.unep.org/about-un-environment.

Lidstone L, Wright T, Sherren K. (2015). An analysis of Canadian STARS-rated higher education sustainability policies. Environment, Development and Sustainability 17(2): 259–278. doi:10.1007/s10668-014-9598-6

Kamal A., Asmuss M. (2012). Benchmarking tools for assessing and tracking sustainability in higher educational institutions. Identifying an effective tool for the University of Saskatchewan: International Journal of Sustainability in Higher Education Vol. 14 No. 4, 2013 p. 449–465 q Emerald Group Publishing Limited 1467-6370 DOI 10.1108/IJSHE-08-2011-0052.

Urbanski M., & Filho W. (2014). Measuring sustainability at universities by means of the Sustainability Tracking, Assessment and Rating System (STARS): early findings from STARS data: Environ Dev Sustain (2015) 17:209–220 DOI 10.1007/s10668-014-9564-3
United Nations Environment Program. (January 2023). UNEP Sustainable University Framework. Retrieved from: https://www.britishcouncil.dz/sites/default/files/un_ar_toolkit-2022.pdf.
Princess Nora bint AbdulRahman University. (January 2023). Sustainable development at Princess Noura bint Abdul Rahman University. Retrieved from: https://www.pnu.edu.sa/ar/Pages/Estadama.aspx
Princess Nora bint AbdulRahman University. (January 2023). Data and statistics of the College of Business and Administration. Retrieved from: https://www.pnu.edu.sa/ar/Faculties/Management/Pages/Statisticsanddata.aspx
Princess Nora bint AbdulRahman University. (January 2023). Teaching staff members. Retrieved from: https://www.pnu.edu.sa/ar/Faculties/Management/BachelorofBusinessAdministration/Pages/Facultymembers.aspx?slrid=666f89a0-e709-300c-7321-252b6ded777b
Vision 2030. (January 2023). A sustainable Saudi vision. Retrieved from: https://www.vision2030.gov.sa/ar/v2030/a-sustainable-saudi-vision/

Digital Synergy – El Emary et al. (eds)

Chapter 16
Foreign direct investment and competitiveness in the 21st century: A systematic literature review

El Bouch Hajar & Abdellaoui Mohammed
University Sidi Mohammed Ben Abdellah Fès, Morocco

Contents

The purpose of this paper is to analyze current research work, both in English and French, on the thematic of "Foreign direct investment and competitiveness".

To this end, we carried a bibliometric study using a mixed approach with a search on the SCOPUS portal, in the form of a systematic literature review. In this respect, we analyzed the content of 107 publications between the period 2020 and 2023.With the aim of presenting the main research work in this area, our methodology is based on a double analysis: a descriptive analysis of 107 articles and a thematic analysis of 5 articles. Our analysis generated multiple scientific landscapes using both IBM SPSS Statistics 27.0 and Nvivo softwares. The results of our review show the main findings in the literature. Indeed, we were able to collect the main factors contributing to the explanation of the link between foreign direct investment and competitiveness.

In summary, the article provides a systematic review of the literature of the key concepts of our research thematic, being to our knowledge one of the first studies to be done on this topic.

Finally, this document acts as a guide for further studies on this field of research.

1 INTRODUCTION

Foreign direct investment (FDI) is at the heart of the debate on globalization because of its role in the growth of international trade (Tathhira & Ashar 2019). In fact, as part of their opening-up to the global economy, emerging and developing countries have adopted a number of policies to attract foreign direct investments (FDIs) (Činčikaitė & Meidute-Kavaliauskiene 2023) due to the benefits FDIs can have on host countries in terms of: infrastructure enhancement, transfer of know-how, job creation, technological advancement and innovation etc. (Anastassopoulos, G. (2007). In order to ensure their international competitiveness, countries implement various strategies, including but not limited to enhancing the business environment, sustaining macroeconomic growth, and impoving labor market efficiency (Clipa, 2011). Competitiveness becomes then a central preoccupation for the host countries (Nguyen et al. 2023).

DOI: 10.1201/9781003440406-16

In this context, our research problem is formulated in the following central question: "To what extent can scientific research explain the link between foreign direct investment and competitiveness?"

In order to answer our research question, our work will be organized as such: Introduction, overview of the literature review, data analysis methodology, presentation of the results including the main bibliographic findings and finally, the conclusion.

2 OVERVIEW OF THE LITERATURE REVIEW

The extensive body of literature on foreign direct investment has consistently highlighted the significance of FDIs for both developed and developing countries. It has been widely acknowledged that FDI inflows play a vital role in stimulating economic progress in host countries (Dinh et al. 2019). In addition to fostering capital accumulation, foreign direct investments (FDIs) have the potential to enhance productivity through increasing competition, creating job opportunities, facilitating the transfer of technology, and fostering the development of human capital (Tsinaridze et al. 2022).

According to the academic literature of the 50s and 60s, FDI was perceived as having a negative impact on the economies of less developed countries. In recent decades however, we have observed a change of perception towards FDIs due to the beneficial impact they can have on recipient nations (Kok & Acikgoz Ersoy, 2009). In fact, starting from the 1980s, there was a substantial increase in FDI flows primarily originating from developed nations.

Furthermore, in recent years, there has been a notable rise in FDI flows from emerging countries to developed nations. This emerging trend has significantly impacted the global landscape, prompting numerous research studies to explore the connection between competitiveness indicators and foreign direct investment. It is now widely recognized that competitiveness plays a crucial role in driving economic advancement, particularly in developing and emerging economies heavily reliant on foreign direct investments (Cristina & Cantemir 2012). This underscores the significance of competitiveness as a key determinant of FDI attractiveness.

3 DATA ANALYSIS METHODOLOGY

The aim of this document is to explain the link between foreign direct investment and competitiveness. In order to accomplish this, we utilized the Scopus Portal, a reputable database that indexes local and global academic journals (Carrera-Rivera et al., 2022). The applied filters consisted of scholarly- reviewed articles in French or English, specifically open access academic papers. The keywords searched were: foreign direct investment, and competitiveness, separately and jointly.

For the purpose of analyzing the data, we have adopted a blended approach based on quantitative and qualitative analysis techniques. The quantitative analysis was conducted using IBM SPSS Statistics 27.0, The objective of this approach is to identify the characteristics of the articles studied by generating frequency tables and univariate statistics, thereby providing a comprehensive description of the data, and thus allowing us to make a breakdown analysis by type of document, year of publication, and number of citations, as well as an analysis of the chronological progression of topics.

The quantitative approach was complemented by a qualitative analysis performed using Nvivo software, the primary objective of this qualitative analysis is to conduct a lexical analysis by word frequency in order to identify the key concepts prevalent in scientific research. This analysis generates a word cloud that highlights concepts with a high frequency of occurrence, providing an initial overview of the overall research subjects' trends.

We then proceeded to conduct a content analysis to assure a comprehensive understanding of the overall context of the 5 selected articles by identifying their main findings.

4 PRESENTATION AND ANALYSIS OF THE RESULTS

We conducted a search for scientific articles on the Scopus website to gather our data on the following concepts: (Foreign direct investment, and competitiveness) on the Scopus scientific portal, and were then provided with the following data:

Table 1. Used keywords in the research.

The keywords used in the research		
Thematics	Total number of articles found on Scopus	Total after reading the abstract
Foreign direct investment	379	47
Competitiveness	318	47
Foreign direct investmentand competitiveness	32	13

Source: by ourselves.

Based on our search of articles according to keywords representing the key concepts of our study and once the themes have been sorted out according to their relevance to our research subject., 107 of these documents published between 2020 and 2023 were examined in this study.

Table 2. Characteristics of the items.

Characteristics of the items					
		Frequency	Percent	Valid Percent	Cumulative Percent
Valid	2020	38	34,9	34,9	34,9
	2021	22	20,2	20,2	55,0
	2022	47	43,1	43,1	98,2
	2023	2	1,8	1,8	100,0
	Total	109	100,0	100,0	

Source: generated by IBM SPSS Statistics 27.

The chosen papers are primarily scientific articles indexed on the Scopus portal. These papers address themes that incorporate concepts such as: (foreign direct investment, competitiveness, foreign direct investment and competitiveness) published mainly during the year 2022. In fact, during the year 2020, 34,9% of the articles were published followed by 20,2% in 2021, then 43,1% in 2022 and finally 1,8% in 2023.

Table 3. Number of citations of articles.

Number of article citations	Mean	Median	Count	Standard Deviation	Minimum	Maximum
Cited by	5,68	2,00	109	11,95	0	98

Source: generated by IMB SPSS Statistics 27.

The majority of the processed articles served as a research reference for at least 6 scientific works. The analysis of the citation counts per article indicates a median value of 2, which indicates that 50% of the analyzed articles were referenced by more than 2 scientific works published on Scopus.

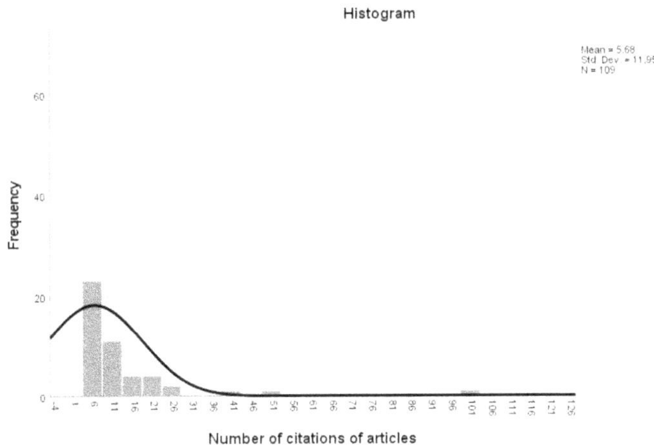

Figure 1. Number of citations of articles (Generated by IMB SPSS Statistics 27).

The histogram represents the results obtained from the table of citation numbers shown above. It is evident from the histogram that over 20 articles have been cited in more than 20 scientific research works, with some articles surpassing 100 citations.

Table 4. Distribution of articles by themes.

Distribution of articles by themes					
		Frequency	Percent	Valid Percent	Cumulative Percent
Valid	Competitive ness	47	43,1	43,1	43,1
	Foreign direct investment	49	45,0	45,0	88,1
	Foreign direct investment and competitiveness	13	11,9	11,9	100,0
	Total	109	100,0	100,0	

Source: generated by IBM SPSS Statistics 27.

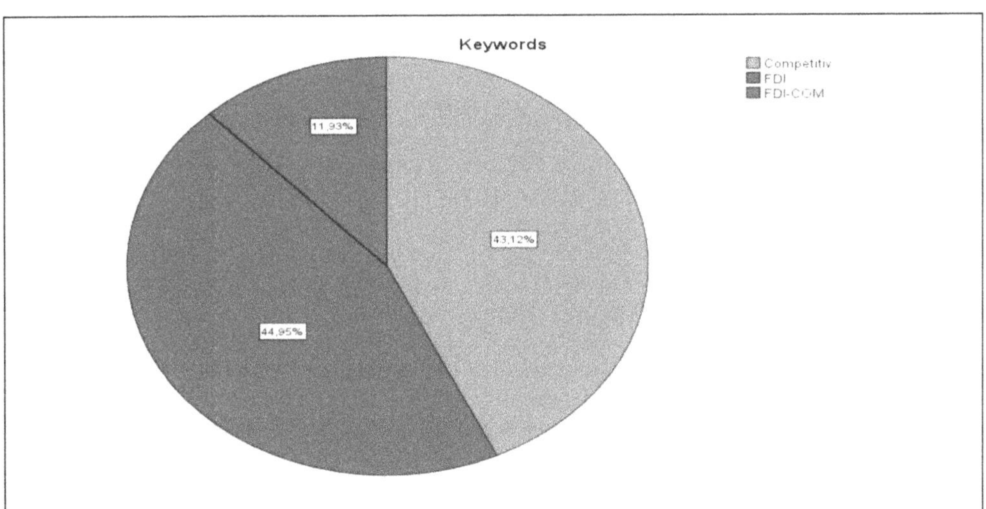

Figure 2. Distribution of articles by keywords (Generated by IBM SPSS Statistics 27).

The chosen articles are categorized into three research themes: (Competitiveness), (foreign direct investment), (foreign direct investment and competitiveness).

Our article database consists of 47 documents related to the topic of competitiveness, along with 47 articles addressing foreign direct investment. In addition, there are 13 clauses dealing with the intersection of foreign direct investment and competitiveness.

The pie chart shows the distribution of key words. Foreign direct investment figures in the articles with a pourcentage of 44,95%, followed by competitiveness with 43,12% and lastly (FDI and competitiveness) with 11,93%.

The pie chart illustrates the distribution of keywords in the articles. Foreign direct investment represents 44.95%, competitiveness follows closely with 43.12%, and the combination of FDI and competitiveness accounts for 11.93%.

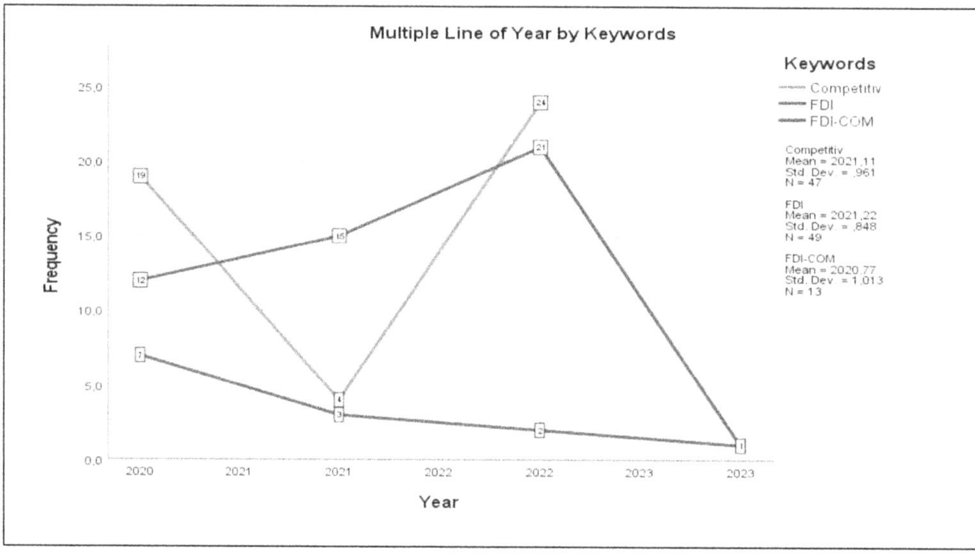

Figure 3. Temporal evolution of the theme (Generated by IBM SPSS Statistics 27).

The comparative analysis of the temporal evolution of articles addressing different concepts has clearly demonstrated that the year 2022 witnessed the highest number of publications on the topics of both "foreign direct investment" and "competitiveness".

Regarding the "foreign direct investment" theme, we have a total of 47 articles, out of which 12 were published in 2020 and 21 in 2022. However, there was a slight decrease in publications related to this theme in the year 2021.

Regarding the "competitiveness" theme, we have a total of 47 articles, with 19 published in 2020 and 24 in 2022. However, there was a decrease in publications related to this theme in the year 2021.

The themes related to "foreign direct investment and competitiveness" contain a total of 13 articles, distributed as follows: 7 articles in 2020, 3 articles in 2021, 2 articles in 2022, and 1 article for the year 2023. This temporal evolution indicates a decrease in research activity on these three themes in recent years, especially in 2022 and 2023.

The keyword cloud reveals that the terms: "FDI," "countries," "growth," "investment," and "competitiveness", are the most frequently mentioned in the reviewed documents. This result indicates that the concept of "foreign direct investment and competitiveness" is extensively addressed in the examined articles, highlighting its significance as a fertile research area within the fields of economics and management. Furthermore, we noticed the pervasive occurrence of the year 2022 as a standout period in the progression of works on FDI and competitiveness, as indicated by the prominent presence of related keywords.

Figure 4. Word cloud (Generated by Nvivo 12).

Table 5. The word frequency in articles.

Word	length	number	Ponderated percentage (%)
fdi	3	258	1,53
foreign	7	179	1,06
investment	10	173	1,02
study	5	150	0,89
countries	9	149	0,88
direct	6	133	0,79
growth	6	115	0,68
economic	8	114	0,67
competitive	11	94	0,56
business	8	91	0,54

Source: generated by Nvivo 12 pro

The word frequency table highlights the most frequently occurring words in the articles. We have chosen to present the first relevant words from the list, which include: FDI, foreign, investment, study, countries, direct, growth, economic, competitive, and business.

In order to complete our thematic analysis, we will present a synthesis of the main ideas emerging from our literature review, this synthesis is summarized in three ideas declined as follows:

(1) First idea: The direct link between FDI and competitiveness is not as commonly treated in research articles, which might explain the amount of articles (5) we chose that deal with this thematic.

(2) Second idea: The results section of our 5 articles shows that the relationship between FDI and competitiveness is treated through the lense of different disciplines (mainly economics and management). The methodology tools are diversified due to the nature of the topic which might be a challenge for our future research works, as it is important to choose the most adequate methodology to treat our subject. It's also worth mentioning that in order to

Table 6. Main bibliographic findings.

Authors/Year / Journal	Country	Research question	Methodology	Results
Huo, D., Chen, Y.,Hung, K., Song, Z.,Guan, J., & Ji, A. (2020). Economic Research- Ekonomska Istraživanja.	Emerging Markets	How do spatial effects resulting from geographic economic factors influence the export competitiveness of agriculture in emerging markets? [11]	Diamond Model	The spatial effects observed across different emerging markets have a substantial impact on the competitiveness of agriculture in those markets.
Latorre, M. C., Olekseyuk, Z., & Yonezawa, H. (2020). The World Economy	United Kingdom	What is the contribution of service multinational enterprises (MNEs) to global trade and their impact on the economy?[12]	General equilibrium model	The impact of barriers to (FDI) is deemed more significant than barriers to international trade in the overall decrease of service varieties in the UK following Brexit.
Tang, Q., Xie, E., & Reddy, K. S. (2022). International Journal of Innovation Studies,	China	What benefits does the global production aspirations of state-owned enterprises, such as outward foreign direct investment, bring to their country of origin?	The study adopts a co- evolutionary approach when examining the development of a state-driven aspiring industrialized economy.	The involvement of state-owned enterprises in outward foreign direct investment (FDI) can strengthen their competitive advantage and contribute to the prosperity of their home countries.
Pazilov, G. A., Bimendiyeva, L. A., Ivashchenko, N. P., & Aitymbetova, A. N.(2020). Polish Journal of Management Studies.	Kazakhstan	Is it essential to take into account the current state of the textile industry in Kazakhstan and strategies aimed at enhancing innovation within textile enterprises? [14]	Literature review	Implementing methods aimed at fostering innovation within textile enterprises has the potential to positively impact the advancement of the textile industry in Kazakhstan.
Bayar, Y, Remeikiene, R., Androniceanu, A., Gaspareniene, L., Jucevicius, R. (2020). Journal of competitiveness.	11post- transition EU members	How does the presence of informal economies and the level of human development affect the inflow of foreign direct investment, and can they be regarded as potential factors shaping competitiveness?	Compaative and systematic literature analysis, combined with second- generation panel cointegration and causality analyses.	While informal economies negatively affected the inflow of foreign direct investment, human development exerted a positive influence on FDI inflows.

Source: by ourselves

measure competitiveness and especially country competitiveness factors, most articles use the global competitiveness Index (GCI) among other indicators. The main questions treated in the articles are related to issues such as: FDI and economic growth, the role of multinationals in international trade and it's impact on the economy, the impact of geographic factors on the competitiveness of an industry, the state owned enterprises' competitive strategies as well as the competitiveness being an important determinant for the attractiveness of FDI.

(3) The fact that we were able to identify such a low number of articles treating the link between FDI and competitiveness might be an opportunity, since we can explore different angles under which we can treat our research topic.

5 CONCLUSION

The objective of this study was to perform an initial analysis of the scientific literature in English and French pertaining to the topics of foreign direct investment and competitiveness. To achieve this, a bibliometric study was conducted utilizing searches in SCOPUS databases. After document selection, a final sample of 107 articles was chosen as the basis for statistical analyses, while 5 articles were identified for content analysis.

Our literature review first examined trends in scientific publications on the subject. We then found out that most of the research works deal with issues related to the impact of FDI on economic progress, the role of multinationals in global trade and it's impact on the economy, the impact of geographic factors on the competitiveness on an industry, the state owned enterprises strategies as well as the competitiveness being an important determinant for the attractiveness of FDI . We can notice the diversification of the topics of the articles selected, this indicates that the our research topic can be treated by different disciplines (mainly management and economics), the 5 articles selected show that searching for the link between FDI and competitiveness, it is more likely to find articles on attractiveness of FDI that treat partially the competitiveness which might be explained by the competitiveness being a component of attractiveness.

Nevertheless, the scarcity of studies on this topic presents a research opportunity to generate further scientific investigations and contribute to the advancement of this theme. Conducting research to validate theoretical studies and incorporating alternative research methodologies would enrich the field. In this work, we confined ourselves to articles in English and French. Therefore, future research could explore other languages and employ additional data processing tools to attain even more sophisticated outcomes.

The results of this work testify to the specificity of our topic that requires more attention from researchers.

REFERENCES

Anastassopoulos, G. (2007). Countries' International Competitiveness and FDI: An Empirical Analysis of Selected EU Member-Countries and Regions.

Carrera-Rivera, A., Ochoa, W., Larrinaga, F., & Lasa, G. (2022). How-to conduct a systematic literature review : A quick guide for computer science research. MethodsX, 9, 101895.

Činčikaitė, R., & Meidute-Kavaliauskiene, I. (2023). Assessment of Attractiveness of the Baltic States for Foreign Direct Investment: The TOPSIS Approach. Journal of Risk and Financial Management, 16(2), 63.

Clipa, P. (2011). Competitiveness Through Foreign Direct Investment. SSRN Electronic Journal.

Cristina, P. O., & Cantemir, C. A. (2012). Competitiveness as determinant of foreign direct investments in central and eastern european countries. Revista Economică, 1.

Dinh, T. T.-H., Vo, D. H., The Vo, A., & Nguyen, T. C. (2019). Foreign Direct Investment and Economic Growth in the Short Run and Long Run : Empirical Evidence from Developing Countries. Journal of Risk and Financial Management, 12(4), 176.

Huo, D., Chen, Y., Hung, K., Song, Z., Guan, J., & Ji, A. (2020). Diamond model and the export competitiveness of the agriculture industry from emerging markets : An exploratory vision based on a spatial effect study using a genetic algorithm. Economic Research- Ekonomska Istraživanja, 33(1), 2427–2443.

Kok, R., & Acikgoz Ersoy, B. (2009). Analyses of FDI determinants in developing countries. International Journal of Social Economics, 36(1/2), 105–123.

Latorre, M. C., Olekseyuk, Z., & Yonezawa, H. (2020). Foreign multinationals in service sectors : A general equilibrium analysis of Brexit. The World Economy, 43(11), 2830–2859.

Nguyen, Phi-Hung, Thi-Ly Nguyen, Hong-Quan Le, Thuy-Quynh Pham, Hoang-Anh Nguyen, et Chi-Vinh Pham. « How Does the Competitiveness Index Promote Foreign Direct Investment at the

Provincial Level in Vietnam? An Integrated Grey Delphi–DEA Model Approach ». Mathematics 11, n° 6 (19 mars 2023): 1500.
Pazilov, G. A., Bimendiyeva, L. A., Ivashchenko, N. P., & Aitymbetova, A. N. (2020). Textile industry: issues of managing the growth of innovative activity in enterprises. Polish Journal of Management Studies, 21(1), 297 315.
Tang, Q., Xie, E., & Reddy, K. S. (2022). Global production aspirations and internationalization by state-owned enterprises: A Co-evolutionary view of state-driven industrialized economy. International Journal of Innovation Studies, 6(4), 276–285.
Tathhira, M. I., & Ashar, K. (2019). Comparative Analysis of the Impact of Competitiveness to Foreign Direct Investment (FDI) Inflows between Indonesia and Vietnam.
Tsinaridze, R., Batumi Shota Rustaveli State University, Batumi, Georgia, Makharadze, N., & Batumi Shota Rustaveli State University, Batumi, Georgia. (2022). The role of foreign direct investment in the national economy and correlation analysis. Access Journal - Access to Science, Business, Innovation in the Digital Economy, 4(1), 46–59.
Usak University, Bayar, Y., Remeikiene, R., Mykolas Romeris University, Androniceanu, A., Bucharest University of Economic Studies, Gaspareniene, L., Mykolas Romeris University, Jucevicius, R., & Vilnius Gediminas Technical University. (2020). The Shadow Economy, Human Development and Foreign Direct Investment Inflows. Journal of Competitiveness, 12(1), 5 21.

Digital Synergy – El Emary et al. (eds)

Chapter 17
Investment in human capital and economic growth

Chamchoune Hind
PhD student in Management Science, LIREFMO Research Laboratory FSJES University Sidi Mohamed ben Abdellah, Fès, Morocco

Abdellaoui Mohammed
University Sidi Mohamed ben Abdellah, Fès, Morocco

Contents

The overarching objective of this article is to analyze scientific production regarding the behaviour of Investment in human capital and economic growth., in English and French, on A mixed-method bibliometric study was conducted using the SCOPUS portal for data collection. This research has synthesized the key findings and identified gaps in the literature concerning this topic, presenting them in a comprehensive summary table.

1 INTRODUCTION

This research holds significant scientific importance as it addresses the critical role of human capital as a key determinant of economic growth within the framework of the knowledge society and the globalized economy.

Countries that invest effectively in human capital tend to be more competitive, attract more foreign direct investment, and prosper economically in the long term.

To what extent can current scientific production be used to understand the impact of investment in human capital to contribute to economic growth?

To address our research question, and considering its relevance in the field of organizational studies, we consulted the SCOPUS database. The structure of this study includes an introduction, a theoretical section covering the key aspects of the impact of investment on human capital and economic growth, research methods, presentation and analysis of the results, and conclusions.

2 REVIEW OF LITERATURE

The establishment of human capital has been recognized as a developmental aim, serving as a primary driver of economic growth, reduction of poverty, and achievement of various developmental objectives.

Human capital encompasses the quantifiable knowledge and skills possessed by individuals, which hold economic value. This extends beyond mere qualifications, including aspects such as health, nutrition, and hygiene, particularly in the context of developing countries (16).

DOI: 10.1201/9781003440406-17

Economic growth is characterized by the long-term rise in real gross domestic product (GDP), reflecting an increase in economic output adjusted for inflation. It should be distinguished from short- term expansions within a business cycle, which refer to temporary increases in GDP (2).

3 AN ADVANCED METHODOLOGY

The aim of this scholarly study is to elucidate behavioral patterns by leveraging the Scopus Portal, a comprehensive and widely recognized database indexing both national and international journals. The search was conducted using the keywords "Investment," "Human capital," and "Economic growth."

During the search process, we implemented various filters to ensure the inclusion of peer-reviewed articles published in French or English, specifically scientific articles. The methodology employed in this study is classified as a mixed-method approach, as it incorporates both quantitative and qualitative investigations were conducted.

The process of statistical analysis was executed employing IBM SPSS Statistics 25 software This method was utilized to generate a comprehensive descriptive summary of the data, utilizing Tabulations of frequencies and descriptive statistics to determine the properties of the studied publications. A comprehensive examination was performed, encompassing the classification of articles based on document type, publication year, and citation count. Additionally, a temporal analysis was conducted to investigate the evolution of the covered themes over time.

The statistical analysis was enhanced by a qualitative study using Nvivo software. The purpose of this analysis was to conduct a lexical examination based on word frequency, aiming to identify the primary concepts that have been the subject of scientific research. This analysis generated a word cloud that highlights concepts with a significant occurrence, providing an initial overview of the prevailing research subjects.

Subsequently, a comprehensive presentation of the results was conducted to gain a comprehensive understanding of the broader context surrounding to examine each concept individually and pinpoint the key aspects ideas advanced by scholarly researchers. This analysis also facilitated the presentation of the research methodologies employed in the respective studies (3).

4 PRESENTATION AND ANALYSIS OF RESULTS

We conducted an extensive search for scientific articles on the research platform, Scopus, with the aim of gathering relevant data pertaining to the concepts of: economic growth, human capital and investment in human capital & economic growth.

Table 1. Keywords used in the research.

Key words	Total count of articles available in Scopus	Count of selected items
human capital	604	57
economic growth	495	57
investment in human capital & economic growth	31	12

Source: ourselves.

After searching for articles on the concepts related to our research topic, we organized and sorted the themes according to their relevance. This approach allowed us to identify 27 articles published between 2021 and 2023, the characteristics of which are presented in the table below.

Table 2. Annual publication percentage.

		Frequency	Percent	Valid Percent	Cumulative Percent
Valid	2021	20	29.0	29.0	29.0
	2022	34	49.3	49.3	78.3
	2023	15	21.7	21.7	100.0
	Total	69	100.0	100.0	

Source: produced under IBM SPSS Statistics 27.

The selected documents primarily consist of finalized research research articles that are listed in the Scopus platform. These articles delve into subjects that incorporate notions including: (human; capital); (economic; growth); (investment; human capital & economic growth) Primarily published during the year 2022, whit 29 % in 2021 then 49.3 % in 2022 and 21.7 % in 2023.

Table 3. Number of citations of articles.

	Mean	Median	Count	Standard Deviation	Minimum	Maximum
Cited by	6.16	2.00	69.00	11.38	1.00	69.00

The majority of the papers reviewed were referenced in minimum 6 scientific papers The statistical analysis of the citation count for each article demonstrates a median value of 2, indicating that 50% of the analyzed articles were cited in over 2 scientific publications released on Scopus.

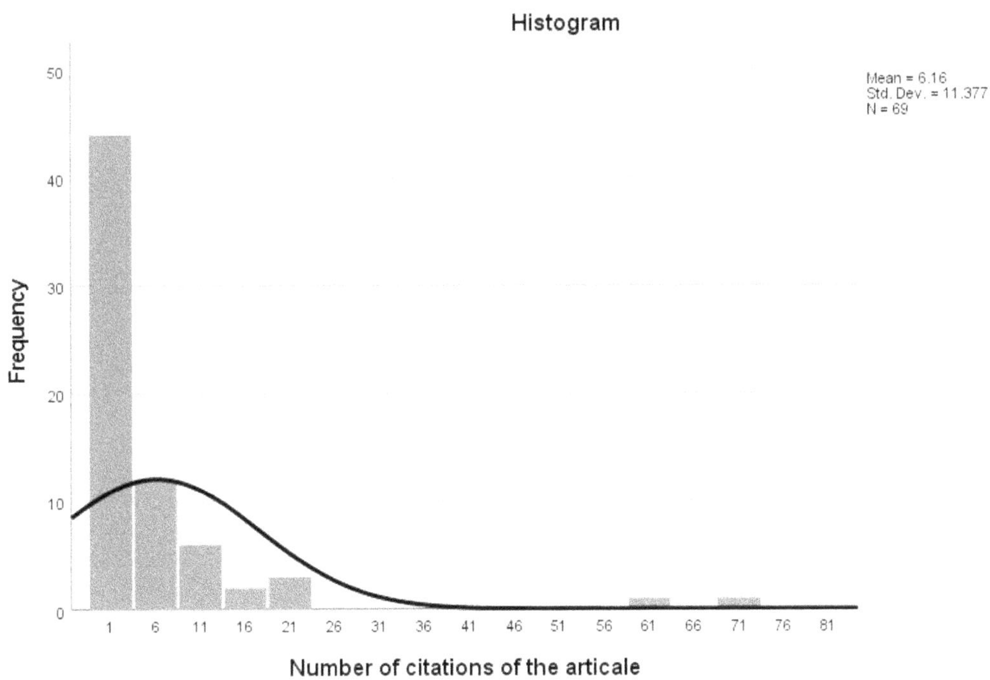

Figure 1. Number of citations of articles.
Source: Produced under IBM SPSS Statistics 27

The histogram illustrates the data from the previously presented table, specifically depicting the distribution of the number of citations. Evidently, over 45 articles have garnered citations in more than 60 scientific papers, with certain articles surpassing 71 publications.

Table 4. Distribution of articles by theme.

		Keywords			
		Frequency	Percent	Valid Percent	Cumulative Percent
Valid	Economic growth	32	46.4	46.4	46.4
	Human capital	29	42.0	42.0	88.4
	investment in human capital and economic growth	8	11.6	11.6	100.0
	Total	69	100.0	100.0	

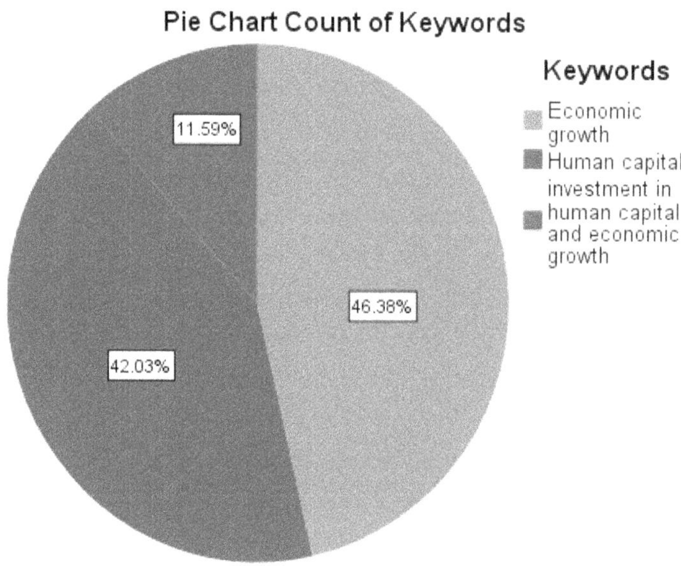

Figure 2. Distribution of articles by theme.
Source: produced under IBM SPSS Statistics 27.

The chosen articles have been categorized into three research themes, namely: (Human, capital), (Economic, growth), (Investment, human capital & economic growth).

Our database consists of 57 documents focusing on the subject of economic growth, alongside 57 articles addressing the concept of human capital, and a further 12 articles specifically examining investment in human capital & economic growth. A substantial portion of the research was conducted in 2021, followed by a notable decline in research activity on these themes beyond that period.

By analyzing the content of the abstracts of the 126 papers, we were able to identify the recurring concepts frequently employed in these papers, along with gaining an understanding of the overarching research context.

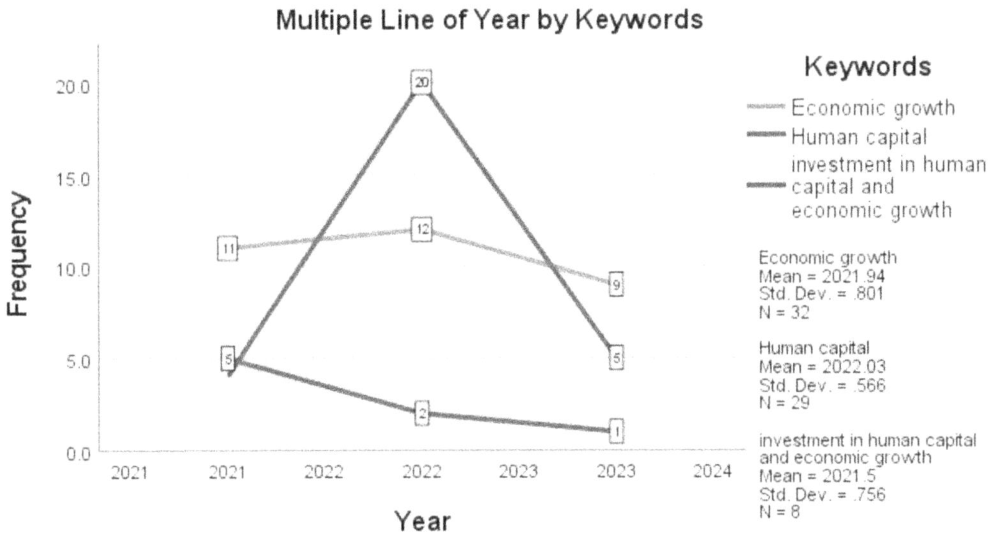

Figure 3. Temporal evaluation of the theme.
Source: Produced under IBM SPSS Statistics 27

The comparative examination of the chronological progression of publications addressing diverse notions has revealed in 2022 stands out as the most prolific in terms of publications on the topics of Human capital. Using the chronological curves, we observed that the 5 papers on the theme of human capital were all published in 2021, with 20 publications on this theme in 2022 and 5 publication in 2023.

As for the theme "economic growth", we have 32, 11 of which we published in 2021, 12 in 2022 and 9 in 2023.

On the investment in human capital & economic growth theme, we identified a total of 8 articles, 5 in 2021, 2 in 2022 and one published in 2023.Considering the current year of 2023, we observe a relatively modest presence of articles across the three themes.

Figure 4. Keywords Cloud.
Source: produced under NVivo 12.

Analysis of the keyword cloud reveals that the terms "economic", "growth", "capital", "Human", "Development", are consistently identified as the most frequently cited among the examined documents. This finding underscores the significant emphasis placed on the concepts of economy, growth, and investment in human capital within the analyzed papers, signifying their pivotal role in the dynamic realm of research related to economics and management. Taking a closer look at the most frequently employed.

5 PRESENTATION OF RESULTS

Table 5. Bibliographic summary of articles consulted.

Author/Year/ Paper	Country/ Region	Research aim	Methodology	Results
Vijaya Kumar (2022) Economic Affairs. All rights reserved.	India	The article delineates the constituents of human capital development & elucidates their influence on the rivalrous progress of the state.	Quantitative methods: The study is founded on the annual temporal data collected from a longitudinal series of observations 2005 to 2019	These results indicate that the effective exploitation of human capital has potential to stimulate economic development and enhance workforce efficiency in India. Given the country's substantial demographic dividend, it becomes crucial to create ample skill-oriented employment options for the current and future workforce, while also providing appropriate training to the existing labor force. Such measures present a viable approach to optimize the utilization of human capital.
Kozhyna Razina Kravchenko Kuprii Melnyk (2022) Economic Affairs (New Delhi)	Ukraine	Analysis intends to determine Ukraine's primary directions for developing human capital in the context of post-war reconstruction.	The approaches of analysis and Integration, comparison, induction, and deduction were also used within the experimental analysis	Based on the study's findings, Based on the available evidence (5).
Innocenti S.; Golin M. (2021) Journal of Economic Behavior and Organization	16 countries	The purpose of this article is to assess the influence of, workers' perceived risk of joblessness resulting from digitization on their intention to allocate resources towards enhancing human capital	Quantitative method: By utilizing innovative survey, data obtained via representative working population samples. in 16 countries	The findings strongly indicate a positive association between intentions to acquire fresh competencies and perceived threats associated with automation.

(Continued)

Table 5. (*Continued*)

Author/Year/ Paper	Country/ Region	Research aim	Methodology	Results
Dadd D.; Hinton M. (2022) International Journal of Productivity and Performance Management	United Kingdom	Objective: The purpose of this study is to examine the increasing utilization alternative financial measures, such as profitability ratios, for performance measurement and assessment of investments in human capital (HC).	Quantitative method	research findings highlight three key points. Firstly, the interpretation of return on investment (ROI) can be ambiguous during implementation. Secondly, it is essential to understand and assess the impact of human capital by considering the subjects' cognitive, emotional, and psychomotor domains of functioning. Finally, alternative approaches focus on measuring changes in individuals' behavior resulting from the intervention.

Source: ourselves.

6 CONCLUSION

The objective of this article was to investigate the scientific output within the domains of investment in human capital and economic growth, with a specific focus on articles published in English and French. To accomplish this aim, a bibliometric approach was employed, which involved conducting searches in the SCOPUS database. Following the selection of relevant results, a final sample of 126 articles was chosen, forming the basis for the analyses presented in this study.

The objective of this study was to analyze the evolution of scientific publications in the field and identify opportunities for improvement in this area of research. The findings reveal that the majority of studies primarily concentrate on issues related to inequality and the tools to promote increased business opportunities, as well as the dissemination of knowledge and technology. Additionally, the inadequacy of skills was identified as another significant focus of research.

This analysis highlights the significance of addressing inequality in various aspects of society, such as access to education, healthcare, and economic opportunities. It underscores the need to develop effective tools and strategies to bridge the gaps and promote equal opportunities for all individuals. Furthermore, the importance of skill development and aligning them with the demands of the labor market is emphasized.

Based on these findings, future research in this field can explore innovative approaches to tackle inequality, propose effective mechanisms to enhance business opportunities, and develop strategies to improve skills matching and reduce skill gaps. By addressing these areas of concern, policymakers and stakeholders can work towards creating a more inclusive and prosperous society, fostering sustainable economic growth and development.

REFERENCES

Crise et faire société sur la planète: un inédit à inventer Avec Vanessa Casadella, Bérangère L. Szostak Dans Marché et organisations 2022/1 (n° 43)

Youness BOUDOHAY, et Abdallah SADIK. « Les organisations de l'économie sociale et solidaire et le développement local : Une revue de littérature systématique par la méthode PRISMA », 31 janvier 2023. https://doi.org/10.5281/ZENODO.7581842.

Ait Benhamou, Zouhair, et Lesly Cassin. « The Impact of Remittances on Savings, Capital and Economic Growth in Small Emerging Countries ». *Economic Modelling* 94 (janvier 2021): 789–803. https://doi.org/10.1016/j.econmod.2020.02.019.

Enilov, Martin. « The Predictive Power of Commodity Prices for Future Economic Growth: Evaluating the Role of Economic Development ». *International Journal of Finance & Economics*, 24 avril 2023, ijfe.2821. https://doi.org/10.1002/ijfe.2821.

Goodfriend, Marvin, et John McDermott. « The American System of Economic Growth ». *Journal of Economic Growth* 26, n° 1 (mars 2021): 31–75. https://doi.org/10.1007/s10887-021-09186-x.

Innocenti, Stefania, et Marta Golin. « Human Capital Investment and Perceived Automation Risks: Evidence from 16 Countries ». *Journal of Economic Behavior & Organization* 195 (mars 2022): 27–41. https://doi.org/10.1016/j.jebo.2021.12.027.

Jin, Cheng, Asif Razzaq, Faiza Saleem, et Avik Sinha. « Asymmetric Effects of Eco- Innovation and Human Capital Development in Realizing Environmental Sustainability in China: Evidence from Quantile ARDL Framework ». *Economic Research- Ekonomska Istraživanja* 35, n° 1 (31 décembre 2022): 4947–70. https://doi.org/10.1080/1331677X.2021.2019598.

Krieger, Alexander, Michael Stuetzer, Martin Obschonka, et Katariina Salmela-Aro. « The Growth of Entrepreneurial Human Capital: Origins and Development of Skill Variety ». *Small Business Economics* 59, n° 2 (août 2022): 645–64. https://doi.org/10.1007/s11187-021-00555-9.

M., Vijaya Kumar, et Balu B. « Estimating the Impact of Human Capital Underutilization on the Productivity and Economic Growth in India ». *Journal of the Knowledge Economy*, 10 avril 2023. https://doi.org/10.1007/s13132-023-01152-9

Nomaler, Önder, Danilo Spinola, et Bart Verspagen. « R&D-Based Economic Growth in a Supermultiplier Model ». *Structural Change and Economic Dynamics* 59 (décembre 2021): 1–19. https://doi.org/10.1016/j.strueco.2021.07.002.

Pfister, Ulrich. « Economic Growth in Germany, 1500–1850 ». *The Journal of Economic History* 82, n° 4 (décembre 2022): 1071–1107. https://doi.org/10.1017/S002205072200033X.

Santos Silva, Manuel, et Stephan Klasen. « Gender Inequality as a Barrier to Economic Growth: A Review of the Theoretical Literature ». *Review of Economics of the Household* 19, n° 3 (septembre 2021): 581–614. https://doi.org/10.1007/s11150-020-09535-6.

Shen, Chengfang, et Xindong Zhao.«How Does Income Inequality Affects Economic Growth at Different Income Levels? » *Economic Research-Ekonomska Istraživanja* 36, n°. 1 (31 décembre 2023): 864–84. https://doi.org/10.1080/1331677X.2022.2080742. « How Does Income Inequality Affects Economic Growth at Different Income Levels? » *Economic Research-Ekonomska Istraživanja* 36, n°. 1 (31 décembre 2023): 864-84. https://doi.org/10.1080/1331677X.2022.2080742.

RAPPORT SUR LE CADRE DE L'OCDE POUR UNE CROISSANCE INCLUSIVE; REUNION DU CONSEIL DE L'OCDE AU NIVEAU DES MINISTRES PARIS, 6–7 MAI 2014

Digital Synergy – El Emary et al. (eds)

Chapter 18
Managing civil servants sustainability competencies – conclusion for global challenges

Marzena Walasik & Andrzej Stępnikowski
Łukasiewicz Institute for Sustainable Technologies, Radom, Poland

Contents

The aim of this article is to present the results of the OECD pilot programme Capacity Building Programme (CBP) for Polish public administration managers with regard to the implementation of the Sustainable Development Goals (SDGs) set in the 2030 Agenda. Given that, despite individual states and public authorities' strong commitment to work towards SDGs, 65% of the 169 SDG targets defined will not be achieved without close involvement of and proper coordination by regional and local authorities, the programme in question is particularly important, as it builds civil servants' awareness of and trains them in SDGs, making it easier for them to reach SDG targets. The results of the programme can also be used in industries and sectors other than the public sector.

1 INTRODUCTION

Faced with the current climate emergency and environmental crises, many countries have shifted their focus to sustainability in an attempt to meet citizens' growing needs for a better life, protect the planet for future generations, and ensure sound economic development. (Song Z, Tong P., 2022; Emina K. A, 2021; Aven T., 2020; UNESCO, 2020). There is a lack of a standard definition of sustainability or sustainable development in the literature. However, most commonly, authors refer to the definition coined by the UN Brundtland Commission (1987), according to which sustainability means "meeting the needs of the present without compromising the ability of future generations to meet their own needs." As a result of the growing awareness of the climate change, global warming and other critical issues, in 2015, 193 UN Member States adopted the 2030 Agenda for Sustainable Development, which covers three areas: economic, social and environmental, and indicates 17 Sustainable Development Goals (SDGs) with associated 169 targets to be met by the countries by the end of this decade. However, to successfully implement the 2030 Agenda, countries need to adopt a systemic approach focusing on interlinkages between goals and targets (Messerli P, Kim EM, Lutz W et al., 2019) and have sufficient knowledge about sustainability and SDGs.

According to the 2020 Sustainable Development Report by the United Nations, Poland ranked 23rd among 166 countries in the performance on SDGs, scoring 78.10%. The Polish

DOI: 10.1201/9781003440406-18

model for economic, social and spatial development, driven by major transition reforms and strong economic growth following the country's accession to the EU, seeks to increase the role of human and social capital as the basis for the development of its economy, and also to build strong industry and develop entrepreneurship (six regional starting platforms for new ideas are about to be launched by the end of this year to establish start-ups). Poland also strives to improve the state of the environment and sustainable management of resources (although there is always the "coal issue", even stronger after Russian invasion of Ukraine). The authorities try to ensure economic development and high quality of life, while guaranteeing development opportunities for future generations. Another objective for Poland is the socially sensitive and territorially sustainable development (East-West, North-South), characterised by a high level of employment, good quality jobs and intensified entrepreneurship development (Poland VNR, 2018).

Five years after the Paris Agreement, the Organisation for Economic Cooperation and Development (OECD) adopted a Roadmap and accompanying Action Plan to define the content and parameters of the planned Capacity Building Programme for Civil Servants in Poland to Deliver on the SDGs. It is based on the findings and recommendations outlined in the Diagnostic Report (OECD, 2021). Capacity building is defined as a process of gaining and increasing capabilities of organisations, individuals and societies to set and achieve goals over a specific period time. Each individual and each organisation has their own set of capabilities.

The Diagnostic Report is based on an in-depth assessment of Poland's institutional mechanisms for enhancing policy coherence for sustainable development (PCSD) carried out at the end of 2020. Key recommendations and findings include the necessity for further integration of the SDGs into all sectoral strategies and greater use of strategic foresight and analytical tools to foster coordination and collaboration between civil servants at national, regional, and local public bodies and stakeholders.

In the Polish context, the scope of the civil service is "rather narrow" as it encompasses only core governmental administration, while excluding, for example, the Chancellery of the Sejm (Polish Parliament) or Senate, customs or police officers, local government, etc. Such narrow scope of Polish civil service brings some challenges in terms of the attainment of SDGs.

2 CAPACITY BUILDING PROGRAMME – ASSUMPTIONS OF THE PILOT IN POLAND

The 2020 Europe Sustainable Development Report ranked Poland 16th (with the SDG performance at 69.9%) among 27 EU Member States, but in the newest version of the Report (2022), Poland ranks 13th (among 34 EU Member States) with the score of 72.4% (EU median of 72%) (URL: https://www.sdgindex.org/reports/europe-sustainable-development-report-2022/).

In general, the Report states that "deep SDG transformations within the EU require broad-based public support. Special attention is needed in Europe to address inequalities within countries and boost education and skills for sustainable development" (Diagnostic Report, pp. IX).

The key areas for strengthening Poland's recovery and sustainable growth are human capital, and going 'green', 'digital' and 'inclusive'. Green investing and containing demographic pressures, together with strengthened environmental policies and increased efficiency of health-related spending, are essential as well.

The so called Social Progress Index (SPI), compiled by the Social Progress Imperative, a US-based non-profit, measures how effectively countries and communities convert their resources into social and environmental outcomes that impact on the lives of people every day. The 2020 Social Progress Index aggregates 50 social and environmental outcome indicators from 163 countries (Poland ranks 31st among 163 countries in the SPI. In the 2022 SPI, Poland dropped to 39th). As the SPI captures outcomes related to all 17 SDGs, it also offers a proxy measure of SDG performance. Considering the total score and ranks, main focus areas for the nearest future may be Health & Wellness (74, 28, rank 46) and

Environmental Quality (80, 90, rank 71) – both areas with the lowest component scores in Foundations of Wellbeing dimension.

3 PILOT METHODOLOGY

The Capacity Building Programme aims to respond to the needs and preferences of potential users regarding forms of development and training. One of the main ideas was to combine online and offline training, as it is crucial to allow participants to gain theoretic knowledge, but also to facilitate interaction in groups to further shape attitudes and build competencies. Another important element of successful capacity building is appropriate follow-up with trainers and experts to broaden the knowledge or consult on specific topics of interest.

The aim was to improve the following SDG skills:

1. Understanding and advancing the 2030 Agenda in Poland;
2. Long-term and horizontal planning and policy integration for advancing the 2030 Agenda in Poland;
3. Multi-level governance and stakeholder involvement for advancing the 2030 Agenda in Poland;
4. Evidence-based policy making for advancing the 2030 Agenda in Poland;
5. Exercising holistic and value-based leadership for advancing the 2030 Agenda in Poland;
6. Managing and motivating teams for advancing the 2030 Agenda in Poland;
7. Professional training ('train the trainers') for advancing the 2030 Agenda in Poland.

Those challenges were divided into the following modules:

1. The 2030 Agenda and SDG implementation (in Poland);
2. Long-term and horizontal planning with policy integration (including foresight);
3. Public management at different levels and involvement of stakeholders;
4. Data-driven policy implementation;
5. Development of competencies of middle managers;
6. Development of competencies of upper-level managers;
7. Training the SDG trainers.

The CPB Pilot was carried out in Poland in 2021. The content of individual modules was developed and tested (except module 7 "training of trainers") at the participants and trainer's levels. Performance indicators were indicated for each module (based on the Likert scale, the minimum level for the pilot was set at 3.5, while for the implementation phase the minimum requirements were set at the level of 4.0 and recommendations were made.

4 PILOT IMPLEMENTATION

As a result of the COVID-19 pandemic, the course was taught only on an e-learning platform. For the purpose of the course, international experts were involved – they shared their experience in the implementation of sustainable development goals, such as:

a. surfacing megatrends (learning ways of framing and understanding megatrends and developing skills for refining our ideas about megatrends and exploring how they could evolve),
b. cross-impacting (learning ways of operationalising megatrends that may otherwise seem too broad to connect to day-to-day work, developing skills for approaching complex futures that are full of uncertainty);
c. transboundary impacts in Agenda 2030 (learning on the transboundary flows relevant to the assessment of transboundary impacts for Poland and developing conviction that we should monitor transboundary impacts in our work and build more agile capacity).

In general, the Pilot was well received as the e-learning course was not overloaded with information and many interactive tools were involved. During each workshop session participants were engaged in discussions (plenary and in break-out rooms), interactive tools were also used (e.g., Mentimeter and Mural). After sessions participants gave their feedback. Reactions were measured on 1–5 Likert scale for each part of the course – including the workshops.

Table 1. Assessment of the CBP Pilot implementation (n=33).

Selected performance indicators/Pilot results		**Module 1**	**Module 2**	**Module 3**	**Module 4**	**Module 5&6**	**General Reaction Indicators**
I.	**Workshop assessment**						
1.1	General satisfaction with the workshop	3.82	4.48	3.88	3.90	4.31	**4.08**
1.2.	Substantive content	4.06	4.69	3.88	4.00	4.38	**4.20**
1.3.	Trainers' attitude, preparation and ability to share knowledge	4.35	4.79	3.88	4.30	4.15	**4.29**
1.5.	Relevance of content to professional practice and its usefulness outside the job	3.76	4.18	3.25	3.60	3.92	**3.74**
II.	**E-learning course assessment**						
1.6.	General satisfaction with e-learning materials	3.88	4.21	3.50	3.60	3.85	**3.81**

Source: authors based on survey results

For the Pilot phase the goal was to have the minimum of 75% of participants with the minimum of 75% of satisfaction (3.5 points). In general, all module elements were assessed higher than 3.5 (although some individual assessments were lower), except "the attractiveness and interactivity of presentations", which was assessed by learners at the level of 3.496. One of the best assessed modules was the second one centred around foresight (which is desired to master for upper-level managers), here are some comments on that workshop: This workshop: "was intellectually stimulating","active and engaging exercises that might be useful at work", "dynamic form of workshop". In the e-learning content there should be more practical examples of foresight (opinion quite often given in evaluation forms), there is an expectation also for more interactive e-learning content. In general, most participants agreed that inclusion of such methods like brain storming, practical training courses with case studies and some introductory lectures was very interesting and effective (however, most participants regret that there were not any face-to-face meetings).

5 TRAINERS' PROFILE AND DEVELOPMENT OF THE COMMUNITY OF SDG TRAINERS

The Pilot showed that at the heart of future SDG trainers' competence profile we should introduce "competencies in sustainability" that serve as a base for the acquisition of other kinds of competencies (e.g. social or andragogical). Case studies – which illustrate concrete and practical experiences – were mentioned in Pilot evaluation forms as the most desired training method. Cambridge University scientists defined "competencies in sustainability" as „complexes of knowledge, skills, and attitudes that enable successful task performance and problem solving related to real-world sustainability problems, challenges, and opportunities" (Cambridge Institute for Sustainability Leadership). There are six key competencies in sustainability according to researchers from the Arizona State University and they are as follows:

1. Systems Thinking Competence
2. Futures Thinking (Anticipatory) Competence
3. Values Thinking (Normative) Competence
4. Strategic Thinking Competence
5. Interpersonal (Collaboration) Competence
6. Integrated Problem-Solving Competence which is the „meta-competence of meaningfully using and integrating the five key competencies for solving sustainability problems and fostering sustainable development" (static.sustainability.asu.edu).

At the beginning of 2022, the European sustainability competence framework (GreenComp) containing twelve SDG competences that are "the building blocks of the sustainability competence for all people" was published. Those competences are divided into four main areas, i.e.:

1. embodying sustainability values;
2. embracing complexity in sustainability;
3. envisioning sustainable futures; and
4. acting for sustainability.

These competences are interlinked and interconnected, and should be treated as parts of a whole. This GreenComp model implies that "sustainability as a competence" is made of 12 building blocks and we should encourage learners to acquire all 12 competences, but they do not need to be achieved at the highest levels of proficiency in all of them (Bianchi G. at al. 2022, pp. 14–15).

Candidates for future SDG trainers should acquire such a set of competencies (preferably) or some of them to be able to conduct at least one or some of five chosen sessions like "Introduction to the Capacity Building Programme", "Soft Skills for SDG implementation" or "Training design and managing SDG module training content". Additionally, they should be able to conduct training courses in the future with the most relevant methods like "story telling", including "good practices" and "success stories" as "the success of change also relies on the strong continuity of efforts across the government" (OECD 2021, p. 6).

SDG trainers must have all abilities connected to this field of professionalisation with strong experiences in the field of sustainability and SDGs' implementation – in different contexts. Civil servants learn their vocation and shape their attitudes walking the road of the professional mastery, where optimal results are achieved in the way of self-improvement. According to Prof. Kotarbiński, it is about "learning from other masters (predecessors) and then going a step ahead" (Tokar J. 2015, p. 232). Training of trainers in public administration is a programme that creates such an opportunity to develop professionally – taking the course of professional mastery and showing your abilities in the interdisciplinary (multifunctional) team.

6 CONCLUSION

The 2030 Agenda is a reflection of global challenges and measures to take to stop global warming and protect the planet for future generations. It also imposes on countries an obligation to achieve SDGs. This means that civil servants need to be properly trained in sustainability and SDGs and networks/communities of SDG Trainers supporting the implement of the 2030 Agenda objectives should be established. The experiences of middle and upper managers from public administration can be also used to develop sustainability-related competencies of managers in companies, higher schools (Lozano et al., 2017), local governments or associations. Civil servants are quite a specific group of professionals with certain abilities and responsibilities – with a similar range of responsibilities around the World; they are also deeply motivated and often driven by a concern for their country. As such, they are experts in their fields, as they have professional, personal, and social competencies required for their positions. However, it seems they do not always see their professional field of interest in the broader context of global challenges connected with other issues such as poverty, peace, environmental protection, water and energy safety, etc., which are pointed out in the SDGs.

People who will become trainers for such officials should know that they would work with professional civil servants who have high expectations also in the sphere of trainers' preparation (regarding substantive, andragogical, personal, and social competencies).

With reference to the trainers' competencies in the Capacity Building Programme context, there is a need to underline the importance of having professional-sustainable and personal-social skills, including those in the fields of pedagogy and andragogy. Trainers and their trainers – especially after COVID-19 – also have to master modern information technologies that will be used in the course or workshops (like Teams, Zoom, etc.).

REFERENCES

Aggarwal A. (2015). Recognition of prior learning: Key success factors and the building blocks of an effective system, International Labour Organization - ILO DWT for Eastern and Southern Africa and ILO Country Office for South Africa, Botswana, Lesotho, Namibia and Swaziland 2015

Bianchi G., Ulrike Pisiotis, Marcelino Cabrera (2022) "GreenComp. The European sustainability competence framework", Joint Research Centre, European Commission, Publications Office of the European Union, Luxembourg 2022

Aven, T. (2020). 'Climate Change Risk – What Is It and How Should It Be Expressed?' Journal of Risk Research 23 (11): 1387–404.

Emina, K. A. (2021). 'Sustainable Development and the Future Generations.' Social Sciences, Humanities and Education Journal 2 (1): 57–71

Dzebo A., Shawoo Z. (2023) Sustainable Development Goal interactions through a climate lens: a global analysis, Stockholm Environment Institute, SEI Report, Stockholm, February 2023.

Kirkpatrick J., Kirkpatrick W. (2015) "An introduction to the new World Kirkpatrick® Model", Kirkpatrick Partners-LLC, Newnan GA

Lozano, R., Merrill, M. Y., Sammalisto, K., Ceulemans, K., & Lozano, F. J. (2017). Connecting competences and pedagogical approaches for sustainable development in higher education: A literature review and framework proposal. Sustainability, 9(10), 1889.

Messerli P, Kim EM, Lutz W et al. (2019). Expansion of sustainability science needed for the SDGs. Nat Sustain 2:892–894.

Mezirow J. (2009). "Transformative Learning Theory" [in:] Mezirow J. & E. W. Taylor (Eds.), "Transformative Learning in Practice: Insights from Community, and Higher Education" (pp.18–32), San Francisco, CA: Jossey-Bass.

OECD (2021a). Diagnostic Report – Poland. Design of 'Capacity Building Programme for Public Administration to support the implementation of the Sustainable Development Goals', REFORM/IM2020/004, OECD, Paris 2021.

OECD (2021b). Draft roadmap and action plan – Design of "Capacity Building Programme for Public Administration to support the implementation and carrying out of actions for the SDGs and sustainable development, OECD, Paris 2021.

Song Z, Tong P. (2022) The Impact of Environmental Regulation on Human Sustainable Development: Evidence from China. Sustainability. 2022; 14(19):11992. https://doi.org/10.3390/su141911992

Stępnikowski A.W. (2022). „Guidebook for Training of sustainable development goal's trainers", OECD, Paris 2022.

UNESCO (2020). Education for Sustainable Development, Paris, France, ISBN: 978-92-3-100394-3

NETOGRAPHY

https://sdgs.un.org/
https://www.un.org/en/desa/products/un-desa-databases
https://www.socialprogress.org/global-index-2022-results/
ecampus.itcilo.org
cisl.cam.ac.uk

Digital Synergy – El Emary et al. (eds)

Chapter 19
An analysis of skill growth through project-based learning activities

Yukio Kodono
Kindai University, Osaka, Japan

Contents

This research investigated whether essential skills can be improved through Project-Based Learning (PBL) activities. Previous studies have already established that PBL experiences can lead to improved essential skills. However, given the variety of projects that can be undertaken using PBL, the development of essential skills in these activities may vary. Therefore, this study compared and examined the data obtained from questionnaire surveys conducted before and after PBL activities, targeting members of a university seminar. The survey results were then analyzed to compare the development of essential skills between team and individual settings. Furthermore, factor analysis was conducted to investigate how the elements necessary for PBL activities are classified into factors. Ultimately, this research aims to provide a clearer understanding of how essential skills can be developed through PBL and how this may vary depending on the nature of the project and the dynamics within the team.

1 INTRODUCTION

PBL (Project-Based Learning) has gained attention as an important educational method in modern education because it allows individuals to acquire problem-solving skills, collaboration skills, communication abilities, and other skills that are essential in real-world society. Since 2008, the author has implemented PBL in their seminar to cultivate teamwork skills and foster individual growth through active learning. To measure individual growth through PBL, the following methods can be considered:

1. Evaluation based on outcomes: In PBL, students actively work on problems and create tangible outcomes. Evaluating these outcomes can measure students' growth in problem-solving abilities, communication skills, etc.
2. Evaluation based on the process: In PBL, the process through which students tackle problems is also crucial. By observing and evaluating students' actions and thinking during the process, their critical thinking skills, collaboration, and other aspects can be measured.
3. Self-evaluation: Students can promote self-growth through self-evaluation. To facilitate self-evaluation, it is necessary to provide students with self-evaluation forms or questionnaires and opportunities to evaluate themselves.
4. Portfolio: Creating a portfolio that combines the outcomes produced in PBL and records of students' processes allows for quantitative measurement of their growth and progress. Additionally, portfolios serve as valuable resources for job hunting or further education.

DOI: 10.1201/9781003440406-19

Furthermore, these methods can be combined to measure growth through PBL. However, since PBL exhibits significant individual differences, careful considerations are necessary when measuring growth. When measuring growth through self-evaluation, it is essential to establish appropriate questions or items for self-evaluation. This study focused on the 12 competency elements of social competency. While previous reports [1] have addressed individual and team growth, this study primarily focuses on factor analysis. Additionally, a study [2] has been conducted to explore the difference in social competency development between team sports and mainly individual sports, with a focus on the development of social competency through sports.

Social competency, proposed by the Ministry of Economy, Trade, and Industry (Japan) in 2006, refers to fundamental abilities required for working with diverse individuals in the workplace and local communities. It consists of three competencies and twelve competency elements. In the current era known as the 100-year life, the importance of social competency has increased, requiring perspectives and approaches unique to the 100-year life era.

Considering this context, in the 2017 fiscal year, the concept of Social Competency in the 100-Year Life Era was newly defined to emphasize the skills necessary for individuals to continue playing an active role at each stage of their extended engagement with companies, organizations, and society. While maintaining the three competencies and twelve competency elements, it was positioned as essential to balance self-awareness, reflection, and the integration of goals, learning, and synthesis to pave the way for one's own career advancement [3]. The three abilities of social foundational skills are the power to take initiative, the power to think through issues, and the ability to work in a team. These twelve competency elements of social competency include the powers to take steps forward;, such as initiative, proactive engagement and execution ability. They also encompass the power to think through issues, such as problem identification, planning ability, and creativity. Additionally, they encompass the powers to work in a team, such as effective communication, active listening, adaptability, situation awareness, discipline, and stress management.

2 POSITIONING AND OBJECTIVES OF THE INITIATIVE

The educational philosophy of Kindai University is practical education and cultivation of character. Through the seminar (Comprehensive Exercise I) in the third year, education based on this educational philosophy is conducted. In the Faculty of Business Administration, there are departments of Business Administration, Commerce, Accounting, and Career Management. The seminar is open to students from all departments, and every year, students from all departments gather. The number of third-year students in this academic year is 29. The theme of the seminar is Project Management - Development of Project Execution Skills and Social Business Foundation Skills through PBL Activities. It should be noted that the number of seminar students in 2008 was about 10 students. Figure 1 shows the composition of the research laboratory in the 2022 academic year.

In the 2022 academic year, there were initially six (from 4 to 6 members each team) teams for the projects. However, three additional projects were introduced during the year, resulting in a total of nine teams (from 1 to 9 members each team). In addition to the project teams, there were also six teams (initially five members each team) for business plans. Due to the increase in project teams, the business plan teams were dismantled and reorganized into two teams (5 members each team). As a result, some students who were initially assigned to one project team and one business plan team ended up with two project teams and no business plan team.

Furthermore, within the faculty's curriculum, there are courses such as Project Management Theory and Management Science, which are effectively utilized.

The objective of PBL in the seminar is to provide practical application of theoretical knowledge and specialized knowledge learned through lectures and exercises in the Faculty of Business Administration. By actively engaging in problem-solving through PBL activities, the aim

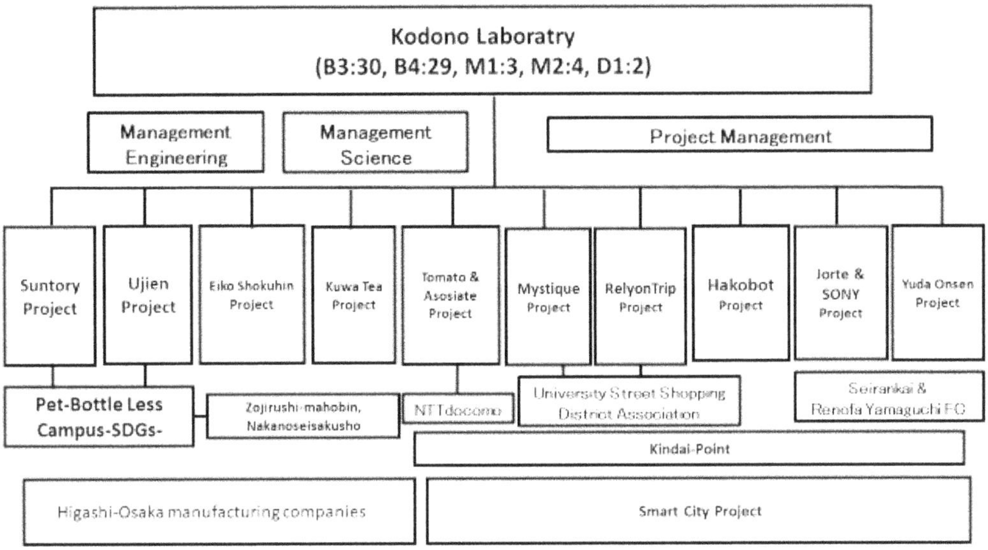

Figure 1. Composition of the research laboratory.

is to cultivate individuals who can utilize their experiences, problem-solving abilities, and teamwork skills in society.

3 RESULTS AND DISCUSSION OF THE SURVEY

Before conducting PBL activities, a brief explanation of the 12 ability elements of social business foundation skills was provided to the seminar participants through a distributed document. Surveys were conducted in December 2021, prior to the start of the project, and in December 2022, after the completion of the project. The surveys used a 10-point scale (1 for not engaging, 10 for fully engaging) to measure the participants' level of engagement with the skills. While PBL activities may not be considered a significant matter, please refer to the literature[4],[5] that utilizes the Likert scale to measure each question item.

Here are some parts of individual results shown in Figure 2 and Figure 3. Additionally, the average scores of the project teams are presented in Figure 4 and Figure 5.

In Figure 2, Student N belongs to Team A shown in Figure 4, while Student T belongs to Team B shown in Figure 5. Both Student N and Student T serve as project leaders, and they show more growth in various aspects after the project compared to

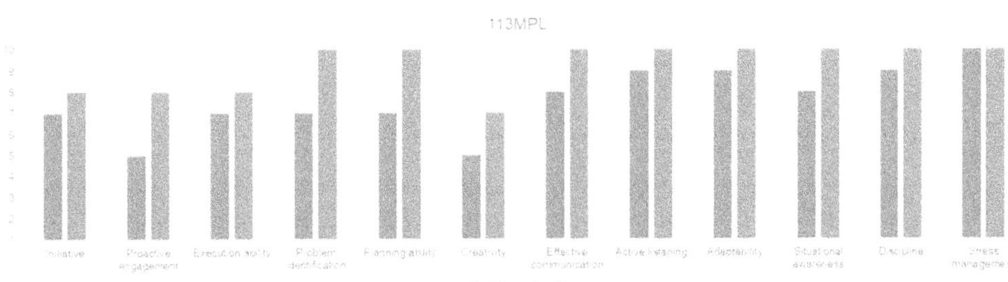

Figure 2. Student N.

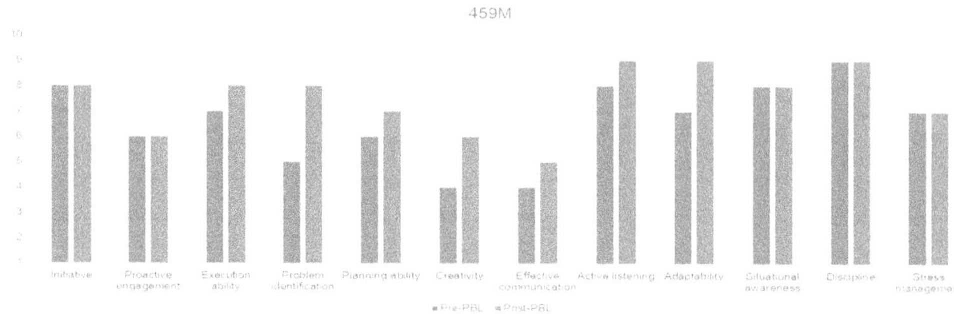

Figure 3. Student T.

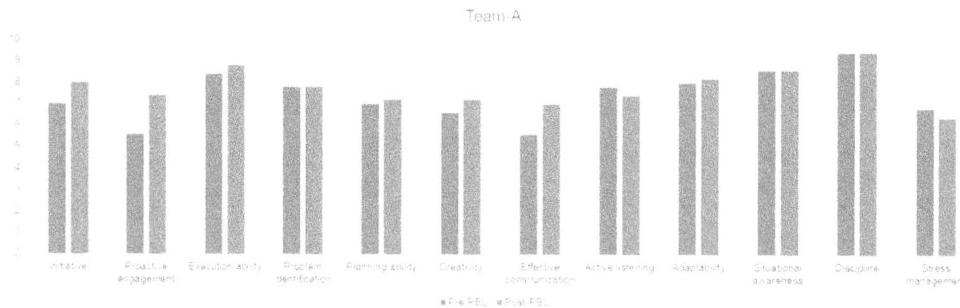

Figure 4. Average of Team A.

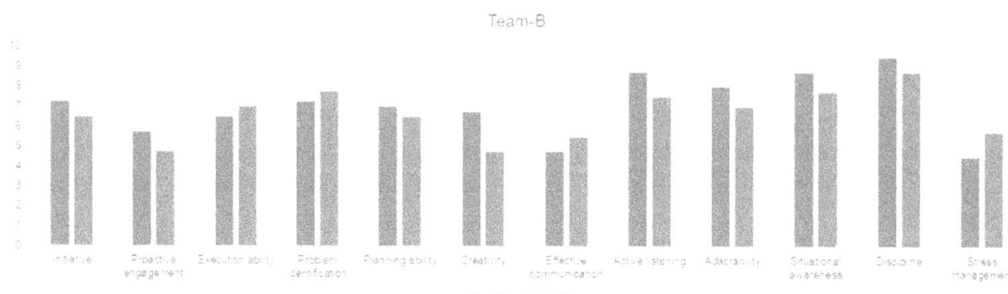

Figure 5. Average of Team B.

before. Furthermore, Team A in Figure 4 demonstrates noticeable improvement, while Team B in Figure 5 exhibits a decrease in several elements. It could be attributed to the ambiguity inherent in self-evaluation through the survey, but it can also be interpreted as follows:

Both Team A and Team B have completed the project, and their deliverables have received certain evaluations. Team A had a duration of 10 months, while Team B had a duration of 6 months. Upon observing both teams, Team A has developed into a highly cohesive unit, whereas Team B appears to have communication gaps within the team. In terms of team building, the Tuckman model [6] is well-known, and all teams have experienced the following five stages in their team activities:

Stage 1: Forming

In this initial stage, team members come together and get acquainted. They are often polite and cautious as they try to understand their roles and responsibilities within the team. There is a sense of uncertainty and members rely on the leader for guidance.

Stage 2: Storming

In the storming stage, conflicts and disagreements may arise as team members start asserting themselves and expressing their individual opinions and ideas. Power struggles and differences in working styles can create tension within the team.

Stage 3: Norming

During the norming stage, the team begins to establish norms, rules, and shared values. Members develop a sense of cohesion and cooperation. They start to recognize each other's strengths and weaknesses and work together more effectively.

Stage 4: Performing

The performing stage is characterized by a high level of productivity and cooperation within the team. Members have established trust and communication flows smoothly. They work towards achieving common goals and produce high-quality results.

Stage 5: Adjourning

This stage refers to the phase where a team disbands or completes its task. It involves the wrapping up of activities, reflecting on accomplishments, and transitioning to new endeavors or individual pursuits.

Therefore, Team A has reached Stage 4, while Team B seems to be in either Stage 2 or Stage 3, indicating a realization of their own skill deficiencies.

A questionnaire survey was conducted before the project activities in December 2021, obtaining data from 30 individuals. After the completion of the project in December 2022, a questionnaire survey was conducted again, and data from 23 individuals were obtained. Using these data, factor analysis was performed.

First, the Kaiser-Meyer-Olkin (KMO) test and Bartlett's sphericity test were conducted using the data from before the project activities. The results are shown in Table I. As can be seen from Table 1, the KMO value is 0.695, which exceeds the threshold of 0.6, indicating that the data is suitable for factor analysis. Additionally, the Bartlett's sphericity test ($p < 0.05$) passed, suggesting that the data is appropriate for factor analysis.

Table 1. KMO and bartlett's sphericity test.

KMO		0.695
Bartlett's sphericity test	*Approximate Chi-square*	234.491
	p-value	0.000***

Factor analysis extracted three factors with eigenvalues greater than 1. The cumulative contribution rates of these three rotated factors were 29.902%, 19.878%, and 11.067%, respectively, resulting in a cumulative contribution rate of 60.846% after rotation. The analysis results are presented in Table 2.

Social competency consists of initiative, proactive engagement, and execution ability which are the powers to take steps forward; problem identification, planning ability, and creativity which are the powers to think through; and effective communication, active listening, adaptability, situation awareness, discipline, and stress management, which are the powers to work in a team. Therefore, in factor analysis, it was expected that each element would be separated into these three powers. However, as a result, three new powers emerged.

They are the first factor, Ideal Leader; the second factor, Ideal Follower; and the third factor, Ideal Team Member. The term ideal was used because it is based on the questionnaire survey conducted before starting the project. It is believed that the ideals of the project leader

Table 2. Factor analysis.

Ability Element	Factor 1	Factor 2	Factor 3	Communality
Initiative	0.821	0.097	0.050	0.686
Proactive Engagement	0.815	-0.003	-0.204	0.706
Execution Ability	0.582	0.035	0.381	0.485
Problem Identification	0.673	0.301	0.367	0.679
Planning Ability	0.648	0.509	0.132	0.696
Creativity	0.588	-0.092	-0.360	0.484
Effective Communication	0.063	0.712	-0.265	0.581
Active Listening	-0.106	0.885	0.043	0.797
Adaptability	0.229	0.794	0.218	0.730
Situational Awareness	0.722	0.067	-0.075	0.532
Discipline	0.078	0.079	0.709	0.515
Stress Management	0.309	0.291	-0.479	0.410

(initiative, proactive engagement, execution ability, problem identification, planning ability, creativity, situation awareness), project manager (planning ability, effective communication, active listening, adaptability), and project team members (discipline, stress management) are reflected in these factors.

Next, the results of the KMO test and Bartlett's sphericity test for the 23 individuals after the project activities in December 2022 are shown in Table 3.

From Table 3, the KMO value is 0.488, which is below the threshold of 0.6 required for factor analysis. This indicates that the data cannot be used for factor analysis due to insufficient data. However, the Bartlett's sphericity test ($p < 0.05$) passed, suggesting that the data is suitable for factor analysis.

Table 3. KMO and bartlett's sphericity test.

	KMO	0.488
Bartlett's sphericity test	*Approximate Chi-square*	142.252
	p-value	0.000***

Factor analysis extracted three factors with eigenvalues greater than 1. The cumulative contribution rates of these three rotated factors were 26.562%, 25.994%, and 12.346%, resulting in a cumulative contribution rate of 64.903% after rotation. The analysis results are presented in Table 4.

From Table 4, three new powers emerged among the 12 elements of social competency. They are the first factor, Leader; the second factor, Follower; and the third factor, Team Member. Since Table IV represents the results of the questionnaire conducted after implementing the project, the data's authenticity is considered to have increased as respondents answered the questions based on their actual project experience.

Based on the factor analysis results, project leaders require initiative, proactive engagement, execution ability, problem identification, planning ability, creativity, and situation awareness. Followers (sub-leaders) need problem identification, planning ability, effective communication,

Table 4. Factor analysis.

Ability Element	Factor 1	Factor 2	Factor 3	Communality
Initiative	0.895	-0.003	0.085	0.809
Proactive Engagement	0.881	0.062	0.273	0.855
Execution Ability	0.584	-0.003	-0.418	0.516
Problem Identification	0.202	0.703	-0.340	0.651
Planning Ability	0.378	0.714	-0.060	0.657
Creativity	0.643	0.176	0.514	0.709
Effective Communication	-0.010	0.734	-0.018	0.540
Active Listening	-0.317	0.830	0.224	0.839
Adaptability	0.149	0.850	0.024	0.745
Situational Awareness	0.725	0.122	0.028	0.541
Discipline	-0.067	0.322	-0.572	0.435
Stress Management	0.136	0.104	0.679	0.491

and adaptability. Project team members are influenced positively by creativity and stress management and negatively by execution ability and discipline.

The Japan Management Association states the following about leaders, members, and followers in their research report on Member Behavior and Roles in Organizations and Teams [7].

"Members are the human resources that serve as the infrastructure (foundation) supporting both leaders and followers in an organization or team. In this sense, leaders and followers are differentiated functional roles that emerge from members. Members do not exist in isolation. By combining leader's 'leadership' (appropriate and effective influence) and each individual's 'followership' (complementary interpretation and translation of the leader), members can exert their power, leading to synergistic effects through teamwork."

Therefore, in this context, individuals with appropriate and effective influence are referred to as leaders, those with complementary interpretation and translation abilities regarding the leader are referred to as followers, and individuals serving as the infrastructure supporting both leaders and followers in a team are referred to as members.

4 CONCLUSION

In this study, survey data was analyzed with the purpose of investigating the changes in individual growth through students' participation in PBL activities. The survey data was collected and compared before and after the implementation of PBL activities using the 12 elements of social foundational skills advocated by the Ministry of Economy, Trade and Industry (METI). The results revealed significant growth in many aspects of individual development, although some elements received lower ratings. Furthermore, a comparative analysis of the average values of the ability elements across different teams was conducted. Again, while growth was observed in several aspects, there were also elements that received lower evaluations.

During the observation of team situations, it became evident that there were teams that reached the final stage of the Tuckman model's five stages of team building, as well as teams that were still in intermediate stages. Therefore, teams that reached the final stage exhibited growth in many ability elements, whereas teams in intermediate stages may have become aware of their actual ability levels during the activities, leading to lower ratings compared to before the PBL activities. This finding can also be applied to individual growth.

Moreover, a factor analysis was conducted to determine if the three abilities would emerge as factors, considering that social foundational skills are subdivided into 12 elements. As a result, the 12 elements of social foundational skills were divided into three distinct factors. It can be inferred that these factors represent an ideal factor before engaging in PBL activities and a realistic factor after participating in such activities. The three factors were identified as Leader, Follower, and Team Member.

Given that the number of respondents was relatively small, with 30 participants before the PBL activities and 23 participants after the activities, it is necessary to accumulate a larger amount of data. Additionally, further analysis should be conducted on elements other than social foundational skills. These are areas to be addressed as future challenges.

ACKNOWLEDGMENT

This research was supported by the 2023 Kindai University Educational Reform/Student Support Project Grant.

REFERENCES

[1] Y. Kodono, "Comparing Self-Assessments Before and After PBL Activities: Essential Competencies for the 100-Year Life," The 33rd Soft Science Workshop, Japan Society for Fuzzy Theory and Intelligent Informatics, pp. 33–34, March 2023. (in Japanese)
[2] Y. Kitayama and Y. Kodono, "A Comparison of the Basic Social Skills in College Athletics," The 37th Fuzzy System Symposium, Japan Society for Fuzzy Theory and Intelligent Informatics, pp. 530–535, September 2021. (in Japanese)
[3] Ministry of Economy, Trade and Industry. (https://www.meti.go.jp/policy/kisoryoku/index.html (2023/05/31 acsess)).
[4] L. Jiang and Y. Kodono, "Interrelationships Among Consumer Attitudes Toward Vlog Promotion," J. Adv. Comput. Intell. Intell. Inform., Vol.26, No.4, pp.542–578, 2022
[5] H. Cheng and Y. Kodono, "The Motivation BehindParticipation in Virtual CSR Co-Creation by Chinese Post-90s: A Case Study of Ant Forest," J. Adv. Comput. Intell. Intell. Inform., Vol.26, No.4, pp.549–554, 2022
[6] B. W. Tuckman, "Developmental Sequence in Small Groups", Psychological Bulletin, Vol.63, No.6, pp.384–399, 1965.
[7] Japan Management Association: Investigative Research Report, "Survey Report on the Way and Behavior of Members in Organizations and Teams" (https://noma.actibookone.com/?cNo=128549m=MV8xXzc=&siteNum=4396&siteTitle=NOMA&pNo=1(2023/05/31 access)) (in Japanese)

SECTION 3
Corporate Social Responsibility and Regional Case Studies Management

Digital Synergy – El Emary et al. (eds)

Chapter 20
The actual level of European enterprises' involvement in the implementation of CSR postulates - a case study from the region of Silesian Voivodeship Poland

Aleksander Pabian
Czestochowa University of Technology, Poland

Contents

I am handing over to the readers an article which is the result of my own research process carried out in the Silesia voivodeship, Poland. It relates to corporate social responsibility - a concept according to which enterprises should take into account social and ecological aspects in their business activities as well as in contacts with its stakeholders. This concept for many years has been attracting interest and recognition of academics, politicians as well as business practitioners. Its postulates contribute to achieving harmony in the contemporary, turbulent environment, the condition of which unfortunately leaves much to be desired. At the same time, however, a research questions arises, whether contemporary European enterprises really undertake activities aimed at the environment and the community, whether the scope of their activities can be considered satisfactory as well as what are the examples of specific initiatives. The author decided to find an answer to them by conducting an interview with practitioners. Conditioned by the will to create ability to capture context and lived reality he decided to develop results in the form of a case study.

1 INTRODUCTION

Every organization has an environment that represents a set of independent variables, i.e. factors that are largely beyond its control. At the same time, these factors always affect company and enter into relationships based on mutual relations (Koźmiński and Jemielniak 2012: 107). Nowadays, the dependence of enterprises on their environment (e.g. social and natural) has become so strong that it has become a necessity for companies to care for the environment in which they operate. Without this, they will not create a platform that will allow them to maintain their position in the future, and thus they will destroy themselves.

The development of any enterprise depends notably on the state of the natural environment and "the health and stability of the community in which it operates asc well as the well-being of members of the socjety" (Pluto 2007: 196). The company is part of its environment. There are certain interactions between him and the representatives of the community. A healthy society in which a company operates is conducive to its own well-being.

DOI: 10.1201/9781003440406-20

The concept and management strategy assuming the need for companies to voluntarily take into account social interests, environmental aspects or relations with various stakeholder groups in their activities is corporate social responsibility. CSR is a kind of duty to take care of everything that surrounds the organization - therefore means the ethical behaviour of business towards its constituencies or stakeholders (including natural environment). Expenses for this purpose should not be treated as a cost (as, for example, in the case of funds spent on improving the level of service), but rather in terms of investment. This is due to the fact that although the outlays incurred to support a social or ecological project do not bring direct and quick profits, at the same time they improve the quality of life in the company's surroundings, which the company itself benefits from. Therefore, the need for companies to act in a responsible manner is not only strongly emphasized in the literature but also specifically, and to excess, supported by the authorities of European countries (Kazoić 2014: 57). The European Commission's Green Paper points out that companies have also obligations other than making a profit, solely. They function in a certain social and natural environment (Bernatt 2009: 19). Therefore, they cannot disregard the needs and interests of this community in their activities.

At the same time, however, a research question arises as to whether contemporary European enterprises really undertake activities aimed at the environment and the community, and whether the scope of their activities can be considered satisfactory. The author decided to contribute to dispel these doubts by conducting research in Silesia voivodeship. They made it possible to reveal whether targeting activities at the environment is one of the key elements of planning development strategy of enterprises participating in the exchange processes taking place on the market of the old continent. They also made it possible to describe the practical experience of companies applying practices aimed at increasing the quality of life in the environment in which they operate. The presented cases allowed to organize and extend the presented theory, provide further explanations and understand the practical course of processes taking place in organizations. This part has also an illustrative, educational and inspiring value. By analogy, this section may inspire readers to design their own activities.

2 LITERATURE OVERVIEW - SOCIAL AND ECOLOGICAL THREATS AS A PREMISE FOR CSR DEVELOPMENT

An enterprise is a unit separated from the environment in organizational, economic, territorial and legal terms. However, the fact of such separation does not mean complete independence. As it has been repeatedly shown by the results of research, environmental conditions affect various aspects of the functioning of any organization.

At the same time, both the social and natural conditions of the environment in which modern enterprises have to function are not generally considered satisfactory (Pabian 2020: 55). „Today's world is struggling with many problems, including issues such as growing social inequalities, increasing unemployment, an aging society, social exclusion, climate change or growing environmental pollution connected with its impact on the health of society" (Wronka-Pospiech 2005: 125). This is related to the fact that traditional forms of counteracting these phenomena have been exhausted or failed. In this context, it is not surprising that researchers express view that "currently there is a phase of civilization breakdown" (Huczek 2011: 43).

As confirmed by the research results, even in the most developed countries there are negative phenomena related to, for example, the exclusion of representatives of certain social strata (Gough and Eisenschitz 2006: 46). „Community of the need has always been, and will probably remain, large and diverse. It includes the disabled, the homeless, the seriously ill, orphans, alcoholics and drug addicts wanting to break free from addiction, and other categories of people struggling to survive" (Pabian 2008: 157). This is the first group of people who need help even in wealthy countries. The second group includes those affected by factors such as various types of natural disasters (victims of fires, floods, epidemics, hurricanes, etc.). The next group includes victims of pathologies resulting from the excess of free time, commercialization of life and excessive consumption, which results, as research shows, in new types of addictions, e.g. to shopping or using Internet.

Fortunatelly, due to the high level of economic development, the majority of inhabitants of the most developed countries are not affected by the serious effects of economic disturbances. They are also usually unfamiliar with major political or military turmoil. Such communities are not oppressed by dictators, their members are usually not victims of internal military conflicts, and religious minorities are not persecuted there, which is primarily due to the high level of democratization and acceptance of differences.

Their members, however, feel the effects of environmental pollution, which is primarily associated with a high degree of urbanization and industrialization. “The natural environment consists of: climate and weather, terrain, shape and elevation above sea level, water conditions, as well as the vegetation and animal world formed in these conditions” (Korzeniowski 2010: 429). L.E. Hinkle points out that the state of the environment defined in this way has an obvious impact on the quality of life of the representatives of the human race. Moreover, this impact is absolutely prominent, because “if we destroy the natural ecosystem on which our survival depends, the civilization we know will collapse, and with it the social system developed over the years” (Hinkle 1980, p. 16). In this context, a source of concern is the fact that current state of the environment leaves much to be desired. As noted by A. Sadowski, "the irrational use of natural resources accompanying economic development has contributed to the creation of a huge amount of waste on a global scale and has given rise to a global ecological crisis, the effects of which are even difficult to estimate” (Sadowski 2010: 13).

Dynamic development, which has already led some countries to achieve the characteristics of the post-industrial era, has its price. As noted by the authors of the Global Environment Outlook report, prepared under the United Nations Environment Programme, the growing number of households and the wealth of people contribute to excessive consumption, high usage of energy and resources such as water, large amounts of municipal and industrial waste, transport problems, heavy urbanization and related air, water and soil pollution (Ekins, Gupta and Boileau 2019: 75).

Currently observed, unprecedented intensification of phenomena disturbing natural environment poses new challenges for man. Data on the state of the natural environment show that we live in a time of so-called: „The Great Acceleration”, which is a phenomenon unprecedented in the 4.5-billion-year history of our planet. We have driven Earth to the brink of exhaustion, increasing demand for energy, soil and water. We have disrupted Earth's biodiversity, referred to as: „the web of life”, which is in fact the infrastructure that sustains life on Earth. This phenomenon is so significant that there is even talk of a new geological epoque, which is called - Anthropocene. Its beginning dates back to the 1950s. Since that period, there has been a permanent increase in temperature on the Earth's surface, carbon dioxide, nitrogen oxide and methane concentration has also increased. There is a loss of tropical forests, degradation of the biosphere, an increase in marine fishing, ocean acidification and other alarming phenomena. According to the Living Planet Report 2019, animal populations have decreased by 40% in the last 40 years. Between 1970 and 2014, the total vertebrate population declined by 60% - it means an average decline of more than half in less than 50 years. Only a quarter of the Earth's land area is free from the influence of human activity (Grooten and Almond 2018).

The sources of many of the above-mentioned problems (mainly those of an ecological nature) should be sought in the activities of enterprises. People began to be aware of this fact in the 50s of the last century, already, when H. R. Bowen proposed a definition considered nowadays in terms of the foundation of the basic conceptual apparatus in the field of corporate social responsibility. It referred to “the obligations of enterprises, which should pursue such a policy and take such decisions and actions that are not harmful to the environment, desirable by society and consistent with its goals and values” (Bowen 1953: xi). Since its presentation, the need for companies to bear responsibility towards society and the natural environment has been constantly and increasingly emphasized in the literature. It has been proven and emphasized many times that in order to reduce the negative impact on the surrounding, changes should be made to the traditional practices of economic entities. Businesses must be able to combine the ability to generate profits with environmental performance (Gregory 1997: 178). As the researchers note: “they should not take advantage of their privileged position as users of the environment by locating onerous production processes in areas with less stringent standards, failing to comply with social and ecological standards, not paying ecological penalties, increasing their benefits at the expense of third parties" (Nahotko 2002: 46). On the contrary - they should adapt to the requirements of the environment, limiting production that burdens the environment, adopting appropriate technical standards, investing in protective technologies, paying environmental fees and taxes. W. Lenart notes that such a responsible attitude will only be effective if it receives full approval from all decision-makers, regardless of the industry they represent or in what geographical area their companies operate (Lenart 2000: 7). Whether modern enterprises really follow these guidelines and take actions in accordance with the CSR canon, the author decided to check later in this article.

3 METHODS

Research should be considered in terms of a specific movement: from the unknown to the known. In order to obtain data for the preparation of theoretical fragments of the article (devoted, among others to approximate conceptual apparatus in the field of corporate social responsibility) an analysis of secondary sources was used. Theoretical aim was then achieved on the basis of the analysis of source materials and literature. The bibliographic query was conducted in accordance with the adopted methodology of a systematic literature review, i.e. one that follows specific standards and constitute method of integrating scientific evidence, which uses explicit methods for the identification, selection, critical evaluation and analysis of data from relevant studies qualified for the review (Orłowska et. al. 2017: 350). Undertaken approach allowed removal of limitations of traditional reviews based on implicit and unsystematic techniques of collection and compilation of studies, allowing demonstration of reliable and credible scientific evidence in an objective manner. The factual data and literature being used allowed to look at the described reality from a sufficiently broad perspective and made it possible to describe and evaluate the phenomena from the expert level of theoretical knowledge.

In obtaining the data needed to develop the empirical part of the work, the method of observation (non-participant) was used, understood as a process of careful and deliberate perception, peculiar collection and interpretation of the data in their natural course, when they remain in the direct field of vision and hearing for the observer (Cybulska 2013: 21). For the purpose of the work, the author also decided to use an interview with middle and senior managers of 17 medium-sized and large companies (employment size criterion). The conversation with them allowed to reveal examples of corporate social involvement - such activity is not always adequately publicized and promoted (Pabian 2021: 55) as well as to delve into the way of implementing CSR postulates in their own companies.

In this study sampling did not depend on chance. The selection of the sample was purposive (non-probabilical sampling). Individuals have been selected based on the arbitrary decision of the author (intention to research individuals who possess expert knowledge what empowers them to answer a research question) and included 25 people. The choice of the non-random method in which not all population members have an equal chance of participating in the study was justified by the desire to select respondents who would be the most valuable source of information related to the problem in question. Their average age was ≈ 42 years. They differed in terms of demographic characteristics, such as age, gender or marital status. They were distinguished by such characteristics as declared level of education (one of them had a doctorate), occupied position in his company or the amount of earnings. They all worked in companies running a business and having their headquarters in the Silesian voivodeship.

It is a region well known and geographically close to him. The present-day Silesia voivodeship is located in the southern Poland. It borders Czech Republic and Slovakia as well as four other voivodeships: Swiętokrzyskie, Łodzkie, Małopolskie, Opolskie. This voivodeship has been functioning since the beginning of the 20th century. It is the second (after Mazowieckie) largest Polish voivodeship in terms of population (over 4.5 million people, which translates into ≈ 12% of the total population of Poland). There is the highest level of population density in Poland (369 people per km^2 with the Polish average of 123 people per square kilometer). Śląskie is one of the strongest polish regions in terms of economic (12.4% of the country's GDP is generated here) as well as demographical indicators. It is also the largest urbanized area in Central and Eastern Europe, with an urban population rate of over 77%. The economy of the voivodship is dominated by the coal and metallurgy industries (Silesian mines generate 90.2% of the sold production of hard coal mining in Poland) as well as electromechanical, metal, chemical and food industries (Official website of the Silesian voivodeship 2023). The voivodeship has the largest share in the production of passenger cars and crude steel. Companies such as General Motors, ING Group, Fiat, Danone, Helwet Packard and many others have located their investments in the considered region.

In the literature it is emphasized that due to the growing importance of economic and spatial units such as regions on the world stage, social, economic and environmental phenomena for which space is an integrating factor should be precisely analised in relation to regions. The priority task of researchers should be therefore to create - with the involvement of many beneficiaries and information providers - a coherent information system, serving to describe the phenomena occurring in regions (Rogalińska et. al. 2014: 2). What is more, thanks to the decision to conduct research in a region known and close to the author, obserwation as well as the recruitment process of sample units for the interview (in-depth), turned out to be relatively simple and cheap. Carrying out research in Siolesia Voideship did not required a complete survey frame what translated into the fact that entire research proces turned out to be relatively fast, easy as well as allowed for inexpensive way of obtaining data. This fact was not without significance because, as R. Alkassim, I. Etikan, S. Abubakar rightly notice: in sampling, workforce, time and money in many times may highly limits researchers from getting true random sample that will represent the entire population (Alkassim, Etikan and Abubakar 2016:6). Reaching people constituting sample was possible thanks to the usage of, so-called: snowball technique. As it was mentioned previously, it is a non-random recruitment technique in which an initially small group of respondents is tested and then each research participant from this group is asked to assist researcher in identifying other potential subjects belonging to the general population. This technique is called "snowball" because the sample group grows like a rolling snowball and it „relies on referrals from initially sampled respondents to other persons believed to have the characteristic of interest" (Johnson 2014: 75). Initial subject serve as seed through which wave one subject is recruited. Wave one subject in turn recruit wave two subjects and the sample consequently expands wave by wave (Heckathorn 2011: 355). As the sample builds up, enough amount of data can be gathered in order to be useful for the purpose of research.

The author decided to present the results of his studies in the form of a case study, i.e. in a form of description of real, applied CSR practices, allowing to draw conclusions as to the causes of their occurrence and the results of their course. It was conditioned by the will to create ability to capture context and lived reality of participants as well as show a relationship between phenomena, context, and people. Author also decided to allow exploration of deeper causes of phenomena as well as make it easy to explain results, also to a non-specialist audience. The work is crowned with the ending in the form of a discussion, in which the conclusions resulting from the study of examples given by practitioners are presented in a synthetic form.

4 RESEARCH RESULTS

This chapter presents practical experience of European enterprises (example of Silesia voivodeship) in the implementation of corporate social responsibility postulates. In order to meet ecological challenges responsibly, some enterprises of this region are trying to locate their operations in buildings erected as a result of clean production processes based on natural, renewable and healthy materials of local origin (e.g. wood, brick). Innovations in the field of construction lead to a situation in which the elements of the static infrastructure of enterprises do not disturb the landscape, and after the end of their life, the elements from which they are made may be subject to reusing and recycling processes. Another feature of the environmentally friendly architecture is energy efficiency. Therefore, the authorities of some enterprises in the region strive to locate their activities in the so-called autonomous buildings, which are considered a model solution in this regard.

The concept of an autonomous building should be understood as a self-sufficient structure to which no external energy is supplied. This is possible thanks to the usage of modern insulation systems for the roof, walls and windows as well as the usage of renewable energy: solar, wind or these, coming from the Earth (Pabian 2011: 5-25). Solar cells and collectors enable conversion of sunlight into heat, which is then used in order to heat domestic water and the operation of central heating. In turn, wind turbines or photovoltaic cells thanks to which it is possible to convert solar energy into electricity can be used to generate electricity.

Rational water management is also important for the canon of sustainable development. Therefore, companies from Silesian voivodeship pursue modern solutions taking into account solutions consisting in equipping buildings with rainwater tanks (rainwater usage) and water purification and treatment stations (used, water resources can be recycled). Water from these sources can be used, for example, to irrigate plants or flush toilets. A rare, but sometimes encountered practice is also to include in the architectural plans of buildings the need to use biologically active surfaces (e.g. green spaces with vegetation - Figure 1). In addition, in order to protect the health of employees and ensure high comfort of staying in company facilities, more and more actions are often undertaken to use furniture and finishing materials that are not harmful to health, efforts are made to create an appropriate microclimate inside the rooms (temperature, humidity, ventilation and air filtration), it is not uncommon for interiors to be protected against noise, finally companies tend to ensure proper lighting (energy-saving light sources) inside their buildings.

Figure 1. The usage of green space within a commercial facility in the Silesian province.
Source: author, Silesia voivodship, 2022.

In Silesia voivodship, there is also an example of the business sphere involvement in a construction project which goes beyond simply improving the properties and transforming the features of one's own building in order to create a technical and functional entirely that is friendly from the point of view of the needs of the natural environment. This example is related to the construction of the commercial eco-town: Siewierz-Jeziorna on the area of 120 square meters (Figure 2). It is a commercial architectural and construction project, which is intended to be environmentally friendly, e.g. by developing appropriate attitudes among the people who form/make up the housing community.

Figure 2. Eco-town at the finishing stage.
Source: author, Siewierz, 2020.

At the beginning of the current millennium, already, as an initiative of TUP joint-stock company, the idea of building a new urban layout in the Silesia voivodeship appeared, taking the form of, so-called: a garden city – an assumption based on the idea of combining an area with intensive development with a clearly separated green area. Such a model is aimed at improving the quality of urban life by combining the amenities of civilization with the idyll of rural life, it is also intended to counteract the threats and problems faced by industrial areas (Baranowska 2007: 15-17). The place is located in the vicinity of Siewierz, a small town with a rich history, near the Upper Silesian metropolis, close to the airport in Pyrzowice and to the left of the national road no. 1, going from Katowice to Czestochowa. Initially, it was considered to build a regional logistics center there. However, it would be kind of waste because it is a beautiful area located directly on the bank of Przeczyce-Siewierz reservoir, in the vicinity of Kraków-Częstochowa (protected recreation area), adjacent to the railway line that will connect Katowice with the airport in the future. Due to the complexity of the project, its costs and limited domestic experience in the implementation of such projects, the implementation of this project was initially planned for many years.

The idea of the spatial concept of the new settlement was developed by an international group of urban planners with the participation of local stakeholders. At the end of 2007, during workshops lasting several days (according to the charrette method), it was possible to define the vision of the new foundation and to tighten cooperation with the majority of people and institutions important for the project (the decisive attitude of the mayor of Siewierz who was looking for appropriate solutions for the development of the commune and good cooperation with the municipality, was of key importance in this case). The adopted concept of the project assumed the construction of a compact urban structure, which is designed in accordance with the requirements of sustainability. It can offer intimacy and contact with nature as well as access to urban and transportation infrastructure. It also has full functionality in the sense of the possibility of providing housing services and an extensive spectrum of various forms of economic activity (the presence of office and industrial buildings protecting residential part and service part from the nuisance associated with intensive traffic).

An equally important issue for involved in the project, architects and planners from the Warsaw-based and specializing in sustainable urban solutions Mycielski Architecture & Urbanism studio was the usage of environmentally friendly solutions. It was considered necessary to separate the central part of the park with a network of ponds and mere. Building materials safe for human health and of local origin were used. It was even planned to build its own water intake and sewage treatment plant. It has been assumed that the energy-independent buildings will be located around city squares, which will ensure quietness and acoustic comfort (Jeleński 2010: 262). Introducing responsible principles of social coexistence, the official statute has been established. It imposed harmonization of colours, waste segregation, due to it excessive noise production was prohibited and car traffic restrictions were adopted.

Thanks to modern solutions in the field of construction art, companies operating in Silesia can contribute to inhibit negative tendencies that occur and are visible in regional natural environment. Among them, however, there are also entities whose activity goes beyond the introduction of pro-ecological solutions only. Some of them undertook modern activities in the form of programs or social actions aimed at the inhabitants of the region, at specific social groups that make up the layer of firms' stakeholders. They are aimed not so much at protecting nature, but at progressive change within the realities of the social environment in which these companies have come to operate. An interesting example was given by one of the respondents. He revealed the fact of existence of initiative called: "hours of silence", undertaken by his company (a large retail chain operating in the Silesian voivodeship). This action was initiated 4 years ago and has been continued in the chain's outlets to this day. The idea arose from the need to ensure that people with autism or related disorders could make purchases.

It consists in setting a day of the week on which the lighting in the store is dimmed at certain times, and voice messages and music are not broadcasted. All radios and TV sets become turned off and a special, privileged cash register is made available to visitors. This initiative has been met with social satisfaction, because without ensuring sensory-friendly conditions, it becomes very difficult (if not impossible) to purchase goods by people for whom too much stimuli cause fear of entering the store (sometimes even panic attacks). There are also examples of other pro-social activities undertaken by commercial entities operating in the Silesia voivodship:

- An educational project of the electricity distributor aimed at the elderly in the form of workshops, in which organizations and associations working for the benefit of seniors (Senior clubs, Retirement and pensioners associations) were also involved. Thanks to the participation of partners from the third sector, the meeting organizers had a chance to reach a large group of recipients. In the form of lectures for a wide audience and small educational meetings, potential threats related to fraud attempts and dishonest practices of some salesmen were presented, as well as ways of dealing with them appropriately.
- Bank's initiative consisting in substantive support (advice, including these in the field of business reporting, customer relationship management or team management) and financial support (development grants) for, so-called: startups, aimed at solving specific social problems. This innovative project was supposed leading to noticeable, progressive changes in the environment in an indirect way. This was to be done by supporting the development of external entities - new enterprises that decided to go beyond the traditional business model and focus on eliminating problems related to, for example: environmental protection, integration of disabled people or people at risk of exclusion from the labour market.
- Project promoting proper eating habits undertaken by a producer of mineral water. The aim of this action was to promote pro-ecological attitudes, healthy lifestyle, proper nutrition and physical activity. It was addressed to children 3-6 years old (preschoolers). As part of the campaign, e.g. packages with educational materials (audiobooks, worksheets for children, a poster with a model food plate, guides for parents and teachers) were prepared and distributed, a competition was announced for the preparation and implementation of the most innovative activity among the preschool community related to shaping the habit of drinking water, a website was created where one can find content and forms of activity tailored to the needs of both parents (e.g. articles, tips) and their children (e.g. educational interactive games).

Several of the respondents provided the example of CSR practices undertaken by a company present in the region and dealing with e.g. trading liquid fuels. This company developed, for example, a project of a mobile application dedicated to the subject of environmental protection (it was later implemented and made available for clients free of charge). The software allows, for example, to calculate the approximate amount of carbon dioxide that its user emits every day (e.g. when driving a car) and to check how his own lifestyle and eating habits affect the environment. Traditionally, this application also allows to collect points that are awarded for changing owns daily habits towards more environmentally friendly behaviour. These points can be later transferred, for example, for the sake of social purposes (Gazeta Bankowa 2022).

It should be also emphasized that described company undertook decisive pro-social activities during the pandemic related to the spread of virus (corona) causing COVID-19 disease. Although it was not its main activity, in March 2020, Orlen initiated large-scale production of hand sanitizer (in the subsidiary's production plant). Due to the high demand from medical services and the others involved in the fight against the virus, the first batch of the product was sent to the Material Reserves Agency which performs tasks resulting from the laws in the field of strategic reserves management (among other things, it creates and maintains stocks of the most needed products in a specific period) (Kulicki 2013: 90).

As part of its corporate social responsibility policy, during the pandemic, the company also decided to reduce fuel prices at the stations it manages. It was, among others possible thanks to falling oil prices, combined with internal and institutional activities related to the optimization of production costs. The premise for the introduction of sale promotion was the belief that uniformed and medical services must maintain the highest mobility abilities in difficult times. It was also noted that many private individuals as well as institutional clients across voivodship are still forced to intensively use vehicles (both for professional purposes and, for example, in order to care for family members).

The unprecedented practice of the corporation led to a situation in which fuel prices were also lowered at other stations. This happened because, first of all, prices were also lowered for retailers purchasing from the company products resulting from oil refining (apart from petrol stations, the company runs refineries, which are one of the main sources of liquid fuels supply to the entire market). Secondly, as company had, and still has, (Polska Organizacja Przemysłu i Handlu Naftowego 2019: 21-24) the largest network of retail outlets in the scale of entire country, it had informal and indirect possibility of influencing the pricing policy of other chains. It is proved that, in situation when a market leader significantly modifies its pricing policy, its competitors are usually forced to verify the advantages of their own offer (lowering prices), in order not to lose their competitive position (Garbarski, Rutkowski and Wrzosek 2001: 356; Bareja 2006: 966).

5 DISCUSSION

The multitude of contemporary ecological and social problems means that there should be no consent to passivity in the field of counteracting them. At the same time, private companies should also join in the implementation of ideas aimed at positive transformations in the environment. The analysis of cases from the Silesia vovoideship area shows that there are many european companies that are actively involved in the implementation of CSR postulates. These are usually large enterprises operating in non-identical industries (e.g. banking or trade). Initiatives undertaken by these entities are not always very extensive and complicated, but they also usually do not boil down to charitable activities, i.e. organizing additional funds to help raise the standard of living of representatives of social strata in the greatest need. It seems that such a degree of involvement is sufficient because corporate social responsibility directly contributes to the implementation of the EU's postulates of sustainability - a concept which, due to the downplay of the importance of economic interests is gradually met with increasing criticism from, both researchers and practitioners of business activities: "there is a need for a more realistic and workable communitarian approach to environmental governance" (Benson and Craig 2014: 777-782).

According to new approach, CSR solutions in order to be considered valuable do not have to be of great importance in shaping new order. It is enough for them to take the form of a small but useful change or only a modification of the current state of affairs (Bessant and Venables, 2010: 3). Maybe, therefore, the initiatives undertaken by some enterprises in Silesia voivodship are not very extensive and have a strictly targeted character (e.g. an action promoting waste segregation under the patronage of a waste processing company or an entertainment event organized by a company from the medium-sized enterprise sector - a festival for children from dysfunctional families). First of all, they are aimed at fulfilling the assumptions related to the necessity of such development, which is carried out with the respect for the values and usage of resources of the natural environment (Skowroński 2006: 3).

At the same time, there are also companies on the market that do not see the potential of CSR in creating a new, better order. Particularly smaller firms do not see the advantages of social involvement and consider the outlays on this aim primarily in terms of additional and unnecessary costs. Therefore, all kinds of publications in which attention is drawn to the fact that nowadays care for economic interests should be wisely combined with care for compliance with ethical principles of responsibility towards society should be considered as valuable (Żmigła 2007: 11). Author hopes that this study will allow less experienced managers to better understand the essence and origin of CSR as well as to appreciate its role. Thanks to the cited examples, it will in turn inspire experienced practitioners of responsible economic activity to develop current and search for further management solutions that can, at the same time, benefit their own enterprises as well as society that makes up the layer of its environment.

REFERENCES

Alkassim R., Etikan I. and Abubakar S. 2016. Comparision of snowball sampling and sequential sampling technique. Biometrics & Biostatistics International Journal, vol. 1, iss. 3.

Baranowska M. 2007. Miasta – ogrody. Utopia a rzeczywistość, Acta Universitatis Lodziensis. Folia Geographica Socio-Oeconomica, no. 8.

Bareja K. 2006. Informacje kosztowe w ustalaniu cen w Systemie Informacji Planistycznej. In A. Karmańska (ed.). *Rachunkowość zarządcza i rachunek kosztów w systemie informacyjnym przedsiębiorstwa.* Warszawa: Difin.

Benson M. H. and Craig R. K. 2014. The end of sustainability. Society& Natural resources. Taylor Francis International Journal, vol. 27, iss. 7.

Bernatt M. 2009. *Corporate social responsibility. Constitutional and international perspective.* Warszawa: Wydawnictwo Naukowe Wydziału Zarządzania Uniwersytetu Warszawskiego.

Bessant J. and Venables T. 2010. *Creating wealth from knowledge. Meeting the innovation challenge.* Northampton: Edward Elgar Publishing.

Bowen H. R. 1953. *Social responsibilities of the businessman.* New York: Harper&Brothers.

Cybulska D. 2013. Wykorzystanie metody obserwacji w naukach społecznych. Obronność. Zeszyty Naukowe Wydziału Zarządzania i Dowodzenia Akademii Obrony Narodowej, no. 2 (6).

Ekins P., Gupta J. and Boileau P. 2019. *Global environment outlook. Healthy planet, healthy people.* New York: Cambridge University Press.

Garbarski I., Rutkowski I. and Wrzosek W. 2001. *Marketing.* Warszawa: PWE.

Gazeta Bankowa. 2022. (April 15). *Ranking firm zaangażowanych społecznie.* https://www.gb.pl/upload/CSR/ranking.pdf.

Gough J., Eisenschitz A. and McCulloch A. 2006. *Spaces of social exclusion.* London, New York: Routledge, Taylor & Francis.

Gregory A. 1997. *Public relations w praktyce.* Wydawnictwo Profesjonalnej Szkoły Biznesu, Kraków.

Grooten M. and Almond R. E. A. 2018. *Living planet report 2018.* Gland, Switzerland: Aiming Higher, WWF.

Heckathorn D. D. 2011. Snowball versus respondent - driven sampling. Sociol Methodol, no. 41 (1).

Hinkle L. E. (1980). *Theme presentation.* In: J.H. Wiggins, C. Hamilton (ed.). *The Importance of the built environment to the quality of american life.* Washington: National Academy Press.

Huczek M. 2011. Kultura innowacyjna organizacji. Zeszyty Naukowe Wyższej Szkoły Humanitas. Zarządzanie, no. 1.

Jeleński T. 2010. Urbanistyka i gospodarka przestrzenna. In J. Kronenberg, T. Bergier (ed.). *Wyzwania zrównoważonego rozwoju w Polsce.* Fundacja Sendzimira, Kraków.

Johnson T. P. 2014. Snowball sampling. Introduction. Wiley Statistics Reference.

Kazojć K. 2014. Koncepcja społecznej odpowiedzialności i jej obszary w organizacji. Studia i Prace Wydziału Nauk Ekonomicznych i Zarządzania, no. 38, vol. 1.

Korzeniowski L. F. 2010. *Menedżment. Podstawy zarządzania.* Wydawnictwo EAS, Kraków.

Koźmiński A. and Jemielniak D. 2012. *Zarządzanie od postaw.* Warszawa: Wolters Kluwer.

Kulicki J. 2013 *Kontrola skarbowa. Komentarz*. Warszawa: Wolters Kluwer.
Lenart, W. 2000. *Rola konsultacji i negocjacji społecznych w procedurze uzgadniania inwestycji zmieniających środowisko*. Gdańsk: Wydawnictwo Eko-Konsult.
Nahotko S. 2002. *Podstawy zarządzania ekologicznego przedsiębiorstwem*. Bydgoszcz: Oficyna Wydawnicza Ośrodka Postępu Organizacyjnego.
Orłowska A., Mazur Z. and Łaguna M. 2017. Systematyczny przegląd literatury. Na czym polega i czym się różni od innych przeglądów? Ogrody Nauk i Sztuk, no. 7.
Pabian A. 2008. *Promocja. Nowoczesne środki i formy*. Warszawa: Difin.
Pabian A. 2011. Ecological aspects of sustainability in building industry. *Proceedings of the 3rd International Conference on Contemporary Problems in Architecture and Construction*, Beijing.
Pabian A. 2020. *Innowacje społeczne w zarządzaniu przedsiębiorstwami komercyjnymi*. Częstochowa: Wydawnictwo Politechniki Częstochowskiej.
Pluto A. 2007. Corporate Social Responsibility. Kierunek zmian w zarządzaniu przedsiębiorstwem. In S. Lachiewicz, M. Matejun (ed.). *Problems of contemporary management practice*. Łódź: Wydawnictwo Politechniki Łódzkiej.
Polska Organizacja Przemysłu i Handlu Naftowego. *Raport: przemysł i handel naftowy 2018*. Warszawa: POPiHN.
Rogalińska D., Mroczkowski M., Kowalski K., Wróbel K. and Dębicka M. 2014. Rekomendacje w zakresie rozwoju analiz regionalnych w systemie statystyki gruzińskiej. Warszawa: Główny Urząd Statystyczny.
Sadowski A. 2010. *Ekonomiczne i ekologiczne aspekty stosowania logistyki zwrotnej w obszarze wykorzystania odpadów*. Łódź: Wydawnictwo Uniwersytetu Łódzkiego.
Skowroński A. 2006. Zrównoważony rozwój perspektywą dalszego rozwoju cywilizacyjnego. Problemy Ekorozwoju, no. 2, vol. 1.
The official website of the Silesian Voivodeship. 2023 (April 20). https://www.slaskie.pl/content/gospodarka.
Wronka-Pośpiech M. 2015. Innowacje społeczne. Pojęcie i znaczenie, Studia Ekonomiczne. Zeszyty Naukowe Uniwersytetu Ekonomicznego w Katowicach, no. 212.
Żemigła M. 2007. *Społeczna odpowiedzialność biznesu. Budowanie zdrowej, efektywnej organizacji*. Wolters Kluwer, Kraków.

Digital Synergy – El Emary et al. (eds)

Chapter 21
Building a corporate social responsibility management system

Joanna Wyrobek
Cracow University of Economics, Cracow, Poland

Contents

The aim of the study was to discuss the basic tools used for the implementation and control of the corporate social responsibility system. CSR is now becoming one of the tools of company management because, due to the publicly available information, business entities must pay particular attention to the reputation and perception of their brand by the business environment and stakeholders. The state of development of CSR tools has already reached the stage of standardization and ready-made tools that quantitatively allow to implement and control the strategy of the company in this regard. Depending on the size of the entity, these tools may be simple or complex, although, given the existence of specific standards, it is worth starting to slowly implement these standards, as the policies of both international organisations and the European Union clearly indicate that sooner or later the standards described will apply to a much wider group of companies than they currently do.

1 INTRODUCTION

In recent years, the concept of sustainable development and building relationships based on trust with the entire social environment of the company has become increasingly important in the management of the company. This is not only due to the good intentions of businesses, but also due to technological progress and changes in legislation. Due to technological advances, any violations of corporate social responsibility rules are almost immediately disseminated via social media and degrade the company's reputation, and most companies adhere to CSR rules for fear of loss of reputation. In addition, legislation is being developed around the world whose goal is to preserve the planet Earth for future generations in a state that allows the further development of humanity. Man has already dominated the planet to such an extent that there is no space for animals or enough forests to maintain oxygen balance in the atmosphere.

One example of legislation aimed at countering the degradation of the planet was the adoption by the United Nations General Assembly in New York in 2015 of the "Agenda for Sustainable Development – 2030", i.e. development that meets the needs of the present generation without compromising the ability to meet the needs of future generations. The 2030 Agenda includes 17 Sustainable Development Goals (SDGs) with 169 specific targets in five

DOI: 10.1201/9781003440406-21

areas – people, planet, prosperity, peace and partnership. In addition to talking about quality of life, health, prosperity, social justice and the environment, the Agenda for Sustainable Development also mentions corporate governance as an important element of the described concept.

Another example of legislation setting ambitious goals for the economy is the European Union, where the Green European Deal Strategy has been implemented, under which important changes have already been made for companies, including:

- Regulation (EU) 2020/852 of the European Parliament and of the Council on the establishment of a framework facilitating sustainable investment, commonly referred to as the EU Taxonomy. According to the Regulation, investments are to be sustainable and make a significant contribution to at least one of the six environmental objectives.
- The Corporate Sustainability Reporting Directive (CSRD) 2022/2464. The Directive imposes publication obligations in the field of non-financial reporting, providing information on environmental, social and corporate governance issues. By 2025, PIEs with more than 500 employees will be required to report, by 2026 all large companies and by 2027 the Directive will also cover small and medium-sized listed companies.

As can be seen from this brief review of legal acts, sustainable development is slowly becoming a necessity rather than a business choice, and given the dynamic pace of imposing new rules on business entities, it is worthwhile to implement both the concept of CSR in the company and the system of monitoring the implementation of the key CSR objectives imposed on companies, especially if the entity is large or is an object of public interest.

2 ELEMENTS OF THE CSR SYSTEM IN THE ENTERPRISE

2.1 *Non-financial reporting GRI G4*

Regardless of whether a deadline has already been set for the implementation of non-financial reporting to the unit or the deadline is not yet known, due to the plans to use this reporting to offer various benefits and facilities, it is worth implementing a system of collecting information and measuring information required in such reporting today. Currently, three very popular non-financial reporting standards are GRI G4 (Global Reporting Initiative), TCDF (the Task Force on Climate related Financial Disclosures) and SASB (Sustainability Accounting Standards Board). These are specific standards already implemented by many entities, hence it is enough to download existing reports to have a good overview of the information that is required in individual reports. Although the choice of the standard that the company will implement for its internal needs is arbitrary, it is worth paying attention to the GRI because it has the same standards for all industries and covers all three areas of ESG. In addition, the GRI G4 standard has become popular and is now used by approx. 10,000 companies. Table 1 shows the general standard disclosures, and Table 2 details the information that should be disclosed in a report prepared in accordance with GRI standards.

Although the list of information required by the GRI is quite extensive, in light of the increasing emphasis on CSR, these indicators very effectively delineate the elements of the system implementing CSR in the enterprise. By defining the expected outcomes (improvement or at least no deterioration of the indicators from Table 2), the entity will strive in the right direction, and additionally, it will prepare in advance for the day when CSR reporting becomes a duty of a wider group of units than it currently is.

Of course, the CSR system does not have to be so comprehensive and extensive. Popular systems strongly linked to CSR and with a much lower degree of complexity include the sustainable scorecard, the London Benchmarking Group model and even the sustainable duPonta model. What all the systems described have in common is their quantitative nature, the assignment of specific goals and the measurement of achievement of these goals.

Table 1. General standard disclosures.

Aspect, Indicators	Explanation
G4-1	Statement from the most senior decision-maker - CEO.
G4-2	Description of key impacts, risks, and opportunities.
G4-3	Name of the organization.
G4-4	Primary brands, products, and services.
G4-5	Location of the organization's headquarters.
G4-6	Countries where the organization operates, and names of countries where either the organization has significant operations or that are specifically relevant to the sustainability topics covered in the report.
G4-7	Nature of ownership and legal form.
G4-8	Markets served
G4-9	Scale of the organization.
G4-10	Employee data
G4-11	Percentage of total employees covered by collective bargaining agreements
G4-12	Describe the organization's supply chain.
G4-13	Significant changes during the reporting period.
G4-14	Report whether and how the precautionary approach or principle is addressed by the organization.
G4-15	Externally developed economic, environmental and social charters, principles endorsed
G4-16	Memberships of associations (such as industry associations) and national or international advocacy organizations.
G4-17	Entities included in the organization's consolidated financial statements or equivalent documents. Any entity included in the organization's consolidated financial statements or equivalent documents is not covered by the report.
G4-18	Process for defining the report content and the Aspect Boundaries. Explain how the organization has implemented the Reporting Principles for Defining Report Content.
G4-19	Material Aspects identified in the process for defining report content.
G4-20	For each material Aspect, report the Aspect Boundary within the organization.
G4-21	For each material Aspect, report the Aspect Boundary outside the organization
G4-22	Report the effect of any restatements of information provided in previous reports, and the reasons for such restatements.
G4-23	Report significant changes from previous reporting periods in the Scope and Aspect Boundaries.
G4-24	Provide a list of stakeholder groups engaged by the organization.
G4-25	Report the basis for identification and selection of stakeholders with whom to engage.
G4-26	Report the organization's approach to stakeholder engagement, including frequency of engagement by type and by stakeholder group, and an indication of whether any of the engagement was undertaken specifically as part of the report preparation process.
G4-27	Report key topics and concerns that have been raised through stakeholder engagement, and how the organization has responded to those key topics and concerns, including through its reporting. Report the stakeholder groups that raised each of the key topics and concerns.
G4-28	Reporting period (such as fiscal or calendar year) for information provided.
G4-29	Date of most recent previous report (if any).
G4-30	Reporting cycle (such as annual, biennial).
G4-31	Provide the contact point for questions regarding the report or its contents.
G4-32	'In accordance' option chosen. GRI Content Index for chosen Reference to the External Assurance Report
G4-33	Policy and current practice with regard to seeking external assurance for the report. Relationship between the organization and the assurance providers.
G4-34	Governance structure of the organization, including committees of the highest governance body. Identify any committees responsible for decision-making on economic, environmental and social impacts.

(*Continued*)

Table 1. *(Continued)*

Aspect, Indicators	Explanation
G4-35	Process for delegating authority for economic, environmental and social topics
G4-36	Executive-level position or positions with responsibility for economic, environmental and social topics, and whether post holders report directly to the highest governance body.
G4-37	Processes for consultation between stakeholders and the highest governance body on economic, environmental and social topics. If consultation is delegated, describe to whom and any feedback processes to the highest governance body.
G4-38	Composition of the highest governance body and its committees by: -Executive or non-executive -
G4-39	Is the Chair of the highest governance body is also an executive officer (and, if so, his or her function within the organization's management and the reasons for this arrangement).
G4-41	a. Report processes for the highest governance body to ensure conflicts of interest are avoided and managed. Report whether conflicts of interest are disclosed to stakeholders, including, as a minimum: -
G4-42	a. Report the highest governance body's and senior executives' roles in the development, approval, and updating of the organization's purpose, value or mission statements, strategies, policies, and goals related to economic, environmental and social impacts.
G4-48	The highest committee or position that formally reviews and approves the organization's sustainability report and ensures that all material Aspects are covered.
G4-49	a. Report the process for communicating critical concerns to the highest governance body.
G4-50	a. Report the nature and total number of critical concerns that were communicated to the highest governance body and the mechanism(s) used to address and resolve them.
G4-51	Remuneration policies for the highest governance body and senior executives
G4-52	Process for determining remuneration. Report whether remuneration consultants are involved in determining remuneration and whether they are independent of management. Other relationships which the remuneration consultants have with the organization.
G4-53	Report how stakeholders' views are sought and taken into account regarding remuneration, including the results of votes on remuneration policies and proposals, if applicable.
G4-56	The organization's values, principles, standards and norms of behavior such as codes of conduct and codes of ethics.
G4-57	Internal and external mechanisms for seeking advice on ethical and lawful behavior, and matters related to organizational integrity
G4-58	Internal and external mechanisms for reporting concerns about unethical or unlawful behavior, and matters related to organizational integrity.

Source: GRI G4 standards.

2.2 *A balanced scorecard*

The sustainable scorecard is probably the best known and most popular tool for implementing the adopted strategy at executive level (Figge, Hahn, Schaltegger and Wagner 2003). To achieve this, the company must first have a formulated strategy, which it wants to achieve over five years in terms of four areas: customers, finance, internal processes, and growth and learning. Once the strategy has been defined, the entity must define the specific objectives it wants to achieve progressively over the next five years and the measures by which it will measure the pursuit of those objectives. Meters must be well thought out, as must targets, so that they are not easily circumvented and form a coherent whole. Meters must be quantitative and calculable and assessable. There are a very large number of examples in the literature of well-defined objectives and measures, as well as examples of mistakes that should be avoided.

Table 2. Indicators of specific aspects of CSR.

Aspect, Indicators	Explanation
G4-EC1	Direct economic value generated and distributed
G4-EC2	Financial implications and other risks and opportunities for the organization's activities due to climate change
G4-EC3	Coverage of the organization's defined benefit plan obligations
G4-EC4	Financial assistance received from government
G4-EN3	Energy consumption within the organization
G4-EN4	Energy consumption outside of the organization
G4-EN5	Energy intensity
G4-EN6	Reduction of energy consumption
G4-EN7	Reductions in energy requirements of products and services
G4-EN8	Total water withdrawal by source
G4-EN15	Direct greenhouse gas (GHG) emissions (scope 1)
G4-EN16	Energy indirect greenhouse gas (GHG) emissions (scope 2)
G4-EN17	Other indirect greenhouse gas (GHG) emissions (scope 3)
G4-EN18	Greenhouse gas (GHG) emissions intensity
G4-EN19	Reduction of greenhouse gas (GHG) emissions
G4-EN20	Emissions of ozone-depleting substances (ods)
G4-EN23	Total water discharge by quality and destination
G4-EN24	Total weight of waste by type and disposal method
G4-EN27	Extent of impact mitigation of environmental impacts of products and services
G4-EN28	Percentage of products sold and their packaging materials that are reclaimed by category
G4-EN29	Monetary value of significant fines and total number of non-monetary sanctions for non-compliance with environmental laws and regulations
G4-EN30	Significant environmental impacts of transporting products and other goods and materials for the organization's operations, and transporting members of the workforce
G4-EN32	Percentage of new suppliers that were screened using environmental criteria
G4-EN33	Significant actual and potential negative environmental impacts in the supply chain and actions taken
G4-LA1	Total number and rates of new employee hires and employee turnover by age group gender and region
G4-LA4	Minimum notice periods regarding operational changes, including whether these are specified in collective agreements
G4-LA5	Percentage of total workforce represented in formal joint management-worker health and safety commitees
G4-LA6	Type of injury and rates of injury, occupational diseases, lost days, and absenteeism, and total number of work-related fatalities, by region and by gender
G4-LA8	Health and safety topics covered in formal agreements with trade unions
G4-LA10	Programs for skills management and lifelong learning
G4-LA11	Percentage of employees receiving regular performance and career development
G4-LA12	Composition of governance bodies and breakdown of employees per employee category according to gender, age group, minority indicators of diversity group membership, and other indicators of diversity.
G4-LA13	Ratio of basic salary and remuneration of women to men by employee category, by significant locations of operation
G4-LA14	Percentage of new suppliers that were screened using labor practices criteria
G4-LA15	Significant actual and potential negative impacts for labor practices in the supply chain and actions taken
G4-HR3	Total number of incidents of discrimination and corrective actions taken
G4-HR4	Operations and suppliers identified in which the right to exercise freedom of association and collective bargaining may be violated or at significant risk, and measures taken to support these rights

(*Continued*)

Table 2. (*Continued*)

Aspect, Indicators	Explanation
G4-HR5	Operations and suppliers identified as having significant risk for incidents of child labor, and measures taken to contribute to the effective abolition of child labor
G4-HR6	Operations and suppliers identified as having significant risk for incidents of forced or compulsory labor, and measures to contribute to the elimination of all forms of forced or compulsory labor
G4-HR9	Total number and percentage of operations that have been subject to human rights assessments
G4-HR10	Percentage of new suppliers that were screened using human rights criteria
G4-HR11	Significant actual and potential negative human rights impacts in the supply chain and actions taken
G4-HR12	Number of grievances about human rights impacts filed, addressed, and resolved through formal grievance mechanisms
G4-SO1	Percentage of operations with implemented local community engagement, impact assessments, and development programs...
G4-SO4	Communication and training on anti-corruption policies and procedures
G4-SO5	Confirmed incidents of corruption and actions taken
G4-SO7	Total number of legal actions for anti-competitive behaviour, anti-trust, and monopoly practices and their outcomes
G4-SO8	Monetary value of significant fines and total number of non-monetary sanctions for non-compliance with laws and regulations
G4-SO9	Percentage of new suppliers that were screened using criteria for impacts on society
G4-SO10	Significant actual and potential negative impacts on socie in the supply chain and actions taken
G4-SO11	Number of grievances about impacts on society filed, addressed, and resolved through formal grievance mechanisms

Source: GRI G4 standards.

The great advantage of a balanced scorecard is its quantitative nature and very clear definition of the path of implementation and implementation of the strategy of the entity. Although the sustainability scorecard is described in a descriptive way (because its parameters have to be adapted to the type of business), in practice it is a quantitative model, setting precise goals to be achieved in each of the five years for which the scorecard is usually planned. Below is an example of goals and measures that can be used in the printing industry based on example given by Cegłowski (2010). Within the Balanced Score Card, either CSR variables are added to the client's perspective or a new, fifth perspective is created.

Financial perspective:

Objective 1: Increase in value for the owner, measures: economic profit, desired target value of PLN 300 thousand, actions: identification of areas generating profits, inclusion of profits in the bonus system, optimization of sources of financing.

Objective 2: Maintaining financial liquidity, metrics: liquidity ratio, factoring limit plus unused credit line balance, target values (respectively) PLN 1. 2 and PLN 1. 5 million, actions: control of receivables, optimisation of cash flow management using banking services, cooperation with debt collection companies, analysis of the profitability of using trade loans, optimisation of the use of warehouse space.

Customer Perspective:

Goal 1: Increase sales, metrics: change in sales, share of revenues from key customers in total revenues, target values (respectively) 15%, 20%, actions: build systems for sales analysis, develop and implement a marketing plan, prepare and implement a care plan for key customers, systematically analyze competitors, record and analyze requests for proposals.

Objective 2: Providing customers with fast and timely delivery of orders, metrics: percentage of orders completed on time, average lead time of typical orders, target values (respectively): 90%, 21 days, actions: systematic analysis of delivery timeliness and reasons for delays, analysis of order execution sequence, optimization of production process, critical path analysis, improvement of distribution system.

Objective 3: Increase customer satisfaction, metrics: degree of customer satisfaction, percentage of customers making subsequent orders, target values: above 7 and above 50%, actions: analysis of customer behaviour, analysis of reasons for loss of customers, analysis of reasons for complaints, determination of personal responsibility for complaints, improvement of the service process, quality control of service with the help of "mysterious customer".

Perspective of internal processes:

Objective 1: Cost rationalisation, metrics: profit from sales to sales revenue, profit from sales to assets, targets: above 5% and above 20%, actions: systematic analysis of prices at suppliers, analysis of costs, search for and use of non-expendable reserves, analysis of employee time use, rationalisation of employment to increase productivity, substitution of fixed variable costs.

Objective 2: Introduction of new products and services, metrics: number of new products and services, number of new products and services prepared for future implementation, targets (respectively): 10 and 15, actions: talking to target customers about their needs and capabilities, promoting R&D activities, creating project groups.

Objective 3: Improve product quality, metrics: percentage of defective products, percentage of returns and complaints, target values (respectively): maximum 3% and 5%, actions: allocate more time for inspection, raise awareness of quality issues.

Development Perspective:

Objective 1: increase in employee satisfaction, metrics: satisfaction rating, number of employees leaving work, target values (respectively): min 7 on a scale of 0-10, maximum 5, actions: survey employees on job satisfaction, analyse survey results and implement solutions to increase the level of satisfaction.

Objective 2: Systematic improvement of employees' skills, measures: training costs to salaries, number of working days per year allocated to training, number of employees attending training at least 24 hours per year, target values (respectively): 5% and 6, 60% of the staff, actions: analysis of training needs, development of internal training and coaching system, improvement of working time enabling participation in training, purchase of professional publications and making them available to employees.

Objective 3: Stimulate rationalisation, metrics: number of rationalisation requests submitted by staff, targets: 60, actions: awards and distinctions for rationalisation activities, use of team-based problem-solving methods.

Objective 4: Development of information capital, metrics: assessment of the usefulness of the reports provided, target values: min 8 on a scale of 0-8, actions: building and supplementing customer databases, developing and conducting employee surveys, developing and conducting customer satisfaction surveys, preparing an analytical report summarizing the company's activities.

Objective 5: Improvement of cost records, metrics: percentage of costs without possibility of precise breakdown, target values: 20%, actions: refinement of the system of division of the company into responsibility centres, allocation of costs to responsibility centres, products and services, integration of the efficiency of centres into the remuneration system.

Social and environmental perspective:

Objective 1: Reduce pollutant emissions: Meters: Wastewater and water consumption, Target: Halve, Actions: Gradual switch to greener technologies.

Objective 2: Taking care of reputation and relations with the environment, metrics: number of publications per year showing the company in a favorable light, target values: 6, activities: supporting cultural events, cooperation with local school (classes with a printing profile).

2.3 *London Benchmarking Group model*

The London Benchmarking Group model is also, contrary to appearances, a model strongly focused on using specific quantities usually measured in money. This is a commercial model offered by the LGB, for the implementation of which individuals have to pay. Conceptually, the model is based on a comparison of the resources involved with the results obtained. The model enables the company to:

- calculation of the value of the various resources involved in social activities, such as the products donated, the working time of volunteers,
- measuring the effectiveness of social actions and assessing the short- and long-term benefits for the company resulting from their implementation,
- improving the quality and transparency of social engagement reporting, including e. g. management and promotion costs related to the implementation of social activities by the company,
- increasing the effectiveness of management of various forms of social engagement of the company,
- comparison – according to different criteria – of conducted social activities against the background of the market and industry.

The model values actions. Charity and philanthropy are at the top of the list. In second place are investments for the community, slightly below commercial ventures in the local environment. Below in the hierarchy are the obligatory contribution to local communities and (at the bottom) the basic activities of the company (these are activities resulting from legal regulations and rules of doing business). The aim of the model is to measure and account for all the company's resources involved in social activities, i.e. funds, time, in-kind gifts and services. The second element is the analysis of actions. The third element is the results and their measurement – according to the form of involvement, the type of activities supported and the geographical regions where the involvement is directed. The model identifies and measures both the immediate and long-term benefits of social engagement. Thanks to its quantitative approach, the model allows companies to compare with each other, of course, using the same methodology in terms of CSR engagement. However, the LBG model is advantageous mainly for large entities, once because of its commercial nature and twice because of the nature of the tool itself. However, even if an individual fails to implement the sense of the strict model, the very concept of a quantitative approach to the issue is feasible also from the perspective of an individual entity.

2.4 *Sustainable du Ponta system*

Another potential element of the CSR control and management system could be the use of a sustainable duPonta model, or at least a model and approach based on that model. The du Ponta model is an approach to the analysis of financial performance and its changes based on the dynamic analysis of changes between two consecutive periods. If the result changes (particularly the return on equity), the change can be broken down into the product of different indicators and these indicators can be broken down until the individual analytical accounts of the entity are reached. In this way, the inquiring accountant can accurately indicate which accounts and, consequently, economic operations, have had the strongest positive or negative impact on the financial result of the entity. The sustainable model treats the impact (both positive and negative) of an individual on the environment as inputs and results.

Among the proposals regarding the possibility of using the DuPonta model in environmental management in the enterprise, we can note three directions (Doś and Błach 2014):

- the use of the DuPont model to demonstrate the rank of a specific area of business and thus justify the creation of an environmental strategy in that area (Alvarez 2012; Chai 2009),
- identification of the impact of environmental impact indicators on profitability indicators (ROE, ROA and ROS) (Dong-Shang and Li-Chin 2008; Waddock and Graves 1997; King and Lenox 2002),
- decomposition of the DuPont model indicators to capture the environmental impact of certain operations and events and the financial results achieved (Castro and Chousa 2006).

The DuPonta model can be expanded with a set of indicators including, among others, the type of energy used, its quantity, the type and quantity of water used, the type and quantity of fuel used, the categories of wastewater and any other pollutants, the costs of waste storage and treatment, the productivity of recycled waste. These elements are interwoven into the du Pont equation, for example, as follows:

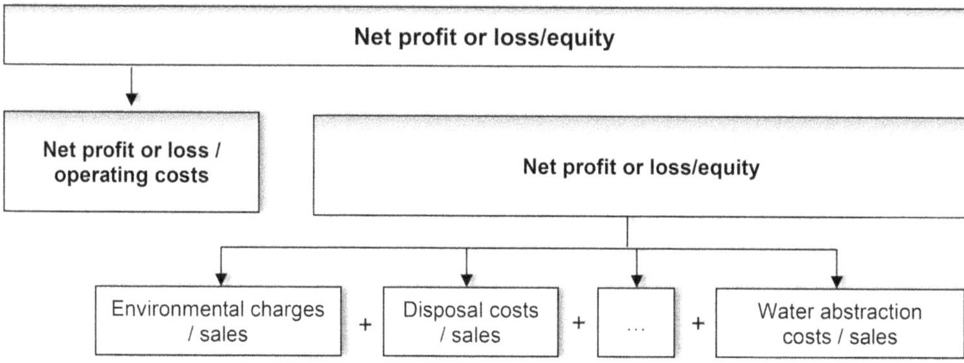

Figure 1. The first concept of sustainable du Pont analysis/model.
Source: own study based on (Castro 2006) for: (Kochalski et al., 2016, p. 222).

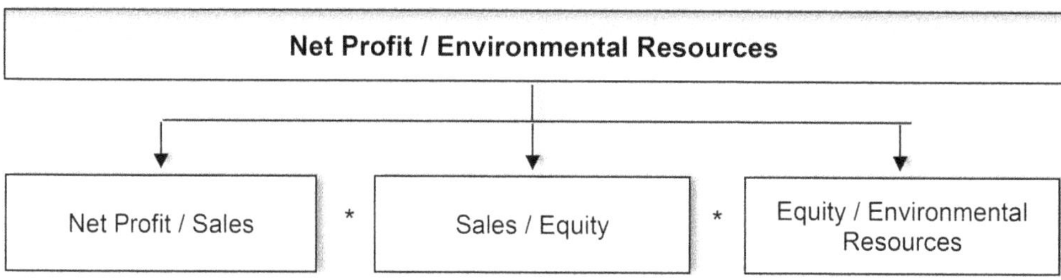

Figure 2. The second concept of the sustainable du Ponta model.
Source: own study based on (Figge, Hahn 2013) for: (Kochalski et al. 2016: 222).

3 FINAL CONCLUSIONS

As with other company control systems, it is not possible to propose a single matrix for building such a system in a company, as it depends on the specifics of the entity: industry, size, needs. Nevertheless, due to the increasing incorporation of CSR issues into reporting and into the legal system, the implementation of even the beginning of CSR control in an entity seems to be a reasonable proposal. However, it is important to push from the outset to quantify this system, because descriptive treatment of CSR issues may at most show the broadly understood intentions of the individual, but not measure action and achievement of objectives. Perhaps in the near future CSR reporting will become mandatory, but even if not for all entities, the reputation of an individual will increasingly depend on its activity in this area. Therefore, it is worth implementing such a system today, setting goals to be achieved and slowly starting to implement the system in order to get used to the new metrics and expectations of employees before changes in the social and legal environment force rapid implementations not necessarily accepted by employees.

The CSR system is not only the employer's outlays, but also the involvement of employees both in the form of charitable activities and saving resources used by the entity. In many respects, the CSR system resembles a cost control and planning system, only those that elude the measurements and definitions of standard controlling.

The benefits appear to be long-term, but they are obvious. In the world of the public Internet, the reputation of a company becomes one of the key intangible assets of an individual. The CSR system is a great way to not only take care of this reputation, but to increase it.

REFERENCES

Ajlouni M. 2008. The Environment as a Fifth Component of a Balance Scorecard for Improving Organizational Performance. In: E.N. Laboy-Nieves, F.C. Schaffner, A. Abdelhadi and M.F.A. Goosen (edd.), *Environmental Management, Sustainable Development and Human Health*. CRC Press, London.

Alvarez I. 2012. Impact of CO_2 Emission Variation on Firm Performance. *Business Strategy and the Environment*, vol. 21.

Castro N., Chousa J. 2006. An Integrated Framework for the Financial Analysis of Sustainability. *Business Strategy and the Environment* vol. 15.

Cegłowski B. 2010. *Strategiczna karta wyników w firmie poligraficznej - case study, Analiza i kontrola finansowa*. 3 listopada 2010, [@:] https://analizafinansowa.pl/controlling/strategiczna-karta-wynikow-w-firmie-poligraficznej-case-study-2897.html (12 05 2023).

Chai N. 2009. Sustainability Performance Evaluation System in Government: A Balanced Scorecard Approach Towards Sustainable Development. Springer, Dordrecht – Heidelberg – London – New York.

Dong-Shang Ch., Li-Chin R. K. 2008. The Effects of Sustainable Development on Firms' Financial Performance – an Empirical Approach. *Sustainable Development* (16).

Doś A., Błach J. 2014. *The application of the DuPont model in the context of corporate environmentalmanagement – evidence from the Polish companies*. Research Papers of Wrocław University of Economics (Prace Naukowe Uniwersytetu Ekonomicznegowe Wrocławiu), 330, 34–42.

Figge F., Hahn T., Schaltegger S. and Wagner M., 2003 The Sustinability Balancescorecard as a Framework to Link Environmental Management Accounting with Strategic Management. In: M.D. Bennett, P.M. Rikhardsson and S. Schaltegger (eds.), Environmental Management Accounting: *Purpose and Progress*, Springer, Norwell, Dordrecht.

Figge F. and Hahn T. 2013. Value Drivers of Corporate Eco-Efficiency: Management Accounting Information for the Efficient Use of Environmental Resources. *Management Accounting Research*. 24. 387–400. 10.1016/j.mar.2013.06.009.

Guerard J., Schwartz E. 2007. *Quantitative Corporate Finance*. Springer, Anchorage.

King A., Lenox M. 2002. Exploring the locus of profitable pollution reduction. *Management Science* 48(2).

Kochalski C., Bartkowiak P., Cieślak M., Chudziński P., Cyfert S., Kubiak J., Matuszak-Flejszman A., Mikołajewicz G., Nowicki J., Ratajczak P., Sierpińska-Sawicz A., Szulczewska-Remi A., Zerbst S. and Zieliński T. 2016. *Zielony controlling i finanse*, Wydawnictwo C.H. Beck, Warszawa.

Schaltegger S., Burritt R., Petersen H. 2003. *An Introduction to Corporate Environmental Management: Striving for Sustainability*. Greenleaf Publishing, Sheffield.

Waddock S.A., Graves S.B. 1997. The corporate social performance-financial performance link. *Strategic Management Journal* 18(4).

Digital Synergy – El Emary et al. (eds)

Chapter 22
Municipal barriers to intellectual capital management in SMEs from the lower Silesian voivodship in Poland

Robert Balcerzyk & Katarzyna Czaińska
Land Forces University, Wrocław, Poland

Contents

The purpose of the research was to diagnose barriers in the process of intellectual capital management in SME's in the Lower Silesian Voivodship in Poland. The diagnostic survey was adopted as the leading method. The research was conducted in the second half of 2022 on a random research sample of 335 people employed in small and medium-sized enterprises in Lower Silesia.

Employees identify the organization's intellectual capital with human capital; perceive intellectual capital as the clarity of minds of employees, their creativity and innovation, reliability, honesty, credibility, consistency in action and teamwork. Companies based on intellectual capital need leaders, rather than managers. Managers focus on systems and structure, while leaders are people-oriented; leaders build trust by removing barriers to information flow, managers rely only on control.

For people responsible for recruiting employees, the results may be useful in developing a candidate profile, in particular when identifying key competences of knowledge workers or talented people. Based on empirical research, the article proposes an original set of system solutions in the field of human capital management to improve the functioning of organizations in an unstable and changing environment.

1 INTRODUCTION

Intangible resources have always existed in enterprises. Many management concepts have noticed and still see the knowledge, skills of their employees, social relations, company image, and inter-organizational networks. They are reflected in such management concepts as human resource management, knowledge management, marketing management or enterprise value management. Therefore, it was necessary to classify individual intangible resources in order to use them optimally. This task was to be met by a concept created in the 1980s, namely the concept of intellectual capital. This concept emphasizes the significant role of man/employee as a source of competitive advantage and success of modern organizations. It allows to practically and properly use the company's intangible resources, which creates the basis for gaining a strategic advantage on the market. Intellectual capital is the coexistence of such assets as people and their competences, various types of organizational systems, technological facilities, knowledge management systems, internal relations between employees and external ones in

DOI: 10.1201/9781003440406-22

relation to business partners and clients. The development of intellectual capital proves the innovativeness of the company (Matinfard & Khavari 2015). The challenge for organizations, that want to develop on new levels, is to locate their intangible assets and then manage these resources appropriately. The reason for such changes in modern management strategies is to cultivate the era of knowledge and knowledge workers. Therefore, it is necessary to diagnose potential barriers in acquiring employees with the highest intellectual capital, in the intellectual development of the organization or the organizational learning process, and to diagnose the benefits for companies that efficiently manage intellectual capital.

The number of active companies in Poland has been constantly growing in recent years and from the economic collapse in 2009 to the end of 2020 it increased by 35%. The ongoing war in Ukraine and the energy crisis in Europe in the near future will cause a slowdown in economic growth in many EU countries, and even recession. Polish entrepreneurs will have to face this problem. Already in 2022, a reduction in expenses can be noticed, as well as conservative investment decisions of entrepreneurs, in particular in the field of research and development. On the other hand, the increase in the number of entrepreneurs' declarations regarding investments in human capital may be encouraging. It should be emphasized that medium-sized enterprises in Poland employ 1.54 million people. Medium-sized enterprises are a very important sector of the Polish economy and account for 43.4% of all actively innovative enterprises that introduced new or improved existing products or business processes in 2018-2020. What allows for the rapid development of these enterprises is flexibility, manifested by quick and effective "adjustment" to the turbulent environment thanks to the competence of employees. Out of 2.26 million Polish enterprises, 99.8% are small and medium enterprises. The vast majority are micro-enterprises (97%), small enterprises (2.2%) and medium-sized enterprises (0.8%), which is 18,080 companies. It is worth noting that, according to the Report of the Polish Agency for Enterprise Development (PARP, 2022), the latter sector is responsible for generating approximately 10.2% of the Polish gross domestic product. One of the leading voivodships in the area of entrepreneurship is the Lower Silesian. In 2020, in 27 analyzed categories, the value of the synthetic indicator of entrepreneurship for the Lower Silesian Voivodeship was 67.5, taking third place in the ranking. The first place was taken by the Mazowieckie Voivodeship with the index of 80.54 (PARP 2022).

The analyzes show that entrepreneurs in the Lower Silesian recognize the importance of human capital, and at the same time a huge reservoir can be seen in the development of this sector. Therefore, it is important to know the development barriers of human capital in medium-sized enterprises. When starting the research, three research questions were defined:

1. What factors constitute a barrier to the implementation of the organizational process of learning in SMEs in Lower Silesia?
2. What are the barriers to the development of intellectual capital in SMEs in Lower Silesia?

Moreover, the following hypotheses were formulated:

H1There is a relationship between the indication of potential barriers to intellectual capital and the size of the enterprise.

H2There is a relationship between the indication of potential barriers to intellectual capital and the type of industry.

H3There is a relationship between indicating the factors that make it difficult for a company to recruit employees with the highest intellectual capital and the size of the company.

H4There is a relationship between indicating the factors that make it difficult for a company to recruit employees with the highest intellectual capital and the type of industry.

2 THE ESSENCE OF INTELLECTUAL CAPITAL MANAGEMENT

The Intellectual capital management is a relatively new trend in research in the field of management (especially in Poland), although the concept of intellectual capital was used for the first time in 1969. The 1980s brought an increase in interest in the idea of intellectual capital (Kucera & Dvorakova 2023: 296-315). W. Wriston, being the president of the American bank

Citicorp, announced that his bank and other enterprises have intellectual capital that creates their value, and is not measured in accounting terms (Stewart 2001: 52-56). At the end of the 20th century, two research trends concerning the concept of intellectual capital could be distinguished. The first emphasizes the need for accurate measurement of non-financial data and the study of the relationship between them and financial data. The second trend mainly concerned the creation and storage as well as the improvement of knowledge and the relationship between knowledge and value creation (E. Gross-Gołacka et al. 2019: 15).

Intellectual capital consists of two factors: human capital and structural capital. Human capital is, of course, the knowledge, skills and talents of the organization's employees. Structural capital consists of hardware, software, technologies, databases and patents. K. Beyer noted that "structural capital is the result of the actions of employees and, unlike human capital, can be owned by the company" (Beyer 2013: 17). P. Wachowiak (2005) presents intellectual capital as the result of studying the value of the company, measuring the hidden dynamic factors underlying parts of the organization. It is the difference between the market value and the book value of the company, creating its non-financial assets (Haji 2015: 756-784). These are hidden assets that are not fully captured in its balance sheet reporting (Mehrotra et al. 2017: 366-387). It consists of employee competences, company organization and customer relations.

In the presented approach, the intellectual capital of an organization is divided into immeasurable elements: social, human and organizational capital. Social capital is a combination of organizational structure, interpersonal relations and cognitive capital. "The development of social capital in an organizational context is based on the assumption that the company's potential is best developed through cooperation between staff members" (Jashapara 2014: 92). The organization is mainly created by interpersonal relations (Todericiu & Stăniţ 2015: 676-681; Balcerzyk 2021: 228-230). Organizational (structural) capital refers to more specific elements of an organization (Claver-Cortés 2018). It consists of the organizational structure, relations with the environment in the form of supply chains, knowledge stored in databases, documents (procedures, regulations, data), IT systems (Hajro 2017: 345-372). Organizational capital is an organization's investments in management systems and a philosophy that accelerates the flow of knowledge, both inside and outside the organization (Aryanto et al. 2015: 874-879). It can be assumed that organizational capital takes a materialized form, and its owner is usually an organization (company) (Madsen & Leiblein 2015: 1097-1127). The company may claim ownership of these assets through patents, copyrights, trade secrets.

B. Hamm believes that human capital is "all the features and abilities that can be attributed to a single person" (Hamm 2004: 52-53). One part of human capital is therefore natural capital, namely everything that can be classified as physical existence and metabolism. The second part is social capital, namely all activities that society undertakes to "ennoble" human nature, and thus change it through upbringing and education. People are the main driving force behind all innovation (Wijaya & Utama 2023: 328-342). It should be noted that intellectual capital in the context of the organization's value is its immeasurable part, creating "added value" (Kalkan et al. 2014: 700-707). Intangible assets are difficult to identify, and the values of its individual components are difficult to add up. Therefore, it seems accurate to say that the potential of an organization is evidenced by the "strength of minds" of its employees (Berzkalne & Zelgalve 2014: 887-896). Thanks to this, the organization gains measurable market benefits (e.g. a new product, technology, patent). Moreover, by using modern technologies, it becomes possible to share the capital held by other employees (e.g. gathering, storing and sharing knowledge).

3 RESEARCH METHODOLOGY

The diagnostic survey was conducted using a questionnaire. It was developed on the basis of literature review. The survey was intended for employees of companies in Lower Silesia. In the study, the following independent variables were assumed: the sex of the respondents, the age of the respondents, the size of the company (place of work), place of residence and the industry of the company's activity. The research was conducted in the second half of 2022. 335 people took part in the research.

The study group was evenly divided by gender. Women constituted 46.87% of the study group, and men 53.13%. About 65.37% of the respondents are young people aged 19-29. 24.78% of the respondents were between 30 and 40 years old. The least numerous group were employees over 40 (9.85%). The respondents were young people at the stage of early professional career, during which crystallization occurs, narrowing the field of exploration and finalizing the choice of profession. 64,77% were employed in small companies; 35.23% in medium-sized companies. The largest group of employees were people employed in production companies (45.87%). A large percentage of respondents are employees in the trade industry (14.43%) and transport (7.16%). The rest are people employed in the financial industry, construction, etc.

In order to answer the research questions, statistical analyzes were carried out using the IBM SPSS Statistics 26 package. Cross tables with the chi-square test of independence were made using it. The level of significance in this chapter was considered to be $\alpha = 0.05$. In order to check the essence of the dependence, a post-hoc analysis was performed taking into account the values of the corrected residuals (Beasley & Schumacker 1995: 82).

4 IDENTIFICATION OF BARRIERS IN MANAGING THE INTELLECTUAL CAPITAL OF THE ORGANIZATION

The research shows that over 58.81% of respondents identify the meaning of the concept of the organization's intellectual capital with human capital (Table 1).

Table 1. Interpretation of the concept of the organization's intellectual capital.

No.	Response categories	n	%
1.	social capital	33	9.85
2.	human capital	197	58.81
3.	organizational capital	105	31.34
	total		100

Source: Author's own analysis

About 31.34% of the respondents identify the intellectual capital of an organization with the organizational (structural) capital. They perceive it as an organizational structure, explicit knowledge stored in databases, documents (procedures, regulations, data), implemented IT systems, processes taking place in the organization that do not disappear when an employee leaves. It consists of built relationships with the environment in the form of supply chains. Structural capital affects the value of the company through its brand, reputation and having loyal customers.

Intellectual capital management brings measurable effects to the company, which take the form of an increase in the value of intellectual capital, the possibility of eliminating errors, increasing innovation, developing intellectual resources, promoting knowledge, knowledge management, increasing creativity and competitiveness, and talent management programs (Table 2). This opinion is shared by almost 71% of the respondents.

The organizational culture of a company is determined primarily by the culture of its management staff and the employees themselves. A high level of uncertainty avoidance or power distance (which is a feature of Polish culture) may significantly limit the full implementation of the organizational learning process. The research attempted to diagnose the factors constituting the greatest barrier to the implementation of the organizational learning process (Table 3).

Table 2. Interpretation of the concept of the organization's intellectual capital.

No.	Response categories	n	%
1.	Definitely yes	72	21.49
2.	Yes	166	49.55
3.	NO	51	6.27
4.	definitely not	10	2.99
5.	I don't know	36	10.75
	total		100

Source: Author's own analysis

Table 3. Factors constituting a barrier to the implementation of the organizational learning process.

No.	Response categories	n	%
1.	creating a vision for the future based only on the opinion of top management	106	31.64
2.	internal competition between parts of the organization	57	17.00
3.	accumulation of knowledge for personal gain	25	7.46
4.	lack of trust in the organization	40	11.94
5.	treating organizational learning activities as extra work	34	10.15
6.	treating unusual events as a threat	20	5.97
7.	punishment for mistakes	20	5.97
8.	no tolerance for dissenting opinions	33	3.88
	total		100

Source: Author's own analysis

Research has shown that the main factor blocking the process of organizational learning is creating a vision of the future based only on the opinion of top management (31.65%). In highly hierarchical and centralized organizations, the flow of information and knowledge is limited. This limits their flexibility and negatively affects the rational behavior of employees. They are characterized by the lack of employee participation in making any decisions. Excessive centralization and formalization cause the boundaries between the departments within the organization to be outlined, but also between the company and the external environment. The lack of information supply from the external and internal environment blocks the free flow of knowledge resources, limits cognitive possibilities and taking initiating actions. Such organizational culture favors passivity of actions.

A learning organization is a kind of social system that has its own internal structure of communication and information flow, and thanks to this, interaction between participants is possible. Clearly defined boundaries create internal competition between departments/ departments of the organization (17.00%). It leads to the avoidance of certain undertakings and the preference for short-term activities with apparent success. The goal of individual organizational units is mainly to increase the effectiveness and efficiency of their employees. Departments (their managers) compete with each other for awards, promotions, organizational prestige, resigning from teamwork and achieving strategic goals of the organization. Such an organizational culture generates further barriers to the functioning of the concept of intellectual capital management, namely the lack of trust in the organization (11.94%). Trust plays an important role in the management of intellectual capital. For a learning organization, the starting point is the recognition of benevolence-based trust and competence-based trust, which determines the level of trust in management and co-workers. Clearly drawn interdepartmental boundaries block or underestimate the innovative ideas of employees. This way of treating employees creates a climate of mistrust and suspicion among people who make up the company's intellectual capital. It is a significant barrier to knowledge management, and in the longer term it hinders the company's development. The respondents considered the treatment of unusual events as a threat (5.97%), punishment for mistakes made (5.97%), lack of

Table 4. Barriers to the development of companies' intellectual capital.

No.	Response categories	n	%
1.	obtaining funds for employee development	48	14.33
2.	acquiring employees with appropriate qualifications	46	13.73
3.	staff turnover	104	31.04
4.	lack of leadership skills among managers	68	20.30
5.	disorganization of work (lack of managerial skills among the management staff)	69	20.60
	TOTAL		100

Source: Author's own analysis

tolerance for different opinions (3.88%) as unimportant factors constituting a barrier to the implementation of the organizational learning process.

The respondents diagnosed potential barriers to the development of the intellectual capital of their companies (Table 4).

It can be assumed that the respondents identified the managers themselves as a barrier to the development of the company, believing that they are responsible for the disorganization of work due to the lack of managerial skills (20.60%) and lack of leadership skills (20.30%). Some believe that the leader is more important than the manager, others that he is an alternative, as research results suggest. Despite the fact that they are mutually compatible, they are also divergent roles. People follow a leader because they want to. Behind the manager because they have to.

Another significant barrier to the development of the organization's intellectual capital is staff turnover (31.04%) and the mere acquisition of employees with appropriate qualifications (13.73%). Human capital is an important element building a competitive advantage. The surveyed organizations struggle with staff shortages. On the Polish labor market, it is difficult to attract employees, it is even more difficult to train them, and it is most difficult to keep the best ones. A high staff turnover indicates that the working environment is hostile to them. Employees feel underappreciated, do not see development and promotion opportunities for themselves, teamwork is not preferred in the company. To put it simply, employees feel underappreciated. Regardless of the reasons, rotation always generates some losses for the employer, especially when employees with above-average performance or employees with rare qualifications who are difficult to replace leave. Problems related to obtaining funds for the development of employees constitute a barrier (14.33%). However, this is not a leading barrier as it might seem. Currently,

Table 5. Barriers in attracting employees with the highest intellectual capital.

No.	Response categories	n	%
1.	changes in employees' life priorities	50	14.93
2.	dwindling talent pools and limited resources	54	16.12
3.	cultural differences	19	5.67
4.	narrow range of employment options	109	32.54
5.	deficiencies in modernizing the working environment	55	16.42
6.	fear of having to comply with the corporate culture	28	8.36
7.	access to the global labor market	20	5.97
	total		100

Source: Author's own analysis

Table 6. Relationship between the indication of potential barriers to intellectual capital and the size of the enterprise.

Which of the potential barriers to the development of your company's intellectual capital pose the greatest threat to the company?		Enterprise size: micro enterprises	Small enterprises	Medium enterprises	Total	$\chi^2(8)$	p	Vc
Raising funds for employee development	n	3	35	10	48			
	%	5.9%	21.1%	8.5%	14.3%			
	Rest	-1.87	3.50	-2.26				
Acquiring employees with appropriate qualifications	n	11	29	6	46			
	%	21.6%	17.5%	5.1%	13.7%			
	Rest	1.77	1.97	-3.39				
Staff turnover	n	16	35	53	104			
	%	31.4%	21.1%	44.9%	31.0%	54.31	<0.001	0.40
	Rest	0.05	-3.91	4.05				
Lack of leadership skills among executives	n	7	24	37	68			
	%	13.7%	14.5%	31.4%	20.3%			
	Rest	-1.27	-2.63	3.71				
Disorganization of work (lack of managerial skills among the management staff)	n	14	43	12	69			
	%	27.5%	25.9%	10.2%	20.6%			
	Rest	1.31	2.38	-3.48				

Source: Author's own analysis

more and more companies in Poland benefit from financial support from the European Fund, in particular for activities related to the development of human capital.

Employee turnover implies the need to acquire new employees, talented, with rare qualifications and the highest intellectual capital (Table 5).

Attracting employees with the highest intellectual capital is mainly hindered by the narrow range of employment options (32.54%). Paradoxically, the COVID-19 crisis had a positive impact on entrepreneurs in terms of hiring employees. The flexibility of managers in managing intellectual capital can be noticed. Meetings with clients took place and still take place virtually, which previously lacked an impulse for this type of activity. Remote work and rotational work were introduced, thus meeting the expectations of some employees, especially the younger generation. A significant number of companies have moved their activities to various types of Internet platforms. This enabled broad access to the labor market for people from smaller towns or those raising children.

Lack of modernization of the working environment is a barrier to finding employees (16.42%). Young people increasingly pay attention to the adaptation of office infrastructure and the functioning of specific security procedures. It is not only about factors such as noise level, lighting, air pollution, temperature, humidity, but also working methods, breaks, modern infrastructure, social security. Harmony is needed. It is also a holistic approach to the workplace, i.e. planning and adapting both the physical environment and the actual work to the staff. Shrinking resources of talented people and their limited sources are also noticed (16.12%). The business environment is becoming more and more complex, volatile and uncertain. Companies are confronted with the VUCA environment, and additionally with unprecedented demographic challenges. So far, employees with professional experience, specific competences, intellect or education were considered people with the highest potential. Currently, such people are considered to be an employee who is successful in a specific position, the ability to cope with and grow up to increasingly complex roles and circumstances, or emotional intelligence. It becomes more difficult to attract not only people valuable to the company, but also to recruit people in general.

Life priorities of employees have also changed, which may be a barrier to attracting employees with the highest intellectual capital (14.93%). The pandemic and the related restrictions on the provision of work have given many people the opportunity to reflect on what is really important in life. The main reason for changing the place of employment is interpersonal relations and the change of employees' priorities. Employees strive for a balance between work and family life. In the fight for employees, foreign companies are considering attracting employees by introducing a four-day working day.

In order to test the hypothesis regarding the relationship between the indication of potential barriers to intellectual capital that pose the greatest threat to the enterprise and the size of the enterprise, a crosstab with the chi-square test of independence was performed (Table 6).

The analysis showed a statistically significant relationship between the variables. Cramer's effect strength factor V indicates that this association was moderately strong. In order to check the essence of the dependence, a post-hoc analysis was performed, taking into account the values of the adjusted residuals, which showed that in small enterprises, three aspects were indicated more often than it would result from the expected values: obtaining funds for employee development, obtaining employees with appropriate qualifications and disorganization (lack of managerial skills among the managerial staff), and less often to staff turnover and lack of leadership skills among the managerial staff. On the other hand, in medium-sized enterprises, the situation was reversed, i.e. staff turnover and lack of leadership skills among the management staff were mentioned more often, and three other aspects less often. In the group of micro-enterprises, the obtained values did not differ from the expected distributions.

Subsequently, it was checked whether there was a relationship between the indication of potential barriers to intellectual capital and the type of industry in which the company operates (Table 7).

Table 7. Relationship between the indication of potential barriers to intellectual capital and the type of industry.

	Type of activity										
Which of the potential barriers to the development of your company's intellectual capital pose the greatest threat to the company?		Construction	Finance and insurance	Production	Transport	Trade	Other	Total	$\chi^2(20)$	p	V c
Raising funds for employee development	n	0	7	18	6	3	14	48			
	%	0.0%	43.8%	11.7%	25.0%	6.7%	15.9%	14.3%			
	Rest	-1.20	3.40	-1.30	1.50	-1.60	0.50				
Acquiring employees with appropriate qualifications	n	0	6	26	0	6	8	46			
	%	0.0%	37.5%	16.9%	0.0%	13.3%	9.1%	13.7%			
	Rest	-1.10	2.80	1.50	-2.00	-0.10	-1.50				
Staff turnover	n	0	0	47	11	16	thirty	104			
	%	0.0%	0.0%	30.5%	45.8%	35.6%	34.1%	31.0%	81.29	<.001	0.25
	Rest	-1.90	-2.80	-0.20	1.60	0.70	0.70				
Lack of leadership skills among executives	n	0	3	27	7	7	24	68			
	%	0.0%	18.8%	17.5%	29.2%	15.6%	27.3%	20.3%			
	Rest	-1.40	-0.20	-1.20	1.10	-0.90	1.90				
Disorganization of work (lack of managerial skills among the management staff)	n	8	0	36	0	13	12	69			
	%	100.0%	0.0%	23.4%	0.0%	28.9%	13.6%	20.6%			
	Rest	5.60	-2.10	1.20	-2.60	1.50	-1.90				

Source: Author's own analysis

The analysis again showed a statistically significant relationship between the variables. Cramer's effect strength factor V indicates that this relationship was weak. The post-hoc analysis, carried out taking into account the values of adjusted residuals, showed that work disorganization (lack of managerial skills among the management staff) was much more often mentioned in the construction industry. In companies from the financial and insurance industries, barriers in the form of obtaining funds for the development of employees and obtaining employees with appropriate qualifications were much more often indicated, and less often - staff turnover and disorganization of work (lack of managerial skills among the management staff). On the other hand, in transport, the acquisition of employees with appropriate qualifications and disorganization of work (lack of managerial skills among the management staff) were mentioned less frequently than expected values. In other sectors, no values significantly different from the expected values were recorded.

Then, it was checked whether there was a relationship between the indication of factors that make it difficult for the company to recruit employees with the highest intellectual capital and the size of the company (Table 8).

The analyzed relationship turned out to be statistically significant and moderately strong.

The post-hoc analysis showed that in micro-enterprises, difficulties in the form of changes in life priorities of employees were more often indicated, and less often the fear of the need to comply with the corporate culture and access to the global labor market. On the other hand, in small enterprises, the fear of having to comply with the corporate culture was more often indicated, and cultural differences less frequently. In medium-sized enterprises, in turn, two obstacles were indicated more often, i.e. cultural differences and access to the global labor market.

Table 8. Relationship between indicating the factors that make it difficult for a company to recruit employees with the highest intellectual capital and the size of the company.

Which of the factors make it difficult for your company to recruit employees with the highest intellectual capital?		Enterprise size: micro enterprises	Small enterprises	Medium enterprises	Total	$\chi^2(12)$	p	V c
Changes in employees' life priorities	n	14	24	12	50	65.63	<0.001	0.31
	%	27.5%	14.5%	10.2%	14.9%			
	Rest	2.70	-0.20	-1.80				
Shrinking talent pools and limited resources	n	9	32	13	54			
	%	17.6%	19.3%	11.0%	16.1%			
	Rest	0.30	1.60	-1.90				
Cultural differences	n	0	0	19	19			
	%	0.0%	0.0%	16.1%	5.7%			
	Rest	-1.90	-4.40	6.10				
Narrow range of employment options	n	20	54	35	109			
	%	39.2%	32.5%	29.7%	32.5%			
	Rest	1.10	0.00	-0.80				
Deficiencies in modernizing the working environment	n	8	27	20	55			
	%	15.7%	16.3%	16.9%	16.4%			
	Rest	-0.20	-0.10	0.20				
Fear of having to comply with the corporate culture	n	0	22	6	28			
	%	0.0%	13.3%	5.1%	8.4%			
	Rest	-2.30	3.20	-1.60				
Access to the global labor market	n	0	7	13	20			
	%	0.0%	4.2%	11.0%	6.0%			
	Rest	-2.00	-1.30	2.90				

Source: Author's own analysis

Then, it was checked whether there was a relationship between the indication of factors that make it difficult for the company to recruit employees with the highest intellectual capital and the type of industry in which the company operates (Table 9).

Table 9. Relationship between indicating the factors that make it difficult for a company to recruit employees with the highest intellectual capital and the type of industry.

Which of the factors make it difficult for your company to recruit employees with the highest intellectual capital?		Type of activity: Construction	Finance and insurance	Production	Transport	Trade	Other	Total	$\chi^2(20)$	*p*	V *c*
Changes in employees' life priorities	n	0	3	23	18	0	6	50			
	%	0.0%	18.8%	14.9%	75.0%	0.0%	6.8%	14.9%			
	Rest	-1.20	0.40	0.00	8.60	-3.00	-2.50				
Shrinking talent pools and limited resources	n	8	4	14	3	12	13	54			
	%	100.0%	25.0%	9.1%	12.5%	26.7%	14.8%	16.1%			
	Rest	6.50	1.00	-3.20	-0.50	2.10	-0.40				
Cultural differences	n	0	0	7	0	3	9	19			
	%	0.0%	0.0%	4.5%	0.0%	6.7%	10.2%	5.7%			
	Rest	-0.70	-1.00	-0.80	-1.20	0.30	2.20				
Narrow range of employment options	n	0	6	55	3	13	32	109			
	%	0.0%	37.5%	35.7%	12.5%	28.9%	36.4%	32.5%			
	Rest	-2.00	0.40	1.10	-2.20	-0.60	0.90		164.59	<0.001	0.31
Deficiencies in modernizing the working environment	n	0	0	35	0	11	9	55			
	%	0.0%	0.0%	22.7%	0.0%	24.4%	10.2%	16.4%			
	Rest	-1.30	-1.80	2.90	-2.30	1.60	-1.80				
Fear of having to comply with the corporate culture	n	0	3	6	0	6	13	28			
	%	0.0%	18.8%	3.9%	0.0%	13.3%	14.8%	8.4%			
	Rest	-0.90	1.50	-2.70	-1.50	1.30	2.50				
Access to the global labor market	n	0	0	14	0	0	6	20			
	%	0.0%	0.0%	9.1%	0.0%	0.0%	6.8%	6.0%			
	Rest	-0.70	-1.00	2.20	-1.30	-1.80	0.40				

Source: Author's own analysis

The analyzed relationship turned out to be statistically significant and moderately strong.

A post-hoc analysis found that construction companies were more likely to cite a shrinking talent pool and limited supply of talent, and less likely to cite a narrow range of employment options. Production companies more often pointed to deficiencies in modernizing the work environment and access to the global labor market, and less often to shrinking talent resources and limited sources of talent, and the fear of having to comply with corporate culture. Transport companies pointed much more often to changes in the life priorities of employees, and less often to a narrow range of employment options and deficiencies in modernizing the work environment. In the retail industry, shrinking talent resources and their limited sources were more often indicated, and changes in employees' life priorities less often.

5 CONCLUSION

The conducted research shows that the surveyed employees identify the meaning of the concept of the organization's intellectual capital with human capital. They perceive intellectual capital as, above all, the clarity of minds of employees, their creativity and innovation, reliability, honesty, credibility, consistency in action and teamwork. Modern forms of organization naturally support the management of intellectual capital. Companies based on intellectual capital need leaders, not managers. Managers focus on systems and structure, while leaders are people-oriented. Leaders build trust by removing barriers to information flow, managers rely only on control. Managers take a short-term perspective, while leaders take a long-term perspective. The change of life priorities of employees is a barrier for many companies in attracting them. The COVID-19 pandemic has prompted many people to reevaluate their work and life priorities. Employees strive for a balance between work and family life. In the fight for employees, companies introduce innovative solutions regarding, for example, hybrid or remote working mode, offering a flexible work schedule, rewarding productivity instead of worked hours. Employers are still looking for ways to attract or at least neutralize the number of leaving workers and are considering a four-day workweek. The flexibility of employers will be a decisive factor in staying on the job or quit your job.

REFERENCES

Aryanto R., Fontana A., & Afiff A. 2015. Strategic Human Resource Management, Innovation Capability and Performance: An Empirical Study in Indonesia Software Industry. *Procedia Social and Behavioral Sciences*, 211(9), 874–879. https://doi.org/10.1016/j.sbspro.2015.11.115.

Beasley T. M., & Schumacker R. E. 1995. Multiple Regression Approach to Analyzing Contingency Tables: Post Hoc and Planned Comparison Procedures. *The Journal of Experimental Education*, 64(1), 79–93.

Balcerzyk D. 2021. The Role of a Leader in Contemporary Organizations. *European Research Studies Journal*, Vol. 24, Issue 1, 226–240, doi:10.35808/ersj/1959.

Beyer K. 2013. *Proces zarządzania kapitałem intelektualnym jako wyzwanie dla przedsiębiorstw*, Uniwersytet Szczeciński, Szczecin.

Berzkalne I., & Zelgalve E. 2014. Intellectual Capital and Company Value. *Procedia - Social and Behavioral Sciences*, 110, 887–896. https://doi.org/10.1016/j.sbspro.2013.12.934.

Claver-Cortés E., Zaragoza-Sáez P., González-Illescas M. 2018. Intellectual capital management: An approach to organizational practices in Ecuador. *Intantgible Capital*, Vol. 14, No 2, https://www.intangiblecapital.org/index.php/ic/article/view/1158/709

Gross-Gołacka E., Jefmański B., Spałek P. 2019. *Kapitał intelektualny przedsiębiorstw w Polsce – wybrane aspekty teoretyczne i praktyczne*. Polskie Wydawnictwo Ekonomiczne, Warszawa.

Jashapara A. 2014. *Zarządzanie wiedzą*. PWE, Warszawa

Haji A.A. 2015. The role of audit committee attributes in intellectual capital disclosures. *Managerial Auditing Journal*, 30(8/9), 756–784. https://doi.org/10.1108/MAJ-07-2015-1221.

Hajro A., Gibson, C., & Pudelko M. 2017. Knowledge Exchange Processes in Multicultural Teams: Linking Organizational Diversity Climates to Teams' Effectiveness. *Academy of Management Journal*, 60 (1), 345–372. https://doi.org/10.5465/amj.2014.0442.

Hamm B. 2004. *Kapitał społeczny z punktu widzenia socjologicznego*, Akademia Ekonomiczna w Katowicach, Katowice.

Kalkan A., Bozkurt Ö., & Arman M. 2014. The Impacts of Intellectual Capital, Innovation and Organizational Strategy on Firm Performance. *Procedia - Social and Behavioral Sciences*, 150(34), 700–707. https://doi.org/10.1016/j.sbspro.2014.09.025.

Kucera M., & Dvorakova D. 2023. Analysis of determinants influencing the level of intellectual capital disclosure: The case of FTSE 100 entities. *Intangible Capital*, 19(2), 296–315. https://doi.org/10.3926/ic.2213.

Madsen T., & Leiblein M. 2015. What Factors Affect the Persistence of an Innovation Advantage? *Journal of Management Studies*, 52(8), 1097–1127. https://doi.org/10.1111/joms.12154.

Matinfard M., & Khavari A. 2015. The impact of intellectual capital on firm performance: Evidence from Tehran Stock Exchange. *Management Science Letters*, 5(11), pp.1005–1016. https://doi.org/10.5267/j.msl.2015.8.011.

Mehrotra V., Malhotra A.K., & Chauhan A.K. 2017. Determinants of intellectual capital disclosure-Indian companies. *International Journal of Learning and Intellectual Capital*, 14(4), 366–387. https://doi.org/10.1504/IJLIC.2017.087374.Raport o stanie sektora małych i średnich przedsiębiorstw w Polsce 2022 (parp.gov.pl).
Stewart T. A. 2001. *The Wealth of Knowledge. Intellectual Capital and the Twenty-Firdt Century Organization*, Nicholas Brealey Publishing, Londyn.
Todericiu R., & Stăniţ A. 2015. Intellectual Capital – The Key for Sustainable Competitive Advantage for the SME's Sector. *Procedia Economics and Finance*, 27(22), 676–681. https://doi.org/10.1016/S2212-5671(15)01048-5.
Wachowiak P. 2005, *Pomiar kapitału intelektualnego przedsiębiorstwa*, Szkoła Główna Handlowa, Warszawa.
Wijaya, A., Utama, C.A. 2023. The impact of busy director on the relationship between intellectual capital and performance of manufacturing companies: Evidence from Indonesia. *Intangible Capital*, 19(2), 328–342. https://doi.org/10.3926/ic.2022.
Wijaya, A., Utama, C.A. 2023. The impact of busy director on the relationship between intellectual capital and performance of manufacturing companies: Evidence from Indonesia. *Intangible Capital*, 19(2), 328–342. https://doi.org/10.3926/ic.2022.

Digital Synergy – El Emary et al. (eds)

Chapter 23
Organization and functioning of the regional crisis management system – on the example of the Warmian-Masovian Voivodeship

Małgorzata Orłowska & Dawid Orłowski
War Studies University, Warsaw, Poland

Contents

The article focuses on the important issue of organising the functioning of a regional crisis management system on the example of the Warmian-Masurian Voivodeship. In the face of an increasing number of hazards, such as natural disasters, pandemics, wars or other emergencies, effective management of the crisis management system becomes a key element among local and regional communities. Analysing past experiences, the article examines what role the provincial level plays in crisis management. The article highlights the importance of cooperation between different sectors of society, and including public administration, emergency services, businesses and the community. Furthermore, the article outlines key aspects of effective crisis management, such as planning, coordination of activities, crisis communication and information technology. The conclusions of this study were intended to provide practical guidance for decision-makers at all levels and to serve as a basis for further research into improving crisis management systems at provincial, district and municipal levels.

This article also contributes to the discussion on building societal resilience to emergencies in individual regions, which is crucial for sustainable social and economic development. The article uses theoretical and empirical research methods: analysis, synthesis, deduction, induction, comparison, generalisation, as well as scientific observation with free observation technique, diagnostic survey method with uncategorized interview.

The main objective of the article was to identify and evaluate the crisis management system at the voivodeship level on the example of the Warmińsko-Mazurskie Voivodeship and to formulate recommendations for improving its functioning. The specific objectives were to characterise selected threats in Warmińsko-Mazurskie Voivodeship and discuss the role of the warning and alert system. The collected material allowed answering the main question: How is the crisis management system in the Warmian-Masurian Voivodeship structured and what changes does it require? and two intermediate questions: What are the characteristic threats in the Warmian-Masurian Voivodeship? and What is the role of the warning and alert system in the crisis management system?

As the main conclusion, the author pointed out the continuous need to invest in the crisis management system at all levels (voivodeship, district and commune). These investments should be linked to the implementation of modern technologies and personnel training.

DOI: 10.1201/9781003440406-23

1 INTRODUCTION

Currently as a consequence of global technical, technological, economic, and social transformations, significant changes occurred resulting in a rapid civilizational development. Simultaneously, the formation of new natural and unnatural threats began to be noticed. These threats contributed to the emergence of crisis situations that had an adverse impact on the level of safety of people, property, and the environment. Furthermore, they caused disturbances in the functioning of the public administration bodies (Act of 26 April 2007 on crisis management (Journal of Laws No. 89, item 590, as amended [accessed: 09/09/2022])). In the subject literature, the causes of the occurence of crisis situations include: natural disasters, technical and construction malfunctions, traffic accidents, chemical and petroleum-derived substances hazards, epidemiological threats, public order disturbances, terrorist acts and others.

Crisis situations are unexpected and sudden phenomena that destabilise people's security. Therefore, it is necessary to prepare and organise actions in advance to counteract them and to ensure the fastest possible reaction in the event of their emergence. The scope and nature of these actions are covered by crisis management (Sienkiewicz–Małyjurek K., 2011), which is a deliberate action executed by authorised entities at all levels of the country's security management (national, voivodeship, county, and communal). Managing entities as well as specialised organizations including services, watch, inspections, and the general public participate in it. According to the Act of 26 April 2007 on crisis management (Journal of Laws No. 89, item 590, with subsequent amendments [accessed: 09.09.2022]), the main tasks of the managing entities include fulfilling the responsibilities contained in four main phases crisis management: preventing crisis situations, preparing to assume control over crisis situations through planned actions, reacting in the event of emergencies and the removal of their effects, restoring resources, means, and critical infrastructure.

The crisis management system in Poland, as already mentioned, has a multi-level and multi-element structure. All levels of government and local government administration belong to it, it has an organisational structure that enables the realisation of tasks in the field of protection of health and life of people, property, and the natural environment (Padovani, Iacuzzi 2021). The system as a whole consists of managing elements and the executive elements assigned to them. The managing elements at respective levels of the crisis management system are public administration bodies, which include the policymaker (Council of Ministers, Voivode, Staroste, Commune Administrator), expert-advisory crisis management teams and crisis management centres which are on round the clock duty (Pietrek 2021). One of the main tasks of the crisis management system is to ensure the continuance of decision-making. This is caused by the necessity to prevent the occurrence of threats, monitor these threats, as well as respond to the ensuing threat and remove the effects of this situation (Falecki 2016).

Executive elements responisble for providing immediate aid to the injured party are various types of services (watch, police, army etc.), organisationally separated inspections, non-governmental organisations, as well as the public. Crisis management system can be defined with five basic steps: The first step is the identification of crisis threats with the help of a created catalogue of threats including an assessment of their risk, determining the adverse effects that may occur among people, property, and the natural enviroment as well as in critical infrastructure. The second step defines a catalogue of structural-organisatory undertakings whose task is to prepare the government and the local government administration as well as a country's resources for an effective reaction to the occurring threat. The thirds step consists in defining the procedures to be followed in the event of the occurrence of a crisis situation. The fourth step is the preparation and maintenance of resources (forces and means) for crisis situations. The last and fifth step is the establishment of the rules of cooperation between involved entities (Sobolewski 2013).

Crisis management is currently an extremely relevant and topical topic for several reasons. First and foremost because of the complexity of today's world: Globalisation, the development of technology and the increase in international links, which are making the world increasingly complex (Maśloch 2023). Crises are spreading rapidly and covering different areas, which undoubtedly requires a flexible and rapid response by both authorities and society. Examples of the biggest crises in recent years were undoubtedly the Covid-19 pandemic and the outbreak of war in Ukraine. Researchers from Poland and around the world are devoting a great deal of attention to this topic. They focus on the analysis of problems concerning the organisation of intersectoral cooperation during the Covid-19 pandemic (Latonen and others, 2023) considering it in Poland and worldwide (Rajca, 2023), (Gotkowska, 2021), (Hassenteufel, 2020), (Warner et al. 2021), (Boin and Rhinard, 2023) . Researchers analyse and evaluate existing crisis management solutions (Hruschka and Rohmann, 2023), (Smolenski, 2023) as well as proposing new solutions (Koska, 2023) emphasising the importance of individual policing bodies (Gorazdowski, 2023) and paying attention to the daily problems of society: education, health (Chatzipanagiotou and Katsarou, 2023), small and large business development (Jaaffar et al. 2023) . The crisis management system is considered in the civilian sphere (Petitta and Martínez-Córcoles, 2023) and military (Stelmach, 2023). Undoubtedly, the topic of crisis management has also gained currency in view of the outbreak of war in Ukraine (Kosowski, 2023).

2 METHODS

In the process of preparing the article, the author used both theoretical and empirical research methods, in particular: analysis, synthesis, deductions, induction, comparison, generalisation, as well as scientific observation incorporating the technique of casual observation, and the method of diagnostic survey with the technique of uncategorised interview. The above-mentioned qualitative research methods were used to analyse the subject literature, nation-wide and local legal acts, regulations, and internal procedures of the Crisis Management Centre in Olsztyn. Analysis, understood as the thought processes leading to an in-depth understanding of specific problems and phenomena (e.g. physical systems), as well as synthesis, which is a comparison aimed at identification and better understanding of the studied elements (Pytkowski 2004), were used to deepen the knowledge in the area of the researched issues as well as to identify their interrelationships and interdependencies.Deduction, which is the process of drawing conclusions from what is known or assumed, was used in the top-down inferring approach. Induction, which is the opposite action, based on drawing conclusions or the verification of general laws and principles on the basis of the observation of individual cases was also applied in the process of observations and interviews. Comparison served predominantly as a tool for identification of similarities and differences between structures, tasks, and the operating scope of the crisis management system recognised by legal acts in relation to the actual state of affairs. Comparison was primarily used to identify similarities and differences between the structures, tasks, and the scope of operation of the crisis management system on the example of the Warmian-Masurian Voivodeship. The conducted interviews allowed the author to thoroughly analyse the discussed questions and to elaborate on selected notations in normative documents. Via the means of induction, conclusions at the end of this article were developed. By using these methods, it was possible to learn how the crisis management system is built at the Voivodeship level in the Warmian-Masurian Voivodeship, characterise the threats occurring in the region and the assessed function of the warning and alarm system in the Warmian-Masurian Voivodeship, which is of immense importance from the perspective of an individual inhabitant.

3 CRISIS MANAGEMENT SYSTEM IN THE WARMIAN-MASURIAN VOIVODESHIP

A voivodeship is the largest unit of territorial division in Poland, subject to the authority of a voivode. It is an authority superior to poviat and municipality. As a unit of local government, its dimension is social, and the qualification of its inhabitants takes place by operation of law (Korzeniowska A., 2005). The WarmianMasurian Voivodeship, the fourth largest region of Poland measuring over 24,000 km2, with the population of 1,442,242 inhabitants. Since the early 1990s, the voivodeship' labour market has been one of the most troublesome areas of socio-economic activity in the country. This is largely due to the low employment level (below average employment level in Poland), low salary level, and the highest unemployment rate in the country. The Warmian-

Masurian Voivodeship is also one of the least industrialised areas of Poland. The low industrialisation level of the voivodeship is determined by its localisation, which is dictated by its agricultural and tourist character (Orłowska M., 2022). The Great Masurian Lake District is located in the voivodeship – the area of 1,732 km2, of which 486 km2 is covered by lakes (Głównego Urzędu Statystycznego, data accesed 2.03.2023).

In accordance with Art. 21. Act of 26th of April 2007 on crisis management (Journal of Laws No. 89, item 590, with subsequent amendments): the duty to take action in the field of crisis management rests with the organ that first received information about the threat. This organ immediately informs the higher and lower level organs, respectively, about the situation, including its assessment of the situation and the current state. The most important legal acts relating to crisis management at the voivodeship level are: the laws on the state of natural disasters, the laws on the state of emergency, and the laws on the voivode and the government administration in the voivodeship. Other executory legal acts are the Act of June 5, 1998 on voivodeship government (Journal of Laws of 2001, No. 142, item 1590, as amended), the Act of June 5, 1998 on poviat government (Journal of Laws of 2001 No. 142, item 1592, as amended), Act of 8 March 1990 on municipality government (Journal of Laws 01.142.1591 as amended). According to the above-mentioned documents, the prevention of regional and local threats lies within the competence of local governments. Higher levels of local governments coordinate these procedures in accordance with the adopted crisis management rules resulting from the administrative division of the country.

As mentioned, the crisis management system in the voivodeship lies in the competence and is the responsibility of the voivode. All undertakings in the crisis management field are carried out by an organizational unit at the voivodeship office. The voivode's auxiliary body in crisis management at the voivodeship level is the Voivodeship Crisis Management Centre. The Centre's with its registered office in Olsztyn operates in the Warmian-Masurian Voivodeship. It is an organisational unit of the Office whose task is to enable the Warmian-Masurian voivode to perform tasks in the field of defence, civil defence, crisis management, public security and civil planning, as well as, public order, fire precautions, and combating the effects of natural disasters and event threatening public security in the voivodeship alike. The tasks carried out by the Voivodeship Crisis Management Center in Olsztyn consist of: 24-hour duty to ensure the flow of information for the purposes of crisis management. Maintaining communication poviat crisis management centers and other institutions. Exchanging information on threats with combined and non-combined administration services as well as services and inspectorate. Daily report preparation describing the situation in the voivodeship. Delivery of reports on the situation in the voivodeship to the Duty Operational Service of the Government Center for Security. Gathering information on threats occurring in the voivodeship. Performing tasks on the behalf of Waarmian-Masurian Voivodeshipe Crisis Management Team aimed at ensuring the circulation of information and decisions in the field of crisis management. Creating and updating a database for the needs of crisis management. Performing tasks associated with permanent after-hours office service. Facilitating the line of communication between Government representatives and the Voivode, Vice-Voivode as well as the General Office Director. Transferring operational tasks within the framework of a constant duty as to ensure the continuity of the decision flow in the event of increasing the state's defense readiness condition procedures. Available at: https://www.olsztyn.uw.gov.pl/index.php?option= com_content&view= category&layout=blog&id=266&Itemi d= 267&lang=en access date [20/ 04/2022] After conducting interviews, it has been found that there are five personnel members on 24-hour duty in the Warmian-Masurian Voivodeship Crisis Management Centre. Warmian-Masurian Voivodeship acts accordingly to a plan prepared in response to the needs of the crisis management proces in the voivodeship, including the Warmian-Masurian Crisis Management Team and the process participants. The developement of this plan is imperative according to Article 5 of the Act of 26 April 2007 on crisis management, which regulates the issues in the field of engagement and responsibility of certain entities in the Voivodeship crisis management process. This plan consists of three main parts: I main plan (risk catalogue, safety net, combination of forces and resources, tasks), II crisis situations venture team (risk monitoring, mobilization of forces and resources, crisis response procedures, cooperation between forces) III functional attachments (procedures, connectivity organization, monitoring system organization, rules of informing the public about the risks, other).

4 CHARACTERISTICS OF SELECTED THREATS IN THE WARMINA-MASURIAN VOIVODESHIP

JAs one of the elements of the Voivodeship Crisis Management Plan of the Warmińsko-Mazurskie Voivodeship, there is a catalog of threats that may occur in this region. 19 of them have been defined in the Warmian-Masurian Voivodeship. Several of these threats are ones commonly occurring across the whole country, such as: strong winds, severe frosts/intense rainfall, droughts/heatwaves, fires, epidemics, epizootics, epiphytosis, chemical contamination, radiation contamination, disruptions in the functioning of the power system, disruptions in gas delivery, construction disasters, floods, terrorist threats. The author's attention was drawn to the threats characteristic for this region due to its topography and agricultural character incl. landslides, cacsualties on water, traffic disasters, threats to public safety, and threats to the coastline. In the further part of the article, the author focused on a short description of the threats related to mass-casualty incidents on water, which concern both the inhabitants of the voivodship and tourists.

Numerous reservoirs and bathing areas in the Warmian-Masurian Voivodeship, which are visited on a large scale during summer holidays, pose a serious risk of drowning. The occurrence of such threats is confirmed by the reported cases of drowning and the rescue and search operations carried out by the State Fire Departament.Threatened areas. Taking into account the statistics of incidents and the calculated risk levels, it should be stated that the poviats most at risk of drowning are: Giżycki, Mrągowo, Olsztyński, Piski, Elbląg, Ostróda and Iława poviats. When it comes to mass-casualty incidents on water, events involving breaking applicable regulations (alcohol, drugs or unfamiliarity with regulations, etc.), collisions, overturning of floating objects, as well as drownings should be taken into consideration. According to statistics published by the National Police Headquarters for 2021, 40 collisions involving the police were recorded on the Warmian-Masurian waters. The Government Center for Security stated, that in Warmia-Masuria in the time period from April 1st to August 31st 2021, the National Police Headquarters noted 286 deaths as a result of drowning.It was also stated, that because every third reported death occurred on or in a lake, lakes were the most dangerous leisure area. The conducted interviews established that entities who were authorised to perform water rescue tasks were assigned and authorised by the Interior and Administration Minister of the Warmian-Masurian Voivodeship. These are the entities that applied to the Warmian-Masurian Voivode for additional financing of the rescue activities and were selected in an open competition for the execution of a public task in the field of rescue and civil protection. In 2021 these included: Masurian Volunteer Rescue Service with its registered office in Giżycko, Masurian Rescue Service in Okartów, Water Volunteer Rescue Service of the WarmianMasurian Voivodeship in Olsztyn, Elbląskie Water Rescue Service in Elbląg and Nadnarwiańskie Water Volunteer Rescue Service in Pułtusk. The Masurian Volunteer Rescue Service with its registered office in Giżycko is on duty all year round at four water rescue stations: in Harsz-Skłodów, Mikołajki, Pisz-Łupki and Giżycko - where the Water Rescue Coordination Center is located. In addition, the Masurian Rescue Service is located in the southern part of the Warmian-Masurian Voivodeship, and covers the following lakes: Śniardwy, Teksty, Bełdany, Mikołajskie, Tałty, Nidzkie, Trykło, and smaller lakes in the Piskie poviat that are not on the route of the Great Masurian Lakes. It should be noted that the safety of residents and tourists is also ensured by the State Fire Service, which also carries out rescue operations in the event of an emergency. As already mentioned, immediate actions in the event of a threat are taken by the administrative level where the threat occurred. In the case of events beyond its rescue capabilities, this assistance is provided at a higher level. In the structures of the Warmian-Masurian Voivodship, there is a position of Command of the Provincial Commander of the State Fire Service, whose task is to direct appropriate forces and resources to the place of the threat not only from within a given poviat or municipality where the threat occurred, but also to other poviats of the voivodeship according to the parameters and taking into account the time of arrival and equipment needs. The competences of the State Fire Service also include the implementation of tasks in the field of ensuring water safety. It was also established that in the Warmian-Masurian Voivodeship, the state and volunteer fire brigades are equipped with 28 motorboats (State Fire Service) and 55 boats, pontoons with a motor (Volunteer Fire Brigade). In addition, there are 7 Specialist Water and Diving Rescue, carrying out specialised tasks in waters, including the search for retrieving of sunken people and objects. Another threat from this category is water pollution caused by petroleum and chemical substances originating from drownings of cars, motor and sailing yachts, or caused by human factors through littering or devastation of the natural enviroment. According to the Main Police Headquarters, in 2021, 33 such reports were received in the area of operation of police officers from the Poviat Police Headquarters in Pisz, half of which concerned Lake Nidzkie. These events mainly concerned motorized cruising within a nature reserve. Five similar interventions were recorded by the police from the Poviat Police Headquarters in Węgorzewo on Lake Dobskie.

5 CONCLUSION ORGANIZATION OF A WARNING AND ALARM SYSTEM IN THE WARMIŃSKO-MAZURSKIE VOIVODESHIP

In the event of a threat from the perspective of a single inhabitant, the warning and alarm system, which is one of the elements of the crisis management system, plays an important role. It is thanks to the immediate information about the threat that it is possible to start actions to minimise or prevent its occurrence. Warning means drawing someone's attention to the imminent danger, and alarming takes the form of the notification about imminent danger or a situation requiring immediate intervention as a result of the danger. In situations that have already occurred, and their effects require action by all residents . It was established that in the Warmian-Masurian Voivodship the procedure of warning and alarming the population about extraordinary threats to people, their property and the environment is carried out via mass media: the local television program: TVP 3 and the local radio station Radio Olsztyn. Also via messengers using the RSO system (Regional Warning System), which is a free system, popularized by the Interior and Administration Ministry. The principles of formulating, delivering, storing, and broadcasting messages are regulated by agreements concluded by the Warmian-Masurian Voivode and the directors of regional centres. Similar agreements operate at the level of poviats that are part of the Voivodeship. To observe local meteorological phenomena, local governments use storm detectors obtained on the basis of individual contracts with producers, e.g. in Mrągowo.

In the Warmińsko-Mazurskie Voivodship there is also an Integrated Weather Warning System used by the Masurian Volunteer Rescue Service in Giżycko, and the RSWS Radio System for Activating Sirens, which is an integrated system managed both at the level of the city/municipality and the province, it includes 483 siren alarms (including 108 electronic sirens).

6 SUMMARY

Using the tools and resources at hand (resources, authorities, legal solutions and institutions), crisis management in Poland aims to protect the local civilian population. Therefore, a properly functioning crisis management system at all administrative levels is crucial. From the perspective of an individual inhabitant, it is the local and regional level that plays the most important role due to the effectiveness, speed of reaction, and immediate assistance in the event of a threat. This will only be possible with a properly functioning Crisis Management System. At the voivodeship level, the voivode is responsible for matters related to crisis management. It implements them with the help of the voivodship office and various services, inspections and guards. In the Warmian-Masurian Voivodeship Office in the Department of Security and Crisis Management, it is the Crisis Management Department, that carries the responsibility for collecting and exchanging information between individual levels of local government administration and central government administration bodies. Additionally, in the event of a threat, the Voivode appoints the WZZK (Voivodeship Crisis Management Team), specifying its composition, organization, place, and operating mode. The following individuals are appointed to this team: the Voivode as the chairman, the manager, as the deputy chairman. Furthemore, depending on the needs, individuals are appointed from among the heads of services, inspections, guards, or members of other necessary organizations. The crisis management system in the Warmian-Masurian Voivodeship has a hierarchical structure and is synchronized with the central level of the country, with territorial self-government bodies and public administration bodies.

The Warmian-Masurian Voivodeship, called the land of thousand lakes and a region of agriculltural and tourism character, is characterized by the occurrence of various threats. The Voivodship Crisis Management Plan of the Voivodship takes into account both the possibility of occurrence of common threats throughout the country (e.g. floods, strong winds, landslides, terrorist attacks, etc.), but also characterizes and predicts threats resulting from the shape and nature of the region. Among them, events on water or events involving tourists, which, as shown by government and police statistics, are frequent, especially in the summer. This plan is updated and adapted to modern threats on average every two years. In the author's opinion, it contains accurate and up-to-date threats and procedures in the event of their occurrence. The warning and alarming system operating in the Warmian-Masurian Voivodeship was analyzed as well. This system plays an important role both in the life of the local and regional population as well as in the functioning of managing and executive elements. By means of this system, the local/regional population is informed about the possibility or occurrence of a threat. So that the population can avoid it, counteract it, or execute preparations for its arrival. From the perspective of the managing elements, thanks to the system, it is possible to apply appropriate forces and means in proportion to the threat. Executives use this system to centralise and specialise their forces and resources. As such, it should be stated that the warning and alarming system plays a crucial role in all the above-mentioned entities. The Warmian-Masurian Voivodeship implements basic solutions in this regard. Therefore, the modernization or implementation of the latest system solutions available on the market, compatible with other systems, may be an important direction of development in the field of the crisis management system in the Warmian-Masurian Voivodeship.

REFERENCES

Book of Crisis Communication. 2017. Basics of information management in crisis, Government Centre for Security https://archiwum.rcb.gov.pl/alertrcb/ksiega-komunikacji-kryzysowej/.

Boin A., Rhinard M. 2023. Crisis management performance and the European Union: the case of COVID-19, Journal of European Public Policy, https://www.tandfonline.com/loi/rjpp2.

Chatzipanagiotou P., Katsarou E. 2023. Crisis Management, School Leadership in Disruptive Times and the Recovery of Schools in the Post COVID-19 Era: A Systematic Literature Review, Educ. Sci.13, 118. https://doi.org/10.3390/educsci13020118.

Ciekanowski Z. Nowicka J. Wyrębek H. 2017. Zarządzanie zasobami ludzkimi w sytuacjach kryzysowych. Warszawa. CeDeWu. p. 239.

Ciekanowski Z., Marjański A. 2017. Determinants of crisis management at the basic level, Zeszyty Naukowe Państwowej Wyższej Szkoły Techniczno-Ekonomicznej w Jarosławiu. Współczesne problemy zarządzania, nr 10, p. 103–122.

Falecki J. 2016. Dilemmas of crisis management in the Republic of Poland. Oficyna Wydawnicza Humanitas, Sosnowiec.

Gołębiewski J. 2015. Crisis management at local government level. Theory and practice. Difin.

Gorazdowski K. 2023. Rola i zadania policji w sytuacjach kryzysowych [w:] Prawne, merytoryczne, organizacyjne i informacyjne mechanizmy zarządzania sytuacjami kryzysowymi w zinstytucjonalizowanym systemie bezpieczeństwa państwa Red. Marek Cupryjak, Marek Jasztal, Piotr Ostrowski, Wydawnictwo Naukowe Uniwersytetu Szczecińskiego Wydanie I. DOI 10.18276/978-83-7972-664-6.

Gotkowska J. 2021. Szwedzkie lekcje z pandemii, Komentarze OSW, https://www.osw.waw.pl/pl/publikacje/komentarze-osw/2021-02-16/szwedzkie-lekcje-z-pandemii, 17.06.2022.

Hassenteufel P. 2020, Handling the COVID-19 crisis in France: Paradoxes of a centralized state-led health system, European Policy Analysis, vol. 6(2). DOI: https://doi.org/10.1002/epa2.1104.

Hruschka C. Rohmann T. 2023, Excluded by crisis management? Legislative hyperactivity in post- 2015 Germany, International Migration, DOI: 10.1111/imig.12926.
Jaaffar A.H, Alzoubi R. H, Alkharabsheh O. H. M., Rajadurai J. 2023. Leadership and crisis management and their link to improvement of hotel performance: A study of the Jordanian hotel sector, Heliyon 9, e17839, https://doi.org/10.1016/j.heliyon.2023.e17839.
Kośka M. 2023. Zarządzanie kryzysowe, ochrona ludności, obrona cywilna – obecne i projektowe rozwiązania prawne dotyczące zadań elementów zarządzających szczebla krajowego, Wiedza Obronna, 2023, Vol. 284 No. 3, ISSN: 2658, DOI: https://doi.org/10.34752/2023-e284.
Kosowski B. 2023. System zarządzania kryzysowego sfery cywilnej RP w obliczu wojny w Ukrainie, the war must go on. Dynamika wojny w Ukrainie i jej reperkusje dla bezpieczeństwa Polski, p. 107–114 https://doi.org/10.12797/9788381388801.10.
Latonen S.H., Suominen R.M., Juppo A.M., Airaksinen M., Seeck H. 2023 Organisation of cross-sector collaboration and its influence on crisis management effectiveness among pharmaceutical supply chain stakeholders during the COVID-19 pandemic, Public Health 222, 19, https://doi.org/10.1016/j.puhe.2023.06.042.
Majchrzak D. 2013. Crisis management as organised activities of responsible authorities and actors, In: Zarządzanie kryzysowe G. Sobolewski, D. Majchrzak (Ed.). AON.
Maśloch P. 2023. The New Age of Management, Shineeks, Las Vegas.
Orłowska M. 2022. Powiat węgorzewski w kontekście obecności jednostki wojskowej – analiza wpływu, In: Społeczeństwo gospodarka siły zbrojne. Działalność podmiotów sektora publicznego na rzecz bezpieczeństwa i rozwoju w dobie kryzysu, M. Piotrowska-Trybull (Ed.). ASzWoj.
Padovani E., Iacuzzi S. 2021. Testing the role of accounting in local governments. Journal of Accounting and Public Policy, https://doi.org/10.1016/j.jaccpubpol.2021.106854.
Petitta L., Martínez-Córcoles M. 2023. A conceptual model of mindful organizing for effective safety and crisis management. The role of organizational culture, Current Psyhology, https://doi.org/10.1007/s12144-022-03702-x.
Pietrek G. 2021. The Crisis Management and the Civil Protection in Poland, The Journal of Organizational Management Studie shttps://ibimapublishing.com/articles/JOMS/2021/847128/, http://doi.org/:10.5171/2021.847128
Provincial Crisis Management Plan of Warmińsko-Mazurskie Voivodship, Olsztyn 2020.
Rajca L. 2023. Zarządzanie kryzysem wywołanym pandemią COVID-19 w czasie jej pierwszej fali w wybranych państwach europejskich, Środkowoeuropejskie Studia Polityczne, DOI 10.14746/ssp.2023.1.2
Leta S.D., Chan I.C.C. 2021. Learn from the past and prepare for the future: A critical assessment of crisis management research in hospitality. International Journal of Hospitality Management, 95(3–4):102915/, http://doi.org/:10.1016/j.ijhm.2021.102915.
Sienkiewicz–Małyjurek K. 2011. Organizational problems of crisis management in local governments, Scientific Journals of the Silesian University of Technology. Z 51.
Sienkiewicz-Małyjurek K. 2015. Effective Crisis Management, Revised Edition, Difin.
Smoleński S. 2023. Crisis management plans in context of contemporary hazards, Zeszyty Naukowe SGSP,86: 257–274, DOI: 10.5604/01.3001.0053.7158.
Sobolewski G. 2013. Model zarządzania przepływem informacji w sytuacjach kryzysowych, AON.
Sobolewski G., Majchrzak D., Sobejko Z. 2016. Public administrations and institutions in crisis management, AON.
Stawnicka J., Wiśniewski B., Socha R. 2011. Crisis management Theory, practice, contexts, research Szczytno, Wyższej Szkoły Policji w Szczytnie.
Stelmach T. (2023). Reorganization of the national defence sector crisis management system, ITV, ISSN 1230-3801 Volume 163 No, DOI 10.5604/01.3001.0053.5917.
The Act of February of Apriel 26, 2007 on crisis management Journal of Laws of 2007, no. 89 item 590, as amended.
Warner S. 2021. English Devolution and the Covid-19 Pandemic: Governing Dilemmas in the Shadow of the Treasury, "The Political Quarterly", vol. 92(2). DOI: https://doi.org/10.1111/1467-923X.12989.
Williams P. 2021. Contemporary Strategy, Theories and Policies. https://doi.org/10.4324/9781003104339.
Wong - Tourism Management, 2021 – Elsevier.
Wut T. M., Xu J. B., Wong S. M. 2021. Crisis management research (1985-2020) in the hospitality and tourism industry: A review and research agenda, PubMed, DOI: 10.1016/j.tourman.2021.104307.
www.gus.pl
www.olsztyn.uw.gov.pl/index.php?option=com_content&view=category&layout=blog&id=266&Itemid=267&lang=pl.

Digital Synergy – El Emary et al. (eds)

Chapter 24
Commercialization in network research organizations

Marzena Walasik
Łukasiewicz Institute for Sustainable Technologies, Radom, Poland

Beata Poteralska
Jan Kochanowski University of Kielce, Poland

Contents

The paper is aimed to recognise how operating in a research network facilitates commercialisation processes at research organisations. The authors analyse the state of the art, by studying publications in the Web of Science database, and present a longitudinal case study. Based on the state of the art analysis, measures used (also at network organisations) to assess the effectiveness of commercialisation endeavours are reviewed and compared with measures used at the analysed entity, i.e. the Łukasiewicz Research Network (the "Network"). Then, commercialisation effectiveness at this organisation operating in a research network (the "research network organisation") is compared with the commercialisation success rate of its affiliates (research institutes) prior to the establishment of the Network. The results of the analyses show that operating in a research network improves commercialisation effectiveness. While the effectiveness of commercialisation processes at the biggest acclaimed research networks in Europe is widely discussed and confirmed in the literature, the success of commercialisation at institutes before and after inclusion in a research network is rarely compared. This article contributes to the analysis of this issue. Future studies will focus on the analysis of drivers of and impediments to effective commercialisation at network organisations.

1 INTRODUCTION

The progressive and growing globalisation leads to the intensification of the following activities:

- Popularising research collaboration networks (Adams, 2012).

DOI: 10.1201/9781003440406-24

- Implementing innovation policies at the state level to strengthen research organisations and create networks of research organisations ("research networks") (Matyjas, Bohdanowicz, 2018)
- Directing activity of research networks towards commercialisation (Lehenkari et al., 2022).

Attempts to create research networks were also made in Poland and they led to the establishment of the Łukasiewicz Research Network, whose primary objective is to commercialise results of scientific and R&D activities.

The article analyses how operating in a network facilitates commercialisation processes at research organisations. Authors pay particular attention to measures of commercialisation success, and compare commercialisation effectiveness at research organisations belonging and not belonging to a research network.

2 LITERATURE REVIEW

As part of the literature review, the authors studied definitions of terms 'commercialisation' and 'network', and analysed the activity of research organisations operating in a network. From the literature review findings it follows that research organisations operating in a network are more successful in their commercialisation endeavours. Such networked research organisations as the Fraunhofer-Gesellschaft zur Förderung der angewandten Forschung e.V. or theTechnical Research Centre of Finland Ltd (VTT) can be used as an example. However, in the literature reviewed, the authors did not find any publications on the relationship between the form in which research organisations operate (as independent entities or as a network) and commercialisation effectiveness.

2.1 *What is commercialisation?*

The authors define technology commercialisation as the design, development, manufacture, and marketing of products based on new technologies (Poteralska, Walasik, 2021). This is a broad definition that treats commercialisation as a process spanning all stages crucial for the effectiveness and for the commercial success of the new solution marketed, which is in line with the approach discussed in the literature (Mitchell &. Singh, 1996, Bhasin, 2023). In the literature 'new solutions' include products, services, and new technologies (Meredith & Shafer, 2002, Matusiak 2005, Atvare et al., 2022). Some definitions clearly stress the process of bringing a product or service to the market (Markiewicz, 2009, Sojkin, 2012, Bhasin, 2023). This is how the authors understand it as well, even though they do not directly use the term 'market' in their definition.

2.2 *What is a network?*

"A network is an institution facilitating innovation processes through collaboration, which is composed of (a) a set of measures enabling affiliated entities to implement joint projects, and (b) a group of entities creating, gaining, processing, integrating, and using knowledge and skills to develop a technologically complex, financially viable, and socially accepted innovation or change" (Blażak, 2010).

When used in the article, a networked structure of research entities is understood as a research organisation established and operating in a formal network of affiliated entities. While the aspect of collaboration between a research organisation and entities other than entities forming the research network is important and treated by some authors as sufficient to talk about a networked structure understood as voluntary partnership of legally independent economic entities (Palyvoda et al., 2018), the authors focus on formal research networks only.

2.3 *Research organisations operating in a network*

In Poland, the Łukasiewicz Research Network composed of the Łukasiewicz Centre and various research institutes is an example of a networked research collaboration. This entity, which is further analysed by the authors, meets the following requirements of a research collaboration network: 1) it is made of scientific and research institutes, and 2) it has a formal structure (established pursuant to the Act of 21 February 2019 on the Łukasiewicz Research Network) of a network of public legal entities not affiliated through ownership or control. In Poland, this is still a relatively new solution. The Łukasiewicz Research Network is a multimodal, decentralised (all institutes retain their autonomy) and resource-diversified (all institutes have a wide range of research specialisations) institution (Kwieciński, 2020). Within its structure, the Łukasiewicz Centre was established to supervise the activities of individual Łukasiewicz Research Network institutes. Taking into consideration the criterion of the dominance level, the Łukasiewicz Research Network is a mix of a dominated network (the Łukasiewicz Centre) and a network of equal partners (Łukasiewicz Research Network institutes).

In other EU Member States, research networks created to strengthen the ties between science and business and facilitate commercialisation of research results have a long-standing tradition and are more common than in Poland (Kwieciński, 2020). The creators of the Łukasiewicz Research Network based their efforts on the EU good practices – mainly on Fraunhofer Gesellschaft, Germany and the Technical Research Centre of Finland, VTT).

The analysis of the experience of other countries where research networks operate indicates that such an organisational solution can offer many benefits, including, but not limited to: the ability to coordinate activities between institutes, synergistic effects at the management level of different areas of institutes' activity, and more effective cooperation with businesses and universities (Matyjas, Bohdanowicz, 2018). While a lot of information on the performance of research organisations operating in a network can be found in the literature, the authors did not come across any studies that compare the performance of network organisations with the performance of individual entities before they became network affiliates. The authors attempt to contribute to this issue by conducting a comparative analysis for the Łukasiewicz Research Network established in 2019.

3 RESEARCH METHODS

The authors formulate a hypothesis that operating of a research organisation in the formula of a research network improves intensity of its commercialisation activities.

The adopted methodological approach includes the following two aspects:

1. A state of the art analysis based on publications in the Web of Science database to indicate measures used (also at network organisations) to assess the effectiveness of commercialisation processes.
2. A longitudinal case study – a case study of the Łukasiewicz Research Network including methods for assessing the success of commercialisation.

3.1 *Web of Science analysis*

The authors studied publications in the Web of Science database to build a pool of knowledge on measures of commercialisation success used at network organisations (Table 1). The articles were selected based on the two search criteria that used words and phrases reflecting the key concepts of the research topic, i.e. 'commercialisation' and 'research network'.

Many articles found deal with the topic of commercialisation, but only few of them concern its effectiveness. As a result of the Web of Science database search, the authors identified 10 articles discussing measures of commercialisation success.

Table 1. Selection of articles in the Web of Science database.

Search criteria	Web of Science	Search criteria	Web of Science
Commercialisation (topic)	4,486	Research network (topic)	422,630
Effectiveness (search within results)	117	Commercialisation (search within results)	164
		Effective (search within results)	11
Years: 2014–2023	79	Years: 2014–2023	6
Database after reading abstracts	13	Database after reading abstracts	1
Final database (after reading whole papers)	9	Final database (after reading whole papers)	1

Source: authors.

3.2 *Case study*

Following the Web of Science database analysis, a case study of the Łukasiewicz Research Network was written.

The case study method was selected because it helps answer the question 'How?' with reference to a contemporary set of events over which the investigator has little or no control (Yin, 2014).

A longitudinal single case study was used. Data were analysed at two points in time, i.e. for periods preceding and following the establishment of the Łukasiewicz Research Network, which meant examining variables for individual research institutes before and after their inclusion in the Network. The use of a longitudinal single case study enabled the assessment of commercialisation effectiveness at a network organisation and its comparison with commercialisation effectiveness at individual institutes before the Network was established. The analysis employed grey literature (in-house reports by the Network). As part of the case study, the following were presented: 1) methods for assessing commercialisation effectiveness and 2) a comparative analysis of commercialisation effectiveness before and after the establishment of the Network.

4 RESEARCH RESULTS

The analysis of articles in the Web of Science database allowed the identification of measures of commercialisation success used at research organisations, also belonging to a research network. The analysis results were used as the basis for a case study of the Łukasiewicz Research Network, which involved the examination of the relationship between the inclusion in the Network and commercialisation effectiveness.

4.1 *Measures of commercialisation success*

The analysis of articles in the Web of Science database allowed the identification of the aspects of commercialisation effectiveness measurement and corresponding measures of commercialisation success used at research organisations, also belonging to a research network (Table 2).

They correspond to measures used at the Łukasiewicz Research Network. The next step included selection of basic commercialisation performance indicators (CoPIs) which best help examine commercialisation effectiveness. This was done based on the literature review and authors' own experience. The results are presented in Table 3.

The use of the presented set of basic commercialisation performance indicators to measure commercialisation effectiveness helps monitor the effectiveness of commercialisation

Table 2. Measures of commercialisation success – literature review.

Aspects of commercialisation effectiveness measurement	Measures	Authors
Economic (Financial) performance	Revenue from commercialisation of research results; revenue from research contracts and consultancy activities; income; revenue to cost ratio; Earnings from consultancy activities	Jonek-Kowalska et al 2021; Gao & Haworth 2019; Hou et al 2019; Žižka et al 2018
Spin-offs	Number of spin-offs	Lopes et al. 2021; Gao & Haworth 2019; Kirby & Hadidi 2019; Hou et al 2019; Hewitt-Dundas & Burns 2016; Matlakiewicz et al 2016
Registered industrial property rights, including patents, utility models, industrial designs, and trademarks	Number of patent applications; number of patents, utility models, industrial designs, and trademarks; total/annual number of patents granted/obtained; income from patent transfer	Lopes et al. 2021; Jonek-Kowalska et al 2021; Gao & Haworth 2019; Kirby & Hadidi 2019; Hou et al 2019; Ardito 2018; Žižka et al 2018 (:); Matlakiewicz et al 2016; Miller et al 2016
Licenses	Number of licenses or earnings from licenses; income from patent transfer and licensing	Lopes et al. 2021; Gao & Haworth 2019; Hou et al 2019; Hewitt-Dundas & Burns 2016; Matlakie-wicz et al 2016
Contract research	Earnings from contract research	Gao & Haworth 2019
Collaborative activities	Level of collaborative activities with quadruple helix stakeholders; number of collaborative activities; number of research joint ventures between university academics and industry or government partners; number of long-term relationships with businesses and entrepreneurs; number of collaborative activities involving academic researchers and non-academic organisations	Lopes et al. 2021; Kirby & Hadidi 2019; Hou et al 2019; Hewitt-Dundas & Burns 2016; Miller et al 2016
Staff development	Researchers/Quality of staff; quality of recruitment, training and retaining processes.	Jonek-Kowalska et al 2021; Kirby & Hadidi 2019; Gao & Haworth 2019; Miller et al 2016

Source: authors.

Table 3. Commercialisation performance indicators (CoPIs).

Aspects of commercialisation effectiveness measurement	Measures: commercialisation performance indicators (CoPIs)
Finance	Total revenue; core earnings; net profit
IP (intellectual property)	Commercialisation profit; number of patents; number of spin-offs
Staff development	Number of researchers

Source: authors.

endeavours, set goals, and justify the expenses incurred. The measurement of commercialisation effectiveness should constitute a key element of managing a research organisation operating in a research network. The selected set of commercialisation performance indicators should be regularly reviewed and verified according to the changing internal and external circumstances.

4.2 *Commercialisation effectiveness at independent and network organisations*

To test the proposed hypothesis, the authors used the presented commercialisation performance indicators and analysed their levels with reference to a group of research institutes before and after their inclusion in the Network. The data were extracted from the grey literature, i.e. 2018–2022 financial statements compiled by the institutes, the financial data reporting system – "Kokpit", and from presentations summarising annual financial results. In the period analysed, an increase in all areas (aspects of commercialisation effectiveness measurement presented in Table 3), e.g. total revenue grew by 14%, and higher net profit were recorded. Income from commercialisation went up by 11%, the number of patent application rose, and two spin-offs were established as a result of the Accelerator project. From these analysis findings it clearly follows that the examined 2022 indicators in the area of finance and commercialisation are much better (significantly higher) that in the pre-network period (2018). As regards staff development, the number of employees, including researchers, dropped by approximately 22%, but given higher total revenue, particularly core earnings (including commercialisation), this is a positive trend directly translating into improved productivity and performance of a network organisation.

Therefore, the analysis confirms the proposed hypothesis that the establishment of a network organisation composed of a supervisory body (the Łukasiewicz Centre) and research institutes not affiliated through ownership or control, but rather through shared brand and image, improves intensity of commercialisation activities.

The network organisation analysed has a significant business potential and, as the examined indicators show, it can add value and generate higher profits also in the field of commercialisation of research results.

5 DISCUSSION/LIMITATION AND FUTURE RESEARCH

The objective of establishing research networks affiliating various research institutes in Poland is similar to the goal set for such entities in other European countries – they are directed at knowledge transfer through commercialisation of research results. Also commercialisation success measures they use are similar (Loikkanen at al. 2013). It is not surprising, given that the Łukasiewicz Research Network was established based on European good practices.

The novelty of the topic discussed in the article lies in the comparison of commercialisation success rate of research institutes before and after their inclusion in a network. The analyses indicate that commercialisation effectiveness improved. Additionally, the establishment of the Network enabled co-development of core competencies, brand, and positive image of individual institutes and the Network itself, which directly translated into higher profits. By becoming a part of the Network, individual institutes got access to knowledge as well as unique resources and infrastructure, and an opportunity to establish close and consolidated cooperation, and thus they built competitive advantage (e.g. by improving the financial result).

The research conducted was restricted by the absence of a detailed examination of what contributed to the improved commercialisation effectiveness. Was it inclusion in the Network and application of verified European good practices? Or maybe such a state of affairs resulted from clear expectations the Łukasiewicz Research Network institutes are to meet and from the introduction of a system supporting commercialisation endeavours and a control system motivating or forcing them to improve commercialisation processes.

6 CONCLUSION

The analyses and the case study show that operating in a research network impacts on the intensity of commercialisation endeavours. Cooperation helps network organisations better respond to the challenges of the socio-economic environment (as evidenced, among other things, by revenue growth). A network enables effective coordination of dispersed activities, helps establish close relationships, and creates new opportunities, also in terms of development. It seems that the good practices of the Łukasiewicz Research Network can be implemented to create other new research networks comprising Polish research institutes or R&D centres.

Commercialisation processes are driven and hampered by various factors. While the literature on factors impacting on commercialisation at various entities is extensive, factors affecting commercialisation at network organisations seem to be understudied. Due to the important role research organisations belonging to a network have when it comes to fulfilling the key task of research networks (i.e. commercialisation of research results), the authors of the article would like to focus in their future research on the analysis of factors affecting effectiveness of commercialisation processes at network organisations and, additionally, compile a comprehensive list of commercialisation performance indicators.

REFERENCES

Adams J. 2012. Collaborations: The Rise of Research Networks. *Nature*, 490(7420), p. 335–336.

Ardito L. 2018. Markets for university inventions: the role of patents' underlying knowledge in university-to-industry technology commercialisation. *International Journal of Technology Management* 78 (1–2), pp. 9–27.

Atvare E., Kudurs E., Blumberga D. 2022. Differences in Commercialization Policies of Innovations. Customer Perspective. *Environmental and Climate Technologies*, vol. 26, no. 1, pp. 1020–1031, https://doi.org/10.2478/rtuect-2022-0076.

Bhasin H. 2023. Commercialization – Definition. *Process and Strategies February* 8, 2023 Marketing, https://www.marketing91.com/commercialization/ [access: 19.05.2023].

Blażlak R. 2010. *Struktury sieciowe a innowacyjność przedsiębiorstw.* In: K. Owczarek (Rd.), *Klastry w gospodarce regionu.* Wydawnictwo Politechniki Łódzkiej, Łódź,pp. 30–45.

Gao J.H.H., Haworth N. 2019. Stuck in the middle? Human resource management at the interface of academia and industry. *International Journal of Human Resource Management*, 30 (22), pp. 3081–3112.

Hewitt-Dundas N., Burns C. 2016. Structural Capital of University Spin-Out Firms: The Moderating Role of University Incubators, Annual Conference of the Technology-Transfer-Society, University Evolution. *Entrepreneurial Activity and Regional Competitiveness*, 32, pp. 71–95.

Hou B.J., Hong J. (...), Zhou Y. 2019. Do academia-industry R&D collaborations necessarily facilitate industrial innovation in China? The role of technology transfer institutions. *European Journal of Innovation Management*, 22 (5), pp. 717–746.

Jonek-Kowalska I. Musiol-Urbanczyk A. (...), Wolny M. 2021. Does motivation matter in evaluation of research institutions? Evidence from Polish public universities. *Technology in Society*, 67.

Kirby D.A., El Hadidi H.H. 2019. University technology transfer efficiency in a factor driven economy: the need for a coherent policy in Egypt. *Journal of Technology Transfer*, 44 (5), pp. 1367–1395.

Kwieciński L. 2020. Sieci jednostek naukowo-badawczych jako istotny element w polityce innowacyjnej państwa. Przykład polskiej Sieci Badawczej Łukasiewicz. *Nierówności Społeczne a Wzrost Gospodarczy*, nr 64 (4/2020).

Lehenkari J., Olesiak M., Pęczek T., Oksanen J. Dönitz E., Loikkanen T., Sarvaranta L., Popper R. 2022. Towards a Single Knowledge Transfer (KT) Strategy for the Łukasiewicz Research Network.

Loikkanen T., Rilla N., Deschryvere M., Lehenkari J., Oksanen J., Hyvönen J., van der Have R., Arnold E. 2013. Roles, effectiveness, and impact of VTT. Towards broad-based impact monitoring of a research and technology organisation. *VTT TECHNOLOGY*, 113.

Lopes J.M., Oliveira M. (...), Zaman U. 2021. Networks, Innovation and Knowledge Transfer in Tourism Industry: An Empirical Study of SMEs in Portugal. *SOCIAL SCIENCES-BASEL*, 10 (5).

Markiewicz D. (Ed.). 2010. *Komercjalizacja wyników badań naukowych – krok po kroku.* Centrum Transferu Technologii Politechnika Krakowska, Kraków 2009, s. 38.

Matlakiewicz P., Matuszak P. and Grodzicki G. 2016. Results of the commercialisation of scientific research in the light of experience gained at the Nicolaus Copernicus University Centre for Technology transfer, *Polish Hyperbaric Research*, 54 (1), pp. 37–39.
Matusiak K.B. (Ed.). 2005. *Innowacje i transfer technologii. Słownik pojęć*. Polska Agencja Rozwoju Przedsiębiorczości, Warszawa.
Matyjas Z., Bohdanowicz L. 2018. Projekt Sieci Badawczej Łukasiewicz – analiza porównawcza na tle rozwiązań międzynarodowych. *Zarządzanie i Finanse Journal of Management and Finance*, Vol. 16, No. 4/2.
Meredith J.R., Shafer S.M. 2002. *Operations Management for MBAs*, John Wiley & Sons, New York.
Miller K., McAdam R. (…), Puthusserry P. 2016. Knowledge transfer in university quadruple helix ecosystems: an absorptive capacity perspective. *R & D Management*, 46 (2), pp. 383–399.
Mitchell W., Singh K. 1996. Survival of businesses using collaborative relationships to commercialize complex goods. *Strategic Management Journal*, vol. 17(3).
Palyvoda O., Karpenko O., Bondarenko O., Bonyar S., Bikfalvi A. 2018. Influence of network organizational structures on innovation activity of industrial enterprises. *Problems and Perspectives in Management*, 16(3), 174–188. doi:10.21511/ppm.16(3).2018.14.
Poteralska B., Walasik M. 2021. Commercialisation Models for R&D Organisations. In: Matos F., Ferreiro MdF, Rosa A., Salavista I. (Eds.), *Proceedings of the 16th European Conference on Innovation and Entrepreneurship ECIE 2021*, vol. 2, Academic Conferences and Publishing International Limited Reading, UK, pp. 782–790.
Sojkin B. 2012. Informacyjne podstawy decyzji marketingowych w procesie komercjalizacji produktu. *Marketing Instytucji Naukowych i Badawczych*, nr 1(2).
Wiatrak A.P. 2003. Organizacje sieciowe – istota ich działania i zarządzania. *Współczesne Zarządzanie*, nr 3.
Yin R.K. 2014. *Case study research: design and methods*. 5th edition, Sage Publications, Inc.
Zizka M., Valentova V.H., (…), Stichhauerova E. 2018. The effect of clusters on the innovation performance of enterprises: traditional vs new industries. *Entrepreneurship and Sustainability Issues*, 5 (4), pp. 780–794.

Digital Synergy – El Emary et al. (eds)

Chapter 25
Retail pricing optimization with Monte Carlo Tree Search

Mauricio Hanono-Gómez & José Daniel López-Barrientos
Universidad Anahuac Mexico, Mexico

Celeste Rodríguez-Carreon & Nataliya Kalashnykova
Universidad Autónoma de Nuevo León, Ciudad Universitaria SanNicolás de los Garza, Mexico

Contents

Dynamic price changes in the growing retail industry can be determined by geography, inventory, and competition, among other relevant factors. A Monte Carlo Tree Search (MCTS) model is proposed to determine the optimal retail sales price for each day, with the objective of maximizing profits with limited inventory. The expected units based on the defined price are estimated through a multiple linear regression model, in which random variables are added to make the simulations effective. The experiment is performed in real- time, on three products of a grocery shopping delivery startup, for five days. The results indicate an increase of 12% in net income and 33% increase in units sold within the test days, in comparison to last week. Since, in essence, the proposed MCTS model must be unsupervised in order to be implemented on catalogs larger than a thousand SKUs, criteria and thresholds must be defined to ensure that the output is optimal.

1 INTRODUCTION

Dynamic pricing has become an important practice within the retail industry to proactively respond to market behavior. As the importance of retail grows in the e-commerce industry, pricing software has become more relevant to adjust prices based on supervised strategies. Commercial pricing strategies can be based on a combination of competition, elasticity, cost, and seasonality, among other popular techniques.

The lack of information on any of these factors leads to a non-optimal pricing strategy, leaving the cost of opportunity of being able to execute other scenarios with high potential. The same permanence in a single commercial strategy reduces the generation of information for the evaluation of other alternatives. It is possible to approximate the optimal dynamic pricing strategy through simulation and their interaction over time to evaluate alternatives without repercussions.

Machine learning and artificially intelligent algorithms are supporting important decision-making in a wide variety of applications. Progres- sively, decision-making algorithms are

DOI: 10.1201/9781003440406-25

taking advantage of advances in Artificial Intelligence (AI) to solve problems of greater complexity at lower computational cost (Kochenderfer et al. 2022).

A dynamic pricing change model is proposed based on Monte Carlo Tree Search (MCTS), with the objective of maximizing profits based on the location and demographic information of different groups of people, on their willingness to pay for the same product and adjusting prices according to inventory control and demand behavior over time. The model also seeks to address the problem of minimizing the opportunity cost of abandoning potential pricing strategies.

The MCTS algorithm is a decision-making algorithm that combines the accuracy of a search tree with random sampling through Monte Carlo simulations. It was originally proposed in 2016 in the AI field called Computer Go, and since then, it has become a state-of-the-art technique for Combinatorial Game Theory (Couëtoux et al. 2013). The MCTS algorithm solves reinforced learning problems through weighting experienced returns. It is an iterative algorithm that relies on intelligent tree search to find promising states and builds statistical evidence through random sampling, and, therefore, take informed decisions.

As for the state-of-the-Art with regard to the usage of the method under study, it is worth noting that MCTS has become a novel and unified framework for game AI, after being tested in most combinatorial games to seek the ideal play in sequential games with perfect information. Regarding the application of the algorithm for purposes other than non-deterministic games, MCTS has been applied in different contexts, including cybersecurity (Wang et al. 2020: 1449-1457), airport patrolling (Jain et al. 2010: 267-290), poaching prevention (Segler et al 2018: 604-610), chemical synthesis with deep neural networks (Mańdziuk 2018: 230-244), vehicle routing with AI planning (Neto at al. 2020: 1115-1126), among other relevant applications (Świechowski et al. 2021). Finally, the authors of (López-Barrientos et al. 2022) used a Monte Carlo-based approach to study and forecast football matches.

Regarding dynamic pricing, MCTS has been applied to maximizing revenue or utilization for electric vehicle charging station operators (Mrkos, Basmadjian 2022: 223-240). The authors propose a Markov Decision Process (MDP)-based approach and implement it using MCTS to address the large-scale problem. The former approach proves near-optimal pricing decisions in milliseconds, significantly increasing their reward over the flat-rate baseline. The work by Puterman (Puterman 1994) gives a concise introduction to MDPs.

Likewise, Monte Carlo Simulations have been applied to different fields of study within retail operations. In (Leepaitoon, Bunterngchit 2019: 67-83), the authors estimated the optimal economic order quantity to save inventory cost in a retail store, under the uncertainty of lead time and demand. The authors of (Taylor et al. M, 2019: 555-566) developed a practical approach for applying Game Theory combined with Monte Carlo Simulation modeling into retail marketing strategies.

Unlike other contributions, the proposed dynamic pricing model is based on an MDP adapted to the retail industry and solved by the MCTS method. To the best of our knowledge, this is the first time this approach has been applied with dynamic pricing in the retail industry with MCTS. This constitutes our major contribution to the field.

In concrete, for MCTS, a search tree is built, node by node, according to the possible outcomes within the simulations. Naturally, as with the Monte Carlo method, the more iterations, the more certain the statistics are, and, therefore, the probability that the best-recommended action is actually optimal increases. MCTS consists of repeated iterations (looped until a predefined stop condition is satisfied), on which each iteration consists of four phases, as shown in Figure 1, which we borrowed from (Chaslot 2010).

The remainder of our work is organized as follows. The next section delves into the description of the model for the retail industry, then in section 3, we present the experiments we performed and the corresponding results. We give our conclusions in section 5.

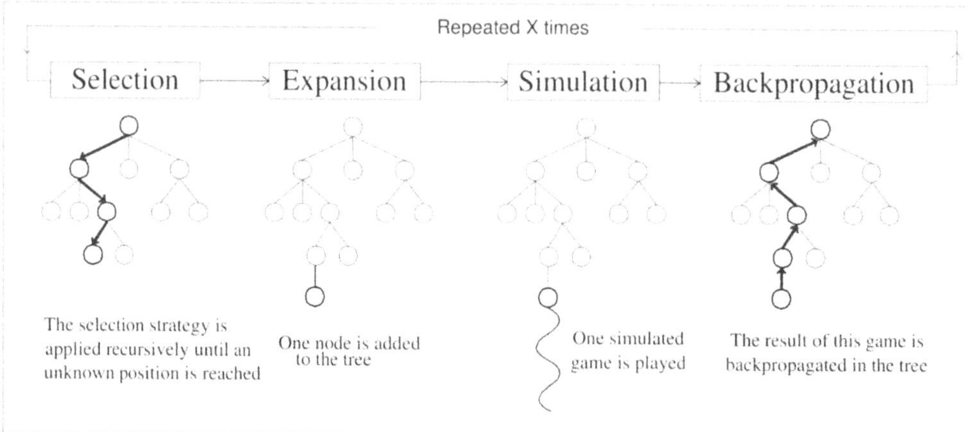

Figure 1. Outline of Monte-Carlo Tree Search.

2 MODEL DESCRIPTION

Formally, MCTS is applicable to an MDP, which allows modeling a simulated environment of sequential decisions to obtain rewards according to the agent's policy. An MDP is defined as a 4-tuple (S, A_s, P_a, R_a) where S is a finite set of possible states, A_s is a finite set of admissible actions when the process is in state s, $Pa(s, s')$ is the one-step transition probability of going from state s to s' when selecting action a; and $Ra(s)$ is the immediate reward for reaching state s' by action a (Puterman 1994). Now, we describe how we use these elements to implement the MCTS.

- Selection. Recall that the state space S_t at time t is defined by the competitive set. Thus, the competitors within the industry are chosen to be considered as a point of comparison. Therefore, it is proposed that the possible states in S at time t, are initially a set of five retail sales price (RSP) options, which include the minimum and maximum, and the quartiles of the distribution of the competing RSP. Additionally, a "win" state is added, which fixes an RSP lower than the minimum competitor by 3%, and a "margin builder" state, which fixes an RSP higher than the maximum competitor by 3%.
  To determine which nodes to add to the tree, the popular Upper-Confidence Bound method is used, since it maintains an appropriate balance between exploration and exploitation (Auer et al. 2002: 235–256). This tree policy allows the agent to do both: improve its knowledge about each action in the long term and choose actions to try to obtain the highest reward in the short term.
- Expansion. Same as with St, the feasible action space A_s can be defined by the competitive set. Thus it is a set of the possible prices in state s'. The proposed limit on S and A is established so as not to iterate on prices that are not profitable, nor on prices that will have no demand at all. To forecast the expected demand with the simulated price changes, a multiple linear regression model is developed, considering elasticity and seasonality. Additionally, random variables that are also statistically significant are added to the model to create a random environment for the simulations to be effective. These random variables can be related to discount strategies, marketing strategies, and traffic, among other relevant factors.
- The defined random variables are fitted to a theoretical distribution through a goodness-of-fit test. The Kolmogorov-Smirnov (K-S) test allows a comparison of a sample with a reference probability distribution (one-sample K-S test), and the parameters can be estimated through Maximum Likelihood Estimation (MLE). Afterward, a random simulation of the

problem is performed until a terminal state is reached. Two conditions are proposed for a state to be considered terminal: whether the inventory in state $s_t \leq 0$, or $t > n$, where n is the parameter to define the number of days to be simulated.

Finally, a phase of backpropagation enters into place. Each node visited during the simulation is updated. There, the transition matrix P_a for each s is updated during each simulation. The reward function R_a is defined by the objective to be achieved. Since the model proposes to maximize profits, R_a will be a function of the Net Income. That is:

$$\text{Net Income} = GMV - COGS - \text{Taxes},$$

where GMV stands for the Gross Merchandise Volume, and $COGS$ is the Cost of Goods Sold.

The pseudocode of the proposed MCTS model is shown in Algorithm 1. Regarding the input values, the root values are the last recorded values of units sold, RSP, GMV, COGS, Taxes, and the added random variables. In addition, the best-performing linear regression model must be provided, as well as the estimators of the fitted theoretical distribution. The output is the path with the highest expected reward, where its child nodes have also the best outcome within the path.

Algorithm 1 MCTS General Pseudocode
Input: Root values
Output: Best Route in the tree
while $i \leq$ x do
$t \leftarrow 0$
while IsT erminalN ode = F ALSE **do**
Selection
Expansion
$t \leftarrow t + 1$
end while
end while

3 EXPERIMENTS

The experiment considers a two-month database containing both daily sales and inventory of a grocery shopping delivery startup in Mexico City. We chose three SKUs from different categories so that their rotations behaved differently from each other. These SKUs are tested in only two of the +20 warehouses located in the city. In this way, the performance of the model is evaluated in real-time, compared to a control group of warehouses. The path of RSPs that maximize the expected Net Income over the next five days was calculated with 1,000 iterations each.

- Available States and Actions. Among the selected SKUs, one item belongs to the bread category. Comparing the prices of the same prod- uct in other retail stores, a range between \$1.75 and \$2.40 dollars is found. Therefore, both our S and A_s are a set of RSPs within {1.65, 1.75, 1.9, 2.05, 2.20, 2.35, 2.45}, rounded to the nearest multiple of 0.05 or 0.1 in US dollars.
- MLR and Fitting Random Variables. In order to develop the best non-supervised performing model regarding the expected units sold, a step-wise selection is made to lower the prediction error. MLR assumptions are validated.

Among the random variables added to the multiple linear regression model is the number of active users per day browsing the website.

In Figure 2, the active users within the study period are plotted. Outliers are removed to continue with the fitting of the empirical distribution.

In Figure 3, performing a supervised analysis on the Cullen-Frey plot, the bootstrapped values suit the theoretical Normal and Poisson distributions.

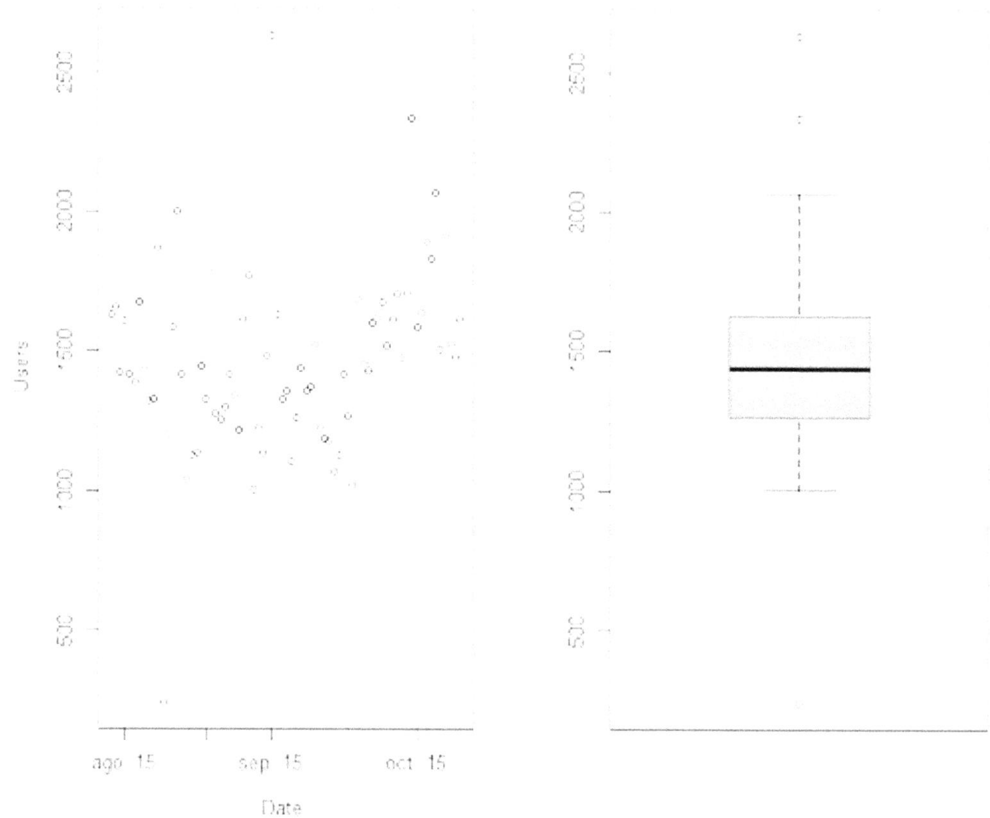

Figure 2. Active users in two months.

A one-sample K-S test is performed to determine whether or not the null hypothesis that the sample comes from a normal distribution is rejected. Likewise, the parameters are estimated through MLEs.

- Before Testing. Once the root values are available, the proposed MCTS model is executed, and compared with a fixed price scenario, considering the initial RSP before trial, in terms of the expected units sold (again with 1,000 iterations) in the following five days. The iterations follow both the MLR model and the simulation of the random variables previously identified. See Figure 4.

Note in Table 1 that the proposed model identifies that the RSP can be slightly lowered on days with lower demand, in order to maximize the Net Income at the end of the 5 days of simulation. Hence there is an expected Net Income increase of 23%, compared to the fixed-price scenario.

4 RESULTS

As mentioned, it has been proposed to conduct a 5-day test starting on a Monday. Overall, in comparison with the previous week, the model achieved an increase of 33% in units sold and a 12% increase in Net Income, whereas in comparison to the control group, the model achieved an increase of 66% in units sold and a 40% increase in Net Income. See Figures 5-6.

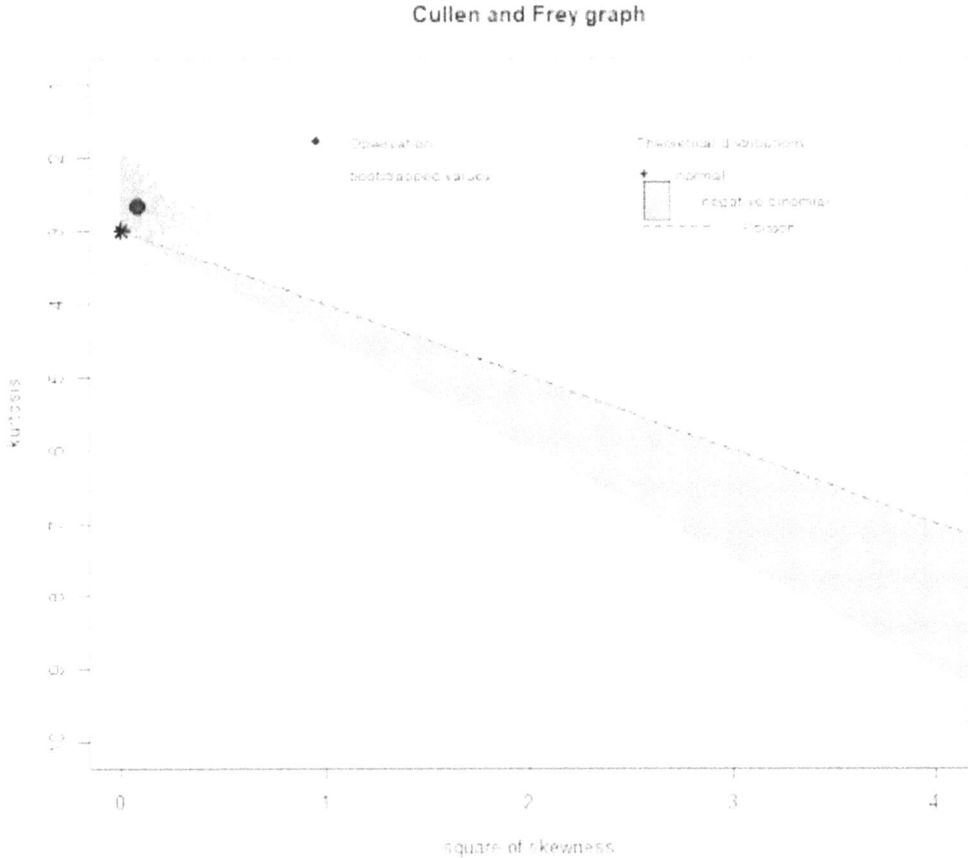

Figure 3. Cullen and frey graph of active users.

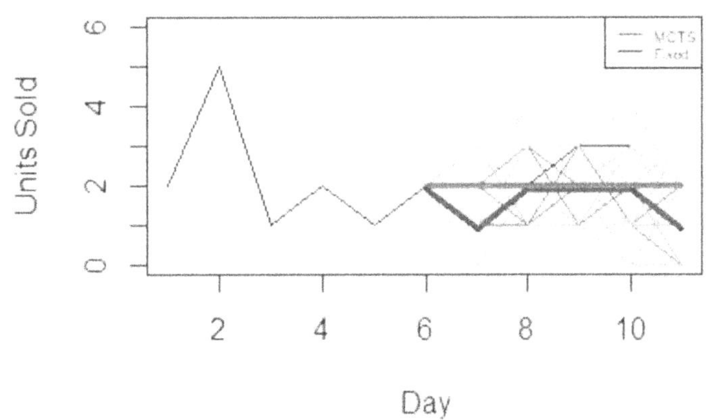

Figure 4. Simulation of sold units.

Considering the SKU that belongs to the bread category, the first tested hub, in comparison to the assigned control group, achieved a 51% net income increase and a 75% in units sold. Likewise, the second tested HUB, in comparison to the assigned control group, achieved a 35% net income increase and a 63% in units sold.

Table 1. Comparison of expected net income.

Day	MCTS: RSP	MCTS: Units Sold	Fixed Price: RSP	Fixed Price: Units Sold
1	$2.35	2	$2.40	2
2	$2.35	2	$2.40	1
3	$2.45	2	$2.40	2
4	$2.45	2	$2.40	2
5	$2.35	2	$2.40	1
Net Income		$7.45		$6.05

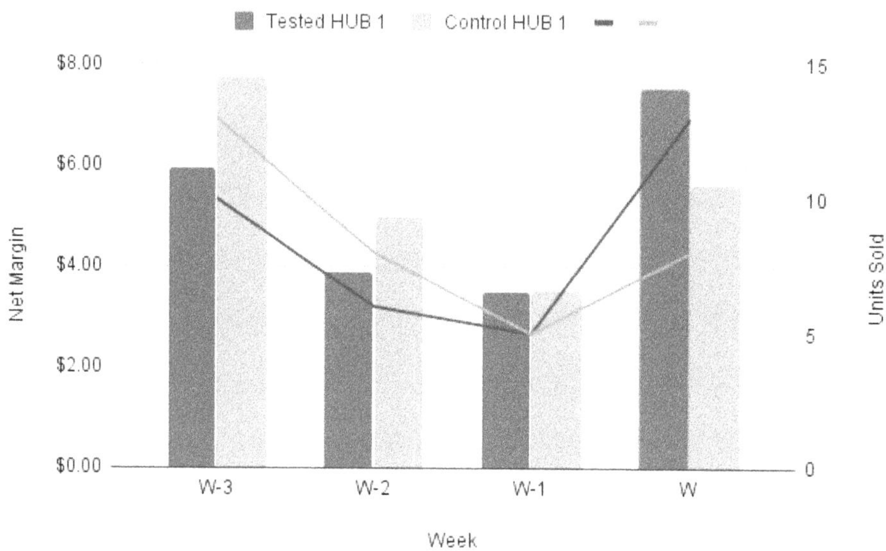

Figure 5. 5-day MCTS Test Results in hub 1.

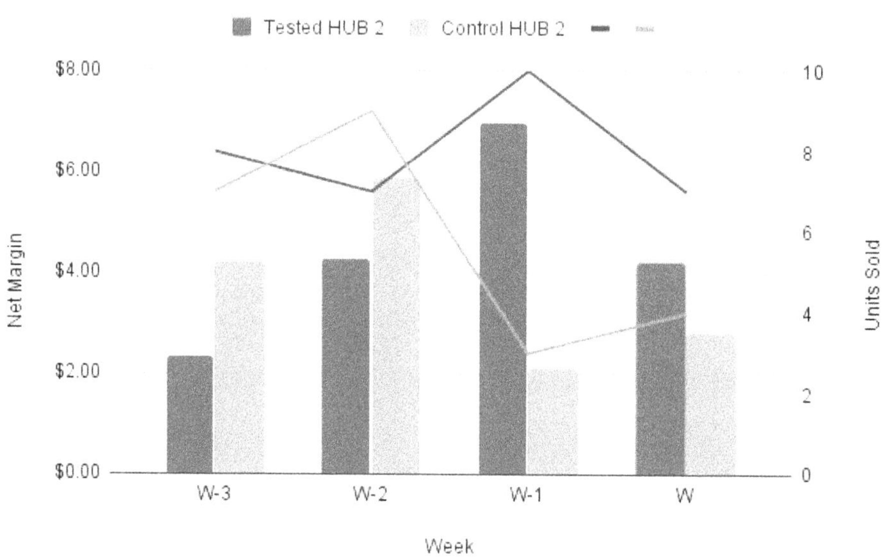

Figure 6. 5-day MCTS Test Results in hub 2.

5 CONCLUSIONS

In essence, the underlying concept of the proposed dynamic pricing model is to sell the selected product at the right price, at the right time, to the right customer; with the objective of maximizing profits. As the retail industry grows, dynamic pricing models are becoming more promising.

Through statistical and machine learning models, unsupervised and data-driven pricing strategies can be developed. Over time, the model itself will learn from the experience of its own outputs, based on real results. Therefore, the model is expected to iteratively improve over time.

5.1 *Limitations*

Since the proposed model is expected to be executed on a catalog of more than a thousand SKUs, at a warehouse level; the development of the LRM model must necessarily be unsupervised. Regardless of the variable selection method (Forward, Backward, Step-wise), there will be cases in which the RSP variable is not statistically significant for the model. Likewise, there will be cases where the R-squared is not statistically significant. For both cases, it is proposed to define criteria and thresholds in terms of p-values, R-squared, and other statistical values. It is suggested that the SKUs that are withdrawn from the model should have their RSP changed continuously to measure elasticity.

5.2 *Next steps*

The proposed MCTS model can be changed to address larger catalogs efficiently. The increase in simulation days or possible RSPs also increases the computational cost. There is an existing wide area of opportunity in developing dynamic pricing models to achieve commercial objectives within the retail industry.

REFERENCES

Auer P, Cesa-Bianchi N, Fischer P. Finite-time analysis of the multiarmed bandit problem. Machine learning 2002; 47: 235–256.

Chaslot GMJBC. Monte Carlo tree search. 24. Maastricht University. 2010.

Couëtoux A, Müller M, Teytaud O. Monte Carlo Tree Search in Go. University of Alberta. 2013.

Jain M, Tsai J, Pita J, et al. Software assistants for randomized patrol planning for the lax airport police and the federal air marshal service. Interfaces 2010; 40: 267–290.

Kochenderfer MJ, Wheeler TA, Wray KH. Algorithms for decision making. MIT Press. 2022.

Leepaitoon S, Bunterngchit C. The application of Monte Carlo simulation for inventory management: A case study of a retail store. International Journal of the Computer, the Internet, and Management 2019; 27: 67–83.

López-Barrientos JD, Zayat-Niño DA, Hernández-Prado EX, Estudillo-Bravo Y. On the Élö–Runyan–Poisson–Pearson Method to Forecast Football Matches. Mathematics 2022; 10: 4587.

Mańdziuk J. New shades of the vehicle routing problem: emerging problem formulations and computational intelligence solution methods. IEEE Transactions on Emerging Topics in Computational Intelligence 2018; 3: 230–244.

Mrkos J, Basmadjian R. Dynamic Pricing for Charging of EVs with Monte Carlo Tree Search. Smart Cities 2022; 5: 223–240.

Neto T, Constantino M, Martins I, Pedroso J. A multi-objective Monte Carlo tree search for forest harvest scheduling. European Journal of Operational Research 2020; 282: 1115–1126.

Puterman ML. Markov Decision Processes. Discrete Stochastic Dynamic Programming. Wiley, New York. 1994.

Segler MH, Preuss M, Waller MP. Planning chemical syntheses with deep neural networks and symbolic AI. Nature 2018; 555: 604–610.

Świechowski M, Godlewski K, Sawicki B, Mańdziuk J. Monte Carlo tree search: A review of recent modifications and applications. arXiv preprint arXiv:2103.04931 2021.

Taylor M, Kwasnica V, Reilly D, Ravindran S. Game theory modeling of retail marketing discount strategies. Marketing Intelligence and Planning 2019; 37: 555–566.

Wang K, Perrault A, Mate A, Tambe M. Scalable Game-Focused Learning of Adversary Models: Data-to-Decisions in Network Security Games. International Conference on Autonomous Agents and Multi-agent Systems 2020: 1449–1457.

Digital Synergy – El Emary et al. (eds)

Chapter 26
Power distance and constraints collectivist cultures

Karolina Julia Helnarska
WSB Merito University, Warsaw, Poland

Contents

The COVID-19 pandemic was an opportunity and reason for re-analysis of existing cubic differences in relation to the wave of the COVID 19 pandemic in the analysed countries. The occurrence of a sudden number of suspicions and the need to introduce restrictions at central level, confirming the impact of cultural differences on the way individual waves run in society. This study is an attempt to answer how the distance of power and individuality affect the security of the individual of society.

1 INTRODUCTION

Hofstede described four cultural dimensions that have become axioms in intercultural research [1] indicating the relationship between culture and functioning in the organization. Thus, individualism and collectivism have become concepts describing cultural differences. According to Schwartz's arguments [5], the more legitimate view is that representatives of a given society tend to be guided by both collectivistic and individualistic values, although at the level of characterization of the whole society, a tendency to choose a specific group of values can be revealed. The values act as criteria determining the methods of operation and the assessment of these activities. Individualistic and collectivist orientation, coexisting in the mind of every human being, means a certain generalized tendency to perceive, value, feel and respond to social reality. In this article, the author in selected countries based on the course of the Covid-19 pandemic, presented the participation of cultural differences in the public's response to restrictions and restrictions imposed by those in power.

DOI: 10.1201/9781003440406-26

2 DESCRIPTION OF THE PROBLEM

February 24, 2020. Tedros Ghebreyesus, announced that the spread of Covid-19 virus around the world is not yet at the pandemic stage, but admitted that it has the potential to become (NewScientist, 2023). March 11, 2020. The WHO director classified the Covid-19 infection wave as (World Health Organization, 2023) pandemic.

In the world as of February 24, 2020, over 124,000 cases of SARS-CoV-2 coronavirus infection and over 4,500 deaths have already been confirmed. Outside China, the virus has already reached 117 countries. Countries have implemented a number of restrictive measures aimed at stopping or slowing COVID-19 transmission, including isolation measures restricting the free movement of their citizens, prohibiting public events and closing shops, restaurants and schools. These measures have frozen public life in almost all countries and have caused social unrest in some countries.

Based on the above information, the author decided to conduct an analysis of the impact of the wave of infections due to cultural differences in societies. Thus, the following research hypotheses were created for the purposes of the article:

Hypotheses 1: Individualistic nations will have a higher growth rate of COVID-19 cases over time than collectivistic nations.

Hypotheses 2: Individualism–collectivism will moderate the relationship between government stringency and the growth rate of COVID-19 cases, such that government stringency will have a weaker attenuating effect on case growth rate in individualistic than in collectivistic nations.

Hypotheses 3: Power distance will moderate the relationship between government stringency and the growth rate of COVID-19 cases, such that government stringency will have a stronger attenuating effect on case growth rate in high than in low power distance nations.

According to Oyserman, the individual's attitude towards the group and the obligations arising from participation in the group are expressed in forming relationships with representatives of their own group, which may be short-term - individualism, or they are a strong, long-lasting bond - collectivism (Oyserman et al., 2002). According to Reykowski, quot. „ the collective is responsible for the entity, but the entity is responsible for the good of the collective and its individual members. Hence the moral order to sacrifice for others and for the good of the collective" (Reykowski, 1990). In addition, Reykowski believes that the quotation „ individualistic approach implies the principle that everyone is responsible for themselves, while the collectivist approach assumes the principle of shared responsibility".

According to Markus H., Kitayama S. (Markus & Kitayama, 1991, p. 224-253) and Triandis H. C. et. al. (Triandis, 1989), cultural orientation shapes the views of individuals about themselves in relation to others and affects the reactions and behaviour of individuals in social situations. Based on the above statements, it was decided to show that collectivist societies put the good of the group over the good of the individual, while individualistic societies, and thus individualistic culture, put the good of the individual first.

In cultures where people depend on a group, there is usually also a strong dependence on power. In the structures of patriarchal multi-generational families, the head of the family also plays the role of moral authority. In cultures where people are not so strongly associated with the group, dependence on power is less.

3 RESEARCH METHODS

3.1 *Research data*

Two countries with extreme values of individualism, collectivism and distance to power presented in Table 1 and Figure 1 were selected for research, where the analysed countries around the diagonal passing from the lower left corner to the upper right corner were grouped, which reflects the described correlation between the distance of power and individualism.

Table 1. Indicators of individualism and power distance for analysed states according to the Hofstede model. (Country comparaison tool, 2023).

Country	Content	Power Distance	Individualism
Costa Rica	South America	35	15
Malaysia	Asia	100	96

Source: author's work based on www.hofstede-insights.com/country-comparison/ [04-05-2021].

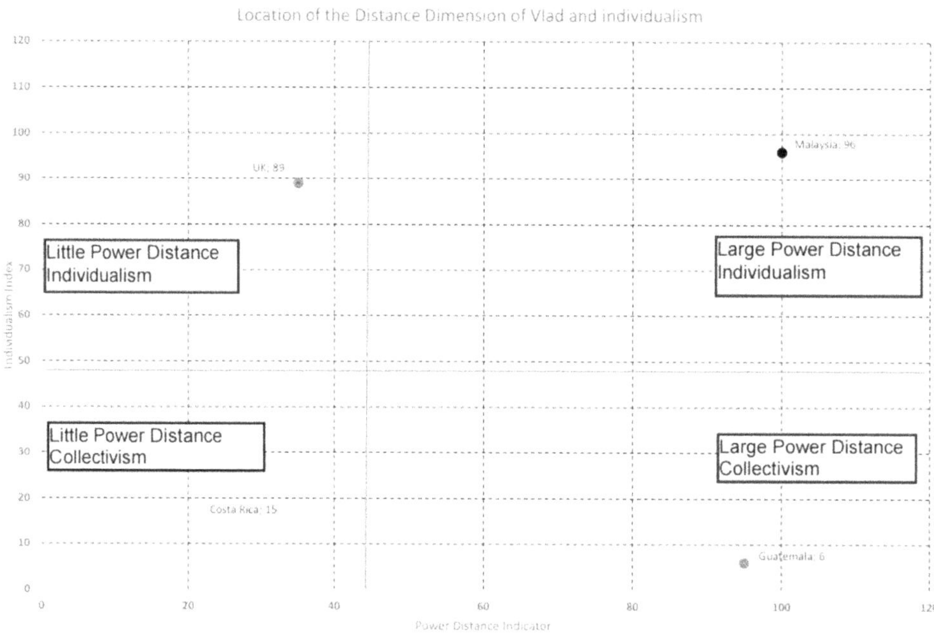

Figure 1. Location of analysed countries in the diagram of the dimensions of the distance of power and individualism. Source: Own elaboration based on data www.hofstede-insights.com/country-comparison/ [04-05-2021].

Malaysia as a country with a high power distance indicator has a low individuality rate, while Costa Rica has a high collective value and low power distance. Countries with a high rate of power distance have a low index of individualism and vice versa, countries with a small power distance are characterized by high individualism. To sum up, both countries (both dimensions) are negatively correlated with each other.

3.2 *Methodology*

In this article, some indicators developed during the implementation of the project have been used Oxford Covid-19 Government Response Tracker (OxCGRT), which will demonstrate the effectiveness of the policy decisions taken by governments to combat the COVID-19 pandemic. 23 indicators were used, e.g. school closures, travel restrictions, vaccination policy. The level of these indicators was related to the scope of government activities. The obtained results allowed us to understand how governments' responses were taken helping in efforts to fight the pandemic.

Stringency Index: The stringency index is a composite measure based on nine response indicators including school closures, workplace closures, and travel bans, rescaled to a value from 0 to 100 (100 = strictest).

Government response index: The index records how the response of governments has varied over all indicators in the database, becoming stronger or weaker over the course of the outbreak. It is calculated using all ordinal indicators. Differential responses can also be seen across the entire period.

For the purposes of this article, a comparison of the policy indicator was made in the form of: Government Response Index (GRI), Stringency Index (SI) In relation to the number of daily new Covid 19 infections.

4 RESULTS OF THE RESEARCH

4.1 *Characteristics of the countries*

Malaysia is a federal constitutional monarchy, executive power is exercised by the government and the prime minister, and legislative power by parliament. It is located in Southeast Asia, where there is a tropical monsoon climate. There are over 33.5 million people in Malaysia, and the population density is about 83 people/km ^{2}. It is an ethnically diverse country - indigenous people make up about 62.5% of the total population, over 20% are Chinese, 6% are Indian, and foreigners make up about 10% of the population. Malaysian society is relatively young (there are few people aged 60 and over).

Costa Rica is the presidential republic, the president and the government responsible for it exercise executive power. Legislative power belongs to the unicameral Legislative Assembly, elected by universal suffrage. Costa Rica is located on the isthmus of Central America, the area of the country is 51,100 km2, and it is inhabited by 5.19 million people. The inhabitants of this country are white people, which constitute 87% of the population. The remaining part is Metysi (6%), Negroes and Mulaci (4%), Indians (1%), Chinese (1%) 1% (. The average population density is 83 people per km2.

4.2 *Covid 19 pandemic course*

4.2.1 *Malaysia*

The first cases of SARS-CoV-2 infection in Malaysia were recorded on January 25, 2020, Malaysian Minister of Health Dzulkefly Ahmad said three infections in people who travelled from Singapore to Malaysia. All persons were related to a 66-year-old man and his son, in whom the Singapore Health Authority confirmed the positive test for the presence of the virus (Siplan & Holmes, 2023), (GardaWorld, 2020), in total, eight new cases were confirmed in the first week. All persons were Chinese citizens. On February 3, 2020, the first positive result of the COVID-19 test of a Malaysian citizen who travelled to the Middle Kingdom was recorded. The first wave of COVID-19, which lasts until February 27, 2020, is called „ imported from China", because in 22 new cases only 2 did not apply to persons who are citizens of this country or traveling there (Shah et al., 2020).

The epidemiological situation deteriorated after a religious assembly attended by 16,000 people from several countries taking place in the Sri Petaling mosque near the capital Kuala Lumpur. Malaysia then became the most affected country in Southeast Asia, increasing the total number of cases to 428 (Ng, 2020). As of March 30, the total number of cases increased to 2,626 active cases of covid 19 in the country. (DG of Health, 2020).

The Malaysian government implemented the Movement Control Order (MCO) on 18th March 2020 to combat the COVID-19 pandemic, which was then extended or switched between the Conditional Movement Control Order (CMCO), the Recovery Movement Control Order (RMCO), and the Enhanced Movement Control Order (EMCO), depending on the country's pandemic situation from time to time. The government remains committed to the National Recovery Plan (NRP) enforced on 1st June 2021. Under the Prevention and Control of Infectious Diseases Act 1988 (Act 342), individuals who violate SOPs stipulated for the pandemic management can be fined up to RM10,000, and enterprises or corporations can be fined up to RM1 million, starting on 11th March 2021. (FlandersTrade, 2020).

In response to the surge of cases in March 2020, the Malaysian government led by Prime Minister Muhyiddin Yassin imposed a nationwide lockdown known as the Movement Control Order (MCO), which came into effect on 18 March 2020. COVID-19 has spread over 135 countries. There have been 162,711 confirmed COVID-19 cases globally. From that number, 6443 deaths have been recorded. In Malaysia, there was a sharp rise in the number of cases:190 cases recorded yesterday and an additional 125 cases today. The total number of cases now stand at 553 cases. From that number, 511 are being treated, whereas 42 have fully recovered. the Government has decided to implement a nationwide Restriction of Movement Order beginning 18th of March until 31st of March. This Order is enforced under the Control and Prevention of Infectious Diseases Act 1988 and the Police Act 1967, and encompasses the following:

- Complete restriction of movement and assembly nationwide, including religious activities, sports, social and cultural events. To enforce this restriction, all houses of worship and business premises are to be closed, except supermarkets, public markets, sundry shops and convenience stores selling essential goods. Specifically, for Muslims, the suspension of all religious activities in mosques and Suraus, including the Friday prayers, is in line with decision of the Special Muzakarrah Committee that convened on the 15th of March 2020.
- A complete travel restriction for all Malaysians going overseas. For Malaysians returning home, they are required to undergo health checks and voluntary self- quarantine for a period of 14 days.
- A complete restriction of foreign visitors and tourists into Malaysia.
- Closure of all kindergartens, public and private schools, including day schools and residential schools, international schools, Tahfiz centers and all other institutions of learning in primary, secondary and pre-university levels.
- Closure of all public and private institutions of higher learning nationwide, including skills training institutes.
- Closure of all government and private premises except those involved in essential services (Water, electricity, energy, telecommunications, post, transportation, irrigation, oil, gas fuel, lubricants, broadcasting, finance, banking, health, pharmacy, fire prevention, prisons, ports, airports, security, defence, cleaning, food supply & retail) (González, 2020).

The MCO, which was supposed to be ended on 31 March 2020, was extended to early May 2020. By early May, the MCO had led to a gradual decline in daily infections. The government progressively relaxed lockdown restrictions in a staggered phase; beginning with the "Conditional Movement Control Order" (CMCO) on 4 May 2020, which allows most business sectors to be reopened under strict standard operating procedures (SOPs) followed by the "Recovery Movement Control Order" (RMCO) on 10 June 2020 The government had planned to end the RMCO on 31 August 2020 but due to the continuous detection of imported cases, measures were extended until the end of the year, with several sectors remaining closed and strict travel restrictions from several countries remaining in place. (Zúñiga, 2020).

The Malaysian government responded by restoring CMCO restrictions in most states since November 2020 to counter the outbreak. By mid-January 2021, the pressure of COVID-19 on the country's healthcare system led to the reintroduction of MCO restrictions across various Malaysian states and federal territories, which was extended to March 4, 2021. (Barquero, 2020).

4.2.2 *Costa Rica*

On February 22, a 54-year-old Costa Rican citizen who arrived from Tocumen Airport in Panama began to feel symptoms, from February 28 the patient was quarantined at San Rafael Hospital in Alajuela, case confirmed on March 7 (González, 2020).

On March 5, the Ministry of Health of Costa Rica announced that it was investigating the possible first case of coronavirus in this country. The suspected case was a 52-year-old Costa Rican from the canton of Pococí, who returned from Italy and Tunisia on

February 29 to the country, the case was not confirmed (Barquero, 2020). As the first case confirmed in Costa Rica, this is the case of March 6, 2020, with an American tourist who admitted to the country on March 1. The couple came to the capital San José from New York. (FlandersTrade, 2020). As at March 7, 2020. The World Health Organization (WHO) in Costa Rica confirmed five cases of Sar Cov - 2 infection. (Zúñiga, 2020a) . On March 8, the Costa Rican authorities confirmed another four new cases. Some patients were in hospitals and tourists stayed in hotels. On March 11, the Minister of Health of Costa Rica announced 22 confirmed cases, (14 men, 8 women), of whom 19 are Costa Rica, and 3 people from other countries (Barquero, 2020a). On March 13, the Ministry of Health confirmed another 4 cases of Sar Cov-2 infection, cases detected in the provinces of San José, Alajuela, Heredia and Guanacaste, and in the province of Cartago (The Tico Times, 2020). On March 15, the Costa Rican authorities closed 350 educational institutions. Three patients were placed in the intensive care unit. The Ministry of Health also confirmed further cases in the cantons of Santa Ana, Grecia, Nicoya, La Unión, Poás, Pérez Zeledón, San Pablo and Barva, the total number of infected is 35 people (Elmundo, 2020). On March 17, a report from the Ministry of Health reported further positive cases of coronavirus in total as at the date of the report, 50 people were concentrated in 19 cantons (Canales, 2020). On March 18, the first death of a patient of an 87-year-old man infected with Sar Cov-2 was recorded, and further cases were reported in the cantons of Goicoechea, Moravia, Santo Domingo and Santa Bárbara (Quesada, 2020). On March 20, the Ministry of Health announced the recovery of the first two patients infected with the virus, American tourists isolated in a hotel in San José (Rodriquez & Cerdas, 2020) . By March 28, 52 health professionals from the Costa Rican Social Insurance Fund (Caja Costarricense del Seguro Social or CCSS) had become infected with the virus. According to Román Macay, the staff were not infected during the treatment of patients, most of the infections were caused by contacts of employees who went abroad and infected employees (Nassar, 2020). On March 30, the Minister of Health warned, that Costa Rica has just started to enter the disease curve due to Sar Cov-2 virus infections (Ministro de Salud, 2020).

4.3 *Restrictions adopted by the government in the fight against the Covid 19 Pandemic*

4.3.1 *Malaysia*

In response to the sharp increase in cases in March 2020, the Malaysian government headed by Prime Minister Muhyiddin Yassin imposed a nationwide blockade known as the Traffic Control Regulation (MCO), which entered into force on March 18, 2020.

4.3.2 *Costa Rica*

On March 8, the Ministry of Health of Costa Rica and the National Rescue Committee (CNE) raised the level of sanitary alarm to yellow (Ministerio de Salud de Costa Rica, 2020). On March 11, the authorities of the University of Costa Rica introduced the suspension of all stationary classes and implementation of the remote teaching mode (Barquero, 2020b). On March 12, the Minister of Health stated, that Costa Rica will not close its borders for foreign tourists (Zúñiga, 2020). CNE launched the 1322 COVID-19 (Quesada, 2020) help line, the Costa Rican film festival (Elmundo, 2020a) was cancelled. On March 15, the Ministry of Education of Costa Rica suspended 317 educational institutions, (7% of all Costa Rica educational institutions) classes, for 150,000 students. Institutions in which cases of COVID-19 have been confirmed, all public special schools, educational institutions in which the case of infection with the Sar Cov-2 virus has been confirmed, and facilities that have been affected by the drinking water access crisis. (Castro, 2020). The President of the Republic, Carlos Alvarado Quesada, has granted the rights of members of the Costa Rican police authorities to supervise and control, both to verify introduced restrictions, close bars, discos and casinos, and to provide 50% visiting opportunities for other meeting centers. Companies that do not comply with the sanitary regime will be closed for 30 days (Elmundo, 2020b). On March 16, the government introduced a state of emergency due to the threat of the Sars Cov -2 virus. In addition, until April 4, classes were suspended in all public, private schools and colleges. From March 18 to April 12, entry was banned, only Costa Rican and permanent residents will be able to enter the country, however, upon arrival, these persons will have to be in quarantine for at least 14 days (Elmundo, 2020a). On March 20, the Ministry of Public Education (MEP) allowed the delivery of food parcels to parents of their students so as not to expose the personnel cooking meals. (Herrera, 2020). On March 23, the Ministry of Health and Government announced the complete closure of beaches, the mandatory closure of temples and the cancellation of services, the restriction of vehicle traffic in major cities of the country. Residents and refugees will lose their migration status if they leave the country (Barquero, 2020c).

On March 27, the government extended vehicle traffic restrictions, further announced that it was considering introducing a temporary solidarity tax on wages above EUR 1.1 million (Alfaro, 2020).

On March 30, the Ministry of Health sent a bill to Asamblea Legislativa, Congress of Costa Rica. Assuming the amendment of Article 378 Ley General de Salud (General Health Act) to impose fines for violation of sanitary or quarantine restrictions, in the amount of 1 to 5 basic salary) (Quesada, 2020a). On March 31, the government opened Centro Especializado de Atención de Pacientes con COVID-19 (CEACO), specializing in the treatment of patients with COVID-19 in CENARE facilities (Presidencia de la República de Costa Rica, 2020).

5 DISCUSSION/LIMITATION AND FUTURE RESEARCH

Despite a proliferation of studies on predictors of attitudinal and behavioral responses to the COVID-19 pandemic (Zettlet et al., 2021), research in this field is still warranted. Hence, we sought to investigate attitudinal and behavioral responses in the first pandemic wave, when uncertainty regarding the spread of the virus dominated societies.

In conjunction with the existing findings, my study provides valuable evidence which can be utilized to compare pandemic responses from different time points during the pandemic.

Moreover, I'll be to statistically test the association between the three related but distinct outcomes – maintaining physical hygiene, avoiding physical contact, and supporting governmental policies related to COVID-19.

This distinguishes my approach from prior research that employed a general factor of preventive behaviors as it allowed us to gain insights both into attitudinal and behavioral responses to the measures aimed at mitigating the spread of the virus. Secondly, we consider potential cultural differences in the meaning of the studied constructs by establishing equivalence of factor scores through (partial) strong invariance (Putnick & Bornstein, 2016). Finally, to determine the efficacy of our independent variables in explaining contact avoidance, hygiene maintenance, and COVID-19 policy support in each country, we applied random forest-based regression algorithms appropriate for complex data sets with possible non-linear and interactive relationships between variables (Breiman, 2001), (Sage, 2018).

6 CONCLUSIONS

Differences in national responses to COVID-19 have been linked in this article to the cultural value of collectivism. This analysis is based on these findings, examining the relationship between individual collectivism and compliance with recommendations in the fight against COVID-19 at the pre-vaccination stage, as well as testing the various features of collectivism, i.e. community care, trust in institutions, perceived social norms.

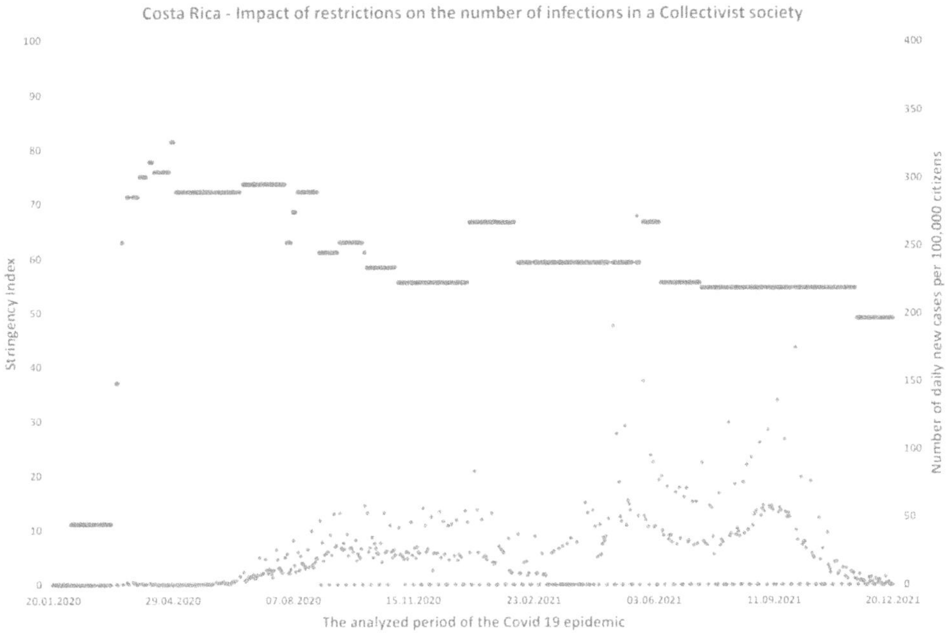

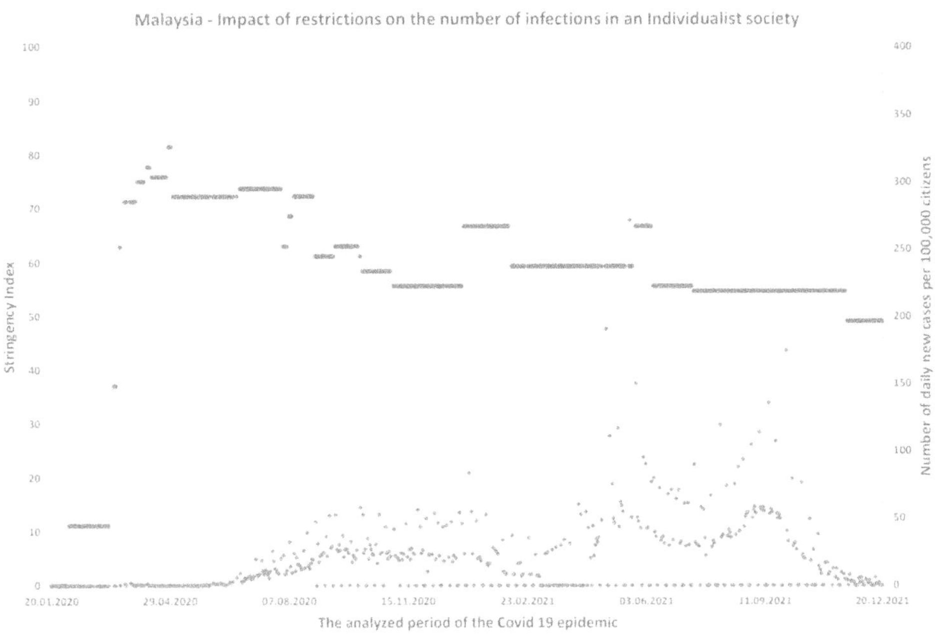

Figure 2. New daily confirmed cases of Covid-19 in correlation of introduced restrictions.

In the face of Covid-19, for people who were at a high level of perceived susceptibility to disease, collectivism was associated with reduced support for xenophobic policy, probably because, that they saw greater protection of their community against the threat of an unknown virus, while individualism was not associated with xenophobic policy support - UK.

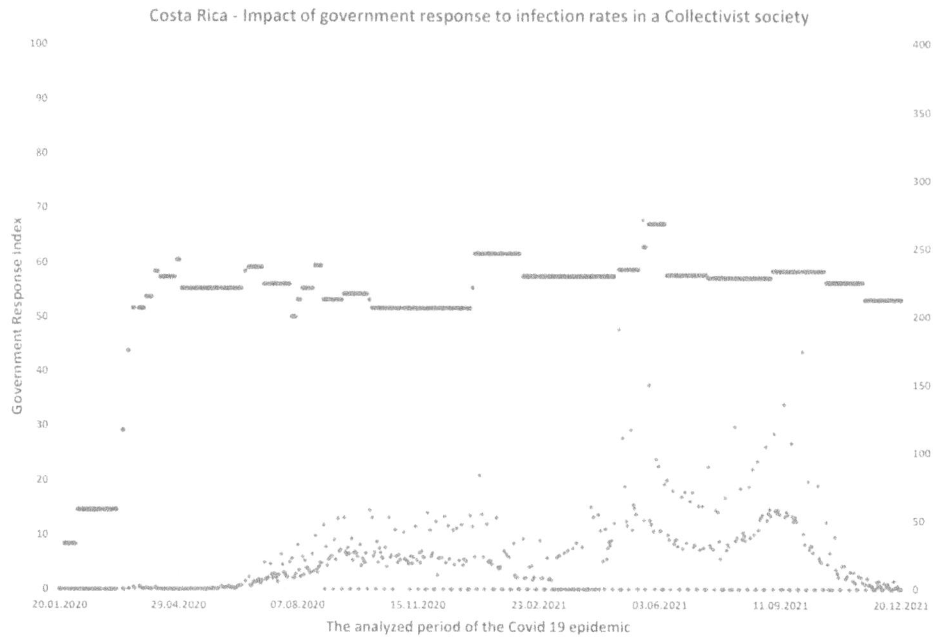

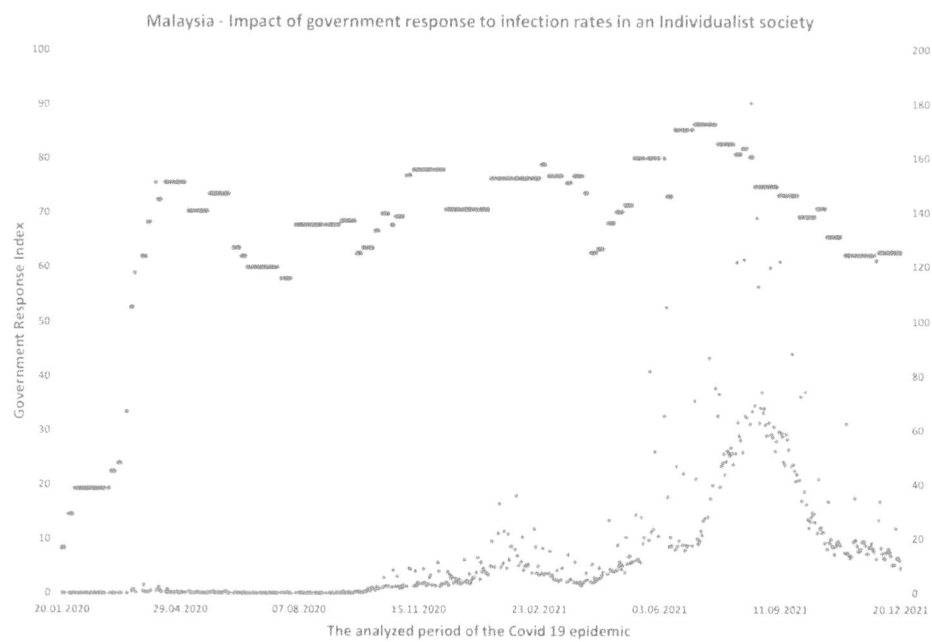

Figure 3. New Daily confirmed cases of Covid-19 in correlation of introduced restrictions.

Orientation to collectivist values is not only a stronger predictor of response to collective threats, but people respond to collective threats by promoting collectivistic values. In the study of the difference in support of collectivist and individualistic values before and after the announcement of the outbreak of COVID-19, it could be observed that individuals supported stronger collectivistic values, but there were no significant changes in support for individualistic values.

REFERENCES

Journal article

Breiman, L. (2001). Random Forests. Machine Learning, 45(1), 5–32.https://doi.org/10.1023/A:1010933404324

Markus, H.R., Kitayama, S. (1991). Culture and the self: Implications for cognition, emotion, and motivation. *Psychological Review*, 98, 224–253.

Oyserman, D., Coon, H.M., Kemmelmeier, M. (2002). Rethinking individualism and collectivism: Evaluation of theoretical assumptions and meta-analyses. *Psychological Bulletin*, 128, 3–72.

Putnick, D. L., & Bornstein, M. H. (2016). Measurement invariance conventions and reporting: Thestate of the art and future directions for psychological research. *Developmental Review*, 41, 71–90. https://doi.org/10.1016/j.dr.2016.06.004 (PDF) Predicting attitudinal and behavioral responses to COVID-19 pandemic using machine learning. https://www.researchgate.net/publication/361836804_Predicting_attitudinal_and_behavioral_responses_to_COVID-19_pandemic_using_machine_learning

Sage, A. (2018). Random forest robustness, variable importance, and tree aggregation. [Doctoraldissertation, Iowa State University]. Iowa State University Digital Repository.https://doi.org/10.31274/etd-180810-6083 (PDF) Predicting attitudinal and behavioral responses to COVID-19 pandemic using machine learning. https://www.researchgate.net/publication/361836804_Predicting_attitudinal_and_behavioral_responses_to_COVID-19_pandemic_using_machine_learning

Shah, A., et al. (2020). COVID-19 outbreak in Malaysia: Actions taken by the Malaysian government, *International Journal of Infectious Diseases*, 97, 108–116. https://doi.org/10.1016/j.ijid.2020.05.093

Triandis, H.C. (1989). The Self and Social Behavior in Differing Cultural Contexts. *Psychological Review*, 96, 506–520. https://doi.org/10.1037/0033-295X.96.3.506

Zettler, I., Lilleholt, L., Böhm, R., & Gondan, M. (2021). Comparing responses in repeated crosssectional and panel studies: Results across eight weeks during the first COVID-19 lockdown in Denmark. *Psychological Assessment*, 33(8), 691–704. https://doi.org/10.1037/pas0001048

Book

Hofstede, G. (1997). *Cultures and Organizations*, Software of the Mind, McGraw-Hill, New York.

Chapter in an edited book

Reykowski, J. (1990). Ukryte założenia normatywne jako osiowy składnik mentalności. In W. J. Reykowski & K. Skarżyńska & M. Ziółkowski (Eds.) *Orientacje społeczne jako element mentalności* (pp. 11–53). Poznań: WN.

Schwartz, S.H. (1994). Beyond individualism/collectivism: New cultural dimensions of values. In U. Kim, H.C. Triandis, C. Kagitcibasi, S. Choi, G. Yoon (Eds.), *Individualism and collectivism: Theory, method and applications* (s. 85–123). Thousand Oaks, CA: Sage.

Internet Documents & Resources

Alfaro, J. (2020). *Gobierno valora impuesto solidario a salarios superiores de ¢1,1 millón, anuncia Alvarado.* ameliarueda.com (in Spanish). https://ameliarueda.com/nota/gobierno-valora-impuesto-solidario-a-salarios-superiores-de-1-millon

Barquero, K. (2020). *Salud estudia primer caso sospechoso por coronavirus en Costa Rica.* larepublica.net (in Spanish). https://www.larepublica.net/noticia/salud-estudia-primer-caso-sospechoso-por-coronavirus-en-costa-rica

Barquero, K. (2020). *Nine cantons with confirmed cases of coronavirus.* La República. https://www.larepublica.net/noticia/nueve-cantones-con-casos-confirmados-de-coronavirus

Barquero, K. (2020). *Confirmed: UCR orders teachers to teach virtual classes*. La República. 11 March 2020. https://www.larepublica.net/noticia/ucr-pide-a-docentes-impartir-clases-virtuales
Barquero, K. (2020). *Actualización: 158 casos confirmados de coronavirus en Costa Rica, se cierran playas y templos*. larepublica.net (in Spanish). https://www.larepublica.net/noticia/actualizacion-158-casos-confirmados-de-coronavirus-en-costa-rica
Canales, D. (2020). *Estos son los 19 cantones con casos positivos de coronavirus*. El Mundo CR (in Spanish). https://elmundo.cr/municipales/estos-son-los-19-cantones-con-casos-positivos-de-coronavirus/
Castro, J. (2020). *Confirmed: Ministry of Education lists 317 educational centers that suspend lessons*. La República. 13 March 2020. https://www.larepublica.net/noticia/ministerio-de-educacion-suspende-lecciones-en-317-centros-educativos
Country Comparaison Tool, (2023). National Culture. www.hofstede-insights.com/country-comparison/
DG of Health. (2020). *Kenyataan Akhbar KPK 30 Mac 2020 – Situasi Semasa Jangkitan Penyakit Coronavirus 2019 (Covid-19) di Malaysia*. From the Desk of the Director-General of Health Malaysia (in Malay). https://kpkesihatan.com/2020/03/30/kenyataan-akhbar-kpk-30-mac-2020-situasi-semasa-jangkitan-penyakit-coronavirus-2019-covid-19-di-malaysia/
Elmundo. (2020). *35 cases of coronavirus are confirmed in Costa Rica*. elmundo.cr. https://elmundo.cr/costa-rica/se-confirman-35-casos-de-coronavirus-en-costa-rica/
Elmundo, (2020). *Se confirman 41 casos de coronavirus en Costa Rica*. El Mundo CR (in Spanish). https://elmundo.cr/costa-rica/se-confirman-41-casos-de-coronavirus-en-costa-rica/
Elmundo, (2020).*Confirmed: Ministry of Education lists 317 educational centers that suspend lessons*. La República. https://elmundo.cr/costa-rica/ministerio-de-salud-anuncia-cierre-de-todos-los-bares-discotecas-y-casinos/
lFandersTrade. (2022). *CORONAVIRUS – The situation in Malaysia*. https://www.flandersinvestmentandtrade.com/export/nieuws/coronavirus-%E2%80%93-situation-malaysia
GardaWorld. (2020). *Malaysia: First cases of 2019-nCoV confirmed January 25*. https://crisis24.garda.com/alerts/2020/01/malaysia-first-cases-of-2019-ncov-confirmed-january-25
González, M. (2020). *Segundo caso sospechoso de coronavirus está grave en hospital público*. https://www.larepublica.net/noticia/segundo-caso-sospechoso-de-coronavirus-esta-grave-en-hospital-publico
Herrera, J.J. (2020). *MEP entregará paquetes de comida ante cierre de comedores estudiantiles*. teletica.com. https://www.teletica.com/coronavirus/mep-entregara-paquetes-de-comida-ante-cierre-de-comedores-estudiantiles_252065
Latiff, R. (2020). *Malaysia defends easing of coronavirus curbs as new infections jump*, https://www.reuters.com/article/us-health-coronavirus-malaysia/malaysia-defends-easing-of-coronavirus-curbs-as-new-infections-jump-idUSKBN22E09R
Ministro de Salud. (2020). *Estamos empezando a subir la curva. Costa Rica Noticias* (in Spanish). https://costaricamedios.cr/2020/03/30/ministro-de-salud-estamos-empezando-a-subir-la-curva/
Ministerio de Salud de Costa Rica. (2020). *Because of Covid-19 cases CNE and Ministry of Health raise the sanitary alert level to yellow*. Ministerio de Salud de Costa Rica. 8 March 2020. ministeriodesalud.go.cr.
Nadirah H. Rodzi. (2021). *Malaysia to reimpose MCO in some states: What do the Covid-19 restrictions entail*. https://www.straitstimes.com/asia/se-asia/malaysia-to-impose-mco-in-some-states-what-do-the-covid-19-restrictions-entail
Nassar, S.P. (2020). *Salud reporta 295 casos de Covid-19, aumentan pacientes hospitalizados*. Teletica.com (in Spanish). https://www.teletica.com/coronavirus/salud-reporta-295-casos-de-covid-19-aumentan-pacientes-hospitalizados_253709
NewScientist. (2023). The WHO Still isn't Describing Covid-19 as a Pandemic. https://www.newscientist.com/article/2235095-the-who-still-isnt-describing-covid-19-as-a-pandemic/#ixzz6F2fq8ncn
Ng, K. (2020). *Coronavirus: Malaysia cases rise by 190 after mosque event as imams urge online services*. The Independent. https://www.independent.co.uk/news/world/asia/coronavirus-malaysia-cases-southeast-asia-mosque-islam-a9403816.html
Presidencia de la República de Costa Rica, (2020). *CCSS refuerza red de servicios para atención COVID-19 con nuevo centro*. https://www.presidencia.go.cr/comunicados/2020/03/ccss-refuerza-red-de-servicios-para-atencion-covid-19-con-nuevo-centro/
Prime Minister. (2020). *The Prime Minister's Special Message on COVID-19 – 16 March 2020*, https://web.archive.org/web/20210811085344/https://www.pmo.gov.my/2020/03/perutusan-khas-yab-perdana-menteri-mengenai-covid-19-16-mac-2020/
Reuters. (2020). *Costa Rica reporta primer caso de coronavirus en Centroamérica en una turista estadounidense*. AméricaEconomía. https://www.americaeconomia.com/politica-sociedad/mundo/costa-rica-reporta-primer-caso-de-coronavirus-en-centroamerica-en-una

Rodriquez, A.A. & Cerdas, D. (2020). *Día 19 de emergencia por nuevo coronavirus en Costa Rica: Gobierno suspende aumento salarial; 177 casos confirmados.* La Nación, Grupo Nación (in Spanish). https://www.nacion.com/el-pais/salud/dia-19-de-emergencia-por-nuevo-coronavirus-17/OFRDSOFRRBCMXO3YZLBMPH4EDE/story/

Sipalan, J.; Holmes, S. (2023). *Malaysia confirms first cases of coronavirus infection.* Reuters. www.reuters.com/article/china-health-malaysia/malaysia-confirms-first-cases-of-coronavirus-infection-idUSL4N29U03A

The Tico Times. (2020). *Costa Rica up to 26 confirmed coronavirus cases: Updates from Friday.* Tico Times. 13 March 2020 – via ticotimes.net. https://ticotimes.net/2020/03/13/costa-rica-up-to-26-confirmed-coronavirus-cases-updates-from-friday

The Tico Times. (2020). *Central America agrees to regional plan vs. coronavirus; Costa Rican film festival suspended.* The Tico Times. https://ticotimes.net/2020/03/13/central-america-agrees-to-regional-plan-vs-coronavirus-costa-rican-film-festival-suspended

World Health Organization. (2023). *WHO Director-General's Opening Remarks at the Media Briefing on COVID-19–11 March 2020* https://www.who.int/dg/speeches/detail/who-director-general-s-opening-remarks-at-the-media-briefing-on-covid-19—11-march-2020

Quesada, J. (2020). *Confirman primera muerte por COVID-19 en Costa Rica.* Crhoy.com. CRHoy.com. Periodico Digital. Costa Rica Noticias 24/7 (in Spanish). https://www.crhoy.com/nacionales/confirman-primera-muerte-por-covid-19-en-costa-rica/

Quesada, J. (2020). *Multa por incumplir cuarentena sería de más de ¢ 2 millones.* CRHoy.com. https://www.crhoy.com/nacionales/multa-por-incumplir-cuarentena-seria-de-mas-de-2-millones/

Zúñiga, A. (2020). *Costa Rica confirms four new coronavirus cases.* Tico Times. https://ticotimes.net/2020/03/07/costa-rica-confirms-four-new-coronavirus-cases

Zúñiga, A. (2020). *Costa Rica announces new measures to slow spread of coronavirus*". Tico Times. 12 March 2020. https://ticotimes.net/2020/03/12/costa-rica-announces-new-measures-to-slow-spread-of-coronavirus

Digital Synergy – El Emary et al. (eds)

Chapter 27
On a predictive model of the box office revenue

Jose Daniel Lopez – Barrientos & Gerardo Ortiz-Arellando
Universidad Anahuac Mexico, Mexico

Manuel Alejandro Jimenez Lizarraga & Viacheslav Kalashnikov
Universidad Autónoma de Nuevo León, Ciudad Universitaria SanNicolás de los Garza, Mexico

Contents

The purpose of this project is to develop a model to predict the box office performance of a theatrical movie. Since it is very risky to invest in this area of entertainment, this tool can help determine how much to invest to make a profit. Also, due to the pandemic we experienced in 2019-2022, the means of distribution are expected to change, so our model determines the best direction of distribution. We develop a model that predicts first weekend revenues using a ranking model called "hard voting". Our main tools are decision trees, Light Gradient-Boosting Machine (LightGBM), and *k*-nearest neighbors classification algorithms. Our model yields a balanced accuracy of 84.62%.

1 INTRODUCTION

The multimedia entertainment business is one of the largest in the world today, and cinema is one of its major contributors. Even with the size of the industry, investing in the production of motion pictures is very risky, this is due to the fact that the financial success of a film is very uncertain. Indeed, only between 30 and 40 percent of the films manage to recover their investment, and only one in ten makes a profit (see: Ghiassi et al., 2015).

For these reasons, being able to predict box office performance has been a challenge, especially because of the uncertainty of the audiences' behavior; and also by virtue of the fact that the biggest movies nowadays are part of existing franchises. An example of the latter is that, in 2021, the four highest-grossing films (in the United States of America and Canada) belong to the Marvel franchise, while the highest-ranked movie not belonging to an established franchise obtained only the eleventh place in the classification (see Table 1).

DOI: 10.1201/9781003440406-27

Table 1. Domestic Box Office (2021). Data obtained from The Numbers as of March 3, 2022.

Position	Title	Franchise	Box Office	Market share
1	Spider-Man: No Way Home	Marvel	$781,623,905	24.4%
2	Shang-Chi and the Legend...	Marvel	$224,543,292	7.0%
3	Venom: Let There be Carnage	Marvel	$213,550,366	6.7%
4	Black Widow	Marvel	$183,651,655	5.7%
5	F9: The Fast Saga	F&F	$173,005,945	5.4%
6	Eternals	Marvel	$164,870,264	5.2%
7	No Time to Die	James Bond	$160,891,007	5.0%
8	A Quiet Place: Part II	A Quiet Place	$160,215,764	5.0%
9	Sing 2	Sing	$151,904,445	4.7%
10	Ghostbusters: Afterlife	Ghostbusters	$128,885,266	4.0%
11	Free Guy	Original	$121,626,598	3.8%
	TOTAL		$2,464,768,507	77.0%

The cinematic industry was directly affected by the COVID-19 crisis, forcing studios to change the original release dates of their films or change the means of distribution. On the other hand, this exponentially boosted the growth of streaming platforms, which could be considered a direct competitor to movie theaters. This caused distribution strategies to change from day to day, shortening the theatrical exclusivity window of several films or even cancelling their theatrical distribution altogether. An example of these new means of distribution was "Warner Brothers", which decided to release all its films in theaters at the same time as on its streaming platform "HBO max" in 2021.

2 THEORETICAL FRAMEWORK AND METHODOLOGY

We carried out the practical part of the project in three main parts. First, we harvested our information from **The Numbers, The Internet Movie Database** and **Rotten Tomatoes** websites. We focused on the financial information of the films (such as recollection and box office of the first weekend), as well as their genre, distributor, and source. Once the database has been collected, we carried out an analysis of the data. According to this analysis, we added some variables that were not necessarily collected at the beginning but were implicit in the data. An example of this is the season premiere. This variable is important since, as can be seen in Figure 1, there is an increase in the recollection variable during the summer (from week 18) and also a drop in the fall (week 36).

On a predictive model of the box office revenue

We also adjusted all the monetary data for inflation. These include the recollection of the first weekend, total recollection, and the budget. To this end, we used the average price of a movie ticket each year from 1999 to August 15, 2022, published by the Motion Picture Association (MPAA) in its annual report and shown in Table 2. Because the annual report is published in March of the following year, there is no average for 2022, so the same price is assumed as in 2021.

Finally, we proceeded to implement the model to obtain the prediction of the film's performance at the box office during the first weekend. We also attempted to match the performance in the remainder of the season of its projection, but unfortunately, the results we obtained were not as accurate as those for the opening weekend. However, it is widely known that the largest amount of money raised in a movie happens during its first weekend. Moreover, since it is then that the film receives reactions from both critics and the general public, it is very difficult to forecast the performance of a film beforehand.

The "opening weekend" phenomenon has been studied and described with an exponentially decreasing pattern, in which product revenue peak immediately after launch and then decline at a constant rate over time (so that the decline becomes less pronounced as time goes by). This is a characteristic feature of most entertainment products. In the case of cinema, this is

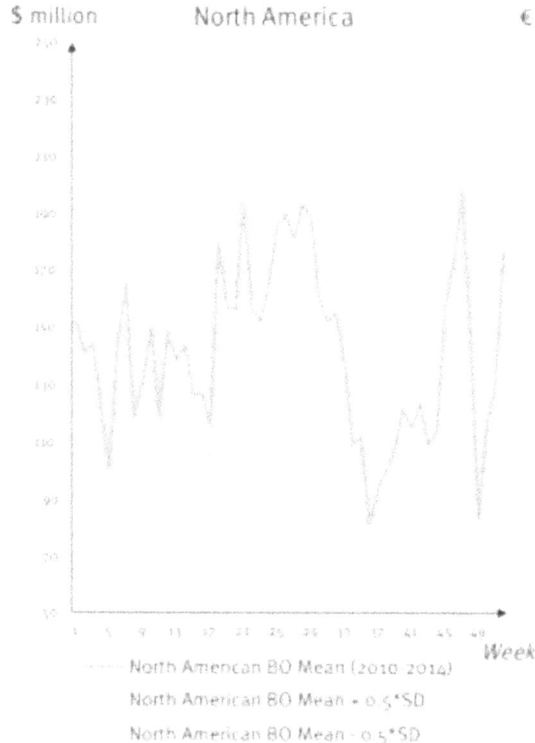

Figure 1. Seasonal revenue from movies at the box office (see: Hennig-Thurau and Houston. 2018).

Table 2. Average price of a ticket at the box office. Data obtained from **The Numbers**.com and **Statista** and provided by the MPAA as of September 14 of 2022.

Year	Average Price	Year	Average Price
2021	$9.57	2009	$7.50
2020	$9.37	2008	$7.18
2019	$9.16	2007	$6.88
2018	$9.11	2006	$7.55
2017	$8.97	2005	$6.41
2016	$8.65	2004	$6.21
2015	$8.43	2003	$6.03
2014	$8.17	2002	$5.81
2013	$8.13	2001	$5.66
2012	$7.96	2000	$5.39
2011	$7.93	1999	$5.08
2010	$7.89		
	TOTAL	$2,464,768,507	77.0%

measured with the first weekend of release because, most commonly, a film is released on Friday and, as can be seen in Figure 2, it is the weekend (Friday, Saturday and Sunday) of the highest recollections at the box office (see: Hennig-Thurau and Houston. 2018).

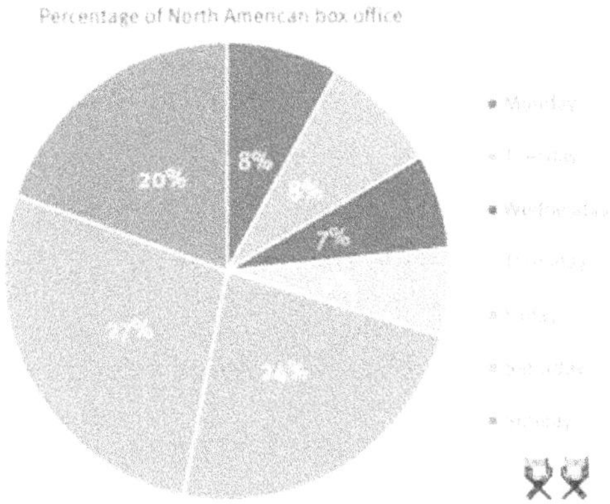

Figure 2. Average box office receipts by day of the week (see: Hennig-Thurau and Houston. 2018).

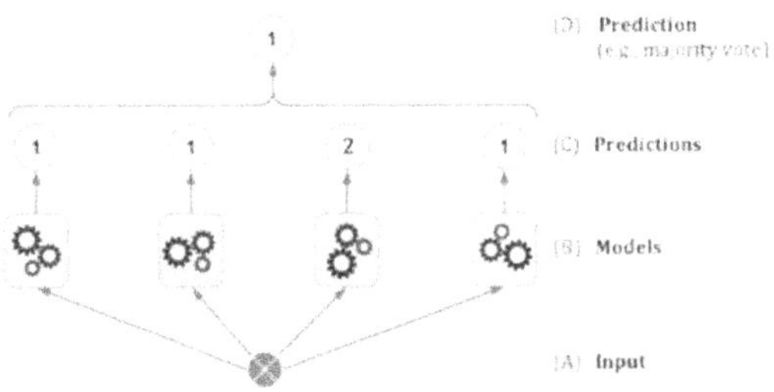

Figure 3. Hard voting classification tree (see: Phelps 2020).

3 HARD VOTING

In this model, we used the "hard voting" assembly. This is an assembly method for multiclass predictive models where the outcome is the option with the highest number of votes. Figure 3 shows the model. Level (A) represents the tickets for a specific instance of a movie: budget, genre, etc. Level (B) represents a subset of optimized models. Level (C) represents the prediction given the input from each of those models. These predictions are added to find the mode. Level (D) is the final level, exemplifying the majority vote of the selected classifiers (see: Phelps 2020).

On a predictive model of the box office revenue.

For the assembly, three multiple classification algorithms will be used: classification trees, LightGBM and *k*-nearest neighbors.

3.1 *Classification trees*

Classification tree algorithms are recursive partitioning methods that use the statistical learning technique of decision trees. *Grosso modo*, the algorithm consists of first quantifying the optimization criterion for the data partition for each variable, and then select the best partition. The process is repeated until a Split that belongs to the same value as the target variable is reached (see: Zelterman 2015). Algorithm 1, which we borrowed from Software testing help, delves into the details of these ideas.

Algorithm 1: Classification tree

Data: Data partition D, *attributes_list*, *attributes_selection_method* (i.e. *split_attribute*, and *split_point* or *split_subset*)

Result: Decision tree

Create a node N;
if all tuples in D are of class C then
return N as a leaf node labeled as class C
end
if *list_of _attributes* = ∅ then
return N as leaf node with majoritary class D⊲ majoritary voting
end
Apply *attributes_selection_method to D* and *attributes_list* to find the best split criteria;
Label node N with split criterion;
if *split_attribute* is of discrete-type and Multidirectional splits are allowed ▷ Non-binary trees are allowed
then
attributes_list ←*attributes_list\split_attribute* ▷ Eliminate *split_attribute*
end
for $j \in$ *split_attribute* do
$D_j \leftarrow$ subset of D that meets j;
if $D_j = \varnothing$ then
Attach labeled leaf with majoritary class in D to node N
else
Attach decision tree for D_j, *attributes_list* to node N
end
end
return N;

3.2 *Light gradient boosting machine*

The main advantage of LightGBM is the speed at which it is trained, which is where the "light" prefix comes from. It differs from other tree-based algorithms in that it grows its tree vertically, while other algorithms grow trees horizontally (see: Phelps 2020). Algorithm 2 presents the details (see: Dunbray et al., 2021).

On a predictive model of the box office revenue

Algorithm 2: Classification tree

Data: Training data set $D = \{(x_{1,1}), \ldots, (x_N, y_N)\} \subset \mathbb{R} \times \{-1, 1\}$, loss function $L(y, \theta(x))$, M, a–Number of sampled data of large gradient, b–Number of sampled data of small gradient.

Result: Minimal loss function θ_M

Combine mutually exclusive features of $x_1, \ldots, x_N$ by means of the exclusive features bundling technique;
$\theta_0(x) \leftarrow \arg\min_c \Sigma_i^N L(y_i, c)$
form = 1 to M do
$r_i \leftarrow \left| \frac{\partial L(y_i, \theta(x_i))}{\partial \theta(x_i)} \right|_{\theta(x) = \theta_m - 1(x)}$ for $i = 1, \ldots, N$;
Re-sample dataset with the gradient-based one-side sampling method:;
topN ←$a|D|$;
randN ←$b|D|$;
▷ | · | stands for the size of the set ·
sort indices in r;
$A \leftarrow$ sort indices from 1 to N;
$B \leftarrow$ random index from the sorted set *topN*, …, $|D|$;
$D' \leftarrow A + B$;
$V_j(\mathrm{d}) \leftarrow \frac{1}{n} \left(\sum_{x_i \in A_\ell} r_i + \frac{1-a}{b} \sum_{x_i \in AB_\ell} r_i \right)^2 \left(\frac{1}{n_\ell^j(d)} + \frac{1}{n_r^j(d)} \right)$;

▷ V represents an information gain
Build a new decision tree $\theta'_m(x)$ over the set D';
$\theta m(x) \leftarrow \theta_m - 1\ (x) + \theta_m(x)$;
end
return $\theta'(x) \leftarrow \theta_M(x)$;

3.3 *k-nearest neighbors*

The k-nearest neighbors' algorithm is a nonparametric supervised learning classifier that uses proximity to make classifications or predictions about the clustering of an individual data point. It is normally used as a classification algorithm, assuming that similar points can be found close to each other. In classification problems, the class label is assigned on the basis of a majority vote, that is, the label that occurs most frequently around a given data point is used (see: Dasarathy. 1991). Algorithm 3 presents the details.

Algorithm 3: k-nearest neighbors
Data: D–Matrix of distances of dimension $n \times n$ and s–index of point of departure
Result: route list of vertices with the path of minimal length
for $i = 1$ to n do
visited $(i) \leftarrow 0$
end
Initialize the route list with s;
visited $(s) \leftarrow 1$;
current $\leftarrow s$;
for $i = 2$ to n do
Find smallest index
end
return $\theta'(x) \leftarrow \theta M(x)$;

4 WORK DEVELOPMENT

4.1 *Database acquisition*

For data collection, we consulted the platform **The Numbers** platform, where the data of the 100 films with the highest domestic grossing for each year from 1999 to July 2022 were captured.

This database was used as a first approach and as a basic dataset for obtaining additional data for each film. These attributes were obtained through a program written in Python using the "selenium" library. This method was used on **Rotten Tomatoes** and **the Internet Movie Data Base**.

Next, we show the attributes obtained in the three consulted platforms:

- Name: The title of the film, this was not used in the models.
- Release date: Data in date format that indicates the first day the film was available to the public, from which the season variable emerges.
- Year of release: Year in which the film was released, used for inflation adjustment in monetary variables.
- Distributor: It oversees promoting and distributing the films, it can be the same production company.
- Genre: A way of categorizing films and a variable commonly used to predict the performance of a film. Within this are genres such as adventure, musical, action, drama, comedy, etc.
- Source: Material on which the film is based, be it a book, historical, or original idea.
- Production method: Indicates whether the film is animated or not.

- Creative Type: Another way of categorizing movies based more on the universe where the movie takes place as fantasy, science fiction, etc.
- Budget: All expenses used to produce the film.
- Cinemas on the first weekend: Number of establishments where the film was shown on the first weekend of release.
- Maximum number of cinemas: Maximum number of establishments where the film was shown on a certain date.
- First weekend income: Box office receipts for the film the first weekend it was shown in the United States and Canada.
- Domestic income: Box office receipts of the film in the United States and Canada.
- IMDB Rating: Rating from 1 to 10 given by the users of the **the Internet Move Data Base**.
- Metascore: Rating from 1 to 100 given by a weighted average of the rating given by critics published on **Metacritic.**
- MPAA: Movie rating system in the United States published by the MPAA, these can be G, PG, PG-13, R and NC-17.
- Duration: Time that the film lasts in hours and minutes.
- Tomatometer: Aggregate rating of a movie given by certified critics on the **Rotten Tomatoes** page, it takes values from 0 to 100.
- Audience Score: Aggregate rating of a movie given by the user of the Rotter Tomatoes page; this takes values from 0 to 100.

4.2 *Database settings*

Adjustments are made to the same database by first removing films with incomplete data such as budget or number of theaters in which they are shown. In addition to adding variables obtained through an analysis of the database and adjusting the monetary data for inflation.

Binary variables refer to categorical variables, where a 1 is identified if this movie belongs to the indicated category.

The variables indicated as *average* are obtained with the data from the same base obtained.

The variables that will be handled in the initial classification model with the recollection response variable on the first weekend are shown below:

- Post-COVID (binary): Identify if the film was released after March 31, 2021.
- During COVID (binary): Identify if the film was released between March 13, 2020, and March 31, 2021.
- Release season: Identifies in which season the film was released, this can be winter (January and February), spring (March and April), summer (from May to the end of August), autumn (from September to the 17th weekend before Thanksgiving) and Holidays (from Thanksgiving to New Years).
- Distributor Average (numerical): Average recollection of films distributed by the distribution company.
- Genre: Indicates the genre belonging to the film, this can be action, adventure, black comedy, comedy, documentary, drama, horror, musical, romantic comedy, thriller/suspense and "western".
- Source: Indicates the origin of the film's story, this can be comic strip/graphic novel, fact book/article, folk tale/legend/fairy tale, video game, play, events from real life, television, original script, "remake" and "spin-off".
- Production method: Indicates whether the film is animated, "live action" or a combination of both.
- Creative type: Categorizes the films more focused on its environment. They can be contemporary fiction, dramatization, factual events, historical fiction, children's fiction, science fiction, and superheroes.
- MPAA: Identifies the classification of films given by the "Motion Picture American Association", these include G, PG, PG-13, and R.

- Duration: Time that the film lasts in minutes.
- Franchise (binary variable): Identifies whether the film belongs to a franchise or not.
- Franchise average (numerical): Average of the recollection of the films within this franchise, in case of not belonging to a franchise it takes the value of 0.
- Average director (numerical): Average revenue from films directed by the same director.
- Average Actor 1 (numerical): Average of the recollection of the films where the main actor appears.
- Average Actor 2 (numerical): Average of the recollection of the films where the second most important actor appears.
- Competition (numerical): How many films had their release date 14 days or less from the film's release date.
- Budget (numerical): How much money it cost to make the film adjusted for inflation.
- Cinemas first weekend (numerical): Number of cinemas where the film was shown on its first weekend of release.
- Limited release (binary): Identifies if the film opened its first weekend in less than 1000 theaters.

For the regression model, where the response variable is domestic revenue, all the variables used in the previous model and the following are used:

- Maximum number of theaters (numerical): Maximum number of theaters where the film was shown in a weekend.
- Income first weekend (numerical): Recollection adjusted for inflation during its first weekend.
- IMDB Rating (numeric): Rating from 0 to 10 of a movie by IMDB users.
- Metascore (numeric): Rating from 0 to 100 of a film by certified critics.
- Tomatometer (numeric): Rating of a movie from 0 to 100 by certified critics on Rotten Tomatoes.
- Audience Score (numeric): Rating from 0 to 100 of a film by users of Rotten Tomatoes

These variables are not the final ones because some may be eliminated due to a high correlation between them.

5 RESULTS

Table 3 shows a normalized confusion matrix for the model. The confusion matrix, also known as error matrix, is a table that allows visualizing the performance of a classifier. It shows the ways in which the classifier gets confused when making predictions. The columns of this confusion matrix represent the predicted classes, while the rows represent the actual classes. The intersection point of these cells represents the correct classification of the data. A perfect classifier has 1.0 in each row that matches the true label and the predicted label.

Table 4 shows the performance of each methodology used in the first model including the Hard-Voting assembly showing the balanced precision of each one. Balanced precision prevents inflated performance estimates on unbalanced data sets. It is defined as a metric that measures what fraction of the class in question has been correctly predicted. It is calculated as the sum of true positives divided by the sum of true positives and false negatives of a class. Algebraically, the mean sensitivity can be formulated as$(\frac{1}{M})\sum_{n_m}^{M}\frac{r_m}{n_m}$ where M is the number of classes, nm is the size of the 21 data in class$m$, r_m is the number of accurately predicted data items that belong to class$m$ (see: Luque et al., 2019).

Figure 4 shows us which variables are more important in model 1, with the highest being the distributor's average followed by the number of movie theaters on its first weekend. It can be observed that the variables with more weight are the numerical ones, while the categorical ones are losing importance. Due to the number of variables (52) the graph only shows the first 30 variables.

Table 3. Confusion matrix.

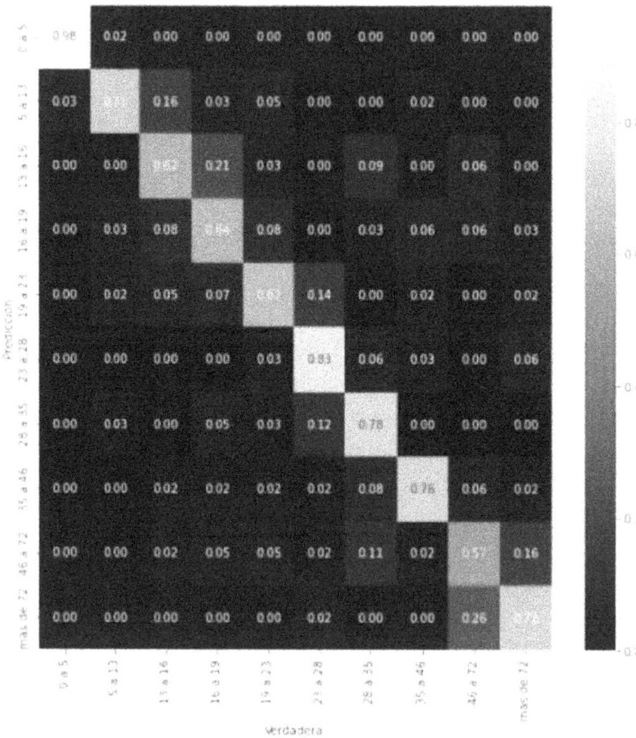

Table 4. Performance of the model.

Classifier	Balanced Precision
k - Nearest Neighbors (k = 45)	59.56%
Decision tree	62.92%
LightGBM	82.99%
Hard-Voting	84.62%

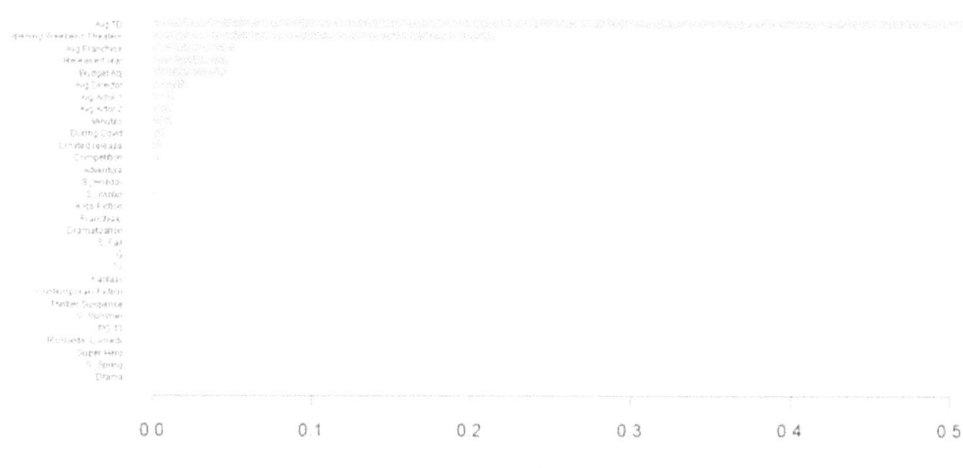

Figure 4. Importance of variables.

6 CONCLUSIONS

Movie production requires a great deal of time and money. Most of these films generate income that is less than what it costs to produce them. This especially affects 24 small distributors and producers where today's competitive film market due to the production of franchised films and competition with streaming platforms in the world has made it more difficult for them to recover the investment. The models ended up giving satisfactory results while there is still room for improvement. In the first model, improvement can be sought by testing different methodologies in the assembly to increase its precision.In the same way, the model could improve if there were a more extensive database, on the one hand, with the number of observations to improve the precision of films with poor performance, as well as variables more focused on distribution and advertising methods.

REFERENCES

Belur V. Dasarathy. 1991. Nearest Neighbor (NN) Norms: NN Pattern Classification Techniques. IEEE Computer Society Press.

Nachiket Dunbray, Rashmi Rane, Sparsh Nimje, Jayesh Katade, and Shreyas Mavale. 2021. A Novel Prediction Model for Diabetes Detection Using Gridsearch and A Voting Classifier between Lightgbm and KNN. 1–7. https://doi.org/10.1109/GCAT52182.2021.9587551

M. Ghiassi, David Lio, and Brian Moon. 2015. Pre-production forecasting of movie revenues with a dynamic artificial neural network. Expert Systems with Applications 42, 6 (2015), 3176–3193. https://doi.org/10.1016/j.eswa.2014.11.022

Thorsten Hennig-Thurau and Mark Houston. 2018. Entertainment Science: Data Analytics and Practical Theory for Movies, Games, Books, and Music. https://doi.org/10.1007/978-3-319-89292-4

Amalia Luque, Alejandro Carrasco, Alejandro Martín, and Ana de las Heras. 2019. The impact of class imbalance in classification performance metrics based on the binary confusion matrix. Pattern Recognition 91 (2019), 216–231. https://doi.org/10.1016/j.patcog.2019.02.023

Brian Phelps. 2020. Predicting Motion Picture Box-Office Performance. Southern Connecticut State University, CT.

Daniel Zelterman. 2015. Applied Multivariate Statistics with R. Springer Cham. https://doi.org/10.1007/978-3-319-14093-3

SECTION 4
The Future of Logistics (Military Logistics)

Digital Synergy – El Emary et al. (eds)

Chapter 28
The contemporary trends in military logistics

Tomasz Jałowiec
War Studies University, Warsaw, Poland

Contents

Continuous improvement of the effectiveness of military logistic processes is a prerequisite for the fulfilment of tasks set for the armed forces in all states of state functioning, i.e. peace, crisis and war. The aim of the article is to indicate the directions of development of military logistics in view of the dynamically changing conditions of the realisation of military logistics security processes. The research problem to be solved was formulated in the form of the question: what and to what extent exerts the greatest influence on the development of military logistics today? A number of research methods were used in the material, among which analysis and synthesis, abstraction, generalisation and methods of inference proved to be the leading ones. In addition, the content of the work was supplemented by the results of empirical research, carried out using the diagnostic survey method with the survey technique. The research results obtained can form the basis for improving the military logistics system in terms of improving the effectiveness of tasks carried out in the framework of support and logistic security of troops. The article contains unique research results, the application value of which has been confirmed in the framework of modernisation activities implemented in armed forces concerning military logistic potential and procedures of logistic cooperation in the military-civilian formula.

1 INTRODUCTION

The dynamic development of military logistics is inextricably linked to the history of armed conflicts, during which the satisfaction of the logistical needs of the fighting soldiers has repeatedly determined the success or failure of a military operation. Over the centuries, solutions have been sought in the military sphere to optimise the use of available logistical potential in a maximally effective manner. The need for an interdisciplinary approach to solving problems related to the management of military and acquired logistical resources has directly translated into the development of military logistics theory and practice both in the past and today. It has resulted in the cyclical emergence of a variety of approaches, concepts, methods and techniques for managing the limited logistical potential that determines the realisation of a wide range of tasks facing the armed forces. Nowadays, the situation is similar, as the military community is constantly looking for ways to improve the relationship between the effects obtained and the outlays incurred in the area of support and logistic security of troops.

DOI: 10.1201/9781003440406-28

In view of the problem situation outlined above, the aim of the article is to indicate the directions of development of military logistics in the face of the dynamically changing conditions of the realisation of the processes of logistic security of the army, trying to seek an answer to the question of what and to what extent exerts the greatest influence on the development of military logistics today?, which in the work took the form of a scientific problem.

2 AN OVERVIEW OF THE LITERATURE

The scope of cognition of military logistics is extremely broad and multifaceted and encompasses the subject of cognition of many disciplines and fields of study. Contemporary trends in military logistics largely boil down to improving interoperability internationally through the use of the latest information and communication technologies. Interoperability is primarily intended to increase the flexibility, sensitivity, as well as the effectiveness of the response to the external environment and, consequently, to increase the potential of the national military logistics system (Kaźmierczak, 2019, p. 57). In the current political and military realities, this is extremely important, as one of the key tasks of the entities forming the military logistics system is to plan and coordinate interaction with allied troops during exercises at home and abroad, as well as during missions.

When considering in detail the basic assumptions, relationships and scope of modern military logistics, it can be seen in the literature that a number of experts unequivocally indicate that it is essential for its further development to develop complex predictive capabilities and to build network capabilities. In this process, military logistics is already giving primacy to the digital sphere. Research in the field of military logistics is moving from planning and optimisation to interdisciplinary studies that combine operations research, analytics, innovation management and new forms of organisation inspired by networks, platforms and ecosystems (van Fenema, van Kampen, 2021, p. 21). In this context, it is also important to refer to technological and digital innovations and the modernisation of supply chains in line with the idea of technology 4.0, the effects of which allow for continuous efficiency improvements in the flow of goods and related services (Minculete, 2021, p. 46). In addition, national and international research seeks to minimise any disruption to the functionality and integrity of military logistics chains treated as threats of strategic importance to the performance of tasks by the armed forces in all states of state operation(Foltin, Repík, Lipowský, Mazal, 2022, pp. 3-8). Another key area in the development of military logistics, which is taken up repeatedly in the literature, is the legislation and procedures for the management of military logistical support and security, correlated with the changes that are constantly taking place in the security environment and the armed forces systems of states, especially in Central and Eastern Europe. In published scientific works, it is also possible to observe trends towards the adaptation of business solutions aimed at optimising logistics capabilities for the needs of military logistics systems (Bury, 2021, pp. 112-136).

Military logistics was developed in two dimensions, as an art and as a science, applying, according to its nature, different historically evidenced concepts, which were useful for the support of armies. However, today, it is necessary to develop a mixed discipline that integrates the two dimensions mentioned and has the capacity to respond to the needs of the troops before they are required, applying avant-garde concepts such as focused logistics, in order for the operation of an army to be improved and its cost and benefit optimized (Serrano et al, 2023, p. 19).

3 RESEARCH METHODS

The research problem addressed required the use of a number of research methods, both theoretical and empirical. The research methods, among which analysis and synthesis, abstraction, generalisation and methods of inference led the way, made it possible to identify and assess the essence of the phenomenon under study. On their basis, the most important trends in military logistics were identified, resulting from the dynamic changes taking place in the armed forces and in their closer and further environment. Furthermore, at this stage of the research process, the trends presented in numerous literature on the development of logistics in the civilian sector were confronted with the possibilities of their occurrence in the military environment. In order to confront the research material collected on the basis of the theoretical methods used, the method of a diagnostic survey conducted with the use of a questionnaire technique was employed. The results presented in this paper are part of an extended empirical study conducted on the development of military logistics processes. The survey, conducted between January and May 2023, included 196 respondents, among whom were representatives of all functional levels of the military logistics system. Of these, 74% were officers, while 26% served in the non-commissioned officer corps. Men made up 86% of the research sample, and all respondents had a length of military service between 17 and 32 years. It is also worth noting that 32% of the respondents had experience of serving abroad, having participated in a foreign mission at least once.

4 RESULTS OF THE RESEARCH

A review of the literature on the subject has clearly indicated that the current geopolitical and military situation is forcing elements of the military logistics system to meet challenges of a new nature or of a hitherto unprecedented scale. The growing problems associated with the unstable geopolitical and economic situation result in new solutions in addition to numerous threats. In addition, customer preferences are constantly changing, as well as the way global supply chains operate (Skowrońska, 2020, p. 197). Flexible adaptation to dynamic changes and meeting the evolving needs of the entities being secured has become a prerequisite for the proper functioning of all entities comprising military logistics systems.

The Global Military Logistics market is anticipated to rise at a considerable rate during the forecast period, between 2022 and 2031. In 2021, the market was growing at a steady rate and with the rising adoption of strategies by key players, the market is expected to rise over the projected horizon. The global Military Logistics market size was valued at USD 376169.5 million in 2021 and is expected to expand at a CAGR of 5.67Percent during the forecast period, reaching USD 523599.17 million by 2027. Logistics services is an essential element for functioning of the armed forces. Timely delivery and supply of essential materials such as ration, equipment, arms and ammunition to the military bases for their sustained operation are very vital for functioning. Effective logistics services act as pillars of the military around the globe (https://www.marketwatch.com)

As past experience shows, well-prepared functional models are indispensable in the face of various emerging threats and disruptions. Their elimination is possible, among other things, through the implementation of the latest organisational and technological solutions into the practice of military logistics systems. These include, above all (https://vervo.eu):

1. Automation of logistics processes - moving from manual to digital processes in military supply chains.
2. The use of artificial intelligence - implementing advanced technologies in, among other things, forecasting demand for particular material assets.
3. Internet of things - the use of an interconnected network of computing devices, enabling the transfer of data between elements of the military logistics system without human intervention.
4. Sustainability - the application of good organisational practices and efforts to use logistics resources rationally and responsibly to reduce the adverse environmental and social impacts of operations.
5. Advanced analytics - providing the necessary data to improve the efficiency of military logistics processes, with the aim of maximising owned and sourced resources; using external data sources to respond immediately to changes.

6. Cybersecurity - protecting IT networks, devices, programmes and data from attack, damage or unauthorised access.
7. Supply chain agility - the ability to adapt quickly to uncertainty and the ability to operate in volatile crisis situations.
8. Supply chain visibility - the collection and real-time display of the location and status of assets across the military supply chain in order to make quick and accurate decisions.
9. Supply chain resilience - the ability to avoid or mitigate risk and the ability to stabilise and recover from unforeseen events.

The key trends in the development of military logistics outlined above were verified through an empirical survey. Respondents were asked to express their opinion on which of the identified trends are of priority importance for the further development of military logistics. Each respondent was able to indicate the two areas that, in their opinion, are the most important. The results obtained are shown in Figure 1.

The research results obtained clearly indicate that a key issue in the development of military supply chains remains that of ensuring their resilience, which should be seen as the ability to respond to unexpected disruptions and restore the continuity of ongoing supply chain processes (Barroso et al, 2011) or as the ability to maintain, resume and restore operations after the impact of a disruption (Gaonkar et al, 2007).

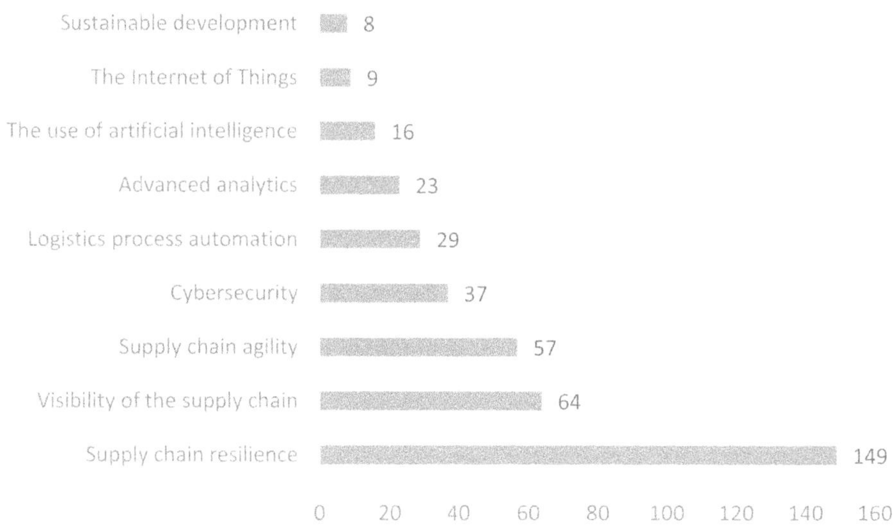

Figure 1. Respondents' views on priority trends in the development of military logistics (n=196). Source: own.

5 DISCUSSION/LIMITATION AND FUTURE RESEARCH

When comparing the obtained results of our own research with materials published in specialist scientific journals, it is necessary to point out noticeable similarities. The issue of ensuring maximum resilience of supply chains is an area of particular interest for many researchers, who agree on its priority importance in modern realities. In the literature, supply chain resilience is considered not only from the perspective of loss of capacity in general - which does not happen often, but if it does, it is in the case of spectacular natural disasters or technical failures - but from the perspective of the value delivered to the end customer. This perspective makes it possible to assess the degree of resilience of the supply chain in the context of its performance. It allows an assessment of the extent to which the occurrence of different types of situations and events affects the ability to create and deliver value (Szymczak, 2015, p. 48).

The above-mentioned areas should be the subject of future, extended research, which it seems reasonable to conduct both nationally and internationally and in collaboration between the military community and managers responsible for supply chains in the civilian sector. Defense operations can catch up with two decades of rapid advances in technology that have enabled commercial supply chains globally. These Industry 4.0 technologies, including artificial intelligence and machine learning used in predictive analytics, supply chain intelligence and more autonomous functionality, can quickly bridge gaps and increase speed in contested defense scenarios. The result can be greater cargo visibility, smarter warehousing and better transportation utilization (https://www.ey.com/en).

For an unambiguous interpretation of the research results obtained, it should be pointed out that some difficulties were encountered in the course of the research due to different interpretations of the concepts defined by the respondents. Depending on their experience and knowledge related to the functioning of military supply chains, the respondents referred their opinions to different functional levels of the military logistics system. After a detailed analysis of the responses obtained, it can be clearly stated that the adopted methodological assumptions and the determined minimum size of the research sample proved to be correct and made it possible to make generalisations and draw conclusions constituting the basis for future research, of this extremely important area from the perspective of the functioning of the armed forces.

6 CONCLUSION

Summarising the research results obtained, priority directions for improving military logistics should be identified (Mokwa, 2009, pp. 321-322):

1. Ensuring resilience and visibility should be a priority in the development of military supply chains.
2. The implementation of advanced information technologies while ensuring maximum security of data flow is a prerequisite for the proper execution of tasks by elements of the military logistics system.
3. Military logistics should be an integrative concept directed towards the search for an integrated approach to the management of organic and procured logistics resources used in the process of military logistics baking.
4. There is a trend towards extending logistical dependencies into inter-organisational relationships (e.g. multinational logistics), involving suppliers and customers in the management of product and information flows on the basis of enhanced (tending to expand) cooperation (partnership) of equal actors.
5. The increasing role of logistics management, as a process of cross-functional integration of those areas of activity to which it relates and with which it is associated.
6. The concept of logistics management should be oriented towards: flexible control of flows taking into account the time dimension, multi-level and multi-directional integration of flows, thinking in terms of process dependencies and structural links within all six subsystems (command, technical, material, transport and movement of troops, military infrastructure, medical) and two functional areas (host nation support, mobilisation of the economy and strategic reserves) of the military logistics system.

In summarising the discussion of key trends in the development of military logistics, it is worth emphasising its multidimensional and interdisciplinary nature. The dynamically growing needs and requirements of secured entities, resulting from changes occurring within the armed forces and in their environment, force the search for newer and better methods and techniques of logistics potential management. In particular, it is these changing requirements that most significantly influence the need for continuous improvement in methods of managing military supply chains, both in the micro and macro dimensions.

REFERENCES

Journal article

Borys T. (2013), *Interdyscyplinarność nauk o jakości*, „Zarządzanie i Finanse" nr R. 10, nr 3, cz. 1.

Bury P. (2021), Conceptualising the quiet revolution: the post-Fordist revolution in western military logistics, "European Security", Volume 30, 2021 - Issue 1.

Gaonkar R.S., Viswanadham N. (2007): Analytical Framework for the Management of Risk in Supply Chains. „IEEE Transactions on Automation Science and Engineering", No. 4(2).

Minculete, G., (2021). Relational Approaches to Modernizing Operational Logistics Related to Industry 4.0 and Supply Chain Management 4.0. Journal of Defense Resources Management, nr 12 (2).

Mokwa Z. (2009), *Zarządzanie logistyczne jako zorientowane na procesy logistyczne zarządzanie siecią dostaw*, „Prace Naukowe Uniwersytetu Ekonomicznego we Wrocławiu" nr 52.

Serrano I., Kalenatic D., Cesar López C., Montoya-Torres J. R. (2023), Evolution of Military Logistics, Logistics, 7, 22. https://doi.org/10.3390/logistics7020022

Szymczak M. (2015): Elastyczność, wrażliwość i odporność jako cechy adaptacyjnych łańcuchów dostaw, Studia Oeconomica Posnaniensia, vol. 3, no. 6.

Book

Skowrońska, A. (2020). Zarządzanie makrologistyką w gospodarce globalnej. Wrocław: Wydawnictwo Uniwersytetu Ekonomicznego we Wrocławiu.

Chapter in an edited book

Barroso H.P., Machado V.H., Machado V.C.: Supply Chain Resilience Using the Mapping Approach, [in:] Pengzhong Li (ed.): Supply Chain Management. InTech, 2011

van Fenema, P.C., van Kampen, T., (2021). Foundational Concepts of Military Logistics. In: Sookermany, A.M. (eds) Handbook of Military Sciences. Springer, Cham, 21.

Report by a Government Agency References

Foltin, P., Repík, D., Lipowský, P., Mazal, J., (2022). Technological Aspects of the Capability Development of the Logistics Support: NATO STO-MP-SAS-165.

WEBSITE

https://vervo.eu/pl/aktualnosci/vervo-aktualnosci/10-najwazniejszych-trendow-w-logistyce-na-2023-rok-2

https://www.ey.com/en_us/strategy/four-actions-to-modernize-military-logistics-and-supply-chain-security

https://www.marketwatch.com/press-release/latest-trends-and-strategies-for-military-logistics-market-during-2023-2031-2023-04-25

Digital Synergy – El Emary et al. (eds)

Chapter 29
Resilience of military supply chains

Dariusz Grala
War Studies University, Warsaw, Poland

Contents

The aim of this study is to present the possibilities of building resilience of military supply chains. In the current reality, the activity of troops, both during training in peacetime and during the implementation of tasks during crisis and war, requires an effective supply of the necessary equipment and materials. The situation in Ukraine shows that the supply of arms and ammunition may be disrupted not only by military but also by economic and political factors. Hence, the approach to building comprehensive supply chain resilience seems to be crucial. Based on the analysis of the literature and research results, the author attempted to answer the following research problem: Whether and to what extent approaches to building the resilience of supply chains in the business environment can be implemented in military supply chains? The obtained results can be used not only in military logistics, but also in supply chains crucial for the security of the state and its citizens.

1 INTRODUCTION

In the conditions of a dynamically changing security environment and the resulting economic consequences in the environment of every functioning organization, and thus also supply chains, there are a number of unforeseen negative phenomena that may lead to interruption of the continuity of basic processes, and thus to failure to achieve previously set goals, and in less extreme cases to achieve them to a lesser extent (Zaczyk 2016: 629). In the business environment, the consequences of such events are: lack of profit, financial losses, loss of customers, and in some cases bankruptcy of companies. In military systems, disruption of supply has serious consequences for the safety of soldiers and for their ability to perform their tasks.

Professionally trained armies equipped with modern technology require effective logistic support. The supply of equipment, materials and spare parts is necessary to maintain the required combat readiness rate, ensure a high level of training and perform a wide range of tasks in peacetime, crisis and war. Supplying troops with the necessary means delivered in the right place, time, quantity and quality, and at an acceptable price is the task of military supply chains. In the subjective dimension, military supply chains should be understood as "a set of cooperating, structural internal and external elements satisfying the logistic needs of the troops by providing them with goods necessary to carry out training, operational and combat tasks" (Jałowiec 2020: 98). Internal elements are units and institutions of the military logistics system, while external elements are enterprises and institutions (allied, coalition, etc.).

DOI: 10.1201/9781003440406-29

The analysis of the literature on the subject indicates that key approaches to achieving the security of processes taking place in the supply chain occurred at various stages of the development of the concept of supply chain management. An increasingly frequently described area in publications in recent years is the issue of supply chain security (Staniewska 2021, pp. 135-148), including the security of transport processes (Staniewska, 2021: 135-148) and management of military supply chains (Jałowiec et al 2020: 972-982), for which properly prepared logistics staff are necessary (Grala et al 2021: 62-68) and modern IT systems (Tae et al 2012: 61-76), in particular those dedicated to the armed forces (Olszak 2017: 65-67). Supply chain security is "a general property of a system consisting in the smooth functioning of the supply chain, enabling its objectives to be achieved by protecting against external targeted threats" (Ivanov et al 2010: 81). Broadly understood supply chain security does not only concern the protection of its resources, but also its environment in which threats occur (Jażdżewska-Gutta 2019: 12). An extremely desirable feature of modern supply chains is the ability to cope with changes in the environment (including sudden and unexpected ones), reducing the risk of loss of continuity and ability to act (Szymczak 2017: 109-119). Supply chains with such a feature are referred to as resilient supply chain (Świerczek 2020: 151).

In order to solve the defined research problem, after conducting a literature review and getting acquainted with the results of the research conducted so far, empirical research was carried out. Due to the nature of the studied area, a diagnostic survey using the expert interview technique was chosen as a method. The prepared interview sheets were addressed to 10 experts representing various functional levels of the military logistics system and the military scientific community. The relevant research, preceded by a pilot project, was carried out in the period 2022-2023. The interview sheet included the following open-ended questions: 1) Please characterize the main threats to the functioning of military supply chains. 2) What elements of the military logistics system are the most sensitive in the context of building the resilience of military supply chains? 3) Which approaches to building resilience of business supply chains can be applied to military supply chains?

2 CHARACTERISTICS OF MILITARY SUPPLY CHAINS

Supply chains in the civil (business) environment have been known and described for many years. Moreover, there are many different approaches in supply chain theory and Supply Chain Management, and their interpretation is disputed among scientists. It should also be emphasized that the perception of the supply chain has been and continues to evolve related to the changes that have taken place and are still taking place in their environment, in particular changes in the field of organization management, technology development and their implementation into industry and logistics systems, globalization, as well as economic, social and even political factors. According to the most common approaches to defining supply chains, they can be treated both in subjective terms (as a system/organization) (Hugos 2011: 15) and in process terms (as a sequence of sequences, or the flow of goods and accompanying information and financial resources) (Bovet et al 2000: 24-28) (Figure 1.)

In military supply chains, the basic links are military logistics subunits and military logistics bases, additional links are civilian companies, so-called contractors (e.g. logistics operators, transport companies), the final customers are troops performing tasks (training, operational, combat). The structure of such a chain may vary depending on the level of logistic support of operations. At the lowest tactical level, the chain will be short and simple consisting only of military cells, at the operational level it will be more extensive and partially supported by enterprises outside the military logistics system (civilian companies) and possibly multinational logistics units (e.g. NATO units), at the strategic level there will already be links of the national economy, civilian logistics operators, manufacturers and even mining companies, national and international creating together a supply network for the needs of the army (Figure 2).

At each level of logistics supply (supply chain), there may be a different range of risks to the supply chain. Extensive supply chains are relatively exposed to various undesirable factors and adversities that increase the risks associated with physical flows. Disrupted physical flows

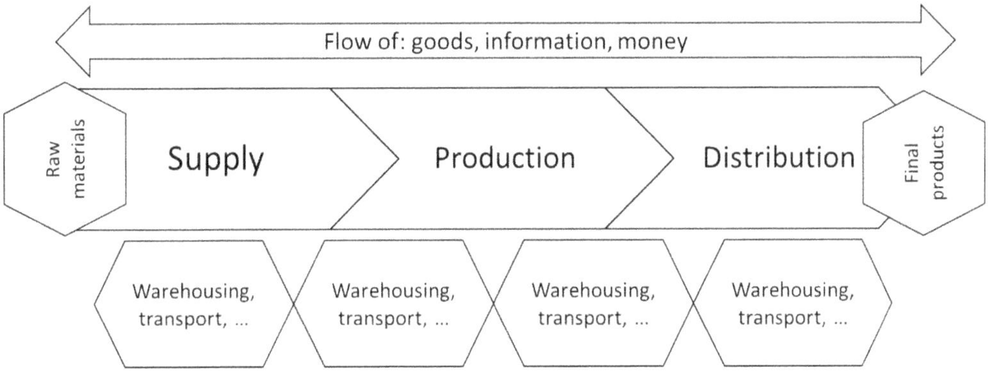

Figure 1. Supply chain idea.
Source: own compilation.

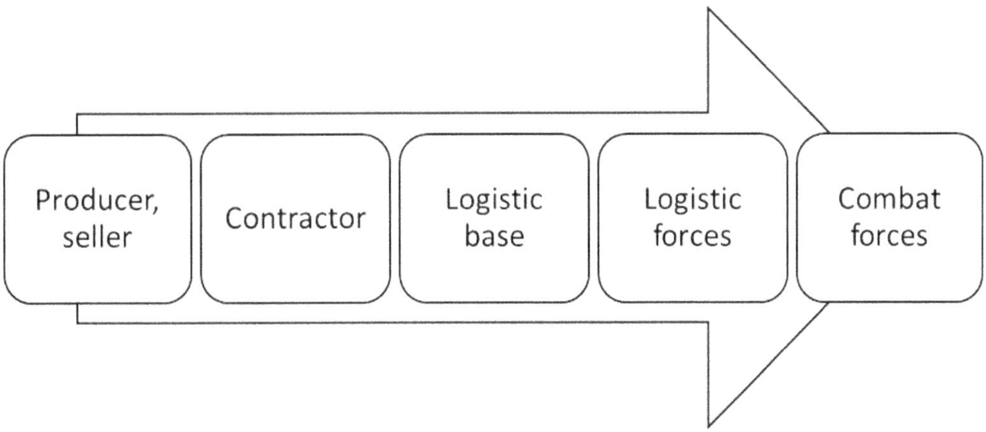

Figure 2. Military supply chain idea.
Source: own study.

may generate various effects of an organizational, technical and, above all, economic nature, meaning in this case additional costs and outlays and related losses (Ficoń 2018: 211). In general, the ability of the supply chain to cope with change is determined by resilience (Wieland et al 2013: 301). Building the resilience of the supply chain consists in preparing it to respond to threats occurring in its environment that may disrupt the continuity of the chain.

3 BUILDING THE RESILIENCE OF MILITARY SUPPLY CHAINS AGAINST CURRENT AND FUTURE THREATS

Supply chain security experts point to factors that have influenced the functioning of supply chains in recent years. These factors can be grouped according to their nature into: political: Brexit, presidential elections in the USA, Russian aggression against Ukraine; economic: trade wars between the US and China; social: mass protests; natural: earthquakes, floods, fires, hurricanes, Covid-19 pandemic; crises: energy crisis in China, gas crisis in Europe; blockade of the Suez Canal caused by ship failure, terrorist: cyber attacks (Hutchings, 2023) (Table 1).

Table 1. Factors that have influenced the functioning of supply chains in recent years.

Group of factors	Detailed threats example
Political	– Brexit (2018-2021); – presidential elections in the USA (2020-2021); – Russian aggression against Ukraine (2022);
Economical	– trade wars between the USA and China (2018-2019); – gas crisis in Europe (2022); – China energy crisis (2021);
Social	– massive protests; – Rapid social and political changes;
Natural	– earthquakes (Japan 7.3 earthquake 2022); – floods; – hurricanes (hurricane season in USA 2020; – massive fires; – Covid-19 pandemic;
Others	– terrorist attacks (for the infrastructure, piplines, ships); – cyber attacks; – blockade of the Suez Canal caused by ship failure;

Source: own compilation based on: https://blogs.gartner.com/salil-joshi/healthcare-provider-supply-chain-resiliency-a-four-step-approach.

Supply chain actors aim to ensure that all operations and flows take place in a risk-free environment (Fischer et al 2012: 141). Supply chain security is "a general property of a system consisting in the smooth functioning of the supply chain, enabling its objectives to be achieved by protecting against external targeted threats" (Ivanov et al 2010: 81). Modern military supply chains should be prepared for a wide range of internal (typical for each organization/system) and external threats, including unintentional and intentional ones. A distinction must be made between threats to the functioning of military supply chains in peacetime, crisis and war (Table 2).

Vulnerability refers to supply chain exposure to disruptions from external or internal sources and depends on the characteristics of the supply chain (Christopher et al 2019: 24-25). Typically, complex global business supply chains are more vulnerable to the environment than simpler and more resilient supply chains built for the military. Some elements of military supply chains are particularly vulnerable to disruption, according to experts (Table 3).

Supply chain resilience does not imply the ability to overcome the difficulties arising from unforeseen phenomena and events once. Resilience should be understood in the context of the continuous process of anticipating threats to business continuity or maintaining existing operational capacity. This means continuous improvement of processes, procedures and structures (Azevedo et al 2013: 131-146). There are many different approaches to building supply chain resilience in a business environment (Dos Santos et al 2015 and Zaczyk 2016: 629-641). According to experts, some of the concepts can be successfully applied to build resilience in military supply chains (Table 4).

According to experts, building the resilience of military supply chains should cover all links in the supply chain from the original supplier to the final recipient at every level of military logistic support. Supply chain resilience should respond to the entire spectrum of real and potential threats.

4 SUMMARY

Supply chains designed for the needs of the armed forces are characterized by a much simpler structure compared to global business supply chains, hence they should generally be less sensitive to external factors resulting from non-military threats. However, in practice, military supply chains are powered by manufacturing companies (and previously mining companies)

Table 2. Threats to the functioning of military supply chains.

Group of threats	Detailed threats
Internal threats	– the need to adapt the structure and potential of the logistics system to the increasing number of troops and technical modernization; – preparation of logistics staff to manage military supply chains in conditions of increased military numbers; – full implementation of IT systems ensuring visibility of the supply chain, compatibility with allied systems and cooperation with civilian entities;
External threats unintentional	– natural disasters (floods, earthquakes, hurricanes);epidemie, pandemie; – crises: economic, demographic, social, political;
External threats factors	**in times of peace and crisis:** – hacker attacks on IT systems of: the state, the armed forces, enterprises of the national economy; – stock market manipulation; – sabotage activities of a military nature (attacks on critical infrastructure) and non-military (incitement to strikes, protests); – political influence aimed at stopping international supplies or reducing production (e.g. munitions) **during the war** – all of the above; – destruction of warehouses and logistics equipment; – attacks on logistics convoys; – destruction of transport infrastructure, in particular key transport hubs;

Source: own compilation.

Table 3. Elements of military supply chains particularly sensitive to disruptions.

Area of military supply chain	Elements of military supply chain
Sources of supply	– warehouses and supply depots, tanks and fuel tanks, tanks and water tanks; – supply and transhipment points, strategic reserve warehouses; – military bases and logistic units; enterprises of the National Economy; – national and international military logistics hubs;
Transport	– transport vehicles and handling equipment; – transport infrastructure, seaports, airports; – roads, lines and interchanges; – logistics convoys;
Management	– systems for managing logistics security processes in the armed forces and the state; – information systems in the armed forces.

Source: own compilation.

and sometimes also operated by logistics operators operating on the civilian market. Although these entities, due to their defence importance, have a privileged position on the domestic market and are usually subject to certain protective measures by the state, they are subject to most market processes and global threats.

The study focuses on the identification of the studied phenomenon, trying primarily to determine the basis for further, extended research of this extremely complex problem. Further research should include observations of military logistic support processes in contemporary armed conflicts, in particular in Ukraine, as well as changes taking place in global supply chains.

The results of the conducted research indicate that some of the concepts of building supply chains used in the business environment can be adapted to the military environment. Nevertheless, this requires great caution and taking into account the specifics of military supply

Table 4. Selected concepts for building resilience of military supply chains.

Concept	Explanation
Redundancy	– maintaining an adequate amount of stocks at every level of logistic security of troops and maintaining strategic reserves; – passive and active protection and defense of inventory; – deliberate use of more suppliers;
Flexibility	– flexible logistical security procedures; alternative sources of supply; – the use of various logistic security options and contractors;
Integrity	– logistical interoperability; cooperation with allied and coalition troops; – use of multinational logistics;
Velocity	– mobility of logistic units; military supply chain management – logistics management and command; – the level of training of managerial logistics staff;
Visibility	– IT systems enabling real-time access to a full database of logistics resources.

Source: own compilation.

chains. It should always be remembered that the purpose of business supply chains is the financial effect – the profit of enterprises, while the goal of military supply chains is the operational effect – providing logistical conditions for the implementation of a training, operational or combat task. Further research into the resilience of military supply chains is certainly needed.

REFERENCES

Azevedo S.G., Govindan K., Carvalho H., Cruz-Machado V. 2013. Ecosilient Index to Asses the Greenness and Resilience of the Upstream Automotive Supply Chain. Journal of Cleaner Production vol. 56, pp. 131–146.

Bovet D., Martha J. 2000. From Supply Chain to Value Net. Journal of Business Strategy, no 21, pp. 24–28.

Christopher M. 1998. Logistyka i zarządzanie łańcuchem podaży, Wydawnictwo Profesjonalnej Szkoły Boznesu, Kraków.

Christopher M. 2000. Logistyka i zarzadzanie łańcuchem dostaw, Polskie Centrum Doradztwa Logistycznego.

Christopher M., Peck H. 2005. Logistyka marketingowa, PWE, Warszawa.

Christopher M., Peck H. 2004. Building the Resilient Supply Chain. International Journal of Logistics Managemen, Vol. 15, No. 2, pp. 1–13.

Coyle JJ., Bardi E.J., Langley Jr. C.J. 2002. Zarządzanie logistyczne, PWE, Warszawa.

Dos Santos M.G., Alcantara R.L.C. 2015. Management capabilities in supply chain resilience. Proceedings of the POMS 26th Annual Conference. Washington.

Grala D., Zadorożny K. 2021. Kształcenie kadr logistycznych na potrzeby Sił Zbrojnych RP - problemy i wyzwania. Gospodarka Materiałowa i Logistyka, no 4, pp. 62–68.

Ficoń K., Krasnodębski G. 2018. Multiśrodowiskowe zagrożenia bezpieczeństwa globalnych łańcuchów dostaw. Gospodarka materiałowa i Logistyka, no 5 (cd), p. 211–2030.

Fischer R.J., Halibozek E.P., Walters D.C. 2012. Introduction to Security, 9th edition, Elsevier, Boston.

Hugos M. 2011. Zarządzanie łańcuchem dostaw. Podstawy, Helion, Gliwice.

Hutchings S. 2023. Defence Supply Chain Strategy. Combat Logistics & Engineering Conference, Warszawa.

Ivanov D., Sokolov B. 2010. Adaptive Supply Chain Management, Springer-Verlag, London.

Jałowiec T. 2020. Paradygmaty logistyki wojskowej, Diffin, Warszawa.

Jałowiec T., Grala D. 2020. The Effectiveness of Logistic Processes in Military Supply Chains [in:] Khalid S. Soliman (red.), Education Excellence and Innovation Management: a 2025 Vision to Sustain Economic Development during Global Challenges, International Business Information Management Association (IBIMA), pp. 972–982.

Jażdżewska-Gutta M. 2019. Znaczenie bezpieczeństwa dla funkcjonowania międzynarodowych łańcuchów dostaw, Wydawnictwo Universytetu Gdańskiego.

Olszak W. 2017. Systemy informatyczne jako element wsparcia decyzji w logistyce sił zbrojnych RP. Rocznik bezpieczeństwa morskiego – rok XI –, pp. 65–76.

Staniewska E. 2021. Wybrane aspekty zarządzania bezpieczeństwem łańcuchów dostaw. Systemy Logistyczne Wojsk, Vol. 54, nr 01, pp. 135–148.
Szymczak M. 2015. Ewolucja łańcuchów dostaw, Wydawnictwo Uniwersytetu Ekonomicznego w Poznaniu, Poznań.
Szymczak M. 2017. Systemy Performance Measurement w budowaniu odpornych łańcuchów dostaw. Zeszyty naukowe Uniwersytetu Ekonomicznego w Katowicach. Zarządzanie, no 9, pp. 109–119.
Świerczek A. 2020. Rezylientne łańcuchy dostaw jako systemy adaptacyjne. Polskie Wydawnictwo Ekonomiczne, Warszawa.
Tae H. O., Young B. Ch., Rajath Ch. 2012. Supply Chain Management for Generic and Military Applications using RFID. International Journal of Future Generation Communication and Networking, Vol. 5, No. 1, pp. 61–76.
Wieland A., Wallenburg C.M. 2013. The Influence of Relational Competencies on Supply Chain Resilience: A Relational View. International Journal of Physical Distribution & Logistics Management, Vol. 43, No. 4, pp. 301.
Yoshi S. 2023. Healthcare Provider Supply Chain Resiliency: A Four-Step Approach,
Zaczyk M. 2016. Strategie budowania i wzmacniania odporności łańcucha dostaw – przegląd teoretyczny. Zeszyty Naukowe Politechniki Śląskiej. Seria: Organizacja i Zarządzanie, z. 99, p. 629.
https://blogs.gartner.com/salil-joshi/healthcare-provider-supply-chain-resiliency-a-four-step-approach

Digital Synergy – El Emary et al. (eds)

Author Index

For Product Safety Concerns and Information please contact our EU
representative GPSR@taylorandfrancis.com
Taylor & Francis Verlag GmbH, Kaufingerstraße 24, 80331 München, Germany

www.ingramcontent.com/pod-product-compliance
Ingram Content Group UK Ltd.
Pitfield, Milton Keynes, MK11 3LW, UK
UKHW052213190926
475702UK00006B/990
* 9 7 8 1 0 3 2 5 7 6 5 8 9 *